Doing Rebellious Research

Critical Issues in the Future of Learning and Teaching

Series Editors

Founding Editors

VOLUME 23

The titles published in this series are listed at *brill.com/cifl*

Doing Rebellious Research

In and beyond the Academy

Edited by

Pamela Burnard, Elizabeth Mackinlay, David Rousell and Tatjana Dragovic

BRILL

LEIDEN | BOSTON

Cover illustration: Artwork by Trisha McCrae (www.trishamccrae.net)

All chapters in this book have undergone peer review.

The Library of Congress Cataloging-in-Publication Data is available online at https://catalog.loc.gov

Typeface for the Latin, Greek, and Cyrillic scripts: "Brill". See and download: brill.com/brill-typeface.

ISSN 2542-8721
ISBN 978-90-04-51604-5 (paperback)
ISBN 978-90-04-51605-2 (hardback)
ISBN 978-90-04-51606-9 (e-book)

This book is printed on acid-free paper and produced in a sustainable manner.

Printed by Printforce, United Kingdom

Contents

PART 4
Rebellious Leadership Leading Differently

A Visual Mapping of Topic Flows

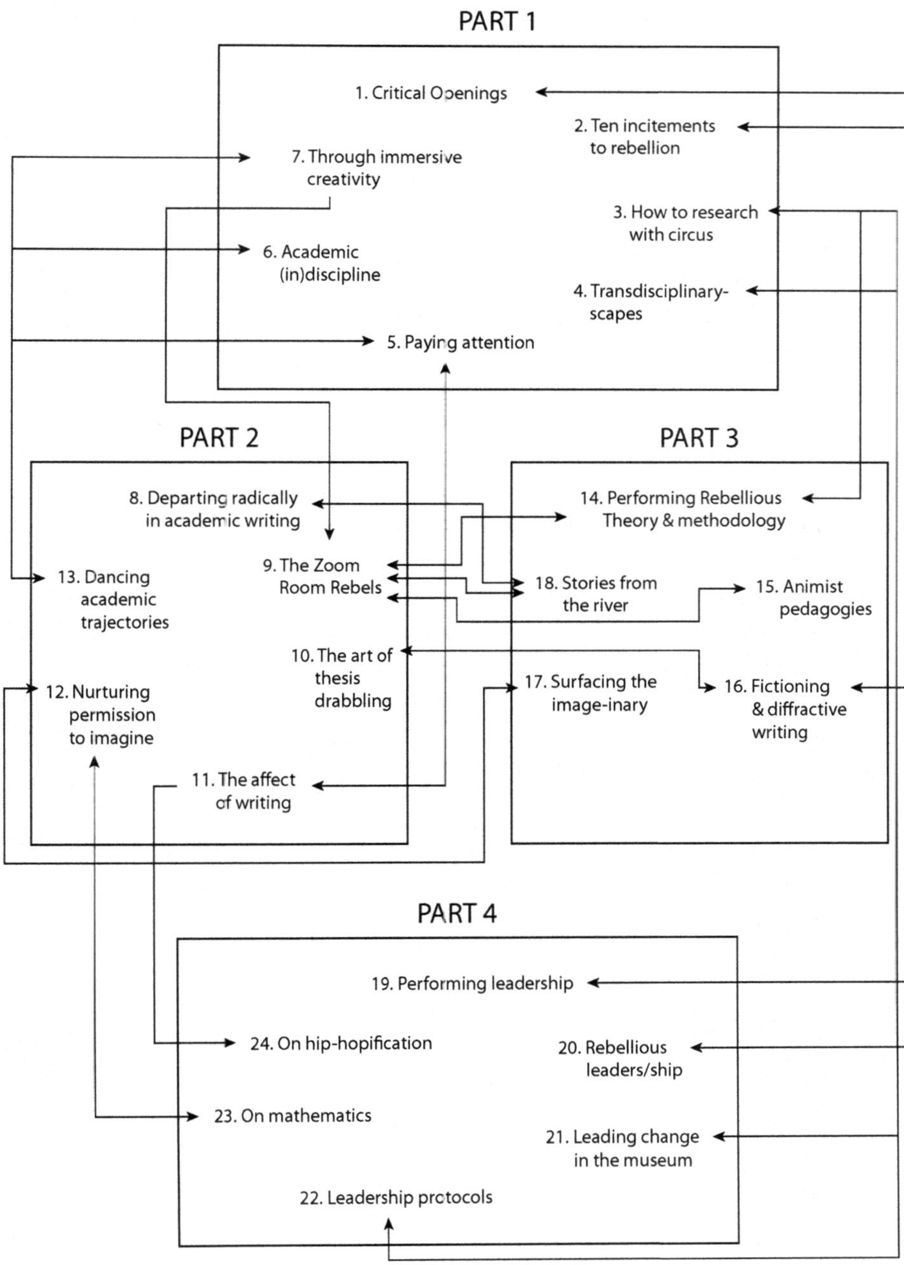

Acknowledgements

> I am forever on the way
>
> MAXINE GREENE

We would like to give heartfelt thanks to our contributors for taking pleasure in performing the gestures that jam the system, dislocating and disrupting things and values. You were all part of the truly generative entanglement that shaped and progressed from the 'Performing Research' Seminar Series – during the Covid-19 lockdowns of 2020–21 – to this collection.

We are deeply grateful to Fiona Eldem, our book administrator, who patiently kept heavy lifting and moving us gently forward as a writing community.

Thanks also to Trisha McCrae (www.trishamccrae.net) whose cover illustration and artwork bring to life the rhythm and movement that frames a line of flight in its orientation to the book.

We would also like to thank our wonderful Series Editors Pam Denicolo, Britt-Marie Apelgren and Nese Cabaroglu for their support and gift of hope. A special thank you to Julia Flutter whose chapter reviews were full of grace and encouragement. We would also like to thank the 'Brill' editors and support team, Evelien van der Veer, Alessandra Giliberto and Jolanda Karada who were open and willing to move beyond their standard publishing format and template.

To future-making writers, researchers, artists educators and their students, thank you for joining us as we both celebrate and trouble how might rebellion become something in and beyond the academy?

Illustrations

Figures

Table

Notes on Contributors

Elizabeth Allotta

is a doctoral student in the School of Education at the University of Queensland. She has over 15 years' experience as a high school teacher, with particular interests in science and STEM education. Her doctoral thesis focuses on the experiences and challenges of continuing teachers in the ever-changing world of education. She is also a member of a research group exploring the experiences of doctoral students. Elizabeth has authored a number of texts and education resources for high school students and co-authored academic papers related to nutrition and physiology in a past life.

Dewi Andriani

is a PhD candidate in the School of Education, University of Queensland, Australia. Using journeys as a metaphor, Dewi's research explores the experiences of Indonesian female students in Australia. With an autoethnographic lens informed by post-structuralist and post-qualitative paradigms, she plays around and experiments with writing in a language which is not her native one.

Bernard Andrieu

is a French philosopher, Professor of Philosophy and Epistemology of Body, and Director, Science and Sport Health Institute, I3SP-URP3625, University of Paris. Author of dozens of books and articles, his research focuses are the theory of body ecology, emersiology and performativity. Since 2006, he has been Coeditor-in-Chief of the *International Journal Corps* and Associate Editor of Movement Science and Sport Psychology in *Frontiers in Psychology*. His current research projects include 'Body perception in circassians performance' with CNAC and he has published about microperformativity.

Danilo Audiello (*aka Alexis Arts*)

is an illusionist, inventor and creative director in the theatre world, having performed in the greatest theatres and arenas. He is currently the fastest escapologist in the world, holding seven Guinness World Records and a long list of awards, including a World Championship of Magic. He is an alumnus of Cambridge University's Accelerator of the Judge Business School, where the Academy of Magic & Science was founded. Danilo holds a PhD in economics and delivers lectures and inspirational speeches around the globe interconnecting economics with illusionism, behavioural sciences, consumer psychology, communication and decision making.

Birgitte Bauer-Nilsen
is an Associate Professor in the Department of Music and Dance at the University of Stavanger, Norway. She is a choreographer for Yggdrasil Dance, an intercultural dance ensemble, which is creating a trilogy about climate change.

Annouchka Bayley
(SFHEA) is an Assistant Professor in the Faculty of Education, Cambridge University. She leads the Arts, Creativities and Education MPhil, is Chair of the Arts and Creativities Research Group and creates new approaches to doctoral research practice through leading the Pathways to Research program at the faculty. She is a long-time practising artist, director and writer and has written, produced and performed over twenty one-woman and ensemble shows.

Bernd Brabec de Mori
received his PhD in musicology from the University of Vienna. He worked for five years in the field among Indigenous people in the Peruvian lowland rainforests. After returning to Europe in 2006, he has been teaching and researching at, among other institutions, the Austrian Academy of Sciences, at Philipps-University Marburg, and at the Centre for Systematic Musicology, Karl-Franzens-University Graz. He is currently employed by the University of Innsbruck, Austria. He has published books and research articles in the areas of Indigenous vocal music, medical ethnomusicology, sound perception and auditory knowledge.

BREIS (breeze)
is the founder of Student of Life, a hip hop-inspired arts organisation that uses motivational talks, live rap performances, interactive workshops and learning strategies to inspire creativity and engage students more. He is a critically acclaimed rap artist. His music and wordplay explore the human condition with an Afro surrealist perspective. His latest project, Arise & Shine, is full of hard-hitting, clever lyrics over a musical backdrop of Hip hop, reggae and funk. BREIS is also the author of *Diary of a creative mind* (Sol, 2020) and *Brilliant rappers educate intelligent students* (Sol, 2011).

Christopher Brownell
is an Associate Professor of Mathematics and STEM Education at Fresno Pacific University in Fresno, California. His research interests include the role

of creativity in teaching and learning, the teaching of data science, humanistic mathematics, the re-humanising of the mathematics curriculum, and joy as a measure of success. He is author of *Math recess playful learning in an age of disruption* (Impress, 2019). As an ambassador for the Global Math Project, his work includes a public service campaign to change the image of mathematics.

Kathy Burke
is a fourth-year doctoral candidate at the University of Toronto, where she specialises in history and food studies. Her work explores the intersections between food, gendered and racialised labour, and the agency of enslaved people in shaping a colonial culture that travelled across the port cities of the Dutch Indian Ocean Empire in the eighteenth century.

Pamela Burnard
is Professor of Arts, Creativities and Educations at the University of Cambridge, UK. With 20 books and over 100 peer-reviewed articles, her research advances the theory of multiple creativities, from early childhood and school sectors to higher education and creative/cultural industries. She is Coeditor-in-Chief of the international journal *Thinking Skills and Creativity/ies* and an elected Fellow of the Chartered College of Teaching, UK. Pam is currently involved in a number of funded research projects including 'Choices, chances and transitions around creative further and higher education' (Nuffield) and 'Contemporary urban music inclusion' (AHRC).

Mindy R. Carter
is an Associate Professor and the Director of Teacher Education Programs in the Department of Integrated Studies in Education at McGill University, Canada. Her research focuses on teacher identity, and on using the arts to foster culturally responsible and socially just pedagogies. Carter's 'CREATE: Creativity Research in Education using artful inquiry for societal Transformation and intercultural Exchange' research program has received Fonds de recherche du Quebec and Social Sciences and Humanities Research Council funding. She is currently the Co-President of the Canadian Society for the Study of Education's Curriculum Studies special interest group.

Tatiana Chemi
is an Associate Professor and Chair of Educational Innovation at Aalborg University, where she works in the field of artistic learning and creative processes. She is the author of many publications, including *Behind the scenes of artistic creativity* (Peter Lang, 2015). With Xiangyun Du she edited *Arts-based*

methods and organisational learning: Higher education around the world (Palgrave, 2018) and *Arts-based methods in education around the world* (River Publisher, 2017). In 2013, Aalborg University Press named her Author of the Year. She is currently involved in research projects examining artistic creativity cross-culturally, arts-integrated educational designs in schools, theatre laboratory and the role of emotions in learning. She is a Visiting Associate Professor at the University of Chester.

Carolyn Cooke
is a lecturer with the Open University in Scotland, focusing on early childhood, primary education and education doctorate courses. With a background in music education and teacher education, Carolyn has recently completed her PhD *'Troubling' music education: Playing, (re)making and researching differently* (Open University, 2020) as well as co-editing the second *A practical guide to teaching music in the secondary school* (Routledge, 2022). She also actively writes and presents in the areas of STEAM education, professional learning, transdisciplinarity, performativity in research and post-humanism.

Emma Cooke
is a Postdoctoral Research Fellow in the Institute for Social Science Research at the University of Queensland, Australia. She is a sociologist, works in interdisciplinary teams, and has expertise in qualitative research. Her research focuses on early childhood education and care, early childhood discourses, children's rights, and children's, educators' and families' experiences – primarily their experiences of relaxation, sleep and well-being. Her recent work 'departs radically in academic writing' to disrupt dominant early childhood discourse that undermines children's agency. She has published in *Contemporary Issues in Early Childhood, Children and Youth Services Review*, *Early Years* and *Children and Society*.

Marta Cotrim
is a PhD student in the Department of Integrated Studies in Education at McGill University. Her doctoral research focuses on post-human pedagogies and drama/theatre education, re-thinking curriculum, knowledge and teacher–student relationships. After years working internationally as an actor and contemporary dancer, Marta has dedicated the last 15 years to teaching drama/theatre in secondary schools and teachers' training. She holds a MA in Dance Anthropology from the University of Surrey in the UK, and diplomas in Theatre Studies from Université Paris 8 France and in Performance and Choreography from the Art School of Amsterdam. Marta is originally from São Paulo, Brazil.

Hilary Cremin
researches conflict transformation and peace building, in and through education, in the UK and elsewhere. She is working on new ways of exploring peace, drawing on feminist new materialist, embodied, affective and aesthetic perspectives, and on arts-based research methodologies such as autoethnography and photo voice. She is also engaged in evaluating and developing restorative practice in global educational settings, and in investigating education and peace building in settings affected by armed conflict and crisis. She has worked in the public, private and voluntary sector as a schoolteacher, educational consultant, project coordinator and academic. Her latest book with Terence Bevington is *Positive peace in schools: Tackling conflict and creating a culture of peace in the classroom*, published by Routledge (2017).

Eloise Doherty
is a PhD candidate and casual academic at the University of Queensland. She holds a Bachelor of Music with Honours in flute performance from the Elder Conservatorium of Music and a Master of Audiology Studies from the University of Queensland. Eloise's research explores the links between music education and auditory processing for children with hearing loss, applying novel research methodologies to explore both outcomes and experience. As an academic Eloise currently teaches across a range of disciplines including the psychology of music, clinical audiology and research methods, as well as practising clinically and supervising Honours and Masters students.

Tatjana Dragovic
is a doctoral educator and a leader of the EdD research community at the Faculty of Education, University of Cambridge, UK. She is also an Associate Professor of Management, Leadership Excellence and Business Coaching at the Faculty of Organisation Studies in Slovenia. For the last 28 years she has worked across different disciplines, sectors and industries and is recognised as an international educator whose interdisciplinary expertise and research interests lie in the fields of creativity, leadership development, coaching, and the professional and personal development of educators.

Mary Earl
has worked in a wide variety of educational contexts. These include secondary schools, universities and informal community settings (including music ones). She was PGCE Manager at the Faculty of Education in Cambridge until her recent retirement and, for twenty years, a subject lecturer (world religions, philosophy of education and disability/capability studies) working at both

undergraduate and postgraduate levels. Research interests include working with artefacts (museum education), dialogism and capability studies.

Simone Eringfeld
is a researcher, artist and musician who uses sound-based methods such as podcasting and spoken word poetry in her academic work. She holds an MPhil in Education from the University of Cambridge and three BA degrees in philosophy, cultural studies and international relations from the University of Amsterdam and the University of London. Simone is the host of the podcast 'Cambridge quaranchats' and the producer-performer of the data music album 'Please hold'. For her MPhil thesis on hopes and fears for the post-COVID university, she received the BERA Masters Dissertation Award (2021).

Bonnie Evans
is a PhD candidate at the University of Queensland in film and television studies. She writes about gendered embodiment in film and television, in ways that attend to the embodied spectatorial experience. Her doctoral thesis explores the relationship between women's embodiment, violence and contemporary feminisms in recent genre film and television, including horror, crime and true crime genres.

Kristóf Fenyvesi
is a researcher of STEAM education and contemporary cultural studies at the Finnish Institute for Educational Research, University of Jyväskylä. Fenyvesi is Community Events Coordinator of the Bridges Organization. He launched Experience Workshop – Global STEAM Network (see www.experienceworkshop.org). Fenyvesi's publications have appeared in various fora, and he has edited several math-art education and STEAM handbooks, including *Aesthetics of interdisciplinarity* (Springer-Birkhauser, 2017). Fenyvesi has organised international STEAM programs at the International Mathematical Science Creativity Competitions in Seoul (Korea), Science Agora in Tokyo (Japan), Open Design Africa in Cape Town (South Africa) and Ars Electronica Festival in Linz (Austria).

Jennie Francis
has worked as a music teacher, and as a PGCE subject lecturer in music education at the University of Cambridge, UK. Her interests include music teachers' agency, enabling students to have authentic musical experiences both as performers and composers, and helping students to explore the relationship between human interests and the music people make. She also enjoys working as a flute teacher and as a musical director for a choir.

Alisan Funk
is an Assistant Professor of circus and head of the bachelor program in circus at the Stockholm University of the Arts. Drawing on her background in circus performance, education and creation, she researches in the intersections of circus and higher education using the fields of curriculum studies, creativity research and gender studies. Her solo and collaborative publications include scholarly investigations into circus education, youth circus and gender in circus. Strongly invested in translating knowledge between circus and academic contexts, she also works towards the ongoing development of international circus education and research with the European Federation of Circus Schools, and the Circus Arts Research Platform.

Caterina Garone
started her scientific research in 2010 in the mitochondrial medicine field at Columbia University, New York, where she discovered the first effective treatment for mitochondrial disorders. In 2014, she returned to Europe to the University of Cambridge with the Marie Skłodowska-Curie Individual Fellowships, European Commission. For her ground-breaking discoveries, she received the Rita Levi Montalcini award from the Italian Minister of Research in 2019 and she has established herself as Group Leader at Alma Mater Studiorum, University of Bologna. She is now inspiring younger generations to become creative thinkers and innovators.

Mel Green
is a PhD candidate with the School of Education at the University of Queensland, Australia. Her PhD research explores student engagement in reading for enjoyment in the primary school context. Following 25 years of primary teaching, with 20 of those in teacher librarianship and five in curriculum leadership, her area of passion is primary literacy, curriculum and pedagogy. She currently teaches in the UQ Bachelor of Education (Primary) program: Early Years Education, Arts Education, the Teaching of English and Literacies, as well as Primary Professional Experience courses.

Helen Johnson
is a Principal Psychology Lecturer at the University of Brighton, UK, and Co-Director of the university's Centre for Arts and Wellbeing. She is a leading voice in spoken word/poetry slam scholarship and an expert in creative research methods. Helen is particularly interested in the intersections between arts-based research, participatory research and social justice, and has developed the 'collaborative poetics' method framed by these concerns. She is also

an established spoken word poet/educator, and has been Stage Manager for the Poetry&Words stage at Glastonbury Festival, the world's largest greenfield music and performing arts festival, since 2008.

Rachel Lai
holds a MPhil in Education from the University of Cambridge. As a postgraduate research student, her research has focused on arts participation, music education, gamelan, global citizenship, and national and cultural identity construction. Outside of her research, Rachel enjoys organising events, participating in music ensembles, as well as teaching piano and music theory.

Elizabeth Mackinlay
is Professor in the Faculty of Education at Southern Cross University, Queensland, Australia, where she teaches research methods, gender studies and arts education. She holds a PhD in ethnomusicology (University of Adelaide) and a PhD in education (University of Queensland). Her books include *Teaching and learning like a feminist: Storying our experiences in higher education* (Sense Publishers, 2016), *We only talk feminist here: Feminist academics, voice and agency in the neo-liberal university* (with Briony Lipton, Palgrave, 2017), and *Critical writing for embodied approaches: Autoethnography, feminism and decoloniality* (Palgrave, 2019). Her new work *Writing feminist autoethnography: In love with theory, words and the language of women writers* will be published by Routledge in 2022.

Karen Madden
is a PhD candidate in the School of Education at the University of Queensland. Titled *Can I be feminist here? A critical autoethnographic perspective of feminist leadership in Australian girls' schools*, Karen's doctoral thesis proposes feminist theory has more to offer leaders of girls' schools than conventional leadership scholarship. As Dean of Research and Engagement in an Australian girls' school, Karen's own story of leadership in educational contexts, and the stories of her fellow leaders of girls' schools, are central to her critical and creative autoethnographic work.

Naomi Lee McCarthy
has twenty years' professional experience in art and education in galleries and museums. She has published peer-reviewed articles and presented performance-based lectures at regional and international conferences. Naomi is currently a PhD researcher supervised between Western Sydney University and the University of Cambridge. Her research explores the practice of intercultural mediation in art galleries as a pedagogy of embodied social interaction

with a focus on how it can increase social cohesion to promote an ethos of social justice. Her research focuses on the intercultural, mediated forms of photography and video art that feature the performed body enacting activism.

Trisha McCrae
is an installation artist, born in Ireland, based in France. She regularly exhibits in site specific venues, galleries and festivals, including Whitechapel Gallery, London; Kings Place, London; Ruskin Gallery, Cambridge, UK; Babylon Gallery, Ely, UK; Hat Factory Arts Centre, Luton, UK; Norwich Arts Centre, UK. Tulca Festival of Visual Arts, Galway, Ireland; Centro de Historia de Zaragoza, Spain; Festival Videoholica, Varna, Bulgaria; Galerie Maison des Artistes, Riberac, France; La Brousse, Sers, France; Traverse Video, Toulouse, France; Sarabandes, St Genis de Heirsac, France. Her work is raw, immediate and provocative. She creates immersive environments that evoke and explore how the surfaces of these spaces can hold, project, contain and inscribe social, cultural and political feelings. She is a founding member of NEUF Film Collective.

Renee Mickelburgh
is a PhD candidate with the School of Communication and Arts at the University of Queensland, Australia. Her PhD engages with ecofeminist, feminist and affect theory to examine the way Australian women communicate everyday environmental issues through written, oral and visual digital storytelling. With a background in journalism and communications, Renee has a keen interest in understanding the ways digital storytelling is used as a communication tool for environmental and social justice advocacy.

Muhammad Ali Musofer
is a PhD student in the School of Education, University of Queensland. His doctoral research engages with the stories of female postgraduate refugee-background students about their journeying to higher education. His research and teaching interests are in youth development; marginalised students' participation in higher education; and globalisation and education. Muhammad Ali has worked as a teacher educator, youth educator and community mobiliser in different community and educational organisations, and a university in Pakistan. He has been part of the creative writing group Departing Radically in Academic Writing (DRAW) for the last two years.

Kate Noble
is Senior Research Associate: Museum Learning at The Fitzwilliam Museum, University of Cambridge Museums, UK. She worked as a primary and early

childhood teacher before moving into museum education, and currently leads the Inspire training program encouraging creative teaching with objects. Kate's research focuses on visual literacy, young children in museums and practitioner-led action research. She was previously Education Researcher for The National Gallery on the AHRC-funded Practical Evaluation Project, the Northampton Primary Academy Trust Take One Picture Project and the University of Cambridge Museums' Early Years Residencies.

Allan Owens

is Professor Emeritus and Co-Director of the Centre for Research into Education, Creativity and Arts through Practice, University of Chester, which specialises in practice-based research into creativity, learning and the arts. The focus of his practice and research is learning through the use of critically creative pedagogy in the arts for understanding of self, organisation and society (*Creativity, democracy and education: The practices and politics of learning through the arts*, with Jeff Adams, Routledge, 2016). His expert practice is in the use of pretext drama as an arts-based research method with a particular commitment to equality and equity in education and research (*Beyond text: Learning through arts-based research practices*, with Jeff Adams, Intellect, 2021). He has published extensively, is regularly invited to contribute to courses and speak at international conferences, and has staged interactive pretext drama workshops around the world.

Anne Pässilä

is Senior Researcher in the School of Engineering and Science at Lappeenranta-Lahti University of Technology (LUT), Finland and Visiting Research Fellow at the University of Chester, UK. She is a pioneer in designing and applying arts-based research approaches and arts-based methodology in technological and industrial management contexts. Her expert facilitation skills in co-creation processes are in demand both within and beyond the academy. Her interdisciplinary and transdisciplinary work involves leading co-design processes of innovative qualitative research and development methods, nationally and internationally. She specialises in the creation and formulation of participatory sense-making activities to allow for learning in perplexed situations; this centres around the arts-based method she has conceptualised as 'collective voicing'.

Antonella Poli

is a PhD candidate, Science and Sport Health Institute, I3SP-URP3625 at the University of Paris under the direction of Prof Bernard Andrieu with a thesis about the dancer's body intentionality. After her Master II in Philosophy,

Aesthetics of Arts (Dance), she focused her research on danced gesture and body memory. A dance critic, she also participated in the seminar Danced Figures' Gesture (INHA, Paris). In 2020 she was published an article in *Annales Medico-Psychologiques*.

Rebecca Ream

Rebecca Ream is an early career naturalcultural geographer addicted to Donna Haraway. They/she writes, among other things, about colonisation, cats, the goat-god Pan, land and queering 'nature' in her beautiful home of Aotearoa/New Zealand. They/she are/is contingently affiliated with the learning centre of Tararua Ranges, Wairarapa, which was first settled by Rangitāne o Wairarapa and Kahungunu ki Wairarapa.

David Rousell

is Senior Lecturer in Creative Education at RMIT University, Melbourne, Australia, and a core member of the Creative Agency Lab and Digital Ethnography Research Centre (DERC). David's research combines affect studies, process philosophy and post-humanism with his creative practice as an environmental artist, educator and ethnographer. His work is invested in an ecological re-imagining of educational processes and institutions through speculative practices of participatory mapping and creative experimentation, an approach he has termed 'immersive cartography'. David has two monographs, *Immersive cartography and post-qualitative inquiry* (Routledge, 2021) and *Climate child imaginaries* (Springer, 2021, co-authored with Amy Cutter-Mackenzie-Knowles).

Eleanor Ryan

was born in New-Zealand and is a violinist, arts educator, researcher and consultant. Her interests span transcultural and transdisciplinary performance, and anticolonial, feminist and post-human theories and their application in performing arts. Eleanor holds a MMus (in performance) from the Royal Northern College of Music (2004) and an MPhil in Arts, Creativity and Education from the University of Cambridge (2020). An Assistant Professor at the University of Trinidad and Tobago from 2009 to 2018, Eleanor is currently a PhD researcher at the University of Cambridge. Her doctoral work focuses on decolonising performance pedagogies in higher education. Memberships include the Arts, Creativities and Education Research Group (ACRG) and the Equality, Diversity and Inclusion in Music Studies (EDIMS) network.

Kieran Sheehan
is a movement artist, researcher and educator currently completing his Educational Doctorate focusing on intuitive movement, diffractive analysis and professional identity. He has worked in leadership positions at UK conservatories in acting and has experience of innovative arts-based curriculum design within this sector in both the US and UK. Since 2005 he has worked as an independent artist, movement director and facilitator within producing venues, community and education settings. His career now spans academic and artistic practice, and he has forthcoming chapter publications focusing on post-human care, higher education and intuitive movement.

Antonia Symeonidou
has graduated from the National Technical University of Athens with honours and a scholarship from the State Scholarship Foundation of Greece. She conducted PhD research in the University of Cambridge in bioengineering and micromechanics. Her research received several awards and sponsorships including the European Physical Sciences Research Council grant, Lundgren Research Award and the Cambridge University Philosophical Society grant. Antonia co-founded and directs the Academy of Magic & Science, endorsed by the Accelerator of the Judge Business School, crafting creative learning experiences for science outreach through lectures, corporate workshops, public engagements, media formats and interactive exhibitions.

Portia Ungley
is an education researcher and poet with over 20 years' experience in academia. Researching at points of flexion where ideas mutate and collide, she interrogates the status quo. She directed the learning and teaching at Kingston School of Art until she launched Raw Light holistic academic and creative retreats. She is currently working on *A playdate with rigour: Reframing understanding of academic rigour through the lens of play in HE learning spaces*, an educational doctorate at the University of Cambridge. She showcases autoethnography and arts-based research to illustrate how the rebellious voice has a place in academic writing.

Preeti Vayada
is a doctoral student at the School of Education, University of Queensland, Australia. She has worked as a school leader and educator in India and is also a special education teacher in a state school in Queensland. Her research interests lie in student–faculty partnership practices in teaching and learning in

higher education, navigating in-betweenness in international students' identities and cross-cultural partnership practices in higher education. Her research examines the experiences of Indian students in a student–staff partnership program in an Australian university. She is an emerging scholar who has participated in various conferences.

Jonathan Wyatt
is a Professor of Qualitative Inquiry and Director of the Centre for Creative-Relational Inquiry at the University of Edinburgh. His book *Therapy, stand-up, and the gesture of writing: Towards creative-relational inquiry* (Routledge, 2019) won the 2020 International Congress of Qualitative Inquiry Book Award.

Prologue

Elizabeth Mackinlay,
Pamela Burnard, David Rousell,
Tatjana Dragovic and Trisha McCrae

 | DOI:10.1163/9789004516069_001

Dear Reader,

Come Join Our Rebellious Research and Writing

As you open this book, we invite you to remember the moment when you did something truly and utterly rebellious; something so unruly, undutiful and ungovernable that, once you had begun, there was no turning back. Do you remember what it felt like – what it really felt like – to dash through and fly, because your 'writing, life' (Stewart, 2018) depended on it? Do you remember that feeling of learning the art of flying in order to 'fly the coop', as Hélène Cixous (1976, p. 887) might say, and 'take pleasure in jumbling the order', changing the furniture, dislocating and disorienting things and values, breaking them all up, emptying structures' and feeling, dreaming, performing the gestures that jam the system? We remember that feeling and it is to this moment of rebellion we return wilfully in this collection of essays because … because we are exhausted, tired and bored by the academic system of abstraction, opposition and objectification which works hard, very hard, to contain us. Anthropologist and literary theorist Mary Pratt (1986, p. 33) observed: 'How, one asks constantly, could such interesting people doing such interesting things produce such dull books? What did they have to do to themselves?' Pratt made this observation decades ago and yet the scene, the sentiment and the incredulity feels familiar, very familiar – indeed, questions of what it is we have done and are doing to ourselves are too clear and present to ignore. Pratt spoke directly and daringly about the ways in which qualitative researchers tend to deaden experience when writing about social life. Her words were written at the beginning of what we might think of as the 'long' crisis of representation in the humanities and social sciences, where the ways in which we articulated particular kinds of truth and knowledges about the social world were beginning to be positioned as partial and problematic.

Thirty years later, as Elizabeth St Pierre (2018) argues, approaches to qualitative research and writing in the academy continue to perpetuate conformity to pre-existing structures, rules and regulations. When considering post-qualitative research and alternative writing methodologies, she urges us to re/turn to writing as a practice of living, of immanent inquiry at no distance from the world's becoming – to do the radical kind of work that the world needs right now, in a time of climate change, the COVID-19 pandemic, and a rise in nationalism and populism. Pratt's and Pierre's words are an urgent call to rise up and 'fly the coop' with our pens and rebel..

We like the word 'rebel' and use it deliberately here to invoke its etymological origins: re-bel, adj. re – 'against, in opposition to, or again' and bel – to be 'obstinate, stubborn', 'revolt' or 'wage war' and rebel, n. 'a person who makes war for political motives'. For us, rebellious researchers and writing rebels are those who battle against the normative standard of conventional academic practices. For us, wilfully finding new ways to do the work that re/turns is a kind of rhythmic regularity that frames a line of flight that is wise, loving, relational and non-violent in its orientation to the world. We are not the first to make such moves towards rebellion; this academic writing rebellion is rooted in previous rebellions that enable us to travel this route from there and then to here and now. Rebellious words and phrases penned by those who have come before us are the lilting refrains you hear on the crest of the waves in your mind as thinking and wondering breaks onto the shores as writing. We hear Virginia Woolf resolve on Tuesday 22 November 1938:

I am, fundamentally, I think, an outsider. I do my best work and feel most braced with my back to the wall. It's an odd feeling though, writing against the current: difficult entirely to disregard the current. Yet of course I shall. (1954, p. 297)

We listen to Laurel Richardson, who rejected the 'sociological verité style' of writing because it is 'not worth reading … [lacks] credibility and it's boring' and instead found discomfort in asking, 'What do we write about? How do we write it? And for whom do we write?' (1988, p. 199). We smile with monstrous delight as Helene Cixous urges us to 'smash everything, to shatter the framework of institutions, to blow up the law' (1976, p. 888). Boaventura de Sousa Santos speaks of 'a sociology of rebellion' which addresses 'goals that are feasible in the foreseeable future and serve as mobilisers' (2004, p. 32). Stefano Harney and Fred Moten (2013, p. 20) call for abolitionist inquiry that refuses to correct or be corrected by institutional politics and its reductive enclosures of intellectual life, adding a fugitive decolonial rhythm to the roots of our rebellious writing when they assert that 'we are disruption, and consent to disruption. We are upheaval.' Eileen Honan and David Bright (2016) are inspired to play their own tune riffing off the contributions that Gilles Deleuze and Felix Guattari have made to thinking/writing language and how these ideas can be put to work performatively to produce a doctoral thesis differently, working through a language that 'stutters' and always threatens to fall apart, undoing itself to the extent that it provides the 'writer-machine' a space to 'pass'. As Brian Massumi (1987, p. xii) wrote in the translator's foreword to Deleuze and Guattari's *A thousand plateaus*, 'A concept is a brick. It can be used to build the courthouse of reason. Or it can be thrown through the window.'

As you read these rebellious refrains, we think and wonder how they resonate in your mind, body and soul to move you to research and write differently – how they join with refrains of your own and of others whose writing has become the lifeblood of the words that pump and course through your veins, shimmering at first, then surging with a force not yet encountered and impossible to ignore. Let yourself listen. Let yourself feel.

> Let yourself go! Let go of everything! Lose everything! Take to the air. Take to the open sea. Take to letters. Listen: nothing is found. Nothing is lost. Everything remains to be sought. Go, fly, swim, bound, descend, cross, love the unknown, love the uncertain, love what has not yet been seen, love no one, whom you are, whom you will be, leave yourself, shrug off the old lies, dare what you don't dare, it is there that you will take pleasure, never make your here anywhere but there, and rejoice, rejoice in the terror, follow it where you're afraid to go, go ahead, take the plunge, you're on the right trail! (Cixous, 1991, p. 40)

This is our Cixousian invitation to you. Come with us as we seek to go beyond the limitations of language and text in analysing ourselves and our practices as part of connected multiplicities, as we pursue and enact collective, political and generative ways to engage with and write research. Come with us as we experiment with new relational forces that call us to change; to research and write as

> a way of leaving no space for death, of pushing back forgetfulness, of never letting oneself be surprised by the abyss. Of never becoming resigned, consoled; never turning over in bed to face the wall and drift asleep again as if nothing had happened; as if nothing could happen. (Cixous, 1991, p. 3)

This is the germinal moment where something is beginning to happen; this is the germinal moment of rebellion.

This invitation to research and write something truly and utterly rebellious is too inviting to pass over; and so, we accept. Our motives are at once critical and creative, and the work in this edited collection stubbornly refuses the censoring correction and coercion back to the 'boring stuff' (Richardson, 1997) of academia – we are rebels *with* a cause, and this is our enticement to you. R-E-B-E-L. Five letters, five words, five refrains now follow. Come ride this pentatonic wave with us as we lay down the roots and routes this edited collection travels.

Yours in rebellion,
Elizabeth, Pamela, David, Tatjana and Trisha.

Refrain One

During COVID, a rebellious collaboration
Research in and beyond here
Returning to transdisciplinary roots/routes
Social-scientists, educators, artists, musicians, performers
Outsider and insider and more inbetween.

Haha! Here we go now!
Watch us fly the coop!
Pushing back and grating grooves
Re-think the chink, re-configure figure
Has the rebellion arrived yet?

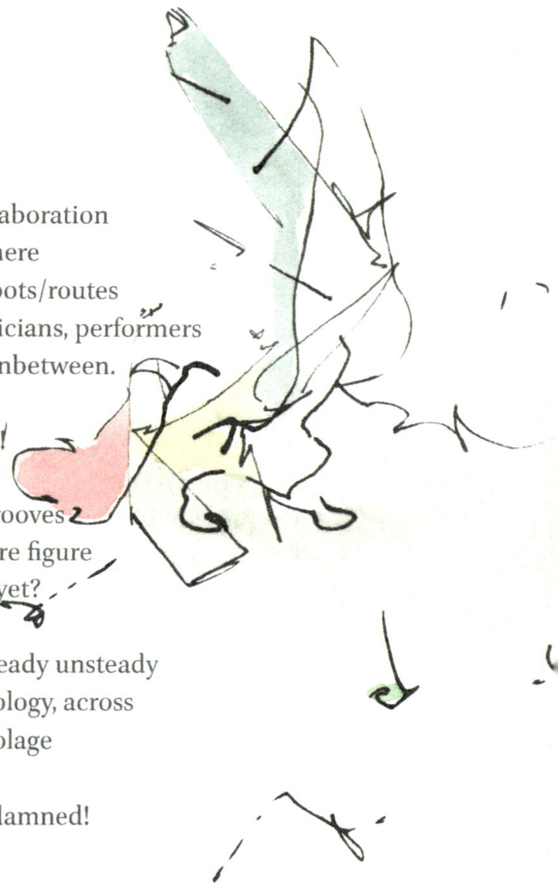

Re-constitute, re-orient, re-search, ready unsteady
Crossing theory, crossing methodology, across
We willingly bear this bricolage
Defy we have, we will
Tradition and convention be damned!

Beginning in the Zoom-i-verse
Online, inline, monthly date lines
Together bringing and creating together
2020 is happening, the host
will let you in soon

Circus balls fly, who knows?
Magic sprinkles as it soothes
Poetry slams and soothes
DRAWing enters the room roaring
Desiring to be wide awake.

Refrain Two

We choose to work in the cracks of neoliberalism
While ignoring its insatiable demands
We choose communion over competition
We choose to throw the
Beads of accountability away, away
And plant seeds of rebellion

We bring an affirmative ethic,
We bring actively standing to
the present to pattern presence
We are bringing this community
We are bringing this rebellion

We are United Kingdom and States
of America, we are Australia
Austria, Canada and we are
Denmark, Finland, France, Greece, Italy
We are New Zealand, Nigeria,
Sweden and we are United.

We see ourselves as experts
With expertise and crafters who
See ourselves as performers and
Practitioners who see ourselves as
Philosophers thinking and wondering, perhaps?

We gift permission to rebel
We gift roots, routes, refrains
We gift affective alternative poetical
Political assemblages embracing others elsewhere
To doctoral students, advisors, educators.

Refrain Three

What is "rebellious" about it?
This research, the practice, the—
writing and the academy/university
Know, resist, and re-imagine it?
Rebellion, what is it about?

Why will this practice (of)
rebellious knowledge production create an
upheaval of or change anything
in the academy or beyond?
Why might you dare to?

We are in crisis, no?
How are critical issues in the
future of my/your/our
work working to become rebellion?
Does it matter, why—why?

How do we research and write
as rebellion without falling, failing
into ruin within neo-liberal performativity?
What techniques and modalities of self
and collective care sustain us?

Why, that twisted little sign
that comes at the end
making power wriggle and writhe
such questions willfully choose carefully
How might rebellion become something?

Refrain Four

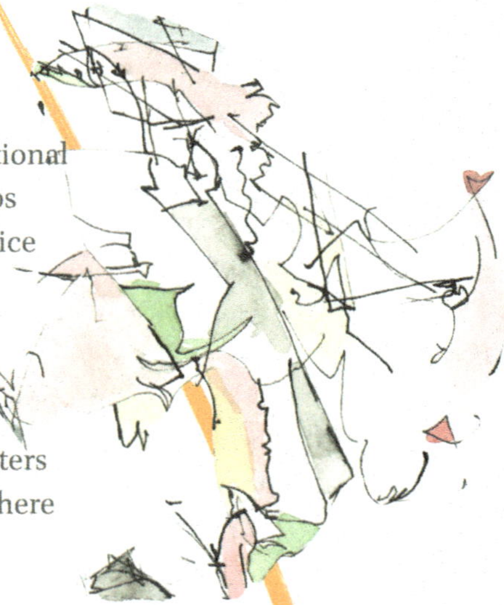

We think and wonder with
Post this, that and t'other
Concepts foregrounded as process-relational
Events as multi-species relationships
More-than-human ecologies of practice

We think and wonder with
Quantum entanglements that cut
And diffract other roots/routes
Along with everyday affective encounters
And ontologies of immanence everywhere

We think and wonder with
Karen Barad, Deborah Bird Rose
Rosi Braidotti, Judith Butler, Hélène
Cixous, Giles Deleuze, Vinciane Despret
Maxine Greene, Donna Haraway, Brian Massumi,

We think and wonder with
Laurel Richardson, Jane Speedy,
Tami Spry, Isabelle Stengers, Fred Moten, Edouard Glissant,
Sylvia Wynter, Bawaka Country,
Kathleen Stewart, Elizabeth St Pierre,
Jonathan Wyatt, Virginia Woolf, etc.

We think and wonder with
The immanent performance of difference
The production of the new made
Event; practice, public and performative
Event; creative, counter-, critical, yes.

Refrain Five

Rebellion; non-fixed moving-way
into being through collaborative exchange
Coming-with, writing-with, making
-with, listening-with, talking-with
Rupturous inquiry in rapture; rebellion.

Rebellion; litterateurs, languages, listeners, lives
In dialogue, in dance, in
A blizzard of slow fused
Fragments, fictions, features, fantastical, flights
Forever on the way; rebellion.

Route one; radical roots more-
Than-humanly reimagined in resistance
Route two; departing radically in
Academic writing, because of roots
To danger we deliberately go.

Route three; disciplinary-posted-notes
Push inter-and-trans-roots
Because this matter matters to
Route four; routes lead roots
That unearth poetically-performatively beyond.

Rebellion; dare to turn ourselves
Over, around and upside down
All the taken-for-granted
Lurch, but for a moment
And question all in; rebellion.

References

Braidotti, R. (2018). Affirmative ethics, posthuman subjectivity, and intimate scholarship: A conversation with Rosi Braidotti. In K. Strom, T. Mills & A. Overns (Eds.), *Decentering the researcher in intimate scholarship* (pp. 179–188). West Yorkshire, England: Emerald Group Publishing.

Cixous, H. (1976). The laugh of the Medusa (K. Cohen & P. Cohen, Trans.). *Signs, 1*(4), 875–893. https://doi.org/10.1086/493306

Cixous, H. (1991). *Coming to writing' and other essays* (D. Jenson, Ed.; S. Cornell, D. Jenson, A. Liddle & S. Sellers, Trans.). Cambridge, MA: Harvard University Press.

De Sousa Santos, B. (2004). *The world social forum: A user's manual*. http://www.ces.uc.pt/bss/documentos/fsm_eng.pdf

Harney, S., & Moten, F. (2013). *The undercommons: Fugitive planning and Black study*. London: Minor Compositions Publisher.

Honan, E., & Bright, D. (2016). Writing a thesis differently. *International Journal of Qualitative Studies in Education, 29*(5), 731–743. https://doi.org/10.1080/09518398.2016.1145280

Massumi, B. (1987). Translator's foreword. In G. Deleuze & F. Guattari, *A thousand plateaus,* (pp. ix–xv). Minneapolis, MN: University of Minnesota Press.

Pinar, W. F. (1998). *The passionate mind of Maxine Green: 'I am ... not yet'.* London: Routledge.

Pratt, M. L. (1986). Fieldwork in common places. In J. Clifford & G. Marcus (Eds.), *Writing culture: The poetics and politics of ethnography* (pp. 27–50). Oakland, CA: University of California Press.

Richardson, L. (1988). The collective story: Postmodernism and the writing of sociology. *Sociological Focus, 21*(3), 199–208. https://doi.org/10.1080/00380237.1988.10570978

Richardson, L. (1997). *Fields of play: Constructing an academic life*. New Brunswick, NJ: Rutgers University Press.

St Pierre, E. A. (2018). Writing post qualitative inquiry. *Qualitative Inquiry, 24*(9), 603–608.

Stewart, K. (2018). Writing, life. *PMLA: Publications of the Modern Language Association of America, 133*(1), 186–189. https://doi.org/10.1632/pmla.2018.133.1.186

Woolf, V. (2008). *Virginia Woolf: Selected essays*. Oxford: Oxford World Classics. (Original work published 1931)

Woolf, V. (1954). *A writer's diary*. London: Hogarth Press.

Walking with-in

Ten Incitements to Rebellion

SPEAK IN FIRE LANGUAGE

e Conundrum of timescapes

PART 1

RebelLIOus Transdisciplinarity Researched Differently

Part 1: Guidance for Readers

Pamela Burnard

This is an invitation to you to read differently. How? Let's start with the fact that you don't have to begin with the first chapter and read consecutively and neatly through. After all, doesn't reading rebellious research invite a rebellious reader to retain the same skin. How? You can you start anywhere and open up to one pathway and yet another pathway through; one that is unexpected, unpredictable and unconnected. As rebellious readers, especially of transdisciplinary research, you are never forced into a singular dimension or generic type. Rather, the reader is invited to reconfigure readings and re-readings; to revel in ways that transgress disciplinary boundaries.

This is an invitation to you to read immersively. How? In a space not without a certain sense of resistance and but also an openness to departures from conventional academic reading. You may well witness your own re-engendering that runs alongside and works like reconstructive surgery to rid oneself of old ways of reading.

This is an invitation to you to intuit the principles behind reflexive reading. How? As Marenko asks 'What does it take to imagine, design, and inhabit spaces of experimentation, collaboration, and reflection together? How can situations of this kind be crafted? How do we – design educators, practitioners, change-makers – come in close proximity with each other to create togetherness' (Marenko, 2021, p. 166), differently?

This is also an invitation for you to read reflexively in ways that can be released by shifting attention to thinking with and of new stories to tell our stories with and by de-coupling the specific language of a discipline from its original context. Not only how, but *why*? Whatever the matter, muse or methodological practice, and however the interrelationalities between reader and writer coalesce, by connecting this learning to the world *we* – you, me, all of us – come closer to redefining ourselves as rebellious readers.

Reference

Marenko, B. (2021). Stacking complexities: Reframing uncertainty through hybrid literacies. *Design and Culture*, *13*(2), 165–184.

 | DOI:10.1163/9789004516069_002

CHAPTER 1

Critical Openings in Performing Transdisciplinary Research as/in Rebellion

Pamela Burnard

The Matter and Materiality of Rebellious Transdisciplinary Research and Writing

Transdisciplinary research and writing require performing differently. By 'performing differently' I mean the capacity to perform ourselves, perform new knowledge configurations, and/or perform multiple creativities differently. As rebellious research, transdisciplinarity emphasises matter, materiality and mattering ('making-with'[1]), resisting being forced into a singular dimension or generic type. Rather, it reconfigures learning in ways that transgress disciplinary boundaries and offers a productive space to research and write within and beyond intersections of scientific and artistic ways of knowing and being with(in) the world.

Transdisciplinary research and writing rebels can be described as waging war against the normative standards of conventional academic practices. Transdisciplinary researchers focus on 'real-world' problems, and methodologies that incorporate critical reflexivity and that are responsive to the particular questions, settings and research groupings involved (Russell et al., 2008). They take a line of flight that invites performative departures from conventional academic writing. The rebellious performance of transdisciplinarity delineates the source of its 'vitality' in mattering a line of flight (see Figure 12.3) that is dynamic, elusive and liminal, intersecting with and open to multiple practice possibilities that articulate, as Jane Bennett (2010) advocates, as 'a vibrant materiality that runs alongside and inside humans' (p. VIII).

Another rebellious performance of transdisciplinarity, as outlined by Sandford (2015, pp. 160–161), is one in which theory and concepts 'are not necessarily identifiable with any specific disciplinary fields, either in their origin or their application'. Sandford suggests that a number of factors are needed

1 *Making-with* is a term coined by Donna Haraway (2016, p. 58) which recognises that nothing makes itself, but we are in a constant state of 'becoming' with materials, environments, bodies and constructs.

 | DOI:10.1163/9789004516069_003

for something to be considered 'transdisciplinary'. The first is the transformation of conceptual thinking into historically based and materialist critique. The second is a focus on, not a neutral philosophical critique, but a politically inflected act of theoretical and practical criticism (p. 171), and the third is the use of methods that transgress disciplinary boundaries to offer a productive means of both unsettling disciplines and developing a space to think and work within transdisciplinary modes. If a disciplinary mode of thinking is defined inwardly and aimed at setting clear distinctions and boundaries of specialist language, focuses of inquiry, and levels and units of analysis, a transdisciplinary mode of thinking is concerned with the 'potential of divergent elements to coexist, communicate, create entanglements; also through friction, dissonance, and disharmony' (Marenko, 2021, p. 167). The same is true of multidisciplinary thinking, which is the model typically adopted when people talk about thinking/working together across disciplines. For me, what is so important about this book is that it really does seek to be radically transdisciplinary and not just pay lip service to thinking/working together by applying the typical additive model of multidisciplinarity.

Yet methodologically, it is not sufficient to assemble an assorted group of people working together in the hope that transdisciplinarity will happen. Rather, the inquiry is still very much at the political level – of unsettling the onto-epistemological underpinnings of our practice/inquiry – and provoking questions such as:

> What does it take to imagine, design, and inhabit spaces of experimentation, collaboration, and reflection together? How can situations of this kind be crafted? How do we – design educators, practitioners, changemakers – come in close proximity with each other to create togetherness? (Marenko, 2021, p. 166)

In reflecting on their own experiences of transdisciplinary working, authors illustrate dispositions and qualities that *transcend their disciplines*. These features, such as empathy, openness to new ideas and experiences, 'bravery' in their openness to failure, and trust, are associated with creativity too (Smith & Henriksen, 2016).

So, from an onto-epistemological point of view, transdisciplinarity is rooted in a system view of reality; a being and knowing which acknowledges the need for multi-levelled and multi-perspectival inquiry (Marshall, 2014). In this realm, I locate not only experiences of collaboration between researchers from different disciplines, but also post-humanist approaches advocating dialogue amongst an extended peer community – one which includes both human and non-human, each one bringing a set of legitimate testimonies. As part of this onto-epistemological questioning, science, rather than being exclusively the source of rigour and objectivity, is socially constructed, 'woven of social relations' (Haraway, 2004, p. 187): it has a class, gender, culture, species and biological context, as well as a methodological context. In taking this more extended and inclusive stance to knowledge creation in transdisciplinary inquiries, post-humanist and feminist theorising, advanced by key authors such as Braidotti (2013), Haraway (2004, 2016) and Barad (2007), can help us understand how transdisciplinary processes can be enacted rebelliously.

In the words of the American post-humanist theorist and quantum physicist Karen Barad, relational knowing is illustrated through the concept of diffraction, meaning 'to break apart in different directions' (2007, p. 168). Diffraction patterns can be observed in water waves, as well as sound waves and light waves. Where the waves interfere or overlap, they create an interference pattern or 'superposition' (Barad, 2007, p. 76). Such entanglements are 'highly specific configurations' that require precise apparatuses to study them, as they alter with every 'intra-action'. The phenomenon that is captured by *intra-action* is transdisciplinarity. Whether in a scientific or artistic context, intra-action emerges from the assemblage and enmeshment of viewer, phenomenon and apparatus. As Barad (2007) explains, 'it is not so much that they change from one moment to the next or from one place to another, but that space, time, and matter do not exist prior to the intra-actions that reconstitute entanglements' (p. 74). Whether we are exploring concepts from/of science, mathematics or arts, these are all *material-discursive practices* that can provide different ways of thinking about how all of us (not just students in the sense of formal education) might engage with our own learning and then, of course, connect this learning to the world.

Diffraction understands phenomena as both inherently different and differing in terms of time, space and matter, as well as deeply relational. Murris and Bozalek (2019), who observe that diffraction is not only a methodological but also a pedagogical tool, caution that 'diffraction troubles humans' epistemic arrogance of locating knowledge intelligence and meaning-making in the subject and only in the human subject' (p. 875). Drawing on Rosi Braidotti (2013), I (along with several authors in Part 1) argue that the post-human helps us to combine/re-instate subject disciplines as inseparable transdisciplinary configurations that are embedded within the real world. The arts and sciences do not operate as opposites. This position limits the value of the arts to at worst handmaidens to science, and at best the tools for emancipation in a dystopian society (Hodgson et al., 2017). Both scenarios reinforce instrumentalist ideas and high-stakes rhetoric on both academic writing and research education by focusing on what academics/researchers should do (e.g., raise interest, deliver outcomes) without regard for field-defining transdisciplinary genres of writing (Dernikos et al., 2020).

In Part 1, these transdisciplinary intersections are performed by scholars who are enthused to invite readers to travel together and who emphasise matter, materiality and mattering or 'making-with' forms of arts/science interaction including reconfigurations of music, science, language, Indigenous and western timescapes, dance, circus arts and spoken word. All describe the doing of rebellious, transdisciplinary research. This research grows out of the sensualism of walking with(in) entangled scapes of north-east Scotland (Chapter 4) or in the spatiality and temporality of a nine-month-long energising conversation on Bakhtin's (1981) dialogics of language which established collaborative writing as a method of inquiry between two teachers (Chapter 5). At other times, the writing ventures far from the traditional territories of academic (in)discipline (Chapter 2) of educational research, to 'performing' new relationships and ideas from transdisciplinary creativity and levels of experience (Chapter 7). There are numerous incitements to rebellion through vibrant, visceral and creative uses of slam/spoken word as a social scientific research tool (Chapter 2) and through a hugely influential claim that academic writing is, or at least can be, a method of rebellious inquiry about circus practice that rebels against circus (Chapter 3). How? By risking the 'traditionally taboo practice' of articulating, understanding and theorising, it reveals the materialities that are constitutive of previously unknowable circus practice and that synergistically both fuel and create rebellious academic writing. Accordingly, pushing against the known and flouting traditions is at the heart of the doing of rebellious transdisciplinarity, which appears at the frontiers of our knowledge. Through pushing against the known and flouting traditions we act out and reveal critical issues in the future of learning and teaching, research and writing. We act out and reveal innovative, affective and sensual encounters and create new and more reflexive transdisciplinary performances.

In contemplating how such rebellious research manifests, authors violate traditional forms of authorship with rebellious intermixings of music with walking (Chapter 4), speaking with listening (Chapter 5), academic (in)disciplinings with different temporalities (Chapter 6), rebellious bodies with a form of *transdisciplinary creativity* (Chapter 7), and other incitements to rebellion that provide a radically different way of doing, being and collaborating in and through research. We see slam/spoken word (Chapter 2) and circus arts (Chapter 3) put to work with new intensities that become battle sites of rebellion. What these scholars make visible are new kinds of (material-discursive) research realities that have important consequences for academic writing.

They follow the example of scholars such as Ken Gale (2018) who, advocating madness as methodology, invites 'the welcome of the unknown' (p. 117) in engaging with new forms of writing as

> a means of challenging, of offering lines of flight and of breaking through ... and working away from fixities, strategies of representation and all those modes of signification that frame thinking and writing practices in static arborescent rigidities of practice. (p. 118)

These authors embrace new forms of writing that are constitutive of, and responsible for, the activation of rebellion. Collectively, these Part 1 chapters offer a juxtaposition and continuous diffractive exchange between different theoretical stances and framings help to not only bring to the surface the structures and cultures that often go uninterrogated, but also turn a critical lens back onto themselves, thus inspiring the enactment of paradigm-shifting transdisciplinary moves.

Collectively, these Part 1 chapters offer a future-making understanding of how disciplines can meet, come to matter and materialise differently in rebellious transdisciplinary research and writing. This challenging of the established demarcations that come with knowledge and subject hierarchies, and bringing forth a renovated understanding of creativity as embedded in sensory experience of the natural world, resonates strongly with the essence of transdisciplinarity.

Petrie (1992) writes: 'The notion of transdisciplinarity exemplifies one of the historically important driving forces in the area of interdisciplinarity, namely, the idea of the desirability of the integration of knowledge into some meaningful whole' (p. 300). Rather, in Part 1, authors seek to embrace *the spaces-in-between the disciplines* – a liminal practice of co-existence – as this *in-betweenness* exists thanks to our own very nature of being enmeshed within multiple levels of relationality, both in society and within the natural world. Such a position does not deny the need to be critical of economic discourses in academia that drive academics towards performativity, but it does recognise that higher education institutions may in fact provide a unique space for reflection on and reconfiguration of relationships amongst humans and more-than-human subjects – a space to enact possibilities that may not be visible, or as yet available, in the present order.

In a similar fashion, Deleuze and Guattari (1987) propose there is no beginning or end to the process or phenomenon of thinking; that is, knowledge making is not static and separable from the living and non-living world, but instead occurs in the form of *assemblages* made up of groups, ideas, elements or systems that are continually intertwining to do something, to produce something rebellious. Inquiry does not follow a linear path made of consequential steps, but is rather more like the shape of a *rhizome* (or tuber, such as, say, ginger), which spreads out in an unruly fashion. As it ruptures in unpredictable directions, it throws us off onto different paths, allowing us to break with old habits and form new ones, making the familiar unfamiliar and offering the space to make the unfamiliar familiar in turn. Accordingly, we conceive of knowledge as *rhizomatic*, organising laterally without hierarchies and constantly open to renovated formulations of the norms and processes that narrowly define disciplines, phenomena and activities. This enables a more fluid exploration of the multiplicities in thinking about and doing arts, sciences, mathematics and other disciplines as 'ways of being' and 'ways of doing' located within learners' sociocultural, economic and political conditions.

What follows is an overview of the encounter with, and contributions of, these authors. The encounter may bring discomfort. The encounter may bring frustration. The encounter may require you to negotiate and revise anticipations. Nevertheless, these authors provide encouragement for others wishing to research and write differently, whether that be in the ruptures shared with a writing partner (as with Chapters 5 and 7) or in the vulnerabilities and eruptions of self-authorship (Chapters 2, 3, 4 and 6).

Inspiring Rebellion When Making-With Music and Musicking Becomes Subversive

In Chapter 4, initial music teacher educator Carolyn Cooke invites us to go for an eruptive walk with/in transdisciplinary-scapes. She makes us an offer to decentre the human in the hierarchy of planetary beings, to rethink and think with nature. It is an invitation not simply to come out to play but also to 'play out together' to 're-see', 're-make' and 're-tell' our relationships with each other and with discipline/s; to rethink research as a practice through a lens of 'making-with'. Carolyn Cooke writes with an incessant drive to rebel against 'teaching' and 'learning' as separate activities occurring in subjective and geopolitical silos and separations.

Using a lens and discourse of 'making-with' in her writing about transdisciplinary music education, she practices a shift in relation to her responsibility towards *doing difference* subversively in research and academic writing. She challenges and fractures the authority and aesthetics of a distinctly patriarchal and colonial academy. Rather than accepting the fabricated dualism of being musical and gifted, or seeing music and ability as a static rather than active condition, Carolyn Cooke challenges societal norms and expectations about specialisation and the infinite possibilities of being musical and music making by dismantling the hegemonic terrain of performing music as a specialism.

Carolyn Cooke rebelliously erodes the bastions of western art music canons by opening us up to a purposively messy transdisciplinary space. She subverts the normalised and destructive logic of knowing music by refusing straightforward stories, explanations and conclusive outcomes. By paying attention differently and subverting the materiality of making with music as something we do 'walking with(in) transdisciplinary-scapes', she calls both researchers and research participants (students) to question, challenge and ultimately redefine the unpredictability of spaces, sounds, images and objects of the classroom (i.e. the research setting). She demands a kind of '(re-)turning' and '(re)-tuning' as generative entanglements that catalyse an unlearning about research certainty and predictability, truth and probability.

Rather than arguing for a research commitment to methodological incommensurability, where logical argumentation cannot be used to assign differential values, where disciplinary differences are fixed to succeeding theories (Kuhn, 1962) or where two theories so differing are methodologically incompatible, Carolyn Cooke rebelliously invites us to engage with/in blurred boundaries as a scape full of transdisciplinary potentials. The disruption and rebelliousness here is about breaking away from our habitual ways of responding and our siloed disciplinary assumptions. It is about seeing research as performative, risky, uncertain, in flux, staying with the trouble of non-linear narratives of normativity, re-turning and re-tuning ourselves with each eruption. The challenge here is to *rethink what we thought we had already rethought*. Interestingly, this was a particular challenge that was shared by all of the authors across all of the chapters in Part 1. For Carolyn Cooke, however, the challenge was about what differentiates landscapes from soundscapes, and about how fixed meanings become fluid by 'paying attention differently' by re-making narratives of transdisciplinarity. Here, researching and rewriting becomes something that embraces discomfort and uncertainty as part of the process undertaken by walking with(in) entangled scapes.

Chapter 5 grows out of, and makes explicit, cross-disciplinary conversations across a nine-month period between two teachers who are now teacher educators of music and religious education respectively. Secondary school teacher educators Mary Earl and Jennie Francis refuse to accept the condition of causality at the intersection of, and space between, teachers and learners. They reflect on the condition of possibilities that their creative research conversation frames as shared experiences, remembering when, as early career teachers, they tried (and often felt that they failed) to find ways to connect with the complexity of students' needs. Their assemblage[2] of encounters include: *dialogic* principles and authenticity in teaching relationships, *care* in education and *alternative ways* of documenting manifestations of teaching inclusively. They put theory to work differently in negotiating and paying attention to what students say. Following Bakhtin (1981), they seek to enact 'dialogue' as a focused conversation which engages the heart as well as the mind, to talk their way into a creative research conversation framed by their shared interest in pupil voice. As Bonnett says about relationships as a form of the poetic, 'no one person initiates the interplay, is wholly responsible for it, or able to control it. It is a matter of co-responsibility' (1996, p. 37).

The social status of being a teacher or student, a performing artist or songwriter, and most notably, the demarcation between expert and lay knowledges, sets clear boundaries between different ways of knowing and relating to different musical worlds. The eruption here is about human–world relationships, about being open to experiment and adjust, researching without re-presentation, non- or post-representational research practices capable of engaging the materiality of language itself (MacLure, 2013), and the language and materiality at the heart of teaching and learning. It is about how two very different teachers (of Religious Education and Music) become performers of inclusivity. The rupture is in the terrain of cross-disciplinary conversations which impact on both of them. The encounter brought discomfort. There were frustrations. They asked, 'What's the point of writing about it as well?' Of course, the point lies in their beliefs and theories; both critical issues in the future of teaching and learning:

> the performance of a teacher does *not* exist to 'programme students in a certain direction so that they will behave in set ways' (Rudduck, 1988, p. 35). It's there to help students towards a reasoned and responsible autonomy – and care about them in the process. Is this rebellion? Who knows? It's certainly, in our experience, counter-cultural at a time when education is full of agendas which seems to be adversely affecting the subjective experience both of teaching and learning. (Earl & Francis, this volume)

The rupture described here is in the terrain of cross-disciplinary conversations between teachers who are caught up in a maelstrom of eruptions

2 Assemblages are ad hoc groupings of diverse elements, of vibrant materials of all sorts. Assemblages are living, throbbing confederations that are able to function despite the persistent presence of energies that confound them from within (Bennett, 2010, pp. 23–24). Examples are the 'thing power' or distributed agency of a guitar, or collaborative song writing between teacher and learner, teacher and teacher, self and other that catalyse teaching inclusively.

themselves. They are also attempting to create a new eruption and rupture. The disruption is in the urgency to rethink so as to reconfigure ways of thinking, feeling and writing about teaching and learning. How, for example, do we (re)address concepts such as 'inclusion', 'autonomy' and the subjective experience both of teaching and learning? The rupture, here, is in the need to recalibrate our sights and pursue the desire to acknowledge the fullness of becoming as inclusive teachers. What use is it, to the next generation, to be given so much information and so much testing that their mental health starts to crumble under the strain and their anxiety about how they will manage to live in the new worlds they are going to inhabit escalates? The authors' answer is that students who are lucky find, in those 'transitional spaces' we call classrooms, a teacher who is *present*. They find a teacher who uses their *voice* and their *ears* and their *eyes* – their whole bodies – *to hear* and inclusively respond.

What is particularly pertinent to their conversation and provides a radically different way of doing and being and collaborating in, and through, research as rebellious teachers is the conversation. This can be the conversation we begin in our everyday classroom teaching between teacher and student, student and student, or the conversations between teachers which are always unfinished and unfinaliseable (Bakhtin, 1984). This is done not just by hearing something and then writing it down, nor by composing something by numbers. Insights come from seeds of discussions, from observations and from deep, attentive listening. They come from being given the opportunity to care about what one is *doing*, not just because it is good for some distant goal, but because it is good for and of itself.

In Chapter 6, Bernd Brabec de Mori, an Austrian musicologist, troubles the notion of 'academic disciplining', '(in)disciplining' and research (in)sanity, and the conundrum of (Indigenous) timescapes. Bernd Brabec de Mori says we need to be rebellious in bridging the 'ontological incommensurability' between Indigenous worlds and westerners, and likewise with the reframing of 'academic (in)disciplining' and transdisciplinarity. He radically puts forward the case for an ontological theoretical shift afforded by the concept of 'temporality', saying

> that a researcher has to understand the timescape of the researched in order to be able to tune into it. Only then can synchronisation occur, and consequently eye-level communication and interaction with the entities becomes possible, both in research and in inter-community life. (Brabec de Mori, this volume)

He disturbs and disrupts the discourse of academic disciplines with the term 'indiscipline', used purposively to open rebellious escape hatches into transdisciplinary encounters that work, and work in, the cracks of neoliberal order. Unlike the either/or approach of reductionist scientific inquiry, where boundaries are set for exclusion, this type of rebellious inquiry is led by questions and interventions that aim to produce ever-richer yet disruptive versions of reality and principles of unrest (Massumi, 2017). This equates to replacing the old way of thinking by taking and arguing for a different stance on the relations between the arts and the sciences, as both ways of thinking can be rather like a continual accretion of multiple descriptions of nature and can, in line with nature's way of working, produce redundancy.

Inciting Rebellion in the Academy

In *Science, order and creativity*, David Bohm and David Peat (1987) emphasise one possible form of creativity in science, for humanity as a whole. Creativity in science stems from metaphorical thinking that, by equating two different kinds of things, establishes an act of perception of a similarity. They emphasise the role of communication and art in this form of creativity in science. Similar insights characterise the communication and artistic work of famous figures such as Leonardo da Vinci. For example, da Vinci's celebrated drawing of 'Water falling upon water' (Figure 1.1) is not a realistic snapshot of a jet of water but an attempt to 'elaborate on several types of turbulence caused by the impact of the jet' (Capra, 2007, p. 195). It is the form of water – its changeable, dynamic shape – and the shifting boundaries of perception that provide the focus of da Vinci's drawings (Figure 1.1).

FIGURE 1.1
Images of Leonardo da Vinci's drawing 'Water falling upon water' (© RCT)

These are, in fact, never realistic renderings of a single instance, but a synthesis of repeated observations through which he attempted to craft a theoretical model. We see this blurring of boundaries in artist Trisha McCrae's sense making of her perceptual encounters with Da Vinci's drawings where, in Figure 1.2, she recognises the 'vital materiality' or 'material vibrancy' (Bennett, 2010, p. XIII) that runs through and across bodies, both human and non-human, and emerges as transdisciplinary renderings. Figure 1.2 brings to life the constant rhythms and movement, likening the constantly changing rips, tides, and flows of ideas that provide new insights into activating transdisciplinary renderings.

FIGURE 1.2
Artist Trisha McCrae's creative exchange with da Vinci (© Pamela Burnard)

The blurring of boundaries is seen, not only in da Vinci's multiple drawings featuring spiral patterning, but also in his effective use of the technique of *sfumato*, which challenged the view of early modern philosophers of aesthetics, and which favoured 'disinterested observation' as a means of making sense of perceptual encounters with the world. Da Vinci's focus on representing what something 'may appear like to the human eye' (Capra, 2005, p. 19) goes in the opposite direction, as it recognises, and rebelliously embodies, how interconnected sensing and acting are.

As mentioned earlier, perception, in arts as well as in sciences, is different from simple 'reception' (as in the process of registering stimuli from an external reality). Perception is very much an active shifting of our own attention to the world, as in the original Latin 'ab-tension'; that is, to draw something or somebody towards. Human creativity is thus central to putting forth new sensory orders and structures that form new perceptions and, for this reason, the disruption and eruption caused by transdisciplinarity is what enables the rebellious act of making sense of the *sensorial relationship* that is being established with, and in, the world (Bergmann, 2018).

In Chapter 7 we see French philosophers and researchers Antonella Poli and Bernard Andrieu perform 'Transdisciplinary Creativity by Emersiology with the Living Body'. They explain that the body is not subject to purposive, language-bound rationality, and can give access to aesthetic experience and to systemic wisdom re-linking us with our context. Similarly, scientists' work is rooted in the individual's own sensorial experience of the world, and such embodied experience is at the heart of the ideas, imagery and conceptions formulating their thinking (Gosetti-Ferencei, 2018). Hence, visual and aural images, kinaesthetic sensibility and sensorial elements play into the repertoire of transdisciplinary creativities (Gosetti-Ferencei, 2018) to constitute a complete 'feel' for and a 'becoming' part of rebellion in the academy. Unlike conventional views, which equate creativity to the linear and analytic thinking that feeds conscious purpose, thinking and knowing in the arts and sciences embrace the unconscious and recursive processes that mean all transdisciplinary creativities, from simple appreciation to the actual process, are embedded in the natural world (Bateson, 1972/2000, p. 478).

In Chapter 2, spoken word artist, performance poet and founder of a 'Collaborative Poetics' method and network,[3] Helen Johnson offers up 'Ten Incitements to Rebellion'. Using spoken word as a social scientific research tool, Helen Johnson makes the case for 'a radically different way of doing, being and collaborating in, and through, research'. Framed as an act of rebellion, spoken word as collaborative poetic inquiry is introduced as a methodological approach to re-territorialising research practice, to unsettling the mainstream view of academic writing and to repositioning poetic inquiry as a rebellious mattering (making with and desiring) that transcends the separateness of arts and sciences. Pursuing a collaborationist agenda, where it is people that make things matter to us, Helen Johnson considers how rebellious 'collaborating across fields (social scientists with artists) acknowledges the specialist skill, craft and knowledge which it takes to produce high-quality creative pieces'.

In Chapter 3, circus artist, circus educator and academic Alisan Funk calls us to a 'rebellious rejection of social norms' that drive perceptions about the practice of becoming/embodying circus and the representation and development of circus itself. Alisan Funk invites us to 'baulk and question, consider the uncomfortable unanswereds' concerning what circus knows about circus and its own theory of performance possibilities. She invites us to reflect on whether we can truly know her experience of circus when we may well have no direct access to her ontology (or experience of being/becoming a circus artist and

3 This network connects research and art with community groups and experts through experience with performative social sciences, exemplified here by interactions between social scientists, spoken word artist-educators and the young people they teach, write, perform and create with.

researcher). For Alisan Funk, research with circus requires immersion in circus. She invites us to expand the space through which her theory materialises.

> Going to practice, practising, and then preparing for the next practice session take precedence. For years. And years. This practical training ensures extensive knowledge of the equipment (corporeal), associated partners (e.g. trapeze, juggling clubs, one or more other humans, and sometimes non-human compatriots), and conditions conducive to research and production (mental, emotional, environmental). (Funk, this volume)

Viewed from different perspectives, re-constructions and voicings of circus practice, circus disciplines and theorising circus, she intermixes encounters of circus practice and research with compelling portraits of entanglement with non-human things in the circus, and both the being of and the storying (knowing) of these things. She introduces a deep ecology of artistic practice manifest in attentiveness to circus encounters of practice, and the differences between performer and audience experiences of circus reality. Then, by engaging us with the theory-in-practice of circus, she goes on to rebelliously ask: 'By entering research, do you risk leaving circus?'

For Alisan Funk, the rebellion is in the threshold between perspectives. In a similar vein, it is about using multiple methods to seek out the traces of an affective and sensual encounter with materiality that matters when people, events and non-human agents make up the multifaceted subjectivity that operates as circus research, that ventures, still, so far from the traditional territories of educational research. What does this all mean? Does it mean that by joining the circus, attending a circus course, engaging in circus research training or writing academically about the circus you have the right to think of yourself as a rebel? She invites us to reflect on whether learning the tools of the trade (as a practising circus artist or as a circus researcher/academic) is not inherently rebellious. Does the topic lead to discomfort and require doing rebellious research?

As is explored in chapters across Part 1, the tools of rebellion are research and writing techniques of power. The matter of discovering what we know and understand about practices, such as those of circus, circus practitioners and the mattering of non-human elements, concerns post-human thinking and the materiality and making of the discipline, as well as the agency of matter. This is where Alisan Funk challenges researchers most vehemently to consider the Baradian materialities (encounters with the particularities of circus) as intra-acting agents where human–non-human partnerships are capable of exploding deeply entrenched ideas. One of these ideas being exploded in this chapter by Alisan Funk is the rebellious need to rethink the relationship and assumed agencies of researcher, research subject (in this case, the circus) and research tools that do not precede but rather *emerge* through their intra-action (Barad, 2007, p. 33). Troubling this relationship and exploring how a post-humanist orientation might enable new readings of circus in the domain of artistic research is another path for researchers without extensive circus practice to engage with circus artistic research.

Embracing Discomfort and Uncertainty as Part of the Process of Doing Rebellious Research and Writing

The chapters that feature in Part 1 are thus presented as rebellious research assemblages that illustrate disruptive and unsettling ways of drawing together differently the affective, discursive, historical, sociocultural and material conditions of academic writing. Why are they disruptive and unsettling? Assemblages are made of and give rise to 'lines of flight', that is, bolts of pent-up energy, trajectories of possibility which exceed the disciplinary 'gaze' to attend to the ongoing folding-unfolding of the self and the world (Figure 1.2). This can involve rebelling by *taking risks* (as told by Alisan Funk through her *circus research* in Chapter 3), by performing rebellious engagement in academic writing partnerships (by Mary Earl and Jennie Francis in Chapter 5 through *language and listening*), by the creative rupture of rebellious dancers and choreographers (as ways of doing transdisciplinary creativity and *emersiology*[4] as told by Antonella Poli and Bernard Andrieu in Chapter 7), and the rebellion at the heart of spoken word (Chapter 2), researching circus (Chapter 3) and within transdisciplinary scapes (Chapter 4) and musicking (Chapter 5).

What kinds of thinking and practice are being advanced by these kinds of de-territorialising practices, and how might this rebellious transdisciplinary way of working de-territorialise academic writing and research? How can rebellious practices generate change and push the boundaries of human-centred thinking towards new territories of transdisciplinary combinations and/or pairings of subject disciplines?

In Part 1, readers are invited to engage in (re-)viewing, (re-)framing and (re-)doing rebellious transdisciplinary research practices and academic writing that breaks away from traditional practices to create new paths in the future of learning and teaching. Understanding how *sciences and arts meet and come to matter* requires the erasure of subject silos and the activation of

4 *Emersiology* is a new method and vision of embodied research which explores the depth of the living body by analysing the emergence of the invisible data of the living body in a person's awareness. The implicit activities of the living body emerge in the awareness of this body without our voluntary control (see Chapter 16).

new ways of entangling subject disciplines, not simply as spaces for acquisition of knowledges and skills but as transdisciplinary creativities with potential for authoring real impact on the individual's life and community. The aim is not simply to re-vision and re-frame transdisciplinary research and writing practice, but to develop ways in which research and writing practices – and knowledge creation itself – may be radically redesigned. Reframing intra-acting binaries through transdisciplinary research – such as art–science, mind–body, material–discursive, discourse–affect, textual–visual, theory–practice – reveals that boundaries are porous, indeterminate, non-permanent and ever changing. This allows us to see differences relationally, to diffract and differentiate, without dominance by any one discipline.

In Figure 1.3 artist Trisha McCrae depicts a non-linear, boundary-crossing constellation of routes into transdisciplinary practices that rebelliously break from traditional ways of researching and writing. Here, Trisha McCrae visually offers a translation of the concept of diffraction as the entanglement of intersecting lines of flight – opening up new possible journeys of transdisciplinary research – through the use of an abstract visual language. Off these abstract shapes are performative departures acting as a communication highway that create assemblages of ideas that are open and porous to generating a flow of new trajectories of possibility. This is a dance of lines, a sounding of music in nature. This is a patterning in sciences and arts where the rebellious energy of transdisciplinarity is emergent and diffractively becoming.

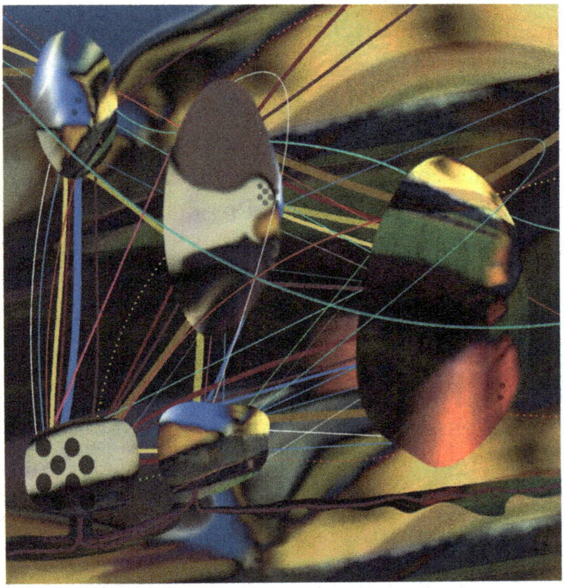

FIGURE 1.3 Artist Trisha McCrae's visualisation of a disciplinary rooting of transdisciplinary research (© Pamela Burnard)

In place of binaries, of siloed disciplines, then, I (along with several Part 1 authors) argue for the imperative/importance of post-humanising, transdisciplinary education with a much greater understanding of the different logics of knowing in the arts and sciences, and the diverse and multiple creativities they shape and cultivate in practice than that which has gone before us. As Marenko (2021) has recently argued, 'trans-disciplinarity is, first and foremost, trans-gression: of boundaries, of expectations, of received assumptions' (p. 179).

This transdisciplinary research and writing assemblage suggests there is scope to reframe our thinking to inquire into not only how arts and sciences purposefully connect, but also how they stimulate different forms of logics, rationality and affect; how they become part of an inquiry that is embedded within post-humanism, which highlights that human beings never act alone and are always *entangled* with/in their environments (Dernikos et al., 2020).

The integration of arts and sciences into transdisciplinary action allows researchers, research educators and academics to develop an understanding of the world that values their affective subjectivities while at the same time enabling their relational capabilities to 'be with' and 'think with' other living things, within a shared 'learning ecology' (Bateson, 1972/2000, 1979/2002).

The integration of scientific and artistic perspectives brings forth both analytical and empathetic thinking, offering a range of different modalities for 'dwelling' with objects of attention, and for thinking and being in the world. Re-uniting these two dimensions in multi-modal, transdisciplinary and real-world activities addresses some of the limitations of current research, education and academic writing structures.

For artists, academics and researchers alike, enacting rebellious, transdisciplinary research and writing practices requires commitment to understanding how scientific and artistic creativities come to matter for sustainable futures. This stance diverges from not only the outcome-based model of education, but also the instrumentalist approach of progress towards a sustainable target, as if sustainability were a point fixed in time. Instead, through the experiences illustrated in this research assemblage, we have endeavoured to show that sustainability as a path, as process, involves multiple creativities, and as such should be allowed to diverge from an original plan in order to remain close to the path of perception and sense experience. 'Sustainable futures' here are thus futures that are enacted through disruptive practices of making with and co-relating, as opposed to co-planning with a fixed outcome in mind. This opens up several new lines of curriculum reform involving a set of negotiated co-authorings with a community of transdisciplinary teachers and learners.

It is essential to note that, for transdisciplinary writing practices to be authentic within and beyond the academy, writing communities can be encouraged and released through:

- *Writing individually and collaboratively* to (co-)author rebellious transdisciplinary approaches which recognise the importance of the intra-action amongst disciplines (Simmons & Singh, 2019).
- *Committing to flattening subject hierarchies* by post-humanising a transdisciplinary curriculum for teaching research and writing that extends and transforms curricula beyond disciplinary traditions and towards sense experience (Braidotti, 2013).
- *Shifting attention to the emerging* material-discursive narratives of reductionist science in education and thinking of new stories to tell our stories with (Haraway, 2016).
- *Being open to diverse creativities* that help to de- and re-territorialise subjects, norms and processes that narrowly define disciplines (Burnard & Colucci-Gray, 2020; Burnard et al., 2021).
- *De-coupling the specific language* of a discipline from its original context, opening up new possibilities for viewing and experiencing the same phenomenon, and the materiality of difference (Braidotti, 2019).
- *Dismantling structures* that deny a turn in future-making education to transgress and transcend disciplinary boundaries, and reposition research education, so that arts and sciences are *not* separate or even separable endeavours, but each discipline acts on the others through a relational materialist approach to transdisciplinary configurations (Gale, 2018).

Globally, research educators and academics are confronting many challenging issues at the forefront of the future of learning and teaching. While transdisciplinary practices are not new, they nonetheless equate to critical issues in teaching and learning in and beyond the academy.

References

Bakhtin, M. (1981). *The dialogic imagination*. University of Texas Press.

Bakhtin, M. (1984). *Problems of Dostoevsky's poetics* (C. Emerson, Trans.). University of Minnesota Press.

Barad, K. (2007). *Meeting the universe halfway: Quantum physics and the entanglements of matter and meaning*. Duke University Press.

Bateson, G. (2000). *Steps to an ecology of mind: Collected essays in anthropology, psychiatry, evolution, and epistemology*. University of Chicago Press. (Original work published 1972)

Bateson, G. (2002). *Mind and nature: A necessary unity*. Hampton Press. (Original work published 1979)

Beadle, R. (2018). On running away to the circus. *Politics & Poetics: A Journal for Humane Philosophy, 4*, 1–28.

Bennett, J. (2010). *Vibrant matter: A political economy of things*. Duke University Press.

Bergmann, S. (2018). With-in: Towards an aesth/ethics of prepositions. In S. Bergmann & F. Clingerman (Eds.), *Arts, religion and the environment: Exploring nature's texture* (pp. 61–84). Brill.

Bohm, D., & Peat, F. D. (1987). *Science, order and creativity*. Routledge.

Bonnett, M. (1996). 'New' ERA values and the teacher–pupil relationship as a form of the poetic. *British Journal of Educational Studies, 44*(1), 27–41.

Braidotti, R. (2013). *The posthuman*. Polity.

Braidotti, R. (2019). *Posthuman knowledge*. Polity.

Burnard, P., & Colucci-Gray, L. (Eds.). (2020). *Why science and arts creativities matter*. Brill Sense.

Burnard, P., Colucci-Gray, L., & Sinha, P. (2021). Transdisciplinarity: Letting arts and science teach together. *Curriculum Perspectives, 41*(1), 113–118.

Capra, F. (2005). Speaking nature's language: Principles for sustainability. In M. K. Stone & Z. Barlow (Eds.), *Ecological literacy: Educating our children for a sustainable world* (pp. 18–29). Sierra Club Books.

Capra, F. (2007). *The science of Leonardo: Inside the mind of the great genius of the Renaissance*. Doubleday.

Deleuze, G., & Guattari, E. (1987). *A thousand plateaus: Capitalism and schizophrenia* (B. Massumi, Trans.). University of Minnesota Press.

Dernikos, B., Lesko, N., McCall, S., & Niccolini, A. (Eds.). (2020). *Mapping the affective turn in education: Theory, research and pedagogies*. Routledge.

Gale, K. (2018). *Madness as methodology: Bringing concepts to life in contemporary theorising and inquiry*. Routledge.

Gosetti-Ferencei, J. A. (2018). *The life of the imagination: Revealing and making the world*. Columbia University Press.

Haraway, D. (2004). Teddy bear patriarchy: Taxidermy in the Garden of Eden, New York City, 1908–36. In D. Haraway (Ed.), *The Haraway reader* (pp. 151–198). Routledge.

Haraway, D. (2016). *Staying with the trouble: Making kin in Chthulucene*. Duke University Press.

Hodgson, N., Vlieghe, J., Zamojski, P., & Ramaekers, S. (2017). *Manifesto for a post-critical pedagogy*. Punctum Books.

Kuhn, T. (1962). *The structure of scientific revolutions*. University of Chicago Press.

MacLure, M. (2013). Researching without representation? Language and materiality in post-qualitative methodology. *International Journal of Qualitative Studies in Education, 26*(6), 658–667.

Marenko, B. (2021). Stacking complexities: Reframing uncertainty through hybrid literacies. *Design and Culture, 13*(2), 165–184.

Marshall, J. (2014). Transdisciplinarity and art integration: Toward a new understanding of art-based learning across the curriculum. *Studies in Art Education, 55*(2), 104–127.

Massumi, B. (2017). *The principle of unrest: Activist philosophy in the expanded field.* Open Humanities Press.

Murris, K., & Bozalek, V. (2019). Diffraction and response-able reading of texts: The relational ontologies of Barad and Deleuze. *International Journal of Qualitative Studies in Education, 32*(7), 872–886.

Petrie, H. G. (1992). Interdisciplinary education: Are we faced with insurmountable opportunities? *Review of Research in Education, 18,* 299–333.

Rudduck, J. (1988). Changing the world of the classroom by understanding it: A review of some aspects of the work of Lawrence Stenhouse. *Journal of Curriculum and Supervision, 4*(1), 30–42.

Russell, A. W., Wickson, F., & Carew, A. (2008). Transdisciplinarity: Context, contradictions and capacity. *Science Direct Futures, 40*(5), 460–472.

Sandford, S. (2015). Feminist theory, philosophy and transdisciplinarity. *Theory, Culture and Society, 32*(5–6), 159–182. https://doi.org/10.1177/0263276415594238

Simmons, N., & Singh A. (Eds.). (2019). *Critical collaborative communities: Academic writing partnerships, groups and retreats.* Brill Sense.

Smith, S., & Henriksen, D. (2016). Fail again, fail better: Embracing failure as a paradigm for creative learning in the arts. *Art Education, 69*(2), 6–11. https://doi.org/10.1080/00043125.2016.1141644

CHAPTER 2

Ten Incitements to Rebellion

Spoken Word as a Social Scientific Research Tool of, and for, Rebellious Research

Helen Johnson

Introduction

For many, the arts and sciences stand at opposite ends of an unbridgeable divide: the sciences, rigid, objective, systematic and authoritative; the arts, fluid, subjective, dynamic and capricious. Yet there are multiple points of interconnection between these fields. Arts-based research represents a particularly fertile form of arts–science interaction. This chapter interweaves creative writing, poetry, theoretical discussion and empirical research to make the case for spoken word poetry as an arts-based method of inquiry that can provide a radically different way of doing, being and collaborating in, and through, research. With reference to the innovative method of 'collaborative poetics' and to the work of youth slam/spoken word educators, I argue that social scientists and spoken word practitioners can learn much from one another's tools, techniques and ways of thinking, creating new forms of knowledge, redefining the relationships between audience, author and participants, and facilitating a 'critical resilience' which enables both individual fortitude in the face of adversity and a means through which to challenge the conditions which give rise to this adversity. I frame this methodological approach as an act of rebellion for participants, researchers and artists alike, considering how spoken word as poetic inquiry enables us to address the critical complexities and challenges of contemporary life, and what this means for the status of both the arts and social sciences.

(Fade in)

In six weeks we write ourselves;
story the silence,
with interview, analysis and poetry;
our lives viewed
like sand through a microscope.

 | DOI:10.1163/9789004516069_004

Each lived experience,
a slither of cerith,
a paring of periwinkle.
No longer lost in tawny drifts,
we hold piece by piece up to the light;
sift rainbows through our fingers.
We are conchologists,
collecting cantles of discrimination;
a poetic inquiry
to splinter
the softness of sands.

This poem describes a study in which I worked with a group of young spoken word artists, using poetry to research discrimination. We mobilised spoken word as a form of poetic inquiry and developed, from this, a method of participatory arts-based research called 'collaborative poetics' (CP). Drawing on CP, this chapter uses a range of poetic devices, including blackout poetry, data poetry and free verse,[1] to creatively embody the background, underpinnings, benefits, applications and challenges of spoken word as a transgressive research method through which to explore lived experiences, promote (critical) resilience and work towards social justice.

For me, CP provides a way of understanding, creating and acting that unites my identities as poet, social scientist and community activist. In doing so, it rebels against the policing of disciplinary boundaries and the hierarchies of power that define these. Accordingly, throughout this discussion, I contend that we should strive to be *rebellious* and *undisciplined*, to question, penetrate, even demolish, the walls that separate different fields, sectors and academic disciplines. Arguably, it is only through such rule breaking that we will create something truly revolutionary and transformative.

This is my rebellion ...

... against forces that would bifurcate my identity ... against a hegemony that elevates academics above those they work with and for ... against the pursuit of 'pure' knowledge as an isolationist rhetoric of privilege.

With incitements to do, think and be differently, I invite you to stage your own rebellion.

1 See Table 2.1 at the end of this chapter for a full list of the poetry forms used.

(Scene)
Introducing Arts-Based Research

No longer lost in tawny drifts,
we hold piece by piece up to the light;
sift rainbows through our fingers.

Arts-based research (ABR) incorporates a wide range of approaches, which use the arts as tools for data collection, analysis and/or dissemination (Leavy, 2009). The 'outputs' of such research challenge the traditional academic form, incorporating images, music and visual art into journal articles, or presenting research in film, poetry, theatrical pieces and other creative formats. Through this, ABR engages larger and broader audiences in social scientific knowledge, presenting them with something which is more accessible, playful, emotional, meaningful and, above all, *human* than the typical academic output. More fundamentally, ABR has the ability not just to convey knowledge differently, but to elicit *different kinds* of knowledge that cannot be represented adequately through other means (Eisner, 2008).

(Freeze frame)

Disrupt
the binary,
resist window dressing,
our art can be radical
research.

As a third research paradigm that transcends the established qualitative–quantitative binary, ABR has the potential to unsettle the metatheory of scientism with its 'gold standard' of objective, controlled experimentation (McNiff, 2018).

Incitement One: In a research landscape dominated by a two-paradigm model …

… stage your rebellion through a third paradigm of arts-based research.

(Cut to)
Autoethnography

Each lived experience,

a slither of cerith,
a paring of periwinkle.

Ellis and Bochner (2000, p. 739) define autoethnography as 'an autobiographical genre of writing that displays multiple layers of consciousness'. As such, it speaks to the radical potential of ABR, embracing researcher subjectivity and emotionality, and subscribing to the view that there are multiple, equally valid ways of viewing the world.

Autoethnography as Autoethnography …

I am image.
I am music.
My life a play.
My whole a poem.
Place me centre-stage,
a story/line to without.
Re-make me visible,
in all fragmented glory.
My inspiration, insight,
my passion, authentic.
I am not irrelevant.
This tangle of plurality
is no corrosive tangent.
I offer you my story,
visceral and vital
for empathy, connection,
healing,
offer you my self
beyond the text.
Song, sketch,
stage and stanza,
reaching out
to rewrite worlds.

Incitement Two: In a context where researchers' positionality is viewed as contaminant …

… stage your rebellion by mobilising subjectivity as a tool of inquiry.

(Cut to)
Poetic Inquiry: Blackout and Beyond

a poetic inquiry
to splinter
the softness of sands.

Like autoethnography, poetic inquiry can embody ideological struggle through the intersection of self and social issues/values, sparking critical consciousness amongst audiences, as they enter into the dialogue (Faulkner, 2009). Furthermore, poetry has the power to condense language and experience to great effect.[2]

FIGURE 2.1 Be …

Incitement Three: In the face of epistemologies based on what can be explicitly demarcated and delineated …

… stage your rebellion in liminality, silence, metaphor and imagery.

Although poetic inquiries typically focus on poetry on the page, there are a few notable exceptions which utilise spoken word, often with teenagers and/or young adults (see Ayala & Zaal, 2016; Fenge et al., 2016; Fletcher et al., 2016;

2 Importantly however, Maréchal and Linstead (2010) urge against mobilising poetry as a means of meeting scientific criteria of parsimony and reductionism, arguing that, while science condenses to reduce and generalise, poetry does so in order to evoke and resonate.

Godwin, 2018; Lashua, 2006; Sethi, 2012; Skinner, 2012). The vast majority of this research, however, uses spoken word as merely one (under-articulated) element of a broader package of methods, bundles spoken word in with hip hop as a presumed synergistic artform and/or labels work as spoken word with little evidence to support this classification. Furthermore, there is little theorisation of the particular benefits that spoken word poetry brings to ABR. As Coemans and Hannes (2017) argue, this failure to articulate a rationale for specific artistic methods/techniques is a common weakness of ABR; yet such work is necessary if we are to rebel in any meaningful way against methodological hegemony. Being *undisciplined* can support this work.

In the context of spoken word, investigations into the work of youth slam and spoken word (YSSW) artist-educators can teach us valuable lessons about the use of spoken word as a radically different tool for research, resilience and social justice. This demonstrates the potential of spoken word ABR to unseat the academic from their throne as sole, authoritative purveyor of knowledge; disrupt the idea of the arts as an exclusive realm for the professionally trained artist/critic; and break away from the page to construct embodied, inter-subjective and dynamic knowledge.[3]

(Enter stage left)
Critical Inquiry in Youth Slam and Spoken Word

we write ourselves;
story
the silence.

YSSW programs typically work with poets who are aged nineteen years or under. They may take the form of regular, year-round after-school clubs, more short-term projects, or be integrated into school curricula.[4] YSSW educators often work with disenfranchised young people, including inner city youth and youth of colour, aiming to explore and reframe these problematised identities as powerful and positive.

3 It is, perhaps, ironic that this discussion is presented through the written, rather than spoken, word. While this arguably limits the extent to which I am able to embody the method, it is worth noting that words presented on the page are not bound to that page, but retain a dynamic, intersubjective quality, as meaning is accomplished through interaction between author, page and audience. This reflects the complex relationship between the written and spoken word in the context of spoken word poetry and poetry slam (Gregory, 2012).

4 For more on YSSW see Gregory (2015) on the UK and Weinstein (2010, 2018) on North America.

Amplify (from) the Margins

'Amplifying
voices of the oppressed,'[5]
on a political journey
through self-exploration.

Voices of the oppressed,
negotiating prescribed identities
through self-exploration,
craft new ideals.

Negotiating prescribed identities,
spoken word artists
craft new ideals,
beyond institutional approval.

Spoken word artists,
connecting with others
beyond institutional approval,
re-write what can be.

Connecting with others,
challenging hegemony,
re-write what can be –
poetry/poets, society/citizens.

Challenging hegemony,
developing criticality,
poetry/poets, society/citizens
reclaim our spaces.

Developing criticality
with self-confidence, resilience,
reclaim our spaces
for empathy and healing.

With self-confidence, resilience,
re-school our teachers,

---

5 Quotation taken from Davis (2018, p. 114).

for empathy, healing,
community.

Re-school our teachers,
amplifying
community,
on a political journey.

Incitement Four: In societies where power rests with the (predominantly white, male, middle-class) academy …

… stage your rebellion by listening to, and learning from, marginalised voices.

In YSSW the audience are invoked as co-conspirators in the pursuit of social justice, to reflect, extend, validate and magnify young people's voices (Ingalls, 2012). For Godwin (2018, p. 238), this is a 'dialogic relationship rooted in solidarity', which challenges traditional power differentials between performer and audience. Fenge et al. (2016) understand this relationship in terms of Bourriaud's (2002) concept of 'relational aesthetics', which emphasises art as a situated, collaborative performance between equal status artists and audience. These encounters are characterised by a sense of 'conviviality' and reciprocally intertwined with macro-level actions.

Incitement Five: In a realm where knowledge is presented as singular, fixed and impersonal …

… stage your rebellion by embracing the performative, dynamic and inter-subjective. … by becoming a co-conspirator in the pursuit of social justice.

(Beat)
Lessons for Spoken Word as Poetic Inquiry

our lives viewed
like sand
through a microscope.

Patmanathan (2013) recognises the potential of spoken word of, and for, research. She echoes the claims of YSSW scholars that slam enables participants (particularly those from marginalised and oppressed communities) to build a critical consciousness, challenge inequalities, develop collaborative relationships and foster empathy. Further, she contends that slam as research method can foreground under-explored perspectives and approaches, challenging dominant western academic notions of what counts as knowledge and documentation, just as slam as artform works to decolonise the limited western model of what the arts are and who they are for.

Incitement Six: In a world where North American and European values are paraded as truth …

… stage your rebellion by striving to decolonise art, research, knowledge.

While Patmanathan makes some valuable points, her work does not live up to its promise. Rather than remodelling slam within a radically new paradigm of ABR, she merely labels existing slam practice as a research process, analysing the content of slam poems and speculating on their potential impact. Collaborative poetics (CP), in contrast, integrates spoken word with established research methods to create a new, robust and creative methodology. In doing so, CP follows third paradigm ABR in: reconfiguring notions of what research and art can/should be; challenging received wisdom around issues such as who has the authority to create art/research and what counts as knowledge; and collapsing distinctions between author and audience, researcher and researched, output and dissemination, theory and practice.

Partnership (1)

Spoken word poets
ally the disempowered,
the marginalised.
  Social scientists partner,
  theorise, network, platform.
Investigating,
articulating our selves,
lived experience.
  Connect micro to macro
  issues, contexts and debates.
Perform, embody.
Unafraid of emotion,

relational art.
Authority promotes change,
systematic inquiry.
Speak the unspoken,
illuminate hinterlands,
disrupt our knowing.

Transforming ...... how .... we .... make
our ...... individual ...... and ...... collective
worlds.

Incitement Seven: In a territory where the researcher is king ...

... stage your rebellion by yielding control to artists, educators and community practitioners.

(Enter stage right)
Introducing Collaborative Poetics

Rewrite the silence.
Our lived experience,
no longer lost in tawny drifts.

In CP lived experiences provide the data through which social scientific topics can be explored and made concrete, while poetry provides the emotion, passion and creativity to engage with an audience. The emphasis of spoken word on (particularly live) performance and on broadening the audience makes it a particularly powerful tool in this respect. Collaboration in CP is two-fold: Collaborating across fields (social scientists with artists) acknowledges the specialist skill, craft and knowledge which it takes to produce high-quality creative pieces. While collaborating with participants, as co-researchers, broadens the ethnographic lens, illuminating multiple subjectivities, as well as the *inter*-subjectivity of their intersection.

Partnership (2)

As co-researchers,
experts by experience

share skills and wisdom.
Academics share power,
collapse research hierarchies.
Through conversation,
co-production builds allies,
new ways of being.
We forego authority,
to democratise knowledge.
Community strength,
harnesses critical thought,
for resilience.[6]
Ditch neoliberalism,
(since no one creates alone).
Learning through process,
teaching truth to those above,
we come together.

Making .... to .... transform
our ...... individual ...... and ...... collective
worlds.

Incitement Eight: In a neoliberal system dominated by productivity, competitiveness and individual performance ...

... stage your rebellion by taking time, valuing process over product ... by confronting neoliberal ideology through critical resilience, collaboration and community.

(Begin flashback)
Founding Collaborative Poetics

We are conchologists,
collecting
cantles of discrimination.

6 'Critical resilience' contests and unsettles the mainstream resilience model, which effectively obscures structural inequalities, individualising social problems by focusing almost exclusively on the individual's ability to cope with adversity (Hart et al., 2016; Traynor, 2018). Rebelling against this neoliberal model, critical resilience takes individual and community strength as a pathway through to social justice and transformation.

CP was founded in a pilot study at McGill University's Participatory Cultures Lab.[7] Over six weeks I worked here with a research collective of seven young spoken word poets, experimenting with poetry as a collaborative research tool for exploring our lived experiences of discrimination and privilege. Spoken word was integral throughout this process. At the data collection stage, for example, activities like free writes were used to elicit discrimination experiences, while poetry composition and editing activities enabled us to organise, clarify and develop our understandings of the topic. At the other end of the process, poetry was harnessed for research dissemination through a chapbook, 'You kind of have to listen to me', and live spoken word show, 'The struggle *is* real'. Finally, during data analysis we mobilised methods like the Listening Guide's 'I' poems (Gilligan et al., 2003) to explore creative writing as an analytic, transformative process.[8]

Incitement Nine: In a field where few are prepared to confront the radical, transformative potential of the arts for research …

… stage your rebellion through a research model that integrates the arts at all stages … through an openness to new forms of knowledge and new ways of writing.

Thinking about artforms like spoken word as *analytic* tools is a particularly rebellious prospect. Accepting that art can be a vehicle for analysis itself, (rather than just providing data for analysis or packaging up findings in an aesthetically pleasing way) disrupts notions of what research and knowledge look like. Yet, if we are prepared to take this step, ABR has enormous potential to reveal new insights and new kinds of knowledge. One of the means through which this can occur is revelation via creative empathy. I experienced this when composing the poem 'Rank' in response to the prompt: 'Write a poem about a murder; do not mention the murder.' I challenged myself to voice 'Rank' in the persona of a white supremacist. In doing so, I experienced chills of horror and hatred, intermingled with the heat of shame; a range of emotions that provided an insight into discrimination that conventional research simply could not have achieved.

7 The study is described in detail in Johnson et al. (2017, 2018).

8 It is worth noting that ABR can disrupt the borders between data collection, analysis and outputs (Jones, 2012). Accordingly, I use these terms here not to establish a rigid, linear divide between them, but as a useful conceptual distinction which enables us to consider the parallels and 'fit' between rebellious ABR and mainstream research methodologies.

Rank

Monstrous fish bloat
these sand-soaked shallows,
eyes empty of love.
They say freedom has teeth.
I will be pliers,
rip slimy spawn
from each ugly shadow,
bring war to their water.
This lake is inspiration.

I'll scythe my hook
through each stupid,
rubber-lipped mouth,
hoick bodies out
into the cold honesty of light,
watch them flip-flap,
on the mottled, gravel beach.
Freedom without teeth.
Caught by the serendipity of God,
laid helpless at my feet.

Bending down
slowly,
to their stinking meat,
penknife pressed
tip to swollen belly,
I will gut them,
neck to tail,
let bloody gills gape
their final, empty complaints.

This lake will breathe anew
and you will thank me,
when the water is safe,
when our children's feet,
no longer need courage
to paddle here.
The lilies will stretch
and flex at last,

iridescent with relief,
petals springing back
like memory foam.

You need me,
to make this water pure again,
the air smell sweet again.
Only when we
are toe to knee,
in unctuous scales
will they realise,
that we
are descended from angels.

(***End flashback***)

(***Jump cut to***)
The Impact and Challenges of Doing Research Differently

hold piece by piece up to the light,
splinter through
the microscope.

The evaluation of the McGill pilot suggests that spoken word ABR can echo and enhance the work of YSSW educators, empowering co-researchers, facilitating the exploration of individual and group identities, supporting healing, and agitating for social change through the development of critical consciousness.[9] There is good reason to suppose that, just as with YSSW and community-based ABR more generally, this approach can be particularly valuable with sensitive topics, vulnerable groups and people who are under-represented in research. Nonetheless, doing research differently presents notable challenges, including issues around anonymity/authorship, vulnerability and time commitments.

Making it Scan?

How do you square
artistry,

9 See Johnson et al. (2017) for more on the evaluation of this research.

authorship with anonymity,[10]
vulnerability with risk,[11]
maximum output
with minimalised outlay?[12]

Resist straight lines,
our art is
relational, not anonymous,[13]
be purposeful with your risks,[14]
maximise time, space,
minimise mundanity.

Incitement Ten: In a market-driven model focused on short-term cost–benefit analyses ...

... stage your rebellion by taking time ... by making space for the intangible.

(Actors assemble)
An Undisciplined Rebellion

The softness of sands
splinter

---

10 Some researchers have approached this dilemma by using pen names; but this only really grants participants authorship if they use those monikers outside of the study, which, in turn, compromises anonymity. In the CP pilot, anonymity was treated as an ongoing, multi-layered issue, and co-researchers were given the option of taking authorship for each respective output (the chapbook, show and academic works).

11 Close, personal investment (from both researchers and participants) is arguably vital in ABR. This is part of its power, and something I have sought to demonstrate in this chapter, for example through the poem 'Rank'. Such emotional openness is risky, however. Thus, Fletcher et al. (2016) argue that we need to balance vulnerability and the risk of re-traumatisation with the need to hear participants' voices and work through difficult issues, while Behar (1996) highlights that we risk our authority as researchers when we challenge the fiction of our objectivity/distance.

12 It has been argued that 'taking time' is vital for the successful conduct of both arts- and community-based research (e.g. Facer & Enright, 2016). This asks a lot of artists, academics and particularly co-researchers (who are often unpaid). In addition, lengthy projects can conflict with the expectations of funders and institutions, who typically seek maximum impact for minimum outlay.

13 This alludes to both Bourriaud's (2002) 'relational aesthetics' and CP's commitment to a 'relational ethics', characterised by 'mutual respect, dignity, and connectedness' between researchers, participants and the communities of which they form a part (Ellis, 2007, p. 4).

14 Behar (1996) calls for researchers to adopt a purposeful vulnerability in which they engage deeply, personally and emotionally with the field.

through poetic inquiry.
Collecting cantles of discrimination,
we are conchologists,
sift rainbows through our fingers.
We hold piece by piece up to the light,
no longer lost in tawny drifts.
A paring of periwinkle.
a slither of cerith,
each lived experience,
like sand through a microscope.
Our lives viewed
with interview, analysis and poetry,
story the silence.
In writing, we right ourselves.

YSSW educators and third paradigm arts-based researchers break the rules and, in so doing, remake the world. Their work reveals the value of being *undisciplined* – talking across disciplines and using this dialogue to question taken-for-granted ways of investigating, mobilising and representing the communities with which we work. Community-engaged social researchers, in particular, have a great deal to learn from spoken word artists, particularly YSSW educators who have decades of experience working with marginalised and disadvantaged communities.

YSSW educators are rarely content with the (laudable) aim of enhancing the writing and performance skills of their students, seeking instead to support critical resilience. Young people are equipped to thrive in adverse conditions and, through voicing their personal, lived experiences, empowered to speak out against inequities. This mirrors the aims of more radical arts-based researchers using methods like autoethnography and poetic inquiry. CP builds on these combined strengths, bringing together the expertise of artists, academic researchers and community co-researchers to present a participatory ABR methodology which draws inspiration from the principles and practice of spoken word.

This approach brings with it challenges around: ethics; financial and time commitments; group dynamics; establishing evaluative criteria (or agreeing whether we need these); and ensuring our impact has both significance and reach. Grappling with these challenges will undoubtedly spark further debate to ignite rebellion. For now though, I close with an extract from a poem composed during the CP pilot, which encapsulates something of the potential of spoken word ABR.

when I'm on stage,
I feel powerful,

from the inside looking out.
I feel safe.
Nothing can touch me.
I'm one of the ones who's right,
has a voice,
Then, I have no choice,
but to take
whatever may come my way.

Incitement: Stage your rebellion …

(Fade out)

TABLE 2.1 List of poems

Title	Form	Source and notes
Untitled	Line palindrome (part one)	Originally published in the National Centre for Research Methods newsletter, 2017, https://www.ncrm.ac.uk/news/show.php?article=5499
(Freeze frame)	Cinquain	Previously unpublished
Autoethnography as Autoethnography	Free verse	Previously unpublished
Be …	Black out poem	Created from an earlier draft of this section written in standard, academic prose
Amplify (From) the Margins	Pantoum	Previously unpublished
Partnership (1)	Renga	Previously unpublished
Partnership (2)	Renga	Previously unpublished
Rank	Persona poem	Originally published in Johnson et al. (2017)
Making it Scan?	Pregunta	Previously unpublished
Untitled	Line palindrome (part two)	Previously unpublished
I'm Not Hiding/ Relief	Data poem (extract)	Originally published in Johnson et al. (2017). This contains the voices of five co-researchers, exploring common themes around discrimination.

Acknowledgements

I would like to thank the University of Brighton, the National Centre for Research Methods and the Independent Social Research Foundation, whose funding and support facilitated the development of collaborative poetics. I would also like to thank the members of the Collaborative Poetics Network for their continued enthusiasm, inspiration and hard work, which have enabled the method to thrive, in particular: Isilda Almeida-Harvey, Polly Blake, Kerensa Bushell, Jenny Fennessy, David Norbury, Carol Rivas, Katherine Wimpenny and Sandie Woods. Finally, I am grateful to the reviewers and editors of this volume for pushing me to rebel ever further in/through my writing.

References

This list has been pared back to a selection of core references, following Richardson's (1993, p. 705) contention that 'references are authority moves; disruptions; invite the reader to disengage from the text, like answering the doorbell in the middle of a lively conversation'.

Ayala, J., & Zaal, M. (2016). Poetics of justice: Using art as action and analysis in participatory action research. *Networks: An Online Journal for Teacher Research, 18*(1), art. 2. https://dx.doi.org/10.4148/2470-6353.1019

Behar, R. (1996). *The vulnerable observer: Anthropology that breaks your heart.* Beacon Press.

Bourriaud, N. (2002). *Relational aesthetics.* Les Presses du Reel.

Coemans, S., & Hannes, K. (2017). Researchers under the spell of the arts: Two decades of using arts-based methods in community-based enquiry with vulnerable populations. *Educational Research Review, 22*, 34–49.

Davis, C. (2018). Writing the self: Poetry, youth identity, and critical poetic inquiry. *Art/Research International, 3*(1), 114–131.

Eisner, E. (2008). Commentary: What education can learn from the arts. *LEARNing Landscapes, 2*(1), 23–30.

Ellis, C. (2007). Telling secrets, revealing lives: Relational ethics in research with intimate others. *Qualitative Inquiry, 13*, 3–29.

Ellis, C., & Bochner, A. P. (2000). Autoethnography, personal narrative, reflexivity: Research as subject. In N. K. Denzin & Y. S. Lincoln (Eds.), *Handbook of qualitative research* (pp. 733–768). Sage.

Facer, K., & Enright, B. (2016). *Creating living knowledge. The Connected Communities Programme, community–university relationships and the participatory turn in the production of knowledge.* University of Bristol/AHRC Connected Communities.

Faulkner, S. L. (2009). Research/poetry: Exploring poets' conceptualizations of craft, practice, and good and effective poetry. *Educational Insights, 13*(3). http://www.ccfi.educ.ubc.ca/publication/insights/v13n03/articles/faulkner/index.html

Fenge, L. A., Hodges, C., & Cutts, W. (2016). Performance poetry as a method to understand disability. *Forum Qualitative Sozialforschung, 17*(2), art. 11.

Fletcher, S., Cox, R. S., Scannell, L., Heykoop, C., Tobin-Gurley, J., & Peek, L. (2016). Youth creating disaster recovery and resilience: A multi-site arts-based youth engagement research project. *Children, Youth and Environments, 26*(1), 148–163.

Gilligan, C., Spencer, R., Weinberg, K., & Bertsch, T. (2003). On the listening guide: A voice-centred relational method. In P. M. Camic, J. E. Rhodes, & L. Yardley (Eds.), *Qualitative research in psychology: Expanding perspectives in methodology and design* (pp. 157–172). American Psychological Association.

Godwin, J. T. (2018). Spoken word as public pedagogy: Conceptualizing a prophetic public. *Journal of Curriculum and Pedagogy, 15*(3), 238–258. http://doi.org/10.1080/15505170.2018.1439787

Gregory, H. (2012). Poetry performances on the page and stage: Insights from slam. In S. Gingell & W. Roy (Eds.), *Listening up, writing down, and looking beyond: Interfaces of the oral, written, and visual* (pp. 77–96). Wilfrid Laurier University Press.

Gregory, H. (2015). Prospecting with the 'poetry pioneers': Youth poetry slam and the U.K.'s WordCup. *Liminalities, 10*(3–4). http://liminalities.net/10-3/wordcup.pdf

Hart, A., Gagnon, E., Eryigit-Madzwamuse, S., Cameron, J., Aranda, K., Rathbone, A., & Heaver, B. (2016). Uniting resilience research and practice with an inequalities approach. *Sage Open, 6*(4), 1–13.

Ingalls, R. (2012). 'Stealing the air': The poet-citizens of youth spoken-word. *Journal of Popular Culture, 45*(1), 99–117.

Johnson, H., Carson-Apstein, E., Banderob, S., & Macualay-Rettino, X. (2017). 'You kind of have to listen to me': Researching discrimination through poetry. *Forum Qualitative Sozialforschung/Forum Qualitative Social Research, 18*(2). http://dx.doi.org/10.17169/fqs-18.3.2864

Johnson, H., Macaulay-Rettino, X., Banderob, S., Lalani, I., Carson-Apstein, E., & Blacher, E. (2018). A Rose by any other name? Developing a method of 'collaborative poetics.' *Qualitative Research in Psychology*. https://doi.org/10.1080/14780887.2018.1442762

Jones, K. (2012). Connecting research with communities through performative social science. *Qualitative Report, 17*(18), 1–8.

Lashua, B. (2006). The arts of the remix: Ethnography and rap. *Anthropology Matters Journal, 8*(2), 1–10.

Leavy, P. (2009). *Method meets art: Arts-based research practice*. Guilford Press.

Maréchal, G., & Linstead, S. (2010). Metropoems: Poetic method and ethnographic experience. *Qualitative Inquiry, 16*(1), 66–77. http://doi.org/10.1177/1077800409349757

McNiff, S. (2018). Philosophical and practical foundations of artistic inquiry: Creating paradigms, methods, and presentations based in art. In P. Leavy (Ed.), *Handbook of arts-based research* (pp. 22–36). Guildford Press.

Patmanathan, N. M. (2014). *Slam as methodology: Theory, performance, practice* [MA thesis]. University of Toronto. https://tspace.library.utoronto.ca/bitstream/1807/67961/1/Patmanathan_Nisha_M_201411_MA_thesis.pdf

Richardson, L. (1993). Poetics, dramatics, and transgressive validity: The case of the skipped line. *Sociological Quarterly, 34*(4), 695–710.

Sethi, B. (2012). Searching for self in a world of labels. *Disability and Society, 27*(5), 717–722.

Skinner, E. A. (2012). *Aboriginal youth, hip hop, and the right to the city: A participatory action research project* [MA thesis]. University of Manitoba. https://mspace.lib.umanitoba.ca/xmlui/handle/1993/8886

Traynor, M. (2018). Guest editorial: What's wrong with resilience. *Journal of Research in Nursing, 23*(1), 5–8.

Weinstein, S. (2010). 'A unified poet alliance': The personal and social outcomes of youth spoken word poetry programming. *International Journal of Education and the Arts, 11*(2), 1–24.

Weinstein, S. (2018). *The room is on fire: The history, pedagogy, and practice of youth spoken word poetry.* State University of New York Press.

CHAPTER 3

Instructions on How to Research with Circus

Or, How Circus Research Rebels against Circus and Research at Stockholm University of the Arts

Alisan Funk

First: Damn Everything But the Circus[1]

Which is to say, let circus become your waking life, and sometimes your sleeping life too. Not only a location (going to see the), not only an action constituting rebellious rejection of social norms (running away to join the[2]), not only monetary exchange for services rendered (see circus, business of the[3]), not only the nostalgically-fuelled fantasy of utopian radical acceptance and communal living (see also running away to join the), nor the well of otherness

1 Him: Precisely; when who should come along but little Mr. Mendel, wheeling a numerical law full of recurring inherited characteristics all wrong side up with their eyes shut on a slackwire tightrope. (*Vehemently*) Damn everything but the circus! (*To himself*) And here am I, patiently squeezing fourdimensional ideas into a twodimensional stage, when all of me that's anyone or anything is in the top of a circustent... (*A pause*). (cummings, *Him*, 1927, p. 12).

2 "Those who have both run away to and written of the circus have often provided stories which contrast the goods pursued in circus and those of money, power, and status that characterize the social order from which they have run" (Beadle, 2018, p. 8).

3 Excerpt from *Falling the Thought of Circus* (Zaccarini, 2018 p. 116).

It's a shame
That in these 5 minutes when I'm flying, we get so swept up in our merriment
That we forget that it's all an act. A game to make you come back
I do not really love you
This is just an experiment.
I'm trying to apologise
For glueing your eyes on me
But I do need two hundred eyeballs
To keep me from falling.
You are my safety device,
My prophylactic in a crisis
So I don't crash,
So the venue can profit from my antics.

 | DOI:10.1163/9789004516069_005

and adventure provoking the protagonist (see literary tropes of the[4]), circus is simultaneously a practice and an identity.[5] Circus is cyclically constituted; those driven to engage with the circus often describe a calling more than a vocation (Stroud, 2000), their identity AS circus drives their practice of becoming/embodying circus, they are constituted by and in turn constitute the representation and development of circus itself.

To research with circus, immersion in circus is primordial. Going to practice, practicing, and then preparing for the next practice session take precedence. For years. And years. This practical training ensures extensive knowledge of the equipment (corporeal), associated partners (ex: trapeze, juggling clubs, one or more other humans, and sometimes non-human compatriots), and conditions conducive to research and production (mental, emotional, environmental). "But this does not mean that by joining the circus, attending a circus course, or engaging in circus training you have the right to think of yourself as a misfit, outsider or rebel" (Priest, 2019, p. 38). In other words, learning the tools of the trade is not inherently rebellious. Nor is it by practicing circus that you will embark on rebellious research – it is through embracing the discomfort and endurance required of rebellion.

Practicing circus builds the vocabulary from which research can be articulated. For some, the practice is not performance, but rather pedagogy and teaching of circus. Circus knowledges, both practical and pedagogical, are still primarily circulated informally between practitioners. Circus practitioners share styles, inventions and sequences within training spaces and across online platforms. Educational experts dedicated to circus build knowledge in their niche which is related to – but not synonymous with – circus performance itself. And then there are those whose practice is studies OF: those who watch and watch and watch and build a nuanced approach to understanding circus itself (and not circus as an extension of another art, whose codes can be uncritically applied).

So, after all this practice, you find yourself with a desire to expand your practice to include research. Ah, you rebel. To do so means you must balk and question, consider the uncomfortable unanswereds, and perhaps undermine your standing in the circus and/or in the academy.

---

4 For a succinct, comprehensive and enjoyable experience of literary circus, I suggest the paired reading of Carter's *Nights at the Circus* with Stoddart's *Routledge Study Guide* to the same book.

5 To better understand circus as identity, I suggest reading Stroud's *Days and Nights at the Circus* paired with Beadle's review of the same book.

Next: "Articulations and Re-articulations of the Questions"[6]

Learning circus, centring circus, has already placed you within a small group. Artistic research places you within another small group. The Venn diagram… well… it is clear, is it not? Then: where within this small overlapping space do we learn to do this circus artistic research? Yet another small circle to overlay. How might we go about "learning the method of teaching the method of artistic research" (Damkjaer & Robitaille, 2009)?

What to Teach? And How?

As head of Artistic Development in the circus BA programme, Marie- Andrée Robitaille, with support from Camilla Damkjaer, sought an answer to this question for the Circus Programme bachelor students at the Stockholm University of the Arts (SKH) (Uniarts, n.d.). To develop the breadth and depth of their disciplines and artistic vision, students persevere through progressions and plateaus, daily difficulties, and aching articulations in both body and expression which ultimately enable each student to create conscious circus constructions for attentive audiences. They learn circus, and in learning they also create the future of circus.

Woven through the three-year programme is a gradually thickening thread introducing and then producing 'Methods of Artistic Research (in circus),' developed by Robitaille, Ana Sanchez-Colberg and John-Paul Zaccarini to help students ask: what might it be to learn *from* circus? How could I represent the questions I ask circus, and the resulting discoveries? Guided by artistic researchers themselves, student research culminates in an artistic research thesis-project performed/presented, written/documented, and defended/discussed with peer and professor opponents.[7]

6 "… some of the first attempts started from the question of what the rhythm of life is, which resulted in a mimetic approach to the topic. But when Quim changed the question in order to address the one of how he as an artist can use images of the rhythm of life to create an independent stage image, the material also changed radically [Quim does a movement sequence developing into the scream] These articulations and re-articulations of the questions are important in order to guide and structure the exploration and the creation of physical material" (Damkjaer & Robitaille, 2015, pp. 138–139).

7 This Artistic Research project stands in complement and contrast alongside it's opposite-partner: the short-form circus act constructed as a calling card by which the expertise and artistic voice of these fledgling artists become known. The circus act is the expected culmination of circus school: a 5–7-minute presentation which can be tidily hired by festivals or companies, and which engages in rather classical performance dialogues between artist (on stage) and audience (watching). Bachelor students in the Circus Programme complete both.

When Luuk Brantjes[8] and Elaine Briant[9] each presented their respective artistic research projects in 2019, they described questions they asked/developed about their circus practice and their situatedness as artists/researchers. Using methods they developed to address the specificity of their particular questions using their particular practice of their particular discipline, within the context of their broader knowledge of circus practices, they represented/presented their questions, methods and discoveries to an informed and constructively critical audience. The dialogue between presenter and watcher is more explicit than within a classical audience-performer relationship (see endnote 7) as each researcher/student must describe and defend the research questions/methods/presentation; the circus is less explicit.

FIGURE 3.1 Luuk Brantjes stands on a teeterboard looking up at a weight rigged on the theatre ceiling, which can drop onto the other end of the teeterboard (Photo: Joel Roxendal)

8 Luuk Brantjes: luukbrantjes.com
9 Elaine Briant: https://www.instagram.com/elainebriant/

The searching student might question the very nature of their discipline, as did Brantjes, who questioned what it is to be dependent upon a group by researching the possibilities of solo teeterboard, a seesaw apparatus that requires at least two people jumping in order to launch one high enough to accomplish acrobatic flips (Figure 3.1). For Brantjes, this research has broadened performance possibilities as he continues to pursue group and solo teeterboard performance. Or the student might draw us into "the minutia, the fleeting, the subtle... the steps within the steps"[10] (Sanchez-Colberg, 2007, p. 42) so closely that the discipline itself becomes as invisible as molecules are to electrons, as did Briant, exploring how her relationship to synesthesia could be used as an artistic challenge to her hand-standing habitudes. Finding resonance between music, movement and spaces based on synesthetic logic brought Briant more intimate and articulated knowledge of the differences between performer and audience experiences.

Then: "Am I the Space through Which Theory Is Materialising?"

It is rare that you, the circus practitioner, will be introduced to artistic research in a formal way. It is far more likely that research questions may form during the practice-performance-practice-performance overlapping cycles.

It is even more likely that answers will emerge for which questions have not yet been formulated.

Your desire to connect questions and answers - or, perhaps, simply to develop better questions – might inspire to re-consideration of your practice as not strictly personal (identity), practical (revenue), or community (social and professional networks). You might wonder what circus knows about circus, or notice that their circus practice approaches ideas, experiences and theories uncommonly discussed in training and performance spaces.

"[A]rt establishes a new reality, whereas the sciences provide a more detailed picture of the one we already have" suggests Efva Lilja (2004), pioneering Swedish choreographer and first Vice-Chancellor of the Stockholm University of Dance and Circus (later re-named Stockholm University of the Arts). You might understand this to mean that the scientific method investigates observable phenomena, while artistic methods encourage imagination and incarnation of experiences which have not yet existed. Perhaps changing one's own experience of reality through the practice of circus (what can be

10 Watch a short excerpt of Sanchez-Colberg's artistic research with circus Bachelor students in 2007, *We: Implicated and Complicated* on videographer Chris Clow's YouTube channel: https://www.youtube.com/watch?v=u-SJkI66688

done in my body and with others', with these or those objects, in this or that emotional state) leads to expanding circus art's potential to influence those who encounter it: through educational dialogues, performance dialogues and now expanding into research dialogues.

Depending upon the experience of practice, the fledgling artistic researcher wielding circus methods must weave their way into a relationship with theory. This ensures reaching research audiences. Yet dialogue with theory remains uneasily accepted in circus practice circles, while circus practice-as-method makes cautious inroads in established artistic research circles.

Becoming Theory; Theory Becoming

Through inquiry and experience during her master's research of Rigging Design as Artistic Research, Saar Rombout discovered that what she perceived as isolated expertises actually form the pillars of her practice (2021). Embodying Barad's (2007) theory of intra-action prompted Saar to re-understand both her 'technical' rigging knowledge and 'artistic' movement discipline as 'objects' through which her artistic practice manifested (Figure 3.2). Like Rombout, you might realize you are uniquely positioned to relate the stories told by your own 'objects' because they have a real, observable, engaged effect on your movements, decisions, and possibilities.

Or you might resonate with Fran-Tank's triple existence as human-object-theory. Conventionally seen as an inanimate, plastic water-holding jug, Tank constitutes half of the performance duo, with Fran suspended by her long braided hair at the other end of a pulley.[11] Face to face, the two are counterweighted. Both containers are visibly at risk of damage from the other, but instead, the graceful, fluid movement flattens the subject/object binary. Embodying, or perhaps only articulating, post-humanist concepts of object-agency, Tank asks:

> How can you truly know my experience when you have no real access to my ontology? We all know that I am a fiction, and a water Tank will never be credited for writing an essay in any meaningful way. What I don't understand is that Fran's 'I' is also a fiction, and I'm wondering how many people have to buy into a fiction for it to become a reality. (Hyde, 2019, p. 136)

Fran-Tank's consciousness and conscious engagement with theory-in-practice was developed during their Master's course in Contemporary Circus Practices at SKH. The practice, theory, bodies and objects living together in Fran-Tank's threshold space reveal truth in tension. They resonate with indigenous

11 Example of Hyde's experimentations with Tank, and the performance of hair-hanging with a counterweight: https://vimeo.com/206207547 (accessed 3 May, 2021).

FIGURE 3.2 Saar Rombout physically explores a rope wall she has created with her knowledge of rigging design (Photo: Joakim Björklund)

relationships to place and space (Hasbe-Ludt & Leggo, 2018), with the pre-positivistic and recently re-emergent knowledge that nature and objects were/are inhabited by spirits and preferences. In short, Fran-Tank experiences the ancient/posthumanist knowledge that we humans and objects constitute each other. The lived realities of Fran-Tank's creation and performance experience embodies theory, is described by theory, and was created through and from embodied practice. To experience Fran-Tank is to experience the conventional division between theory/practice as akin to the perception of light, which might seem to be waves or particles only due to the observer's position. Perhaps Fran-Tank's triple existence will also illuminate the inextricabilities in your own relationships to humans, objects, and/or embodied theory.

Or: "For Circus to Extend Its Practice into a Field beyond Its Reach"[12]

Consider your liminality, you who want to research artistically with circus. Consider the thresholds you hover in, the new risk you embrace, for "thresholds

12 "There is nothing new here, circus traditionally extends its practice into new areas, new objects, new challenges, and so for circus to attempt to extend its practice into a field beyond its reach, namely the immaterial, was for me a way to suggest a new path but also

contain both entries and exits; they are both/and" (Jackson & Mazzei, 2011, p. 6). By entering research, do you risk leaving circus? The "artistic" is your salvation. From the practice emerge the questions. The unusual reality you inhabit gives you access to embodied theory. Retain your liminality, set ups shop in the threshold, live in the intersection and, as you have now become quite used to in your practice, use the tension you have created to develop your technique: use your circus to research your questions, question your research with your circus.

Creating Theory; Theory Creating

Expanding the understanding of circus across theoretical, disciplinary and personal intersections is inherent to artistic doctoral research. Jonathan Priest seeks to "retroactively establish a theoretical practice, a circus approach to theory, that could then act as the basis from which the physical practice could be the praxis" (2019, p. 55). Through his dissertation[13] research and writing, Priest explored "the trick" in relationship with the fields of Gravity, Language and Capitalism. For Priest, the 'trick' in circus as embodiment of three different relationships to a system/field – one trick reveals the limits of a system within the system, the second trick relies on those limits but hides them from view, and the third escapes the system itself. A practitioner, educator, creator, and theorist, Priest pursues the circus-ness of circus practice to understand how participating in circus reifies different sets of 'tricks': those played before audiences (tricks of technique), tricks contrasted-against-and-therefore-necessarily-in-play-with gravity (the fabricated freedom of weightlessness), and tricks played upon circus performers themselves who buy into Romantic conceptions of circus-as-freedom and find themselves monetizing required individuality within the circus tradition's unexamined intimate relationship with capitalism.

Engaging circus within its social, ecological and institutional fields, Marie-Andree Robitaille's doctoral research situates circus practices within contemporary rebellions such as Extinction Rebellion and Black Lives Mater. By re-orienting material and bodies away from their usual functions – and through the diversion of audience/participant senses and perceptions – Robitaille assembles relations between body, environment and human constructions to find a "practice of hope." For Robitaille, experiments with small-scale

---

to retroactively establish a theoretical practice, a circus approach to theory, that could then act as the basis from which the physical practice could be the praxis" (Priest 2019, pp. 55–56).

13 Priest received the first artistic research doctorate in circus Choreography at SKH.

intra-actions (Barad, 2007) guide artist and audience/participants towards a broader understanding of how we can (hope-fully) move our global assemblage towards social, environmental and political justice (Robitaille, 2022). Robitaille's questions provoke circus practitioners to examine fundamental assumptions about their interconnectedness with, and implication and accountability in the systems defining our world(s).

Alternately: Translating Professional Practice: "This Constant Dialogue between the Body in Motion and Its Environment"[14]

You've been reading this and, while you resonate with the desire to question your practice through circus, you feel that your expertise has not yet been recognized. You are immersed in circus, but perhaps your practice is not on your own body. Perhaps you are an educator, or a director, or bringing embodied knowledge from another field.

If you are approaching from the experience of a circus educator, a coach, a teacher, you know that teaching circus artists is a form of daily nuanced research into pedagogy and personality. The one-to-one nature of circus coaching, and the pursuit of building safe replicable technique while also discovering and experimenting asks circus coaches to be simultaneously centred in historical knowledge (what has worked) and responsive to queries, provocations and ideas (what could work), all while keeping their students physically and emotionally safe (what CAN'T work) and being pushed to question their own assumptions about technique and aesthetic (what shouldn't work… but just might). After enough time enacting this iterative process yearly with individual students, and through the years with many students over time, coaches are rich sources of knowledge about circus practice and evolution.

And yet… Coaches are often relegated to physical interests and removed from documented discussions about circus practices and progressions. They are, after all, 'just' coaches…

Discovering What We Know

The practice does not exist without practitioners, yet not all practitioners have had access or encouragement to investigate, represent and disseminate

14 "Understanding balance means understanding how the *different senses interact.* This constant dialogue between the body in motion and its environment is the system that is at stake in balance work" (Dumont, 2017, p. 54).

the knowledges they hold. In recognition of the need for a translation zone between pedagogic practice and research product, SKH circus educators are supported to conduct artistic research and supported through time-allotment, seminars, collaborators and presentation opportunities. Artistic research conducted from pedagogical perspectives has contributed to a broader understanding of circus practices for researchers in other SKH departments.

Multidisciplinary coach Thierry Maussier questioned how students understood and embodied coaching interactions while inverted. In collaboration with dance and circus researcher Camilla Damkjaer, Maussier phenomenologically investigated student experiences of balance during the practice of handstands (Damkjaer, 2015). The method and outcomes of this research using sensation as a guide to developing balancing technique has also been included in renowned circus pedagogy manuals (Dumont, 2017). The burgeoning research of teeterboard coach Jan Rosén has also pushed on common assumptions around his heavily acrobatic discipline (2021). Exploring rhythm, patterns and sound across multiple boards with multiple jumping acrobats, Rosén and his collaborating artists have increased communication strategies within teeterboard training between artists themselves, and artist-coach dialogue. In a discipline which relies heavily on partners for safety and security, these explorations uncover more than the visual documentation: they change how artists and coaches understand the discipline. Students, observers, educators and researchers may each draw different knowledges and inspirations – seeing waves or particles – as pedagogues bring their perceptions to bear in the domain of artistic research.

Also Possibly: Translating Professional Practice: "Who Gets to Call Themselves Artists and Their Work a Piece of Art"[15]

Perhaps, instead, you have been directing and creating circus performance for many years, and now desire return to the questions that have been nagging at you. Perhaps you are seeking to share the insights you have gained in dialogues other than the performer-audience contract. Perhaps you want to challenge

15 "During these days at CARD, the question about what artistic research is and of who gets to call themselves artistic researchers has been under constant debate and I have noticed the need for a clear definition. I would argue that these questions are equivalent to the question of what art is, and of who gets to call themselves artists and their work a piece of art" (Björfors, 2012, pp. 24–25).

some of your own ideas by testing them in another medium: that of writing and research. Perhaps you want to apply some of the processes that generate performance to how you yourself understand and experience circus. Perhaps a better understanding can better feed you yourself, or feed circus itself, or feed the audience/readers themselves.

Stepping Back, Stepping Between

Contemporary circus pioneer Tilde Björfors created Cirkus Cirkör in the late 90s in Stockholm (Björfors & Lind, 2009). Performances rapidly escalated to large-scale provocative events, cultivating an audience and an awareness of contemporary circus in Sweden, which had been visited by few non-traditional circus companies at that time. Circus requires artists, and Björfors collaborated with other artists and educators to create educational programs which turned into social circus projects, a high school program, and the Cirkuspiloterna, the program that would eventually become the bachelors programme in circus at the Stockholm University of the Arts. Björfors was invited as one of the first visiting circus professors; she was initially driven by frustration with the inadequacy of the University College of Dance's institutional structure for supporting the actual practical needs of circus education – and even more frustrated by a lack of ability to articulate what those needs were from within circus (2015, p. 16). Undertaking artistic research and collaboration with the University was a way for her to understand circus and defend it to itself, within and against existing university structures. Björfors created a website to document and disseminate this research – openly accessible by all, researchers and practitioners alike[16] (Björfors, n.d.).

Embracing the rigorous challenge of researching circus, supported to explore connections with other domains (history, neuroscience) to enhance an understanding of circus, and documentation methods to enhance communication of knowledge, Björfors's research is an excellent example of how universities can support practitioner artistic research that enriches the researcher, the field, and enhances communication. Circus actively engages risk and chaos through practice and performance: can studying circus inform more nuanced or collaborative relationships with risk and chaos? Researching risk developed knowledge of her own creative process, which became – in part – the Cirkus Cirkör performance *Wear it Like a Crown* (Björfors, n.d.). Exploration of intrinsic qualities of different circus disciplines revolutionized her approach to the business of running a circus business, a philosophy explicated and explored in Inside a Circus Heart (Björfors & Lind, 2009).

16 All Swedish-speakers, that is, and those with a translation plug-in on their browser.

Another Path: Translating Professional Practice: "The Enterprise of the Homemade Academic Circus"[17]

Sometimes it is possible for artistic researchers without extensive circus practice to also engage with circus artistic research. From a position in another field of artistic research, an artist-academic might discover that circus practice offers new perspectives on their field(s) of interest, perspectives which can only be gained through circus.

From Another Perspective

Assistant professor and artistic researcher Camilla Damkjaer became curious about what information the practice of vertical aerial rope could shed upon certain theoretical postulations. Approaching the technique of rope work with the lens of Butler's performativity (1990/1999), Damkjaer explored whether moving in a gendered way was possible or replicable. Instead of gender determining movement, Damkjaer found that circus disciplines themselves enacted performative muscularity in practitioners.

> The circus disciplines and their training so to speak regulate the materialization of the body, including its sex and gender. … This materialization, however, was not permanent and every time I present the lecture I have to train again in order to manage. Working with the "Ropresentation of Gender" therefore led to an embodied experience of the performance of gender, of the lack of a "natural" or "given" gender, and to the experience of the plasticity of my own body, including its gender, and even possibly its sex if understood as performatively materialized. (Damkjaer, 2016, pp. 122–123)

The construction and re-construction of physically legible identities, performed (enacted) in training by the artist, affected by the physical realities of rope and gravity (Priest, 2019), and performed (presented) for audiences is a reality of all circus practice. Approaching the practice through theoretical performativity enriches our knowledge of both theory and practice and, counterintuitively, might gesture towards a way of using the reality of daily performativity as a type of circus apparatus which we can work with to create new, more conscious, performances.

17 "…the professional circus amateur and the academic freak are not simply me and about me. They occur when the enterprise of the homemade academic circus causes my body to be caught up in the historical and cultural constructions of professionals and amateurs, theory and practice, science and circus, art and academia" (Damkjaer, 2016, p. 9).

Now You: "We Have No Idea What an Adult Circus Might Look Like"[18]

Be warned: they will look at you askance, and you will find yourself awash in translated words and concepts. To circus communities, describing research may mark you as heading towards the exit, leaving the precarious threshold of circus professionalism. You do that 'academic thing' now, and it undermines your trustworthiness. Additionally, established research communities will likely express scepticism that much can be garnered from circus, imagining exclusively, as most still do, the sawdust and spectacle of yesteryear. You do that 'circus thing' now, and it undermines your authority.

The intersection of the youthful discipline of artistic research with the youthful field of contemporary circus studies[19] amplifies upon itself. Look to the drive that committed you to daily practice – it will also guide you in your research practice. Look to the curiosity that insisted upon investigation – it will illuminate connections. And balancing in the threshold (decidedly not on a tightwire, please retire this tired and untried simplicity), you will constantly enter and exit: through your fields of inquiry, through your practice and questions and questioned practice. To choose artistic research in circus is in some ways to rebel against the conventions and histories of both circus and research, and yet it is also to reveal each to themselves.

Where Are We Growing?

Circus performer, creator, doctor(ate), professor and researcher John-Paul Zaccarini viewed contemporary circus through a Lacanian lens (2018). Perceived as acting for fun and sensation, he finds this relatively new incarnation of contemporary circus to be in its adolescence. Zaccarini queries what the form might become when it matures, when it stops "acting (out)" and develops self-reflection (p. 88).

It may occur to you that another archetype of adolescence is rebellion: pushing against the known to discover the new, questioning conventions and flouting

18 "The faster, bigger, more dangerous, skillful, difficult things I can do, the less time I have to consider. Circus is uncritical of itself. It's having too much fun. It's self-satisfied. New Circus is 40 years old but it still behaves like an adolescent. I am 40 years old but I am expected to act (out) like an ambivalent teenager. We have no idea what an adult circus might look like" (Zaccarini, 2018, p. 88).

19 Which is not only the study of contemporary circus, but includes contemporary approaches to studying circus history through the lenses of contemporary study. See, for example: Arrighi and Davis (2021).

traditions. We might imagine circus in its maturity as both rebellious and inquisitive, both acting out and self-reflective, both wave and particle.

I believe the rebellion of circus has shifted. Rather than circus *itself* being an act of rebellion, the rebellious edge in circus is now articulating, understanding and theorizing circus from within the circus. For circus *itself* is not very rebellious when there are well-regarded educational institutions (FEDEC, n.d.) and established, relatively accessible pathways to professional recognition (Sizorn, 2014).

Rather, the rebellion is in the threshold between perspectives, between the waves and the particles, between conventions and imagination. The present is always a threshold between the past and future. By rebelling against the norms, codes and conventions of circus practice through their research of that practice, circus artistic researchers are creating the as-yet-unknown future of circus. As researchers, they tirelessly envision and integrate circus possibilities within academic structures, creating that reality around them and changing the future of academic knowledge.

And you, dear reader, dear potential researcher, perhaps you also see what I see: that these multiple rebellions fuel the fires of inspiration and persistence. These researcher-artists – perhaps like you – are driven by the curiosity and mystery of the edge as they find previously hidden knowledge in the overlap of their particular embodied expertise(s) and the traditionally taboo practice of articulating and revealing their process and discoveries to audiences outside of the circus.

Will you risk joining us?

References

Arrighi, G., & Davis, J. (2021). *The Cambridge companion to the circus*. Cambridge University Press.

Barad, K. (2007). *Meeting the universe halfway: Quantum physics and the entanglement of matter and meaning*. Duke University Press.

Beadle, R. (2003). Book review: Stroud, N. (1999) Josser: Days and nights at the Circus, London: Little Brown & Co. *Culture and Organization*, 9(2), 139–144.

Beadle, R. (2018). On running away to the circus. *Politics & Poetics: A Journal for Humane Philosophy*, 1–28.

Björfors, T. (2012). What stories are worth risking one's life for? And what is the risk? In C. Damkjaer & A. Skönberg (Eds.), *Documentation of CARD – Circus artistic research development* (pp. 11–25) The University of Dance and Circus.

Björfors, T. (n.d.). *Circus research*. Retrieved May 3, 2021, from http://www.circusresearch.com

Björfors, T., & Lind, K. (2009). *Inuti ett cirkus hjärta/ Inside a circus heart*. Cirkus Cirkör.

Butler, J. (1999). *Gender trouble: Feminism and the subversion of identity*. Routledge. (Original work published 1990)

Carter, A. (1984). *Nights at the circus*. Chatto & Windus.

Cummings, e. E. (1927). *Him*. New Boni & Liveright.

Damkjær, C. (2015, April 17). The circus body articulating. *International Conference Semiotics of the Circus*. Cirque Bouffon & University of Munster, Munster. Retrieved May 3, 2021, from https://www.youtube.com/watch?v=gMPLMTzdsgc

Damkjær, C. (2016). *Homemade academic circus: Idiosyncratically embodied explorations into artistic research and circus performance*. John Hunt Publishing.

Damkjaer, C., & Robitaille, M.A. (2011). Learning the method of teaching the methods of artistic research. In A. Arlander (Ed.), *Artistic research in action: Proceedings of CARPA 2-colloquium on artistic research in performing arts* (pp. 135–143). Theatre Academy Helsinki.

Dumont, A. (2017). *Pedagogical guide: Support and alignment: In search of balance sensation, development and creation in equilibristrics*. FEDEC. Retrieved May 3, 2021, from http://www.fedec.eu/en/articles/2116-support-and-alignment-in-search-of-balance

FEDEC. (n.d.). *European Federation of Circus Schools*. Retrieved May 3, 2021, from http://www.fedec.eu/en/

Hasebe-Ludt, E., & Leggo, C. (Eds.). (2018). *Canadian curriculum studies: A métissage of inspiration/imagination/interconnection*. Canadian Scholars.

Hyde, F. (2019). A plastic text. In B. Lievens, Q. Ketels, S. Kann, & V. Focquet (Eds.), *Thinking through circus* (pp. 135–141). Art Paper Editions.

Jackson, A. Y., & Mazzei, L. (2011). *Thinking with theory in qualitative research: Viewing data across multiple perspectives*. Routledge.

Lilja, E. (2004). *Dance – For better, for worse* (F. Perry, Trans.). E.L.D.

Priest, J. (2019). *KNOTCIRCUS: Or 'Being the adventures of happy down-river'* [Doctoral dissertation]. Stockholms konstnärliga högskola.

Robitaille, M. (2022). Circus as a practice of hope. In C. Daigle & M. Hayler (Eds.), *Posthumanism in practice*. Bloomsbury Academic (forthcoming).

Rombout, S. (2021). *Rope design and rigging design as artistic practice: An audiovisual essay*. Retrieved May 3, 2021, from https://vimeo.com/535564051

Rosén, J. (2021). *Språngbrädans akrobatik och koreografier*. Retrieved June 20, 2021, from https://www.uniarts.se/forskning-utvecklingsarbete/forskningsprojekt/sprangbradans-akrobatik

Sánchez-Colberg, A. (2007). "Making the invisible visible: We: Implicated and complicated. In E. Grönlund, G. Gustafsson, A. K. Ståhle, & H. Blomqvist (Eds.), *Close encounters, Artists on artistic research* (pp. 41–78). Danshogskolan-University College of Dance.

Sizorn, M. (2014). Le cirque à l'épreuve de sa scolarisation. Artification, légitimation… normalisation ? *Staps*, *1*(103), 23–38. doi:10.3917/sta.103.0023

Stroud, N. (2000). *Josser: Days and nights in the circus*. Virago Press.

Stoddart, H. (2007). *Angela Carter's nights at the circus: A Routledge study guide*. Routledge.

Uniarts. (n.d.). *Stockholm University of the Arts* [Bachelor programme in circus]. Retrieved May 3, 2021, from https://www.uniarts.se/english/courses/bachelor-programmes/circus-bachelor

Zaccarini, J. P. (2018). *Falling the thought of circus*. Stockholm University of the Arts.

CHAPTER 4

Walking with(in) Transdisciplinary-Scapes

Carolyn Cooke

Setting Off

Transdisciplinarity asks us to do, be and think differently, transgressing and transcending disciplinary boundaries, requiring a different 'way of being' with(in) the world. But how do we make such a shift in being? How can we learn to pay attention differently? How can we learn to transcend the habits and assumptions we have of research? This chapter is an offer to remake narratives of transdisciplinarity, research and writing as we walk with(in) entangled scapes of north-east Scotland and my PhD project which explored teaching as an improvisatory act. In bringing together the sensorial, the bodily, the natural and research, we expose different languages, sensations, images and experiences with which we can think and do in a transdisciplinary-scape.[1]

This chapter is an offer[2] to go for a walk, an offer to travel together in company (with each other but also with materials, images, words). It is an offer to 'play out together'[3] in a transdisciplinary-scape to see what happens, bringing with us our experiences, and paying attention to how we think and make with them as we walk.

This isn't a walk to reach a particular destination, it isn't about where we end, but it is about what happens along the way, where paying *attention* and

---

1 All photographs are my own with relevant permissions gained from those in the workshops as required by the ethics procedures of Aberdeen University.

2 In theatre improvisation 'an offer' relates to the opening up of a situation through an activity or a verbal interjection which enables others to join in. Accepting the offer, and making with it, allows the improvisation to move forward (Johnstone, 1979).

3 Transdisciplinarity, as a practice that transgresses and transcends disciplinary boundaries, has potential to respond to new demands and imperatives (Russell et al., 2008, pp. 460–461). De-coupling the specific language and practices of a discipline from their original contexts opens up new possibilities for *viewing and experiencing* the same phenomenon in many ways. This requires a different 'way of being', which Perry (2021) refers to as 'pluriversality', referring to the 'surplus' of meanings and ways of learning which may be generated to enable the complexity of a changing world to come into the realms of our experience. 'Playing out' in the transdisciplinary-scape, experiencing transdisciplinarity with all our bodymind, is to allow ourselves to rebel against static, habitual, expected ways of being writer/researcher/educationalist.

 | DOI:10.1163/9789004516069_006

noticing what is occurring makes us re-see, re-make and re-tell our relationships with each other. As we walk, our encounters mobilise material-body-environment performances, revealing new narratives, new experiences of transdisciplinary doing, being, becoming. Our walk begins from my front door, into the fields of Aberdeenshire, Scotland.

FIGURE 4.1
From my front door

As I sit here looking out over the fields of north-east Scotland, I can see the very beginnings of spring arriving. The broom bushes that line the fields have started to turn yellow, reminding me of the Scots song about gypsy-travellers with the line 'I'll tak ye on the road again when yellow's on the broom'.[4] *On the trees, I can see the little pockets where the leaves will burst out in a few weeks' time. And yet, at this distance, through a window, the landscape looks very still, as if yet to be woken up fully. To see what is alive, what is moving, we need to venture out and go for a walk. We need to be in and with it, and pay attention with all our senses, not just viewing it from afar. We need to 'tak the road' and go travelling with the landscape and all that it offers.*

As we take our first steps, out of the front door, across the road and onto the earthy fields beyond, the cold wind pulls at us, the sound of the trees rustling draws us in, the smell of the flora wakes us. We think with the word landscape, playing with it as we go …

Landscape *scape-lands*
land-scape *scape-spaces*

4 'The yellow's on the broom' is a Scots language song (MacNaughtan, 2001), based on a book by Betsy Whyte about the experiences of Gypsy-Travellers in Scotland. The song is threaded with issues of social justice and being with(in) the landscape.

space-scapes *discipline-spaces:*
discipline-scapes …
Transdisciplinary-scapes …

The words, as rhythms, as patterns, as sounds, entangle themselves with my recently completed PhD project, raising questions. What 'scapes' had I walk with(in)? What sort of movements had I made? What had pulled at and awakened me? What had I moved across, between, through to make the project transdisciplinary?

Despite completing my PhD four months ago, I am still in a state of 'play', where the materials and ideas are still *with* me, making all the time. Memories, jogged by photos or objects from the workshops, take me back to the music education suite at the university where I, a group of music student teachers and their course leader, explored the idea of teaching as an improvisatory act. We played, we made, we explored, and in doing so we troubled[5] disciplinary notions of improvising with transdisciplinary encounters (with theatre improv, improvisation in nature, contact improv dance, and improvisatory pedagogies in early years education). We entangled ourselves with playdough and pipe cleaners, images and quotations, videos of improvisations and improv games, and of course musical instruments.

Thinking with my project while walking and playing with the language of landscapes makes generative action. I want to play. I want to entangle. I want to allow the experience of walking with(in) the landscape outside my front door to lead the way. To make me write-think-feel-do in different ways, as if it is almost like a diffractive grate, creating wave patterns that amplify, interfere or make change as they come into contact with other waves or materials.[6]

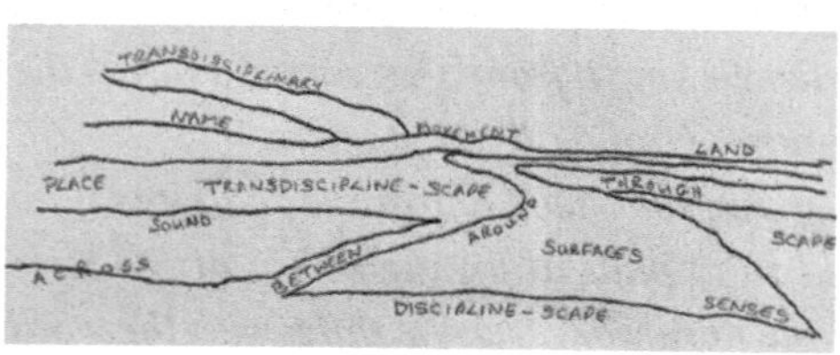

FIGURE 4.2
Movements with(in) the transdisciplinary-scape

5 Haraway (2016) draws on the term trouble, meaning to 'stir up, to make cloudy, to disturb' (p. 1). Haraway argues that living in troubled times requires us to 'stay with the trouble … requiring learning to be truly present' (p. 1).

6 Diffraction, as both a physical phenomenon, and a metaphor (Barad, 2007; Haraway, 2016; Murris, 2016) enables a more fluid exploration of the multiplicities in thinking, creating diffractive patterns of interference which allow us to engage in practices of thinking and doing differently.

The *movement* of the horizon as the trees bend violently in the wind.
Spaces and *places* as leading me in to explore their unending pluralities.
The felt and explored *surfaces* of different fields, of different features in the terrain.
The *scape* not as one view, but of many, asking for different ways of gazing.
The *sensing* of the travelling, as *between, across, through and around.*
The *fields* and *disciplines* not as bounded, abstracted, separated spaces, but as woven together.
The *names* of features, the *sounds* we can hear, the lines we can follow, as understandings of our experiences.

Surfaces

Down the concrete steps onto the moss-filled grass of the sloping front lawn, down we go, crossing the worn-out road, the loose stones move under and around our feet, sending up tiny fragments in dusty clouds until we reach the field track, full of heavy clay mud in heavy worn divots made by the tread of the tractor wheels. As we walk over the crispy mucky frozen ground it feels solid, hard, compacted beneath our feet. Contorting ankles in response, keeping upright and moving. It hurts. It makes us look down, using what we can see to help predict how best to move. We walk in this slightly contorted, uncomfortable manner, until reaching the gate – reaching, touching, its cold metal surface, before quickly recoiling our hands as we feel the 'bite' on our fingers and palms. As we climb it carefully, our shoes, full of mud and stones, hit the gate and it resonates with us. Beyond, we gaze across the fields, noting the patchiness of the new crops emerging from between the soil, their tiny green shoots almost invisible to the eye unless looking across to see the green haze of their collaborative effect.

I think with the experiences of these different surfaces. The moss, the slope, the stones, the mud, the hard, unforgiving ground, the gate, and looking across the surface of the field. Noticing, paying attention, to what we are experiencing. We are not merely travelling across these surfaces; these surfaces as making with[7] us …

7 In defining sympoiesis Haraway states, 'Sympoiesis is a simple word; it means "making-with." Nothing makes itself; nothing is really autopoietic or self-organizing' (Haraway, 2016, p. 58), but instead we become entangled with material-body-environments.

Surfaces in Motion Together

Changing the patterns of lose stones on the road.
Transferring materials as we walk, picking up grass, mud and stones in our shoe treads.
Tiny fragments of skin stuck to the metal as we peal our hands away as quickly as we can.
The gate resonates.

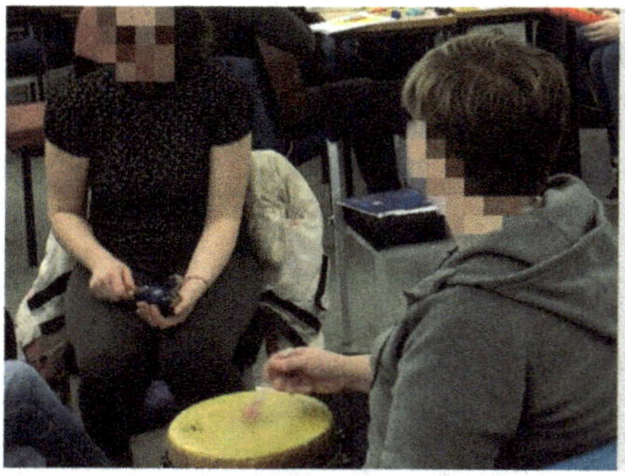

A djembe drum's surface struck not with the hand or a drumstick but with a pen, unexpectedly resonant in multiple directions. The skins, both drum and human, resonate with the vibrations set in motion, the 'buzz' moving up and down and through the bodies (both drum and human). The surfaces in motion, troubling boundaries of what is considered separated, fixed, controllable and what is allowed to resonate, to be alive and to entangle itself.

FIGURE 4.3 Improvising together

Surfaces as Entangled as Felt

Feeling the slope as we descend as our feet crunch forwards in our boots.
Feeling the looseness of the stones between us and the solid road below.
Feeling the shape of the heavy divots in our contorted bodies.
Feeling the cold of the metal.

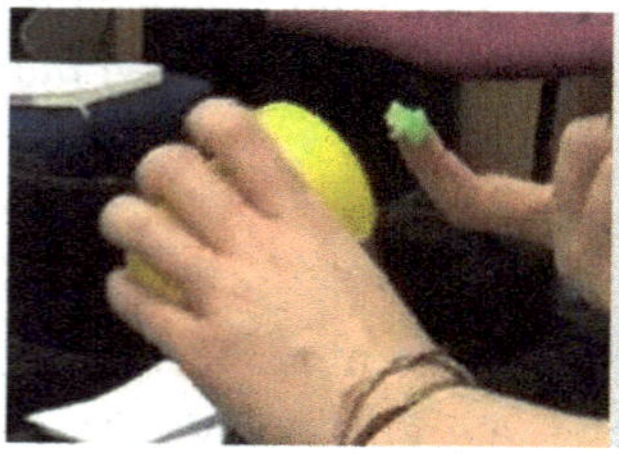

Research notes, March 2019: Tentative. Playdough kept at the very end of the fingers. Playdough doesn't stick to the body, remaining in touch, but is containable and separable.

FIGURE 4.4 First encounters

Research notes, March 2019: All reaching in and forward – hands together. Hands in proximity with materials, each other, table.

FIGURE 4.5 Becoming entangled

Porous Surfaces of Emergence

Moss, resiliently becoming, sheltering in place.[8]
Tiny strong shoots emerging between the soil.
From somewhere beyond gaze.
From somewhere with nourishment.
From somewhere, into here, emerging and connecting above and below,
here and there.

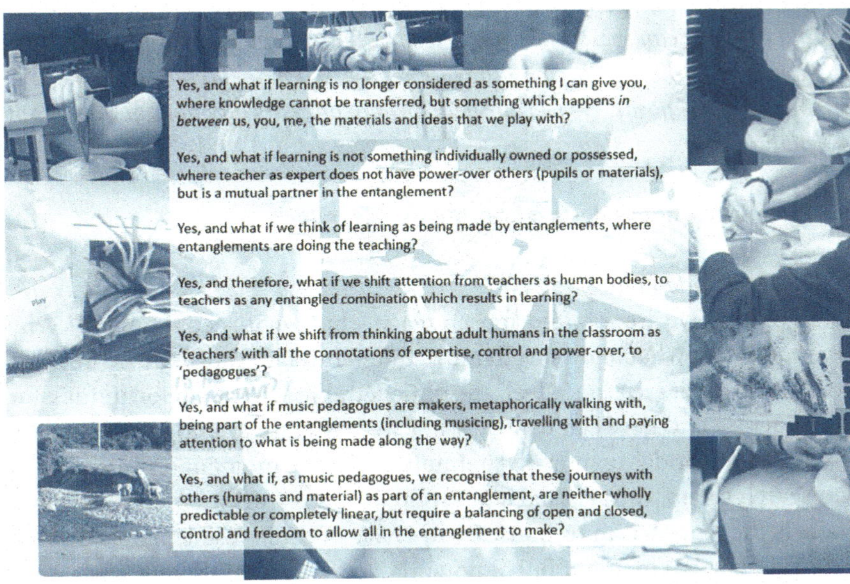

FIGURE 4.6 Yes, and what if? A poem of emergence

Places

There are different places we can go. Do we climb the slopes to reach the tree line? Do we climb the fence and weave our way along the rough land between the river and field of crops? Do we aim for the narrowing of the field where the boundaries of different fields all meet? Or are we going to meander, walking without an intended 'place' in mind? We decide to just set off and see what happens. Walking through the field, the edges, the boundaries come in to meet us, making our scope for changing direction feel more limited. Wondering whether we were coming to a dead end, we pause to pay attention to our options. At first, we just see barbed wire fences, more

8 See Cooke (2021).

and more entangled, impenetrable spikes, keeping us 'in place'. But as we look closer, we see a gate we could climb, we see a broken fence in the distance which has been pushed down by a fallen branch and we see a small bridge over the stream to our right. We choose the bridge, watching the very small brown trickle of water passing under our feet as we cross. And suddenly we are into a much wider space, rising up towards the hill and down towards a line of trees which blocks our view of what is beyond. We want to see. We want to know. We want to understand the scape beyond, so we climb up, deliberately changing our position, changing our place, changing what we can see. We warm up, feeling the heat pushing out between our layers of clothes and we breathe differently, in a more laboured, deliberate, more knowing way. We feel our heartbeat in our ears and hear our bodies in motion with each step.

These are places, not as destination, but as *becoming.*[9]

Unbounded Places

Kept in place – we are so often kept in place – but what keeps us there? Why do we stay? And what allows us to move differently? To travel? To go beyond, or over boundaries we may feel are impenetrable? What opportunities for moving across and between can we *see* if we pay close attention? Seeing the potential of the bridge on our walk reminds me of the moment one member of the research group, Anya, asked a question during a workshop. Her question, 'Where is the teacher?', in response to an image of three young people playing music together, is a moment full of potential to move to a different place. This is a little like the bridge in the field, an opening, an offering to do somewhere differently. We paid attention to it, and in doing so created movement in thinking, doing, imagining.

Displacing Ourselves

*Dis-**place**-ment: to remove, change, or be out of place.*[10]

9 Barad (2007) argues that all the world's matter (human and non-human) is in a constant state of becoming. However, this constant becoming is not individual and bounded, but is a process in which we are all mutually entangled, always intra-acting with everything we are entangled with (Barad, 2007) where 'companion species [both human and non-human] are relentlessly becoming-with' (Haraway, 2016, p. 12).

10 www.etymonline.com

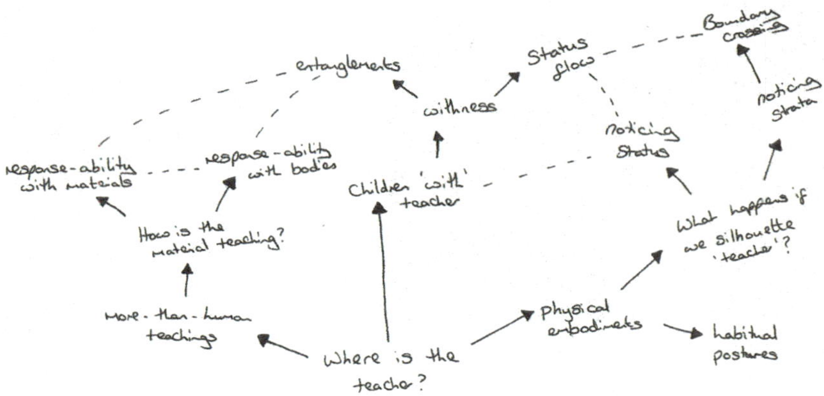

FIGURE 4.7 Tracing movements from Anya's question

How do we dis-**place** ourselves to make something different occur in living-research-practice? How does changing *what we do, what we experience and what we think with* help us displace habits, intentions and assumptions? How do we allow ourselves to be displaced, which involves making ourselves vulnerable and open?

I rip, I tear, I move around, I repeatedly reposition, playfully making with the materials

FIGURE 4.8 Making with materials

Multi-dimensional, embodied and felt (Springgay, 2018), this same process of ripping and tearing applies as much to our experiences of improvising. We displace our existing relationships with materials, our habitual ways of responding and our disciplinary assumptions.

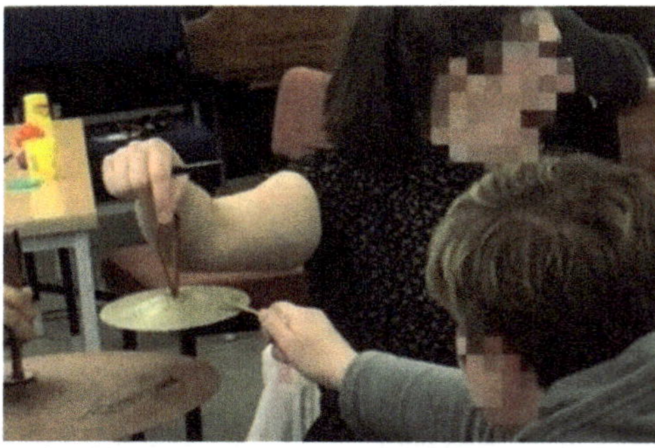

Research notes, April 2019: Key on cymbal. Disrupted expected norms about material relationships. What is instrument? Challenging sight and perceptions more than ears? Changing, repositioning our thinking, and bodies with each other.

FIGURE 4.9 Displacing materials and bodies

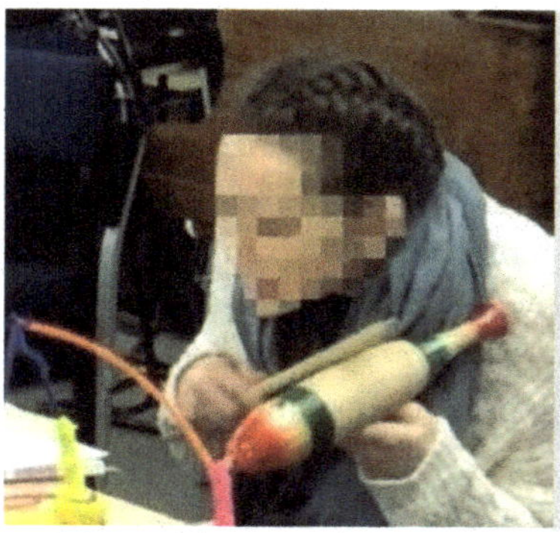

Research notes, April 2019: Listening with whole body, as listening beings. Not just with ears, but leaning, reaching in, deliberately making across the space, connecting both in sound and body.

FIGURE 4.10 Displacing materials and bodies

Friction

Reaching the top of the slope, being able to see across, down, between the places we have travelled together, we take a moment to consider where we are and where we go next. The shortest, easiest route down is the way we have come, retracing, reflecting in mirror image, the journey we have so far taken. We know what we are likely to encounter, what we are likely to feel, as we have only just travelled that path. It feels the safest option. And yet, our attention is pulled by the potential of continuing our explorations, of taking a more tricky, unknown, unplanned route. We set off again, following the edge of the field to our right, following a robin as it flies ahead of us along the stone wall. As we reach the corner, the robin flies over the wall. We want to move with it, we want to continue to travel in its company. We want to know where it takes us. We crunch flat the frozen grasses with our feet. We scramble over the wall, which has more lose stones than we realised at first.

> *It is uncomfortable, as the stones scratch at our legs and hands, making us adjust our position constantly. As you begin to step down the other side you realise the field on the other side is lower, creating a larger drop. There is a moment of hesitation, of concern, of friction between the wall and ourselves, between the two fields we are traversing, between where we have come from, and where we are going into. Are we allowed to climb this wall? Are we going to land safely on the other side?*

I want to understand what one member of the group had meant by the collage picture he had made, but he refused to tell me ('Ah, I think I'll leave that up to you'), capturing in a single moment the tension between trying to understand to represent and research as performative.[11]

Research notes, February 2019: The picture – full of movement, sound reaching outwards, it can't be kept in place. And therefore, full of friction between improvisatory ways of being with materials, and more common relationships in music education of accuracy and interpretation.

FIGURE 4.11 Frictional matters

> *The friction is 'sounded' in the movement of the stones as we scramble over them and in our voices as we discuss what is happening. Sounding frictions, as generative moments, where expectations or assumptions are challenged*[12] *and we are forced to make with in the moment.*

---

11 As MacLure (2013) states, representation is an important part of research, and performative views of research should not aim to completely remove 'representationalism'. Instead, she describes a 'pervasive representationalism that has rendered material realities inaccessible behind the linguistic or discourse systems that purportedly construct or "represent" them' (Maclure, 2013, p. 659). It is this reliance on, and embodiment of, representative forms of 'being researcher' which this encounter with the collage picture disrupted.

12 'Just as an analysis of landscapes can provide important information about the contours, contexts, and histories of a particular environment, collecting and analysing sound can similarly enhance our understandings of a given terrain and the contexts that inform that environment' (Gershon, 2011, p. 69).

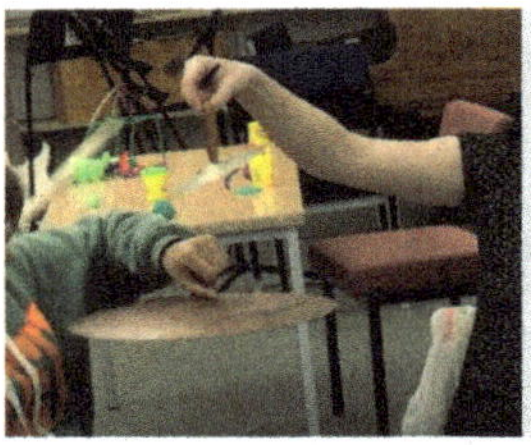

Research notes, April 2019: The slowing of time, the hesitant, awkward pauses in bringing together their bodies, cymbals and then the sounds. A highly charged sensorial moment of attention, drawing in all who were in the room to be part of it.

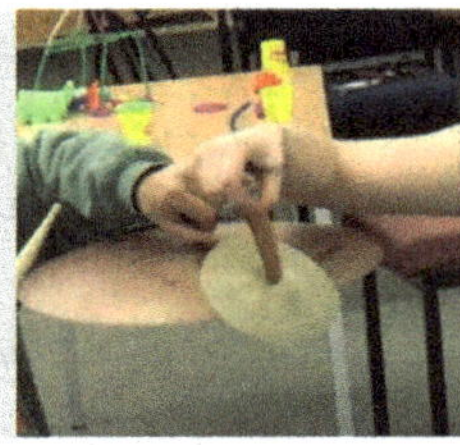

FIGURE 4.12 Frictional entangling

FIGURE 4.13 Frictional entangling

The friction is 'felt' in our scratched skin, our caught clothing, our nervous excitement at how to tackle the descent.

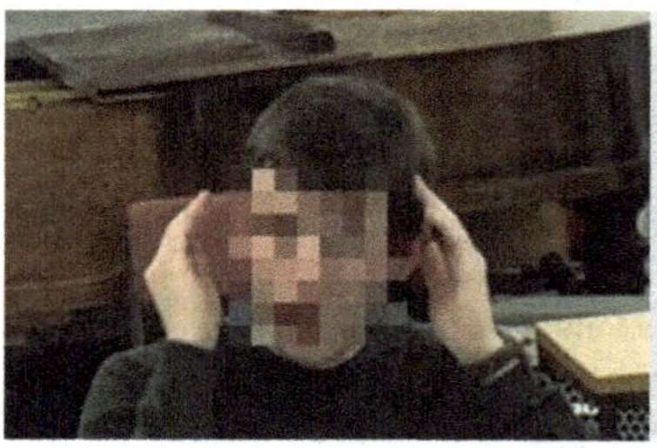

'Yes, [improvising is] making it up but only once you've got a *full understanding* [hands by head – knowing in the head] of what you have rather than just go and play ... you have to have an understanding in the first place ... Jazz improv, 12-bar blues, *you couldn't just go and play* whatever without having a complete understanding.'

FIGURE 4.14 Frictional understandings

The friction is 'materially negotiated', making different understandings and relationships with the wall, with the stones, with the field behind and in front of us.

'Can it be a guitar?' His question threw me. It made me uncomfortable. The question has continued to play, making with the idea *of legitimation to touch, and play* with materials.

FIGURE 4.15 Frictional touch

These frictions leave their mark as we reach the field on the other side. The wall has left its mark on us, on our skins, on our bodies, on our clothing, but we have also left a mark on it. Where we moved stones, their undersides once protected from the elements are now exposed. The shape of the wall, changed by our presence, our movements. The flora around the wall, temporarily squashed from our landing.

These frictions constantly 'tugged' at us; they are more than a 'moment'; they are part of our stories now. As one member of the research group commented in the final conversations, 'thinking with improvising, like we've done here, has really made me so much more aware of what is actually going on in class'. We have 'co-composed frictionally' (Springgay, 2018, p. 67), not stopping where there was friction, but 'staying with the trouble' (Haraway, 2016, p. 1) that it created in the in-between.

(Re)Turning/(Re)Tuning

(Re)turning to the landscape, now imbued with more-than disciplines, where we (re)tune ourselves to the inseparable entanglements of nature, culture, education, becoming, research, practice, instruments, materials, bodies.

(Re)tuning to the sensorial, the movement, the experience as powerful awakening forces to what was always there.

(Re)turning to re-see, re-make, re-experience, re-materialise.

FIGURE 4.16
From my front door *again*[13]

Spring Landscape

As I sit here looking out over the fields of north-east Scotland, I can see the very beginnings of summer arriving. Now there is so much to capture our attention, feeling the rhythms of our walking across time and space. Noticing difference.

Now the movement of the scape isn't just of the trees on the horizon being buffeted by the wind. ***Now everything moves.*** *The clouds, the shadows, the*

13 'Yes, and', a theatre improv game (Johnstone, 1979), permeated my PhD. It provided a generative way of 'making with' the materials of the project, as well as lending itself to the final few pages in the form of this poem. The poem, as a 'porous surface' was where the 'new shoots' of thinking emerged from the rich, nourishing spaces of the project.

trees, the lengthening crops, the swallows, the pheasants, the deer in the far distance. Movement becomes more visible and visceral.

Now the spaces and places are more obviously in flux, in sequences of change, moving with the rhythms of the seasons, the growing and decaying of the flora and fauna, the changes of the weather. They are 'practiced places', where 'myriad stories' (Massey, 2013) are happening with us as we walk, bringing together histories and futures in generative entanglements.

Now the surfaces are more varied, no longer contorting ourselves to deep divots of frozen ground, or stinging ourselves on frozen metal, finding ways to adapt ourselves to the challenges presented by such unforgiving touching encounters. But now, having more generous 'bounce' in our step from the slightly soft, flora-covered surfaces. Having a little 'give', a little 'play' in how and when we move. Where we can make with, explore and allow different wways of being to emerge through, beneath, within, between our movements.

Now the boundaries of the fields, once stark against the topology of the landscape, have become blurred by the life of the flora that has risen up and in some cases grown over. While we can still make out the shapes of the fields, their distinctive characteristics, they are more entangled, creating an impression of 'flowing spaces', where, while there may still be tensions in travelling across and between, there is less definition of where our travelling could go, or could extend itself.

This is a scape which is alive. It is one which we haven't just visited but one we have made with as we walked, as a scape full of transdisciplinary potentials for difference making, future making, and re-making ourselves.

From our walk, we have (re)turned and (re)tuned ourselves to paying attention to different movements, different positionings, different methodologies and different writings.

References

Barad, K. (2007). *Meeting the universe halfway: Quantum physics and the entanglement of matter and meaning*. Duke University Press.

Cooke, R. (2021, June 20). Interview: Robin Wall Kimmerer: 'Mosses are a model of how we might live'. *The Guardian*. https://www.theguardian.com/science/2021/jun/19/robin-wall-kimmerer-gathering-moss-climate-crisis-interview

Gershon, W. S. (2011). Embodied knowledge sounds as educational systems. *Journal of Curriculum Theorizing*, *27*(2), 66–81.

Haraway, D. (2016). *Staying with the trouble: Making kin in the chthulucene*. Duke University Press.

Johnstone, K. (1979). *Impro: Improvisation and the theatre.* Faber and Faber.

MacLure, M. (2013). Researching without representation? Language and materiality in post-qualitative methodology. *International Journal of Qualitative Studies in Education, 26*(6), 658–667.

MacNaughtan, A (2001). *Yellow on the broom.* Scots Language Centre. https://www.scotslanguage.com/articles/node/id/373

Massey, D. (2013). *Social science sound bites: Doreen Massey* (Interview by D. Edmunds & N. Warburton). Social Science Space. www.socialsciencespace.com/2013/02/podcastdoreen-massey-on-space/

Murris, K. (2016). *The posthuman child: Educational transformation through philosophy with picturebooks.* Routledge.

Perry, M. (2021). Pluriversal literacies: Affect and relationality in vulnerable times. *Reading Research Quarterly, 56*(2), 293–309.

Russell, A. W., Wickson, F., & Carew, A. (2008). Transdisciplinarity: Context, contradictions and capacity. *Science Direct Futures, 40*, 460–472.

Springgay, S. (2018). 'How to write as felt': Touching transmaterialities and more-than-human intimacies. *Studies in Philosophy and Education, 38*(1), 57–69.

CHAPTER 5

Paying Attention

A Bakhtin-Inspired Dialogue about Embodiment and Inclusion in the Musicking Classroom

Mary Earl and Jennie Francis

Intro

Mary: I want to tell you about a conversation which I think is important ... We can't listen in from the beginning because it's been going on for a while ... But you'll catch up ...

It's about speaking with authenticity rather than the tokenistic language of 'meeting targets' and 'flight paths' current in education in the UK today.

The chapter has grown out of a nine-month conversation between two teachers who are now teacher educators. We have written it as a dialogue because that was the way it came into being. We both remember times when, early in our careers, we tried, and failed, to find ways to connect authentically with our students' concerns. Either institutional or personal issues of our own seemed to find a way to distort our behaviour in the classroom – and it was hard to discover, in ourselves, why this might be happening. In our dialogue here, as in the actual conversations it is based on, we looked into the dialogic principles of Mikhail Bakhtin, alongside the existentialist writings of Michael Bonnet (on authenticity in teaching relationships) and Nel Noddings' philosophy of care in education in order to try to understand this phenomenon. In this process we traced the links between both Jennie's and my own early career exploration, over three years, of our own identities as teachers, singers and songwriters. This led us to see that what we gained, over time, from our respective identity 'crises' was greater insight into the importance of 'paying attention', 'presence' and 'embodiment' in learning to teach inclusively. In the spirit of layered conversation, the subheadings are lyrics from one of Jennie's students and from Jennie's songs.

 | DOI:10.1163/9789004516069_007

1, 2, 1, 2, uh, huh, Here We Go

Jennie: Well let me tell you the story … I'd been teaching music in a secondary school for a while and I wasn't really flourishing there. What I was doing didn't feel like 'me', and I wasn't sure that what I was trying to do meant anything much to the young people I taught. I was a flute player, I could analyse a piece of Beethoven for you, and I'd conducted the choir at university, but for most of the young people I taught none of that really connected. Somehow I didn't know how to be in the room with *them* and their concerns and with who they each were. In fact in those early years it probably had not dawned on me that that was what I *needed* to do.

So … I was miserable … and as a result of being miserable I decided, extremely, that I needed to leave the country and stop music teaching … And then BAM! I found myself at the piano and the guitar creating an explosion of songs – something I'd never done before – and that changed everything.

Mary: Something like this happened to me too a few years after I started teaching. I was miserably 'doing as I was told' with my classroom teaching (with minimal support) and was feeling really hurt that I couldn't find a way to share the fire I had in me with my students. I knew the way I was teaching didn't meet their concerns, so I tried everything to find a way to connect with them. I wrote simulation games. I laboured over lesson planning into the small hours. I changed classroom seating arrangements. I read a good deal about 'how to' teach. I asked other people's advice. Then, when nothing worked, I decided I had to give up.

In fact … I let go of the 'who am I in a classroom' question for a while, because I couldn't see how to solve that problem. I was still there, present, trying but I had also started exploding, and exploring, my 'other side' in stage management, and later directing for school plays, cabarets and musicals, even operas. I didn't even know I had those skills in me! I had been so embarrassed by myself and was feeling a bit of a failure in teaching before this but when I saw (and my students saw) what I was like when I was 'on fire' I found that our relationships and our conversations changed – both 'on stage' and in the classroom. They could see *me* more authentically – and I them. So I took heart and started paying attention to what *really* worked when I was teaching in a classroom. That transformed classroom teaching for me.

Jennie: I know what you mean. I knew – not just in theory, but in practice – that music is transformative; it's a medium in which you can think and dwell and feel included, where you can step forward and be heard. And I found that knowing that meant that I felt I had an ethical responsibility to try to create spaces in which students might experience that too. Here's an example.

I had a class of Year 10 students who had been given a reduced diet of General Certificate of Secondary Education (GCSE) subjects. They were excluded from the full curriculum – they'd been put in their own special, reluctant, disengaged music class. The class consisted of socially and economically disadvantaged children. And, in the story that I'm going to tell you now, none of the girls had turned up – it was just boys.

So on this day, I had decided that we should write a song about something that they actually cared about. I insisted that we keep talking until we found a subject ... it took us 50 minutes ... until the local cattle market's transformation into a shopping centre got them all in the conversation. The cattle market was a big carpark-type space where they had been able to hang out and do what they wanted. The conversation snowballed along and I took notes. One boy was particularly fluent and expressive. After a while I said, 'Wow! Listen to what you've just said.' I read a few of his lines. 'You need to be our lead singer. You are really persuasive ...' I introduced them to an E-minor chord ... and off we went.

So this gives an example of how an aspect of my practice changed. We didn't listen to any music or try to make any music (or any of the things you traditionally do in a music lesson – I didn't know what was going to happen) until we found something that they wanted to think about and tell about. Everything was driven by a desire that they discover the experience of embodying something in music – and that required me to really pay attention to the people in the room.

Mary: When I became a teacher educator, like you, later on, I knew that it had been experiences like these which helped me explore with trainees what 'paying attention' in a classroom means. I asked them to consider that paying attention isn't something we just demand of our students. We have to demand it of ourselves too. Bonnet calls this a triadic and 'poetic' relationship – between teacher and student, student and the 'thing being learned' and, of course, the *teacher* and the thing being learned (Bonnet, 1994, p. 179). If we are paying attention to all three aspects of this classroom relationship, it seems to me, then both the learner's own engagement with things is celebrated and, also, the teacher's role as essentially receptive-responsive (Bonnet, 1996, p. 27).

But how *do* you teach, in a triadic way and still have time or energy to express qualities like 'integrity, vitality, perceptiveness, aptness?' (Bonnet, 1996, p. 36).

Jennie: I did find, after my song-writing experience, that the integrity and the vitality came through more easily. I had a more in-the-moment musicianship which meant that it was much easier for me to respond musically, sympathetically, helpfully, to the kind of situation I found myself in with that class. It also helped with the perceptiveness and aptness. I felt that students should be able to make the music they *wanted* to make. I also felt it was my job to understand the curriculum and its elasticity in more depth so that I could invite people in and say, 'No, it's fine, you're welcome here. Look, you can do this!' That perception led me to make different choices, ask better questions and, in the end, take a very different approach to working with students who might otherwise have been seen as 'problematic'. I needed my 'fire language' (a term that arrived in a song lyric) in order to work effectively in really inclusive classrooms. Inclusion started to come when I knew I was telling students what I now really believed: that they all could 'do this' music-making, make their own fire language. That confidence, in turn, gave them confidence – so we all made progress together.

Mary: That feels very different to saying, 'We're doing this because it's in the curriculum!' Pring says that teachers 'mak[e] personal that which arrives parcelled up in an impersonal way'. Large class teaching involves 'social interaction within which the learners explore their competing meanings' and can safely 'confront together the uncertainties which, though informed by art and literature, (or history or any other subject) will never be solved' (Pring, 1995, p. 135). That – and Bonnet's way of seeing each and every lesson as the 'product of a set of constantly evolving mutual relationships … the expression of an interplay' – is what led me to Bakhtin. He's a literary theorist, one of the post-revolutionary thinkers and actors of Russia in the early twentieth century. Stravinsky was another. Bakhtin says dialogue is a focused conversation which engages the heart as well as the mind. It's different from everyday conversation *because* it has a focus and a purpose and is used to increase understanding, address problems, and question thoughts or actions. But, as Bonnet says – and we've both experienced, 'no one person initiates the interplay, is wholly responsible for it, or able to control it. It is a matter of co-responsibility' (Bonnet, 1996, p. 37).

Jennie: I was surprised and delighted to be able to embody how I was feeling inside my songs – and once that happened I needed my students to feel that too. For example in my very first song – it's called 'There's no escaping mediocrity' – you can hear that as well as all of the worry and sadness, I'm excited. I've begun to find something in me that means that I can escape mediocrity and that I don't need to leave teaching to find it. I found a more confident, more expressive, more musically generous self inside the process of writing my *own* songs and that's what gave me, I believe, the freedom to really pay attention to my students.

So I didn't leave … but I did, alongside my daily teaching, also properly indulge my inner adolescent for three years. I felt as if I was unflinchingly paying attention to different parts of me. I was in a musical dialogue with myself … with people I knew but also with Randy Newman, Norman MacCaig, all sorts of people and … all kinds of ideas. I felt more and more like I had a space in the world … and that I could participate eye-to-eye in musical conversations – I wasn't staring up at Mozart or Randy Newman or whoever – I was looking across. I'm not suggesting I was writing anything approaching that quality, but I was, like them, being a composer.

You can hear in the final song that I wrote in this three-year flurry (which is the first song I'd ever multi-tracked) that I've explained to myself how to be included in this multi-voiced untidy musical conversation: 'You've got to glitter by music, smile slow days, learn to speak fire language and listen always.' The music becomes messy, a bit dissonant, unresolved but it's also settled and confident. I'm allowing my *self*, by then, to be part of this conversation …

Bakhtin: Perhaps I could come in here? The trouble with modern western thinking (and a lot of your curriculum is based on that) is that it tries to understand events 'according to a pre-existing set of rules to which they conform or structure that they exhibit' (Morson & Emerson, 1990, pp. 49–50). But for me, art is not about this, it's about being 'answerable' for who we are – and about the moral responsibility that goes with that. 'I have to answer with my own life for what I have experienced and understood in art, so that everything I have experienced and understood would not remain ineffectual in my life' (Bakhtin, 1990, p.1).

Mary: That's why it makes absolute sense to me, Jennie, that when you were struggling it wasn't knowing more *about* teaching in some general sense which helped. It was understanding that the curriculum is full of abstract things (music's theory, if you like), but that embodying means that you have to engage in a different, more present way with your students.

Bakhtin: Yes, and the dialogue you then found opening up was like the conversation you and Jennie have been having for so long. It's *open-ended.* I believe that dialogue *is* 'the single adequate form for verbally' – or in your case musically – 'expressing authentic human life' (Bakhtin, 1984, p. 293).

Mary: Bonnet's work has this existentialist sense of the importance of authenticity too. He says that 'the heart of a genuine teacher-pupil relationship is the engagement of the personhood of the teacher with the personhood of the child; a genuine mutual responsiveness initiated by the teacher's desire to enable authentic learning' (Bonnet, 1996, p. 37). He adds that 'the truth – often only tacitly recognized – is that what motivates such a teacher-pupil relationship is knowing that thinking proper is not simply a matter of applying certain cognitive strategies and techniques to some unformed, inert, material, but is a response to what calls for attention, a sensing of what is at issue, what is 'on the move', as it were, in an engagement with a living tradition of thought' (Bonnet, 1996, p. 35).

Bakhtin: Bit of a fourth wall moment there, but interesting. I suppose then, that he'd understand when I say that dialogic means working with the assumption that you can't be authentic unless you're embodied. Dialogism is about participation in an unending conversation so, just as your song writing can go on endlessly because there's always something more for you to be in the space, so everyone 'participate(s), our whole lives, with eyes, lips, hands, soul, spirit, with our whole body and deeds' (Bakhtin, 1984, p. 293).

Mary: I wanted to move onto something else for a minute. Jennie, you were able to persuade a group of people who hadn't asked to be in a music class that their time wouldn't be wasted there. What about people who come into your class with a *strong* sense of musical identity – and then find that that clashes with the music curriculum?

Jennie: I clearly remember a student, Nathan, who was brought to me because he was in danger of dropping out. He had been asked to write a minimalism piece for his GCSE composition. But he was a very good rapper and he was frustrated.

Our dialogue started by me telling him that he didn't need to write minimalism and he could do something that he wanted to. I asked him to tell me about artists he was influenced by. This led to a 'YouTube safari' into Busta Rhymes. I took notes about the music and asked him whether it was typical and then he'd show me another track and so on. We had a really eye-to-eye conversation, enthusiastic and serious on both our parts. After a while we got to the point where I felt that I knew what I needed to teach him in order for him to be able to make his music and be pleased with it.

He was always going to be fine with the rapping; it was the backing track that was going to be the challenge – he didn't play a musical instrument. So I showed him how he could do what he wanted to do just using the black notes on the keyboard, how he could create his own beats and some basic moves on the computer he was working with.

I knew he'd be fine. The whole thing was like starting to roll a snowball down a slope. Once he knew enough then off he went under his own musical momentum – and it was good! You can hear in the recording how pleased he is … and how proud he is. The first part of the song mentions his own tag name – he really owns it.

Mary: I know it might sound a bit pompous but yes, he needed to invest 'his entire self' in the discourse and you made that happen by investing *your* entire self, including the authenticity of your own song composing experience, in it too. That's two sides of the triadic relationship Bonnet talks about. You're relating your musicking self to the student's musicking self – and, lo and behold, it's when you do that that you get into this bigger conversation.

Bakhtin: If I hear you right that's what I call a conversation about the 'dialogic fabric of human life' (bringing us) into the world symposium' (Bakhtin, 1984, p.293).

Jennie: (to Mary) Do you remember when you sent me that image of a face?

FIGURE 5.1
Veiling and unveiling

Mary: Yes. I made it over a few months. I think it embodied (because I tend to do that in images) the fragments I sometimes see of myself in my early teaching world – and I was hearing you talk about too. I had a feeling, back then, like you, that I tended to constantly 'veil' whatever I really wanted to say in classrooms. Like you, that hadn't made me, or my working life, happy. The image helped me 'say' how that felt (to both of us, it seems).

Jennie: When I saw the image I saw a mask, but a scary one – stifling, uncomfortable, monochrome. It was becoming detached from a face, a much more colourful, more subtle, more revealing, human face (although in the image we can't see it yet). The mask has an open mouth and it looks stiff and stuck to me. At the same time, though, it's disintegrating. It's becoming see-through. It's falling away into the past. A memory, perhaps an unreliable one (it's too monochrome to be real). There's lots here that reminds me of what I was singing about and through when I really got down to composing. I sang about being stuck in 'hologram chains', 'going round in circles', 'shuffling up and down'; about speaking and acting in disembodied, not-true-to-me and lonely ways – keeping myself away from the real world – 'polythene promises', 'didn't have a clue', 'never be captured, only be killed', 'you're on your own', 'not sure I dare face the air or the glare of a world that's up there'. Later, I realised that that's exactly how some of students felt too – and that song composition could liberate them too, from those feelings.

Feelings I've Kept Under Wraps, Hopes I Never Spoke of …

Mary: Maybe it was because we were talking so often, over this last year, that our conversations sparked a lot of reading; a lot of writing, too, for me. Remember the poem I sent when you first let me hear your songs?

Jennie: I remember.

Mary: Poems are like an adventure for me. I get engaged in all sorts of struggles and that's quite enlightening. Quite transformative. Like your songs were for you. It's not that I need my poems to be seen as 'good' (though that kind of reward is nice sometimes!). I need them to *mean* something; to put me back in touch with the gaps between myself and 'out there.' It was April when I wrote this, as I remember. Songs and song composition seems to be a similar adventure for you – and for your students.

April-like, your songs bear their youth-in-age theme bravely,
Changeable, fascinating, catching me unawares.
Working with them, this April, reminds me that we
Cannot predict – or tame
All of who we will be (or is it: 'might become?')

We can though, be glad, sad, stand, fall, fail, together,
Paying attention to our deepest selves
And turning them,
April (un) clear, to song.

Jennie: I liked the way you called that experience 'April-like'. The song writing did feel a bit like weather – like something happening to me, something to go along with ... sunshine, showers, desolate winds, stillness. Not tidily going along in a straight line. Not a gradual transition from ambiguity and dark minor sombreness into sunny major certainties and a perfect cadence. But a swirl, more of a dance, a going with the flow. And the joy of it was that my musical self *could* go with the flow. There was always a song when a song was needed. How lucky! What a joy. What a discovery. I found this quotation, the other day, from Bob Dylan: 'composing songs can make sense of things and what is being made sense of is the way we're living, and not living, now' (2005, p. 71).

But music teaching isn't just a 'floaty' thing where you wait for inspiration to hit. There are any number of musical *fields* to explore, to have knowledge of and to come to understand when you teach someone to write songs. The actions, the interventions, the stepping back and the stepping in to find a place where you 'meet' with your students' concerns though is something very different. I found that to teach you need to find inner coherence even, or especially, when there appears to be none in the room. I had to be able to motivate, adapt and learn new knowledge, daily. I needed to be able to leave my lessons and spend time being reflective about them. I needed to be surprised by just how able my students are – and by just how much they will respond if you meet them halfway with the right gifts. There is no 'one-size-fits-all' in teaching – and inclusion is not a 'one-size-fits-all' experience either. I needed to *embody* the ways I had learned myself, in other words, what 'the point' of song composition is, not just talk about it.

I Want Someone to Stop Me Wasting My Time...

Jennie: In the process of creating songs my inner thought patterns about music making were changing and I was now 'believing possibilities that I wouldn't have allowed before' (Dylan, as cited in Hentoff, 1963).

Mary: Isn't that what we want every student to do? Bonnet (1962, p. 26) says that we all want our children to know more than they did before, to be able to think what to do in new situations, to discuss or explain something that they

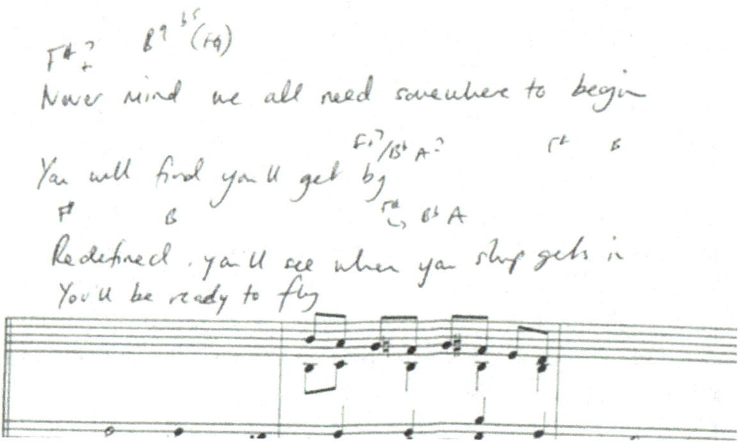

FIGURE 5.2 Somewhere to begin ...

could not before, to feel differently about something, to work something out for themselves that they could not before, to have some new thoughts, feelings, understanding, appreciation, awareness. Learning is about growing and changing, not just about repeating and memorising!

Jennie: Yes. I got more experienced at encouraging people to compose confidently. I found that for students, composing became more satisfying if:

- There is time to play, explore and change.
- Your ideas are listened to and responded to.
- There is a sense of confidence that you will be successful.
- You work in a medium in which you feel comfortable and in which you are interested.
- You understand (through playing, listening, experimenting) sufficient technical and stylistic features to enable you to create and develop ideas that you think are worth hearing.
- You know that you can express something through your music (Francis, 2011, paras. 23–24).

Mary: Was it like that between you and Nathan?

Jennie: Yes, I realized that the task he'd been set wasn't allowing him to do any of these things.

Mary: We've seen something about how you managed to get him to connect. Noddings talks about this as having to expect the conversations we have as teachers to be 'a constellation of encounters, both planned and unplanned, that promote growth through the acquisition of knowledge, skills, understanding and appreciation' (Noddings, 2002, p. 283). Does that resonate with you?

Jennie: Yes, I had no idea that he was going to be brought to me, so the initial encounter was entirely unplanned. Then we got into a conversation which, like an improvisation, was a mixture of a semi-planned interaction, insofar as this was a way of working with students that I habitually used and knowing that I would lose him if I didn't keep paying attention. This moves into a more planned teaching episode in the course of the conversation as I work out what we are dealing with, and what Nathan still needs to know to be able to succeed. After that, the conversations that took place when I visited him were improvised based on what we had before us.

Mary: Hang on! I remember a teaching situation where that happened to me. Dan couldn't connect with lots of words I was using and couldn't see that they meant anything. That was driving me mad because that lack of connection meant that he was excluding himself from the conversation. Then, by chance, his sixth form group went on a theatre trip and saw Marlowe's *Faust*. There's a bit in that story where Faust realises he's doomed himself to an *eternity* in hell because the Devil has trapped him into selling his soul. He's scared witless and immediately tries to bargain his way out of the situation by saying something like: 'maybe a million million years? A hundred million years?' 'No', says Mephistopheles. 'I mean it. You'll be in hell. Forever.' Dan came up to me afterwards and said he'd just twigged what eternity was about, so I asked what he thought about the idea. F*****g terrifying, he said! Now that may not be something you can write on an exam paper, but it was a pretty good reflection, to me, of the fact he'd 'got' the idea! It was this unplanned encounter which in fact promoted growth. But it's also the fact that I could improvise on what he brought to me and use that to connect him to a whole set of otherwise alien ideas.

What I Mean Depends on Being Seen: You Give My Meaning to Me

Jennie: You're covering over something there…

Mary: What?

Jennie: The fact that he wanted to come and talk to you about it. He knew that you had been caring about his connection with this idea and he sought you out to tell you. That shows something reciprocal in your relationship.

Mary: Yes, I remember it as being a really satisfying moment. Nel Noddings puts her finger on this. We 'recognize something admirable, or at least acceptable, struggling to emerge in each person we encounter'. Then, because 'the goal or attribute must be seen as worthy both by the person trying to achieve it and by us', we confirm that they're going in the 'right' way (1998, p. 192). I think that Dan was recognizing in me, just as I was recognizing in him, that there was somewhere we could connect on this idea, but that we hadn't arrived at it yet. He was keen to tell me that he had and I was delighted that he did that. That sort of care is essential. We 'show in our behaviour what it means to care' rather than merely telling them to care and giving them texts to read on the subject, we *demonstrate* our caring in our relations with them' (Noddings, 1998, p. 190).

Bakhtin: What does she have to say about dialogue? Because I think that that's about caring too.

Mary: You're right. She says that 'dialogue is such an essential part of caring that we could not model caring without engaging in it' (Noddings, 1998, p. 190). That's why I agree with her that teachers shouldn't be 'shouting formulas and slogans' or trying to 'posit a single ideal for everyone and then announce high expectations for all' (Noddings, 1998, p. 190).

Bakhtin: Bravo. I've always said that things, people, exist in relationship. We are always in dialogue, not only with other people, but also with everything in the world. In a monologic novel, characters exist solely to transmit the author's ideology. That's why I liked Dostoevsky's novels. He has the courage to be dialogic. To let the different characters be fully, uniquely themselves – and then let the reader decide what to make of them for themselves. I think monologic kinds of writing are deaf to difference and diversity. They're not inclusive. Dialogism is a contrast because it *does* recognise the multiplicity of perspectives and voices.

Mary: Dialogic teachers teach with multiple perspectives in mind, not just with their own ideology in mind. Also as they have care as their primary 'ethic' (rather than Kantian logic), they can *be* those multiple perspectives and teach their students to 'perspective take'. Noddings calls that reciprocity. A lot of child and adolescent development takes place in 'transitional spaces' like classrooms and being inclusive in those spaces 'requires an embrace rather than eschewal of ambiguity, and the capacity to continue to dwell in the transitional space between relatedness and separateness' (McMahon, 2020, p. 37). Neuroscientists give us some insights into how those actions show up on a brain map but teachers need to know how to embody it.

Make It All Mine Then I Boo the Sky…

Jennie: Thing is, we're *all* concerned with growing and changing. Adolescence (and, as I said, I thought of my song writing as a bit of a delayed one) is always saying 'Who am I? How do I fit in? What can I do? What makes me happy?' In the final rap that my GCSE student Nathan wrote you can hear what really concerns him. 'Tell no lie, Say my name, But *capitalise* them letters.' And: 'I'm fresh, I'm raw, I'm right off the bone, never felt so right …'

This – and the whole sound world of that composition – is his creativity nurtured through all those conversations (with me but also with his hero, Busta Rhymes and with so many other people that I'm sure he didn't tell me about).

Nathan's rap was him at that time and in that place. That's what makes it more than just another target met: 'I mean it, I sing it, I deem it, I really can't redeem it like an out-of-date fashion man' If he couldn't find that voice he would be, as the rap says: 'done, I'm leaving.'

Mary: But like you, Jennie, he *wasn't* leaving. The musicking gave him a reason to stay.

Outro

Mary: Educational knowledge exists in, and is verified by, its performance (Rudduck, 1988, p. 35). Two teachers have been the performers here. We've been involved in a conversation, over nine months, which has had an impact on both of us – and which is not over yet. What's the point of writing about it as well? The point is that we strongly believe that the performance of a teacher does *not* exist to 'programme students in a certain direction so that they will behave in set ways' (Rudduck, 1988, p. 35). It's there to help students towards a reasoned and responsible autonomy – and care about them in the process. Is this rebellion? Who knows? It's certainly, in our experience, counter-cultural at a time when education is full of agendas which seems to be adversely affecting the subjective experience both of teaching and learning:

1. Management is altering social connections and power relations to less democratic and caring forms.
2. Performativity and accountability agendas are radically undermining the professionalism of teachers.
3. They are in the hunt for measures, targets, benchmarks, tests, tables, audits to feed the system in the name of improvement (Ball, 2016).

What use is it, to the next generation, to be given so much information and so much testing that their mental health starts to crumble under the strain and their anxiety about how they will manage to live in the new worlds they are going to inhabit escalates? Our answer is that students who are lucky find, in those 'transitional spaces' we call classrooms, a teacher who is *present*. They find a teacher who uses their voice – and their ears and their eyes – their whole bodies, to hear and inclusively respond. The conversations we begin in our everyday classroom teaching are unfinished and unfinalisable (Bakhtin, 1984) and through them both teacher and student develop insight. They do this not just by hearing something and then writing it down, nor by composing something 'by numbers'. Insight comes from 'seeds of discussions, readings, and observations' (Shafak, 2020, p. 16), and to this we might add 'musickings', of the kind we've described here. Noddings (1998) argues that teaching of the kind we are describing tends to produce a 'mentality': if we want to encourage people to care for one another, then it makes sense to give students 'practice in caring and reflection on that practice' (p. 191). In addition to this, students need to be given the opportunity to care about what they are *doing* and not just because it is good for some distant goal, but because it is good for and of itself. Of course, the 'knowledge debate' behind all this matters. But if foregrounding that means that teachers' performance loses both its dialogic character in relation to knowledge *and* an underlying dialogue of care then we will be (and, some would argue, already are) losing something very precious.

References

Bakhtin, M. (1984). *Problems of Dostoevsky's poetics* (C. Emerson, Trans.). University of Minnesota Press.

Bakhtin, M. (1990). *Art and answerability*. University of Texas Press.

Bakhtin, M. (1994). Social heteroglossia. In P. Morris (Ed.), *The Bakhtin reader: Selected writings of Bakhtin, Medvedev, Voloshinov* (pp. 73–80). Arnold.

Ball, S. (2016). Neoliberal education? Confronting the slouching beast. *Policy Futures in Education, 14*(8), 1046–1059.

Bonnet, M. (1994). *Children's thinking: Promoting understanding in the primary school*. Cassell.

Bonnet, M. (1996). 'New' era values and the teacher-pupil relationship as a form of the poetic. *British Journal of Educational Studies, 44*(1), 27–41.

Dylan, B. (2005). *Chronicles: Volume one* (2nd ed.). Pocket Books.

Flood, L. (2020, February 6). Michael Rosen condemns UK education system's 'fear of laughter'. *The Guardian*. https://www.theguardian.com/books/2020/feb/06/michael-rosen-condemns-uk-education-system-fear-of-laughter-awards-laugh-out-loud

Francis, J. (2011). Composing at GCSE – Exploring pathways. *National Association of Music Educators Magazine*, 35.

Hentoff, N. (1963). *The freewheelin' Bob Dylan* [Liner notes]. Columbia Records.

McMahon, L. (2020). 'The separation that is not a separation but a form of union': Merleau-Ponty and feminist object relations theory in dialogue. *Human Studies, 43*(1), 37–60.

Morson, G. S., & Emerson, C. (1990). *Mikhail Bakhtin: Creation of a prosaics*. Stanford University Press.

Noddings, N. (1998). *Philosophy of education*. Routledge.

Noddings, N. (2002). *Starting at home: Caring and social policy*. University of California Press.

Pring, R. (1995). The community of educated people: The Lawrence Stenhouse Memorial Lecture, given at the Annual Conference of the British Educational Research Association, September 1994, at St. Anne's College, Oxford. *British Journal of Education Studies, 43*(2), 125–145.

Rudduck, J. (1988). Changing the world of the classroom by understanding it: A review of some aspects of the work of Lawrence Stenhouse. *Journal of Curriculum and Supervision*, *4*(1) 30–42.

Shafak, E. (2020). *How to stay sane in an age of division*. Welcome Institute.

CHAPTER 6

Academic (In)Discipline, Research (In)Sanity and the Conundrum of (Indigenous) Timescapes

Bernd Brabec de Mori

> Discipline is never an end in itself, only a means to an end.
>
> KING CRIMSON (1981, back cover)

∵

Prologue

In 1981, one of my favourite progressive rock bands, King Crimson, published an LP entitled *Discipline*. The title refers – probably – to the complex and virtuoso rhythmic patterns the band polymetrically intertwine through most of the tracks. There is one exception, though, which is called 'Indiscipline': this piece appears much more chaotic (though well composed), with drummer Bill Bruford playing against everybody else. It ends with the singer Adrian Belew bursting out: 'I like it!'

FIGURE 6.1 Excerpt from a transcription of King Crimson's 'Indiscipline' (Riccio & Gunn, 2020, p. 55)

 | DOI:10.1163/9789004516069_008

Indiscipline vs Academic Disciplining

As a music and sound researcher, I like indiscipline, too. Both the King Crimson song and the thing *per se*. Usually, in academia, musicology is thought of as a 'discipline' in humanities, but most often it is used as a synonym for what would be called a 'subdiscipline', namely historical musicology, which often shares departments with epistemologically quite contrasting 'subdisciplines' like ethnomusicology, music psychology and popular music studies (aka music sociology). We can see, however, that these 'subdisciplines' are all definitely part of their 'mother disciplines' history, anthropology, psychology and sociology. Similarly, an ethnomusicologist could be (and often is) employed at an anthropology department. So what? Shouldn't our area of research be thought of as inter-, cross- or trans-disciplinary, or even as an undisciplined endeavour? Would we like 'indiscipline'?

I would. And 'the more I look at it, the more I like it!'[1]

In 2012, I graduated with a doctoral dissertation about vocal music among Amazonian Indigenous groups (Brabec de Mori, 2015), thus subjecting myself to being called an ethnomusicologist for probably the rest of my academic life; despite my current employment at a music psychology research centre and my publications appearing in anthropological, linguistic, historical, sociological, medical or pharmacological journals and books. Becoming an ethnomusicologist was then bound, similar to cultural and social anthropology, to an extensive phase of fieldwork. I was able to start my fieldwork with three consecutive small grants offered by my university, and later was awarded a two-year major doctoral grant from the Austrian Academy of Sciences. With all this, and by bridging the phases between grants by teaching English and German at a local language school, I was able to stay for five years in the western Amazonian lowlands. After five years, I just started understanding some basics of Indigenous vocal music. I also had enough time and discipline to transcribe hundreds of song melodies and lyrics.

I tell this story because it connects with the foundation of music and sound, that is, time. And time is not only crucial for sounds to be able to unfold in perception, but also for understanding what research is about. I get the impression that nowadays it is nearly impossible for students to do what I did. My application for the two-year grant actually stated that I would spend all the time in the field in order to gather as much data as possible. Try to base a grant proposal in 2021 on a plan to hang out with your research associates for the whole period of the grant. Contemporary academic practice binds research to

1 From Adrian Belew's lyrics to King Crimson's 'Indiscipline' (1981).

highly selective, competitive and time-restricted project grants, and it deems it impossible, or close to it, to start understanding your research area and what people 'really do'. How could you reach deep understanding in six months of fieldwork (which already sounds quite extensive)? The most important thing to do in order to understand is *to listen*. And listening takes time. Therefore, I ask for the reader's time to read on and be taken on a journey that crosses psychology and history, then touches on the ontological incommensurability[2] between Indigenous and modern worlds, and finally returns via some possibly unexpected curves to the (in)discipline from where we set out.

Time and Its Cycles: Vibrations, Synchronization and Sanity

Perception is a function of time, but in different ways. Take visual perception, for example: light enters the eye, and triggers some light-receptive cells to activate a complex interaction of neurons resulting in firing electro-chemical impulses through the optic nerve, cascading through a couple of brain-stem nuclei, passing the midbrain and being projected towards the neural cortex, where it becomes 'conscious' – meaning that the firing was filtered through an embodied space and time construction in the brainstem and midbrain, where emotional and remembrance associations were added, resulting in an enchantment of the momentary with time, with the *longue durée*. Practically, you can get the whole picture in a glimpse. Imagine looking at an image, say, a Van Gogh painting. You see the whole picture in perhaps one second, but of course by looking longer you notice the details, and by gazing closely and patiently, you may be rewarded with many insights.

Now take sound, as a different function of the temporal: the psychophysical processing of hearing is far more complex than vision, but similarly results in neuronal firing through the brainstem and midbrain into the auditory cortex, where sound becomes 'conscious'. However, you don't get it in an instant: if you visited a concert by King Crimson in the 1980s, they probably played a full set of *Discipline* along with older tracks, lasting for maybe an hour and a half. If you drop into the concert, you cannot get a 'glimpse' of the performance in one second. Nor are you rewarded with anything if you listen for longer than its duration. It's 90 minutes, and in order to 'get it', one hour and half is the time it takes, not more and not less. The sonic, and related performing arts,

2 Ontological incommensurability refers to problems that arise from contrasting basic assumptions about the existence of things, e.g. Indigenous worlds inhabited by spirits versus modern worlds wherein spirits do not exist (cf. Ludwig, 2016).

treat time quite differently than the visual arts. Listening, in general, is related to synchronisation in a very distinctive sense compared to other perceptual domains. Vibrations, the basic events of acoustics, are in turn essential for synchronisation, especially in a form known as entrainment: the 'tuning in' of two or more vibrating bodies towards each other.

Dutch astronomer and mathematician Christiaan Huygens observed something peculiar which he called an 'odd sympathy', and which is now known as 'entrainment': when two pendulum clocks, devices he invented in 1656, were mounted close to each other, their pendula would after some time swing in perfect tune with each other. By the way, for historian David S. Landes (1984), the higher temporal precision achieved through said pendulum clocks, especially so-called *regulators*, was a precondition (more, he argues, than the steam engine) for the Industrial Revolution that followed – timepieces: mechanical public and domestic clocks allowed humanity to adapt to the rapid pace of industry. Let us remember this association, this odd sympathy between the measurement of time and the pace of human life for the remainder of this chapter, but for now return to Huygens, and proceed.

Time seems to be somehow magnetic. Cyclic movements (like pendula) lean towards each other, they tend to entrain, coupling attractors, in many instances of our environment and likewise interior processes. Huygens' clocks were, as is known today, not merely sympathetic to each other, but, mounted on the same wall, transmitted their vibrations to each other, thus instantiating a prominent example of entrainment, mutual resonance. In *Reason and resonance*, Veit Erlmann (2010) resorts to Diderot who mused about the curious fact that we tend to trust in the visualism of *reflection* for examining truthful reasoning despite reason's closeness, not only terminologically, to *resonance*, a term from acoustics that describes a body's – e.g. a guitar string's or a clock pendulum's – immersion into vibrations emerging from another body. Resonant bodies thus adapt to the impulse of the other, in frequency ranges from ultrasonic vibrations to planetary revolutions, as for example our Earth's year-long round trip, the so-called circannual period, or even longer cycles – maybe even the 120 ka interstadial.

Bodily resonance is also important when empathically perceiving other human beings. In order to be empathic, that is to feel emotions felt by the (human) being you face, your body responds by imitating the other's embodied emotions, a process often described with the metaphor of *resonance* (e.g. Fuchs, 2016). If emotional consistency, however, would prove to be bound to synchronisation of periodic neuronal firing with periodic processes perceived outside of the body, the use of 'resonance' here could be more anchored in physicality than expected.

Fuchs (2013) also builds on much older observations (e.g. Minkowski's 1933 study on the perception of the mentally impaired) when investigating the correlation of temporal disorientation and desynchronisation with serious psychotic episodes like schizophrenia and major depression. Vogel et al. (2019) further build on Fuchs and others when studying in more detail the disturbance of time perception and experience during and after major schizophrenic episodes. This occurs on various scales: while Fuchs concentrates on the orchestration of implicit and explicit temporal experience embedded in a social, and also beyond-the-human, environment and its dysfunctional uncoupling during psychosis, Vogel et al. provide an empirically based verification of Fuchs' (and others') theoretical approach and confirm the causal relation of loss of synchronisation between the individual and the environment to different phases of schizophrenic illness. On the other hand, synchronisation and decoupling also plays an important role in early psychotic (schizophrenic and bipolar) onset. The causally replicable entrainment effect between auditory (binaural or steady-state) stimulation and EEG responses is remarkably disturbed, especially during the first and early phases of the illness (Spencer et al. 2008). On different scales, it is suggested that the loss of entrainment of temporal interoception[3] with the social and environmental temporal cycles and events results in mental illness of considerable severity. Let us therefore closely monitor phenomena related to time, (de-)synchronisation, entrainment and pace.

Time and Change: Indigenous Communities in Transition

I have been discussing academic questions with my colleague Carolina Rodríguez Alzza, a visiting scholar at my research institution, about the state of research with Iskonawa Indigenous people (Brabec de Mori, 2014b, 2015, pp. 334–362). In brief, this group of people who live in the Peruvian Amazon lowlands and speak a variant of the Pano linguistic family was contacted in 1959 by US missionaries.[4] Prior to contact, the missionaries dropped mirrors, glass jewellery and sweets from an airplane close to the Indigenous camp. With this, the inhabitants were seduced and addicted to 'civilization's' provisions, and later

3 Interoception describes a person's sense, conscious or unconscious, of the physiological states of and processes in one's own body, such as heartbeat, breath, hunger, movements of the limbs and so on.

4 For a more extensive description of the Iskonawa's history see Brabec de Mori (2014b), and on change in this community see Rodríguez Alzza (2020).

were transferred to a village closer to the missionaries' base. The group consisted of only 27 individuals, and a third of them died of disease and stress soon after contact. Only four of them are still alive, and among their families they are the only ones who can speak their language fluently or sing the old songs (Mazzotti et al., 2018). We can observe the slow demise of knowledge, songs, material arts, language and medical techniques among people who are still physically alive. With the old ones dying, knowledge is taken to the grave, too. An oft-employed saying, 'When an elder dies, a library burns down' (attributed to Malian writer Amadou Hampâté Bâ), suggests that this combined bodily-mental-social loss is permanent. In times of COVID-19, with its death toll being highest among Indigenous populations everywhere, this proverb haunts the news again.

The idea, however, that native, Indigenous or Aboriginal people will die out physically or lose, by assimilation, all forms of identity and knowledge and thus will disappear completely, is not new: W. H. I. Bleek, in 1875, tried to raise funds from the British Cape Governor with his *Second report concerning Bushman researches* by suggesting its urgency, terming the Bushmen 'a dying-out, and in many ways an exceptionally primitive nation … doomed to such quick extinction' (Bleek, 1875, p. 1). Other South African 'aboriginal nations' would equally, 'under the now fast-increasing sway of civilization … lose rapidly much of that originality on their life and ideas, which is of such great scientific importance' (p. 1). Much contemporary anthropological research aims at collecting data of 'scientific importance' before their carriers perish. Bleek finished his letter[5] with a plea to the politicians 'to do now for the cause of science that which cannot be done later' (p. 3). By 1939, anthropologist W. E. H. Stanner (as cited in Gray, 2014, p. 3) urged that 'we know the aborigines are dying out', due to the problem that 'the aborigines cannot preserve themselves' in the face of western 'civilization'. Anthropologists, and some politicians and medical practitioners, thus became interested in the causes of this decline, in order perhaps to save, preserve and nourish these peoples (not without first pondering, as Stanner did: 'When we are sure that we can keep them vigorously alive and breeding, we can start to think what we really mean by preserving them. Preserving them for what? … Do we really believe we are conferring a benefit upon them by preserving them?', as cited in Gray, 2014, p. 3). If physical preservation was unsuccessful, at least one could preserve their cultural achievements and

5 The original carriers of Indigenous knowledge should stay alive for data collection, but also the researcher. Although Wilhelm Bleek was allowed a small stipend by the Cape Government during these times, he could not even cover his research expenses, let alone live on it. In summer 1875, Bleek died shortly after composing this letter and submitting his report.

their memory for the future. W. H. R. Rivers (1922) tried to understand how Melanesians, who formerly suffered from massive violence and disease, were still prone, despite a more stable environment, to die from weakness and hopelessness due to what this scholar called the 'psychological factor', Indigenous despair. This translates as the Aboriginals' recalcitrant acceptance of their alleged Darwinian, evolutionary, 'natural' inferiority to the Caucasian.

This Indigenous-to-be-preserved is often referred to – in contrast to moderns – as 'traditional'; and many Indigenous customs are promoted as 'ancestral'; the latter creating temporal distance, honouring customs for their (alleged) antiquity, and the former shaping how the Indigenous is shaped through passing time, hinting at a 'cold', conservative practice of repeating what has been passed on for uncountable generations (thus tauto-lodging in ancestrality, too).

Why do Indigenous developments, treatments of time, appear traditional, ancestral, conservative, in comparison to modernity? One quick answer, opening a vast field of inquiry and analysis, a Pandora's box, which must quickly be shut again in order not to change this chapter's direction, would be: because it sells.[6] Besides economic stereotyping, there may be other reasons, phenomena of entrainment maybe. I first tackled the idea in an essay about Indigenous and non-human co-creativity (Brabec de Mori, 2016, p. 55), and will further develop it here.

With the future death of the four living members of the original Iskonawa clan, will four libraries burn down and all be lost forever? Their offspring still do not show much motivation to adopt their elders' language, learn the old (unintelligible) songs and myths, and re-acquaint themselves with a harsh and short life in the forest with snakes and without smartphones. However, there are now more than four: today's Iskonawa are estimated to number around 100 (well kept 'vigorously alive and breeding', as Stanner would have it), if we count everybody who is somehow genetically related to the aforementioned group without taking into account their self-identification, cultural knowledge or language proficiency. Among this hundred, there are a couple of individuals, though, who engage in *doing indigeneity*: we do observe not only death, but also a nascent reinvention of what it means to be Iskonawa (cf. Rodríguez Alzza, 2020). The younger Iskonawa sometimes listen to and watch the elders when talking to anthropologists. They become interested and ask the elders what their old handicraft was like, maybe they could live better by producing

6 Pandora's box: tourism, 'eco-tourism', 'ethnic tourism', 'cultural tourism', 'spiritual tourism', and so forth. See for example Comaroff and Comaroff's influential *Ethnicity Inc.* (2009), among many other works on tourism and selling, and constructing-selling stereotyped Indigeneity. I too had to add my two cents (Brabec de Mori, 2014a).

and selling artwork? An Iskonawa nation reunion in early 2021 took place in a space well decorated with new Iskonawa-style patterned textiles and with people dressing in fancy Iskonawa-style embroidered shirts. The young people do not have the elders' knowledge of songs, plants and myths, but keep in mind that formerly the elders did not have contemporary youngsters' exceptionally patterned shirts, wallpapers or Isko smartphone sheaths.

In short: there is loss among Indigenous peoples, without doubt, and often amounting to intensities unfathomable for average westerners. Loss, however, engenders invention and re-invention; re-construction of the lost and construction of change. One temporally oriented observation with Indigenous peoples around the world highlights change. It is subtle at times, and sometimes violent, but it involves steadily adapting to new circumstances, constantly employing innovation and creating novelty. If we take them seriously, the terms 'ancestral' and 'traditional' refer much more precisely to European-born thought, where peoples' ways are bound to definitely ancestral ancestors like Aristotle, Christ, Ptolemy, or at least to not-as-long-dead almost-ancestors like Foucault, Gandhi or Stravinsky. Modernity is surprisingly traditional: fast only in technological innovation, while so many institutions (think of schools, universities, hospitals, churches) seem to eternally resist substantial change. Amazing, that pace is so hurried in a society that changes so slowly. And there is an unchanging attitude in this society that thinks that Others would not be able to keep up with it and would be left behind to die out. The communities-to-die, though, usually have a different grasp on reality.

Synchronizing, Understanding, and Finding Empathy

Indigenous peoples, as common knowledge tells (and many ethnographies confirm), very often base their sociality on reciprocity. Reciprocity among the family, village, with its surroundings, the non-human environment, spirits and demons, in war and peace, in health and illness – that is, a taking and giving; as opposed to modernity, which is entirely based on taking.

But there are more particularities around Indigenous worlds: direct interaction with the non-human environment, for example, not only to exploit what can be found, but likewise to prevent reciprocity-based retaliation by contacting and communicating, say, dealing out things with the beings of the outside world. These beings involve, on the one hand, neighbouring Indigenous groups, and with time progressing, soldiers, missionaries, settlers, traders and tourists; and on the other hand, animal, plant and landscape beings, spirits, ancestors or deities. The former are usually efficiently dealt with by applying thought, speech or weapons. The latter require more sophisticated forms of communication.

Take for example, the ritual for preparing a tapir hunt called *parishara* among the Venezuelan Indigenous Pemón (Lewy, 2015): these song-dance performances were staged by a human collective (usually the village's adult, or initiated, population) in order to attract prey prior to a hunt. Killing big game, like tapirs, has to be dealt out with the 'shaman' of the animals in question (Lima, 1999). Therefore, the animals have to hear the songs, be able to listen to them and to 'understand' the lyrics. The Pemón's *parishara*, for instance, is performed for tapirs, who should hear the song and think that there is a tapir-people festival going on. The tapirs should feel invited, and approach the 'party' – only to be surprised and slaughtered by cannibal trickster demons (that is, by the human hunters). A society that works in such ways has to observe environmental cycles and adapt to them. It doesn't make sense to perform *parishara* when no tapirs are around, in the same vein as it lacks any sense to perform a rain dance during dry season.

An oft-told joke, possibly inspired by Evans-Pritchard's (1937) work among the Azande, tells us about a white person asking a Central African rainmaker to perform a rain ritual during dry season in order to test his ability, trying to prove him wrong, of course. The ritualist, however, is said to have turned to his community with some words in his language, like 'only a white could utter such a stupid request, believing that one could make rain during dry season'.

A naïve 'white' understanding of ritual magic misunderstands the sense of the whole: no Pemón would perform *parishara* when there is no prey around – they do not 'call' for the animals when they cannot hear, just as no Massai would perform a rain ritual in dry season (see e.g. Gumo, 2017 for current climate-change challenges for rainmakers in Kenya). The sense of such performances is not to dominate nature, which is obviously a mere white fantasy, but to perform synchronisation with the listening and responding environment. The performance creates a ritual timescape – delusional, if analysed from a distance – and within this world that is chanted-into-being, a copy-of-the-world is created (Taussig, 1993, p. 103), wherein the listening and approaching tapir-people are modelled by the singer-dancers, and this copy-of-the-world convincingly appears congruent to what is happening in real life. Thus, such performances construe a consistent logic that allows for an integrative processing of time and change among humans-in-environment collectives. This also includes explanations in cases of failure, that is, drought when the rainmaking fails, or hunger due to misguided hunting magic.

Another naïve 'white' understanding misunderstands the temporal relation between the human mind-body and its environment when pursuing enlightenment or other forms of non-modern knowledge: from 1960s LSD fantasies to instant enlightenment best-selling books to becoming an Amazonian 'shaman'. The longing for an alleged 'primitives' paradise' proves as old as the eighteenth, maybe even the seventeenth century, thus corresponding with Huygens' invention: 'primitives' don't have clocks. To escape from the ever-accelerating pace of increasingly precise timepieces, an illusion has been built around clockless timelessness among the beautiful nudes depicted by Paul Cezanne.

On many occasions, especially during my 2019 fieldwork in Peru, I observed westerners drinking the hallucinogenic plant decoction called *ayawaska* (see Labate & Jungaberle, 2011; Brabec de Mori, 2014a; Fotiou, 2021). This field is broad and there are many phenomena to be described, so let me only mention one prominent aspect of interest here: many westerners believe that if they drink *ayawaska* a couple of times (sometimes even once is deemed sufficient) they will be rewarded by a deep understanding of Amazonian rainforest ecology, by divine inspiration, or even by being initiated as an Indigenous healer. What it takes to be a healer in traditional Indigenous terms, though, is not connected to the hallucinogenic drink but to year-long training periods of following a set of taboos, which in local Spanish is called *dietas* ('diets'): apprentices are required to abstain from sexual and most other social contacts, and to follow strict alimentary taboos (LeClerc, 2003; Brabec de Mori, 2014a). This means that the disciple has to submit to an extreme form of discipline in order to 'tune in' with plant and animal spirits. The idea is to get in contact with such spirits during dreams or awake-time visions in states resulting from prolonged fasting, in order to learn how to call for these entities in later healing (or hunting or rainmaking) rituals. Traditional Amazonian healers would usually proclaim that four to five years of 'diets' are the minimum; most practitioners would report that they had endured up to ten years of such training. Some whites do understand: I witnessed cases of visitors who planned to spend two or three weeks in the Amazon in order to learn to be a 'shaman', but soon understood that this would take years. Only a few of these visitors would then decelerate their pace, leave behind ongoing education, jobs or even families in their home country and embark on the long arduous path of the 'diet'.

In the same vein, there are many researchers who visit an Indigenous (or other) community for a relatively brief field trip, conducting interviews and recording some rituals or festivities but who do not have the opportunity to 'tune in'. Few are those who may be sufficiently privileged, or daring, to stay for years or to return many times. Menezes Bastos (2013) analyses an Indigenous musical festival in the Xingú region of the Brazilian Amazon. The festival itself takes one entire month to perform, and preparations and post-festival social repercussions shape life during the whole interval between performances. One may document the discourse around such events by conducting a couple of interviews, but in order to understand what is happening in real life and how people actually perform and act, sharing time is indispensable. Listening takes time, real time, and requires tuning in, resonating and empathising.

These examples show that, in order to obtain Indigenous knowledge, disciples have to synchronise with the environmental cycles of plant and animal life and take the time to listen to the spirits (who mostly do not use instant messaging services but are rather bound to rain clouds or tapirs); and in order to understand Indigenous life, the disciplined researcher has to listen to the people, that is, to synchronise with the slow cycles of Indigenous worlds which are, in turn, based on listening to spirits and the environment.

Research (In)Sanity, and in the End (In)Discipline

Resorting to Fuchs' (2013) theory about desynchronisation and psychosis, please allow me to construct a possibly rebellious analogy: research that is not 'tuned in', that is not synchronised with its object, runs the risk of psychotic, delusional constructions of realities. In the previous sections, I invited you to ponder the discrepancies between momentary 'dying out' diagnoses and transgenerational processes of revival, reinvention and innovations, between instant enlightenment fantasies and year-long listening to plant spirits, and between short-term and long-term field research results. Although my examples are taken from the anthropology of Indigenous worlds, my own research 'object', I dare to extend the claim: there is a risk that approaches which are not synchronised with the research objects' temporal cycles can result in delusion – perhaps in all forms of research.

Depending on the research discipline, or the discipline of the involved researchers, such psychotic constructions may pass unnoticed, conform to reality by accident, or cause disastrous effects[7] (take nuclear fission, for example: developed in the pace of current and Cold War competition, now go and witness life and death in Hiroshima, the Bikini Atoll or Chernobyl).

Delusion can often be acceptable, though, for example in scientific modelling: contemporary SARS-CoV-19 research was sped up immensely in order to find medications or vaccines, and successfully so. The vaccines are proven to

7 You can read this, if you wish, as a very general criticism of a possible psychotic desynchronisation of modern humanity with the Earth system, or even in an expansive sense like Deleuze and Guattari (1987). It is up to you.

work in a model, a world calculated-into-being, based on high-pace laboratory studies and tests, and this copy-of-the-world convincingly appears congruent to what is happening in real life. But in order to understand how the pandemic works, including mutations, reproduction, spreading and responses, we can only resort to the pace of the virus, observing the mid- and long-term effects of said vaccines and their efficacy with newly emerging strains. Here, it is rather obvious that the model must not be confused with the world. Although the model always tries to predict the future (which is utterly important), it has to be refined in real time, including to adapt future vaccines or medication to new variants of the virus.

If Huygens' pendulum clock measured the time in congruency with the emerging Industrial Revolution and thus enabled (or forced, as a pessimist would have it) people to adapt to a faster, technologically prescribed pace, so did the telephone, TV, the internet and smartphone feeds (Keib et al., 2021).[8] Ontological incommensurability, in my view, is less dependent on assumptions about whether plant spirits exist or not, than on desynchronisation versus temporal commensurability. The colonial endeavour, I have tried to show in this chapter, was based on either forcing Indigenous worlds into the industrial pace, or leaving them 'behind to die out'. Some did, but most survived by keeping their own pace, or by adapting to industrialisation and post-industrial innovation frenzy by their own means and paces; in contemporary cases like 'ayawaska shamanism', even by forcing (or enabling, as an optimist would have it) western postmodernists into deceleration and months- or even year-long 'dieting retreats'.

I suggest, therefore, rewriting academic discipline. Departing radically from restricting researchers to an established pool of methods within one 'discipline' (psychology or history, for example), I call for indiscipline here I call for creatively overlooking such boundaries, and occupying those methods you need for your project, disrupting methodological conservatism. On the other hand, I wish for the researchers' discipline to heed time, to co-vibrate with the research objects' temporal cycles, to resonate for reasoning. By establishing resonance between researcher and researched, a process of scholarly empathy would be established that allows the researcher to experience the states of her or his observed.

---

8 An interesting side note: as I was writing this chapter, the Facebook-owned smartphone messaging service WhatsApp introduced an automated 1.5x speed playback for speech messaging. One can now listen to a former 1:30-minute message in just one minute, forcing more focused attention in order to grasp what the speaker said, thus 'saving' half the time in doing so.

FIGURE 6.2 Excerpt from a transcription of King Crimson's Discipline (Riccio & Gunn, 2020, p. 89)

Epilogue

On the final track of their 1981 LP, King Crimson perform an interlocking polyrhythmic piece called 'Discipline'. It is based on the same motif (A-C-A-C-D) of 'Indiscipline', but here, everybody plays different time patterns in a highly disciplined manner, interweaving frame by frame, always in perfect sync. The piece makes us hear the sonic analogy of academic disciplining as I would reframe it. Synchronisation does not enforce speed or slowness, but slower parts can be in sync with faster ones (and vice versa), if discipline is maintained. This is how I envision transdisciplinarity: disturbing academic disciplines with indiscipline, and interweaving the scholarly discipline of establishing an entrained 'odd sympathy' between researcher and researched with the discipline of the Amazonian disciple learning from the spirits, the musicians' discipline in performing in synchrony and synergy, and the listener's tuning into empathic resonance in synchronised bodily processes. In the end, discipline is never an end in itself, only a means to an end.

References

Bleek, W. H. I. (1875). *A brief account of Bushman folk-lore and other texts*. Trübner & Co.

Brabec de Mori, B. (2014a). From the native's point of view: How Shipibo-Konibo experience and interpret ayahuasca drinking with 'gringos'. In B. C. Labate & C. Cavnar (Eds.), *Ayahuasca shamanism in the Amazon and beyond* (pp. 206–230). Oxford University Press.

Brabec de Mori, B. (2014b). Los Iskobakebo: la historia de un pueblo originario en peligro de extinción. *Lengua y Sociedad, 14*(1), 21–32.

Brabec de Mori, B. (2015). *Die Lieder der Richtigen Menschen: Musikalische Kulturanthropologie der indigenen Bevölkerung im Ucayali-Tal (Westamazonien)*. Helbling Academic Books.

Brabec de Mori, B. (2016). What makes natives unique? Overview of knowledge systems among the world's indigenous people. *Taiwan Journal of Indigenous Studies, 8*, 43–61.

Comaroff, J., & Comaroff, J. (2009). *Ethnicity Inc.* University of Chicago Press.

Deleuze, G., & Guattari, F. (1987). *A thousand plateaus: Capitalism and schizophrenia.* University of Minnesota Press.

Erlmann, V. (2010). *Reason and resonance. A history of modern aurality*. Zone Books.

Evans-Pritchard, E. E. (1937). *Witchcraft, oracles and magic among the Azande.* Oxford University Press.

Fotiou, E. (2021). Shamanic tourism in the Peruvian lowlands: Critical and ethical considerations. *Journal of Latin American and Caribbean Anthropology, 26*(3), 374–396. https://doi.org/10.1111/jlca.12508

Fuchs, T. (2013). Temporality and psychopathology. *Phenomenology and the Cognitive Sciences, 12*, 75–104. https://doi.org/10.1007/s11097-010-189-4

Fuchs, T. (2016). Intercorporeality and interaffectivity. *Phenomenology and Mind, 11*, 194–209. https://doi.org/10.13128/Phe_Mi-20119

Gray, G. (2014). 'We know the Aborigines are dying out': Aboriginal people and the quest to ensure their survival, Wave Hill Station, 1944. *Health and History, 16*(1), 1–24. https://doi.org/10.5401/healthhist.16.1.0001

Gumo, S. (2017). Praying for rain: Indigenous systems of rainmaking in Kenya. *Ecumenical Review, 69*(3), 386–397. https://doi.org/10.1111/erev.12301

Keib., K., Wojdynski, B. W., Espina, C., Malson, J., Jefferson, B., & Lee, Y.-I. (2021). Living at the speed of mobile: How users evaluate social media news posts on smartphones. *Communication Research.* Advance online publication. https://doi.org/10.1177/00936502211018542

King Crimson. (1981). *Discipline* [LP record]. E. G. Records.

Labate, B. C., & Jungaberle, H. (Eds.). (2011). *The internationalization of ayahuasca.* LIT-Verlag.

Landes, D. S. (1984). *Revolution in time: Clocks and the making of the modern world.* Harvard University Press.

LeClerc, F. R. (2003). *Des modes de socialisation par les plantes chez les Shipibo-Conibo d'amazonie peruvienne: Une étude des relations entre humains et non-humains dans la construction sociale* [PhD dissertation]. Université Paris Nanterre.

Lewy, M. (2015). Mas alla del 'punto de vista': sonorismo amerindio y entidades de sonido antropomorfas y no-antropomorfas. In B. Brabec de Mori, M. Lewy, & M. A. García (Eds.), *Sudamérica y sus mundos audibles: Cosmologías y prácticas sonoras de los pueblos indígenas* (pp. 83–98). IAI.

Lima, T. S. (1999). The two and its many: Reflections on perspectivism in a Tupi cosmology. *Ethnos*, *64*(1), 107–131.

Ludwig, D. (2016). Overlapping ontologies and Indigenous knowledge: From integration to ontological self-determination. *Studies in History and Philosophy of Science*, *59*, 36–45. https://doi.org/10.1016/j.shpsa.2016.06.002

Mazzotti, J. A., Zariquiey R., & Rodríguez C. (Eds.). (2018). *Tradición Oral Iskonawa*. Revista de Crítica Literaria Latinoamericana.

Menezes Bastos, R. J. (2013). *A Festa da Jaguatirica: Uma Partitura Crítico-Interpretativa*. Editora UFSC.

Minkowski, E. (1933). *Le temps vecu: Études phénoménologiques et psychopathologiques*. D'Array.

Riccio, G., & Gunn, T. (2020). *King Crimson: The Discipline era transcriptions*. Music Scores.

Rivers, W. H. R. (1922). The psychological factor. In W. H. R. Rivers (Ed.), *Essays on the depopulation of Melanesia* (pp. 84–113). Cambridge University Press.

Rodríguez Alzza, C. (2020). *Los diseños de nuestra memoria: Registro y continuidad de los diseños de los Iskonawa del río Callería*. PUCP.

Spencer, K., Salisbury, D., Shenton, M., & McCarley, R. (2008). γ-band auditory steady-state responses are impaired in first episode psychosis. *Biological Psychiatry*, *64*(5), 369–375. https://doi.org/10.1016/j.biopsych.2008.02.021

Taussig, M. (1993). *Mimesis and alterity. A particular history of the senses*. Routledge.

Vogel, D. H. V., Beeker, T., Haidl, T., Kupke, C., Heinze, M., & Vogeley, K. (2019). Disturbed time experience during and after psychosis. *Schizophrenia Research: Cognition*, *17*, 100136. https://doi.org/10.1016/j.scog.2019.100136

CHAPTER 7

Performing Transdisciplinary Creativity by Emersiology with the Living Body

Antonella Poli and Bernard Andrieu

Introduction

Performing difference consists not only in *making visible* a conscious intentionality in bodily gestures. The activity of the living body becomes the place and time for renewed creativity by listening to what passes through the consciousness of the lived body. The bodily intentions are unconscious but not inactive because the perception sets up scenarios in the brain before the action can be visible. The body embodies meaning before it can be expressed in a linguistic structure that can be recognised by the community during the proxemic interaction. The difference between *bodily intention* and *bodily awareness* of intention is useful in understanding the unconscious anticipation of the voluntary activation of the body. The works of choreographers such as Isadora Duncan, Pina Bausch, Boris Charmatz, Jérôme Bel and Anna Halprin, and the experiences of the circus artists in CNAC (National Centre for Circus Arts, France) highlight the relationship between *bodily intention* and *bodily awareness* of intention. In the middle, affects, emotions and associative memory come to feed the semantic production of the body, sometimes without the consciousness reaching it.

Academic performance sets standards for validating beauty according to an aesthetic hierarchy. Anything that does not conform to these standards will be viewed at best as a variation and at worst as a transgression in bad taste. Academic schools transmit and teach good taste based on strict rules, methodologies and official disciplines that grant the reproduction of techniques in order to develop what Kant calls talented artists, without particular genius.

The artist who invents new rules of art appears to be a rebel who must first be excluded from any academy. Rebellious performance puts the artist directly in contact with the activity of its living body. It has a great sensitivity to what is happening in it and around it. This sensitivity is an active and permanent rebellion that opposes the agreed world of standards based on pre-constituted conceptions that do not recognize the importance of the inner activity of the body.

 | DOI:10.1163/9789004516069_009

In the history of philosophy, phenomenology showed the importance of the body, pointing out the value of its perceptions to open new ways to explain our experience and the world. But the limit of this theory was that it focused its attention on the lived body (experiences, habits, memories). On the contrary, our purpose is here to show the importance of a living body that has its own activity, escaping our consciousness. Involuntary and instinctive gestures are a good example. Thanks to emersiology (Andrieu, 2016), the theory that elaborates and studies the structure and the representations of the living body, we can point out how this leads to rebellious creation which invents new aesthetic rules from its sensibility against the traditional academy, which preserves the rules by excluding any rebellion. In particular, we will also explore in this chapter how the living body appears in the arts of choreography and circus. With the examples of choreographers such as Isadora Duncan, Pina Bausch, Boris Charmatz, Anna Halprin and Jérôme Bel we can understand how dance, answering to the needs of an *inclusive society*, offers the coexistence of abled and disabled bodies, and professional artists and amateurs.

The body succeeds in allowing its nervous system to be embodied in spontaneous movements, defining an emersive dance using, for example, trance and improvisation. Contact with internal movement, which is possible through bodily techniques of release to eliminate any conscious control, opens to dance the perspective of learning and recognising the forms of the living body in order to renew our perception of the lived body.

Rebelliousness by Ecological Vivacity

To be alive is to feel alive without managing to contain it in the usual perception of our lived body. What is raw comes to exceed its representation by the trouble we have to live with. The living body is a living thing against which we can do nothing, neither by will nor by freedom.

This intensity of living brings our creativity to life. Being lively is not just about being quick to react, either physically or in character, in anger or in self-defence. The liveliness of body and mind is an intrinsic quality of the living body. By spontaneously going green, the living in our body anticipates its responses even before we are aware of it. Being alive is not a conscious movement but an ecological adaptation to the environment in order to make oneself as alive and liveable as possible. Like Varela (2017) developed with the concept of enaction, the embodied self becomes a new perspective for describing the ecological relation between the world and the body. There is a continuous and circular relationship between humans and their environment. The consequence for creation is land art, opening the possibility for an experience of immersion. Thus Christo and his wife Jeanne-Claude modified the environment by the inclusion of art into nature.

For Guattari (1989), this context of decentralisation, multiplicity, antagonisms and singularity processes brings new ecological problems on the individual and collective scales, in particular regarding everyday life or processes like the reinvention of democracy, urbanism, artistic creation, sports and leisure. Body ecology (Andrieu et al., 2018) is a micro-ecology. That's because we transform the practices of individuals, which transforms ecology. The idea is to make micro-micro-situations and experiences. With body ecology, *cosmotic*, an aesthetic with the cosmos, does not stand in nor distance nor idolise natural elements. Nature is neither good nor bad, but it questions our relentless physical interaction with it by the limits of our body and green inventiveness of our techniques.

Vivacity goes hand in hand with ecological vitality. It is not living beings whose age has come that would finally bring to light in the Enlightenment 'our corporeality and our dependence on ecosystems'; with the vitality of the living, of which with vivacity we share the thesis, the philosophers Andreas Weber and Hildegard Kurt demonstrate that the politics of the living connect each and every one of us in 'a culture of responsibility which is capable of realizing its own vitality' (Weber & Kurt, 2021, p. 44). It would be advisable to free oneself from technoid thought and the deadly ideology of the end-of-the-world atmosphere: to get rid of our powerlessness to act in the face of technological dismosis, it would be necessary to dispense with all beings – all without exception! – and their right to experience vitality, that is to say, to be fully themselves while remaining deeply linked to the rest of the world.

Against Academic Performance

Academic performance is very coded: it must meet the aesthetic standards of a very established cultural community. This considers aesthetic novelty at best as an avant-garde rebellion; at worst it excludes those who would protest the established order.

Yet if art rebels constitute this avant-garde, it is first of all because of the new link established by these artists between what they feel in their living body and what they produce as a new form. By referring to their internal life, the emotional level is now more important: the ecological situation of the body influences perception by the intensity and variety of experiences.

- Creative rebels oppose the official forms of the academy by departing from the classical education they received. They create against the established aesthetic normality: on the one hand because their sensitivity makes them perceive the world through a new attention to the condition of the living; on the other hand, their own living body releases in them new emotions and images that nourish creation.
- The rebellious generation, like the beat generation, postcolonial studies, subaltern action, LGBTI+ revolt and Black Lives Matter, is constituted as a minority counter-culture until it becomes the majority: either by the renewal of the generations of the academy, or by genius, in the sense of Kant, which shatters the defenders of the classic shapes through the innovative radicality of new shapes. The counter-culture is coming through the empowerment and agency of the many creators who propose the new rules.

  The academy decides what is beautiful and what is not in the name of tradition and classism. It socially reproduces the established norms and excludes any new ones, as demonstrated by Pierre Bourdieu (1996). In the name of academicism, it rejects what could disrupt the reproduction of standards in art schools: teaching transmits the tradition, which must be repeated as desired until it is perfectly incorporated into the creative gesture.

FIGURE 7.1 Evolution of creativity forms

The Rebellious Object in Emersive Creativity

The opposition between rebellious object and academic discipline is only resolved if a new academy emerges from emersive creativity. By grouping together as a school, a stream and a network, rebel artists gradually impose a contemporary style on traditional academicism. The rebellious object such as the body, emotion, gender, disease or pain must justify its originality by producing new shapes and styles. Conservative opinions and the exaltation of nationalism would be forbidden during the emergence of the new possibility of life, because censure limits rebelliousness like transgressions of academic art, like the punk movement which developed at the same time as critiques of society and the incarnation of a new aesthetic.

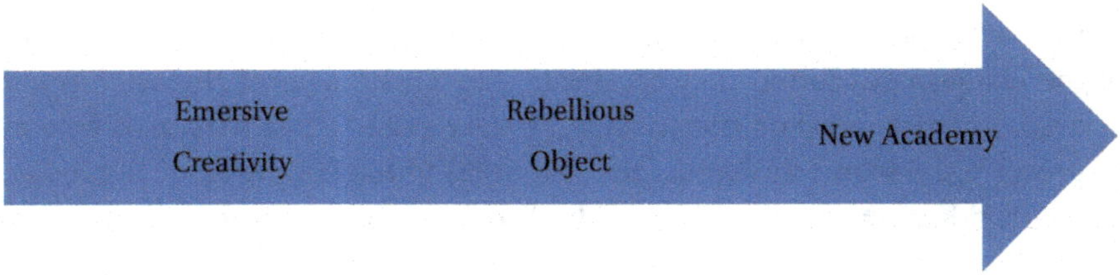

FIGURE 7.2 The movement of emersivity creativity

Emersive creativity refers to this singular listening that the artist experiences through the emergence of their moods, dreams and other emotions. The living body has a liveliness that cannot always be controlled by the consciousness of the lived body. The living body is rebellious because it cannot be controlled by the sole awareness of the lived body. Its activity produces very lively sensations which surprise the creator in its inspiration.

Rebellious Experiences in Dance

For creation to be rebellious against aesthetic standards imposed by ballet, you have to surrender to living this bodily liveliness.

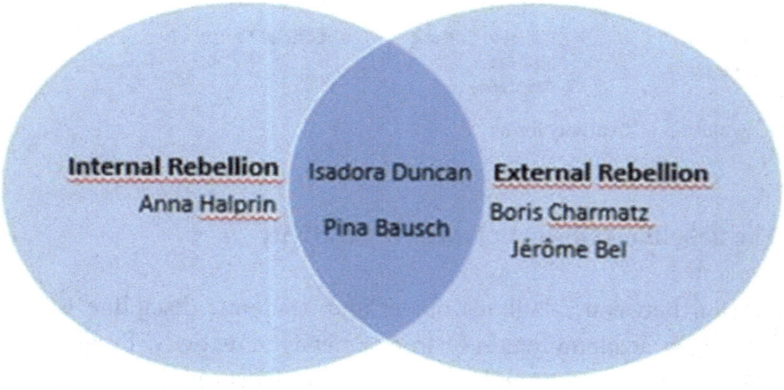

FIGURE 7.3 The different rebellions in dance

First of all, body techniques such as improvisation promote the translation into creative forms of these movements of moods, emotions and sensations that arise: these improvised gestures directly illustrate the language of the living body. The way in which the body feels the world is immediately embodied in uncontrolled gestures like the trance of Jackson Pollock, who throws the paint onto the canvas to the rhythm of the possession which crosses it.

FIGURE 7.4 Happening Tempête, choreography Boris Charmatz (© Antonella Poli)

One of the pioneers in affirming rebellion and a new form of thinking in dance was Isadora Duncan (1877–1927). She conceived a new conception of the origin of movement focusing on the importance of the solar plexus. She opposed the classical theories that placed the centre of motion in the middle of the back. She was absolutely convinced that this method created only puppets able to produce mechanical and artificial gestures. They are not dancers. She looked to develop the internal forces of the body, vibrations, beaming from its centre. She identified three categories of 'dancers' (Maurevert, 1927): (1) those who execute pretty arabesques, transforming dance into a form of gymnastics; (2) those who create their movements from a willing intentionality, led by their brains; and (3) those who transform their bodies led by their internal inspiration. In the latter case, their bodies become pure energy, imagined as a continuous flow. For this reason Isadora's dance was a form of ecstasy that went beyond reality.

From her first performances danced in Europe from 1899, in London, Paris and Munich, she shocked the public with her free dance where the physical, psychological and spiritual elements were strictly bound together: bare feet, and wide, flowing and simple tunics inspired by classical Greek antiquity on one hand de-emphasised the scenery and costumes typical of the classical ballet of the nineteenth century, and on the other hand valorised spontaneous and wide movements. She loved nature and its forces because they produce true images, not artificial ones, and for this reason she was particularly inspired by them.

In spite of her solitude, her revolutionary style based on improvisation touched artists of other arts, especially during her life in Paris from 1900: the painter Eugène Carrière (1849–1906), who was one of the first to recognise her innovative scope, and the sculptor Auguste Rodin (1847–1917), with whom Isadora established a deep friendship based on the same conception of creation in their arts: externalising and shining light on interior forces. Isadora Duncan's revolution influenced the evolution of dance, especially Mikhail Fokine's choreography and Diaghilev's Ballets Russes.

From another point of view, the rebellious body comes to manifest itself in disordered and discontinuous forms to, like Anna Halprin (1920–2021), deform the movement: the dance of life, dancing the life and its feelings. She taught that dance had to be liberated from the 'constricting armor of stylized, preconceived gestures, an innate feedback process between movement and feeling is generated' (Halprin, 2000, p. 24).

Her particular attention to the expression of the body led her to show her cancer through the rebellion of lines. Unlike the dance which simulates death in *Swan Lake*, the rebel dance uses the body's revolt against disease to manifest its energy and anger through the transformations of the body. In fact for Halprin, 'every thing is motion, all time of life is motion. Every day moments can take awareness of dance ... Dance is not what you see but what you feel, you hear, you smell' (Gerber, 2009). In 1972 when she first discovered her cancer, her internal sensations lead her to draw her body and place a little ball, like a golf ball, in her pelvis. Three years later, she relapsed with a new cancer. This time, she drew the two sides of her body, front and back: she detested the frontal view; she loved the back one. Through it, she felt all her rage, pain and rebellion against her disease, and she created an intensive, powerful and dark dance (Caux, 1975). These experiences were the basis of Anna Halprin's process of psychokinetic visualisation, based on three steps: imagination, which lets us reach internal images to open our senses; visualisation, which leads us to build and visualise internal images represented by drawings or inspired by movements; and movement translation, which drives the dancers to move in three-dimensional space what they feel or see in the drawings. This provokes the discovery of surprising directions, dynamics and rhythms.

Figure 7.5 shows the four levels of human mind conceived: physical, visual, ritual and spiritual. They are separate but at the same time connected, as appears in the blue zone in the middle of the human brain.

Anna Halprin reworked her rebellion dance against disease in 2006 with the performance 'Intensive care' inspired by her personal experience when her husband was in intensive care. He was between life and death for one month and she went to see him daily. She was inspired by the sensations she received from him ('he seems to speak, touches his throat, stretches his head') and tried

FIGURE 7.5
Flyer with hand-drawn and coloured sketch for Anna Halprin's Reorganisation Ritual. Anna Halprin Papers, Elyse Eng Dance Collection, Museum of Performance + Design

FIGURE 7.6 Anna Halprin in intensive care, 'Reflections on death and dying'. Anna Halprin Papers, Elyse Eng Dance Collection, Museum of Performance + Design (© English Irene)

to translate these impressions with her hands, with intermittent movements touching her face. She showed, in a sense, her husband's internal sensations.

Rebellion against academic thoughts can be developed in two other ways: on the one hand, using the academic as the basis to create new forms of expression and, on the other hand, a total rupture that completely denies any predefined structure.

If we refer to dance, for example, we can consider two choreographers who revolutionised choreographic language: Pina Bausch (1940–2009) and Boris Charmatz (1973–). Pina Bausch, a German choreographer, joined the movement of expressive dance and studied at Tanztheater principally with Kurt Joos, famous for its creation 'The green table' (1932) where the artists condemned the rise of dictatorial systems in Europe. The aims of Tanztheater were to create a new form of dance that also had political aims, where the representation of emotions replaced academic technique.

In spite of her complete adhesion to these ideas, Pina Bausch was drawn to classical ballet until she became a dancer at the New York City Ballet. When she became the director of Wuppertal Tanztheater (1973) her project was very clear: she wanted to express her point of view about human nature and in particular she was inspired by common and instinctive gestures. For each creation, she worked with her dancers, giving them a topic that they had to develop according to their sensations and emotions. Her ballets showed the different aspects of the human relationship with violence, irony, tenderness and love. Sometimes dancers cried out on stage, or ran impetuously, to the astonishment of the public.

But in spite of this freedom and this inner research, she did not completely eliminate academic language. Every day, dancers began their training with a classical class with the best methods, for example the Cecchetti method, and with the best ballet masters in the world. For Pina Bausch, dancers' bodies cannot forget technical instructions: classical ballet was essential for musicality and for work on the arms, shoulders and feet. The second part of the day was dedicated to creation and dancers had to delve deep within themselves to find new gestures to express particular themes.

We can ask how these bodies which incorporated such a strict classical language could forget it to express themselves in a freer way. Often, a classical dancer has difficulties dancing contemporary works; their bodies and their movements are too formatted even though, in recent years, all dance academies have incorporated contemporary classes into their curriculum.

In the case of Pina Bausch, the dancers worked all afternoon, so they had time to disrupt their ballet training. To fix the final choreography Pina Bausch waited until the evening, the time where the bodies of the dancers could be completely free. Her method was based, we can say, on a process of construction and deconstruction able to raise up the living body of the dancers.

If we consider Pina Bausch's masterpiece, 'The rite of spring' (1975), in which the choreographer points out the ancestral conflict between men and women, the principal artist, 'the elected', who is sacrificed and dies, feels unconscious sensations during her visceral dance of death, discovering a new vitality in her body. One of the principal dancers, Cristiana Morganti, who interpreted this role for many years, confirmed this. At the end of the performance she was completely detached from reality, completely captured by a new perception and vitality of her body. Fast movements executed with great intensity helped by the force of the music of Igor Stravinsky contributed to the creation and emergence of new forces in her body.

The point we would like to make here is that, in spite of the ballet technique imposed upon the dancers, Pina Bausch's conception of dance allows the 'appearance' and 'makes visible' internal forces of the human body that are more powerful than any strict and rigid form of training.

FIGURE 7.7 The Rite of Spring, choreography Pina Bausch, Tanztheater Wuppertal 2018, T Tsai Wei and Ensemble (© Ursula Kaufmann, Essen, Germany)

This aspect seems to substantiate French philosopher Gilles Deleuze's (1993) conception of the body that underlined the presence of invisible and active forces able to give it life. Consciously, Pina Bausch did not want to be a rebellious choreographer, but her dance was rebellious, to such an extent that many times she provoked the rebellion of the public.

On the other hand, we shall consider the approach of French choreographer Boris Charmatz. At thirteen he attended the Ballet School of the National Opera of Paris. After three years he left, as the codes and the training methods were opposed to his conception of dance. He could not envisage spending one or two hours learning a port de bras. He wanted to be a dancer, open dance to everyone, explore the potential of bodies, and their richness, and how to feel and represent concepts such as weight and heaviness, and eliminate the distance between artists and the public. His rupture with the traditional vision of ballet had to be total since dance can be represented anywhere. This idea brought him to produce the performances 'Three collective gestures', at MoMa in New York (2013), 'A dancer's day' in the former airport Tempelhof Hangar 5 in Berlin (2017) and 'La ronde' at Grand Palais in Paris (2021).

He became famous in France as one of the artists belonging to what is now called 'non danse conceptuelle'. The body had to speak by itself and often the choreographer used the nudity of his dancers to highlight his vision. The body does not have an erotic or sexual meaning; it is only a sign that is evidence of the relationship between the frame and the skin that wraps it.

In 'Herses' (1997) nude bodies explore their shapes. They touch each other; every part of their bodies becomes a support for the other, creating an imaginary ground (their bodies) where they can dance. This performance was censured in Japan and Australia, the French public was shocked, and critics did not accept the idea of the body as a simple instrument to describe and discover the space and itself. The meaning of nudity remained embedded in cultural stereotypes.

FIGURE 7.8 Herse, choreography Boris Charmatz (© Jean-Michel Cima)

The two choreographers, Pina Bausch and Boris Charmatz, produced rebellious styles of dance but their relationship with academic dance is the opposite. Bausch did not reject the classical tradition, as we explained, but she integrated it with her deep sensibility, her ideas about creating and allowing the expression of the inner sensations of bodies; Boris Charmatz created a total rupture with the academic, showing and creating a new function for the body considering only its physical powers.

In another opposite direction we can approach Jérôme Bel's works. With Boris Charmatz, he is another French representative of 'non danse conceptuelle' but his relationship with the body goes beyond the usual conception of dancing and the trained body. After the first period of his career in which he created a portrait series of professional dancers (Cédric Andrieux & Lutz Förster, 2009; Veronique Doisneau, 2004), he oriented his choreographic research towards employing common or disabled people (Disabled Theater). From the experience of these bodies without any particular choreographic qualities, the public could retain the image of a fragility or an indiscipline, of a grotesque or an artistic rout for the most defeatist.

In October 2016 he was invited to the MoMa to participate in the event Artist's Choice, created in 2009 and organised by FIAF's (French Institute Alliance) Crossing the Line Festival at MoMA, New York. In the Marron Atrium, 25 employees of the museum danced in proximity and scenic simplicity; they felt like professional dancers, shaping a colourful crowd, a delightful choreographic patchwork where everyone found their place. Eleven qualities of danced movements followed one after another, led each time by a leader to facilitate the synchrony and the memory of the steps borrowed from historical and more contemporary styles, supported by complementary music (Vaysse, 2020).

The show 'Gala' (2015), produced employing non-professional dancers and people with disability, invites us to abstain from aesthetic judgement. The performance is composed of seven parts (Ballet, Valse, Improvisation in three minutes, Michael Jackson, Saluts, Solo and Compagnie compagnie) where all the performers execute the same movement or reproduce a particular style of dance (classical or waltz). But what diversity! In fact, what Jérôme Bel wants to valorise is everybody's gestures. For example, the pirouette accomplished by a body who never studied classical dance can have a sense, can release an expressive value that exceeds any technique. This reminds us that our body has its own neuromotor systems able to develop a personal and singular movement. This appears also in a woman in a wheelchair. The pirouette's meaning is to turn around the axis of the body and she does it turning the wheelchair, an extension of her body.

We can perceive in raw and unformatted bodies, in their approximation, awkwardness and spontaneity, a form of choreographic language totally different from virtuosity. To the codified language of academic training, these bodies oppose their mobility and irregularity, and therefore their inventiveness. In fact, the public is never dealing with a neutral or generic body, but conversely with a particular body, which surprises, astonishes and therefore questions. Also, the coloured and eccentric costumes highlight this aspect.

FIGURE 7.9 Gala, choreography Jérôme Bel

The value of failure or of an imperfect gesture helps us to deconstruct models to take advantage of their distortions. Jérôme Bel urges the performers to make their failures fruitful, to 'Try again. Fail again. Miss better', to turn their imperfections into opportunities for an alternative plasticity, for another way of producing dance.

Their desynchronisation offers the possibility of discovering strongly differentiated personalities, observing the qualities of grace or energy in their movements or how they are related to rhythm. Starting from this attitude of making a handicap a performance, the body is not considered only in terms of pain or deficit. It is invested with support, allowing a form of self-evaluation, a refusal to hide one's body, to let the living body appear.

The powers of the body, led by its neuromotor systems, escape any form of logical comprehension or codification. This approach to the living body opens up an ecological dimension linked to interactions between the body and the world. Dancing with a disability challenges conceptions of the dancer's body: its usual image is transformed by the new abilities produced by the living body.

Gala's performers simply moved with a desire to perform and were motivated only by personal feelings, which implicitly poses the question of the *primum movens* of the choreographic impulse and of the origin of dance. If this is a natural aptitude, a simple expression of a body's relationship to its kinesthetics sensations, the excuse of 'I can't dance' no longer holds. For Bel, the valorisation of an intuitive and unconsciously absorbed knowledge, which puts intelligence at the service of the will, is capable of disinhibiting the desire to dance. 'Gala' ending up reading itself as a hedonistic manifesto for an uninhibited dance.

The Process of Emersive Creativity

The activity of the living body becomes the place and time for renewed creativity by listening to what passes through the consciousness of the lived body: bodily intentions are unconscious but not inactive because perception sets up decision scenarios in the brain before any action is achieved. The body embodies meaning before it can be expressed in a linguistic structure that can be recognised by the community during the proxemic interaction. This particular language of the body is not simply visible; we must look for it. For this, we can use methods such as vigilance/attention (Varela, 2017), which, inspired by Buddhism, invites our minds to remove our feelings, thoughts and concepts to allow our natural mind to emerge.

The difference between bodily intention and bodily awareness of intention is useful in understanding the unconscious anticipation of the voluntary activation of the body. Between the two affects, emotions, and associative memory come to feed the semantic production of the body without always allowing the consciousness to reach it. So …

Emersiology was developed as a new method for analysing the emergence of the invisible data of the living body in a person's awareness. The implicit activities of the living body (cardiac frequency, involuntary gestures, stress, reflex, emotional regulation, interaction expression) emerge in the awareness of the lived body without our voluntary control. It also prompts unconscious body language and is evidence of the body's ecological activation and production of new living data.

A new vision of embodied research explores the depth of the living body to collect these new aesthetic and sensorial possibilities. The depth of the living body exceeds, however, the quality of the attention and conscious listening to what arises in the phenomenon of presence. The permeability and porosity of sensitivity go beyond consciousness: in the immersion during its lifetime the subject is no longer able to mentally represent what is happening there. This implicit living body arises in an emotion that overflows cognition. So … what is the question/the problem then?

To perform differently, through body art or gender deconstruction, emersive creativity relies on the awakening caused by the activity of the living body. This includes:

- exploring the capacities of our body by combining it with the modification of its motor and representational habits;
- new gestures for yourself and for the performative scene by reconstructing your body diagram and the image of your body; and
- learning from your living body by producing new forms of movement.

The circus artists in CNAC (National Centre for Circus Arts, France) produce drawings with an explanatory text, extracts of which are presented as descriptions of the body's theory of internal sensations (Andrieu, 2018). The recognition of chronic and persistent internal sensations makes visible here the internal areas that have become hypersensitive by the repetition of the training. While pain may be visible on the surface of the skin, the circus artist, who trains three hours a day, nevertheless experiences invisible internal sensations.

In Figure 7.10, Liam L (33rd Promotion, CNAC) is an artist of the fixed trapeze. She declares to herself: 'I am hypersensitive' along the whole extent of the skin which is in contact with the trapeze. She repeats it several times defining a kind of skin in contact. Here Liam describes her tactile hypersensitivity as 'the pectorals contracted all the time when touched is 8/10'.

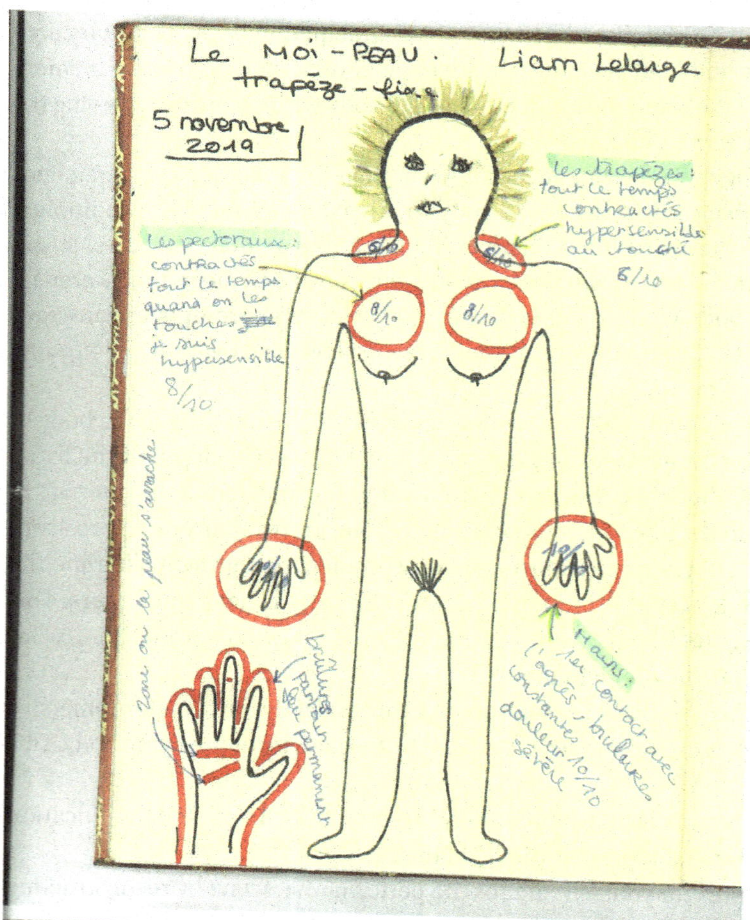

FIGURE 7.10 Liam, 33rd Fixed Trapeze, 5 November 2019

Liam (33rd Fixed Trapeze) uses perceptual memory to perceive what is 'behind me because I know the place, I analysed it before getting on the trapeze'. With contact with the apparatus 'constant burning and severe pain, 10/10', with 'permanent fire' around the fingers with an 'area where the skin rips off'. During the training the skin should be hardened, and wedges made, but the muscle pain does not go away. What would be her 'skin self' goes beyond human anatomical representation. She certainly represents herself naked but reveals her sensitivity by exposing herself, by linking this imaginary to her own internal sensitivity. She underlines here in red by surrounding them six extremities of her body – her hands, her pectorals and her trapezoids – thus giving another meaning to the motor action: that is to say, she shows less its efficiency than its consequences for chronic pain.

Conclusion

The creative rupture of rebellion, in dance and in the circus as we have just shown, is based on a new relationship with the living body. The performance is based here on a microperformativity of the living (Andrieu et al., 2020), which pushes the artist to create more living forms: these must, in the manner of the organism, produce a mobility and a rhythm which corresponds to the internal liveliness and the internal vitality of the artist.

The new forms of artistic rebellion are inspired by the consequences of social distancing measures for COVID-19, pollution, poverty and hunger. They touch the internal movements of the body, invading the sensibility and the consciousness of the artists. They do not seek to idealise the world but to build it from their internal perception. Thus, leads to new creative models and places rebellion at the heart of performance. It removes academic movements because their origin is the intimate emotion that destroys and restructures the mobility and the conception of the body.

References

Andrieu, B. (2018). *Learning from your body: An emersive method at the CNAC.* Purch/CNAC.

Andrieu, B. (2016). *Sentir son corps vivant.* Vrin.

Andrieu, B., Marussich, Y., Bernard, A., Cipoletta, G., & Nobrega, P. (2020), Emersive microperformativity in living bodies. *Performance Research: A Journal of the Performing Arts*, 25(3), 137–144. https://doi.org/10.1080/13528165.2020.1807775

Andrieu, B., Parry, J., Porrovechio, A., & Sirost, O. (Eds.). (2018). *Body ecology & emersive leisures.* Routledge.

Bourdieu, P. (1996). *The rules of art: Genesis and structure of the literary field.* Stanford University Press.

Caux, J. (Producer). (1975). *Dancing my cancer* [Documentary film].

Deleuze, G. (1993). *Critique et clinique.* Minuit.

Guattari, F. (1989). *The three ecologies.* Bloomsbury Academic.

Halprin, A. (2000). *Dance as a healing art: Returning to health with movement and imagery.* Life Rhythm.

Maurevert, G. (1927, September 18). *Journal L'Eclaireur du Soir.* L'Eclaireur de Nice.

Ruedi, G. (Producer). (2010). *Breath made visible: Anna Halprin* [Documentary film].

Vaysse, J. (2020). *Mouvements pensés, Mouvements dansés.* L'Harmattan.

Weber, A., & Kurt, H. (2021). *Ré-ensauvagez-vous!* Le Pommier.

Part 1: Reflective Questions

Pamela Burnard

Linking to Futures of Teaching and Learning

1. What do the concepts of 'transdisciplinary' and 'trandisciplinarity' mean to you? Think about a moment where you see yourself performing transdisciplinarity – What did you do? How did you know? How did it feel?

2. What 'incitements to rebellion' invoke and invite you as a researcher, academic, educator and artist to perform/research/write differently?

3. What are the transdisciplinary practices that various chapters perform? How might these be applied in your own academic writing?

4. What does 'immersive creativity' uniquely offer in terms of your practice?

5. Write down a list of theorists you encounter as you read each chapter. What do you see, do, and think differently because of these theories?

6. What 'academic (in)discipline' is performed in your rebellious research?

7. What is performed differently, for you, in these chapters?

8. If you were to perform transdisciplinarity rebelliously, what would it do and say differently?

 | DOI:10.1163/9789004516069_010

PART 2: Rebellious Writings WriTTen DifferENtly A Manifesto

Part 2: Guidance for Readers

Elizabeth Mackinlay

Dear reader,

I am writing this letter to invite you to immerse yourself in academic writing which has the explicit intent to depart radically from the usual way of doing business in this literary space. Many of the contributors to this part of the book are doctoral students, seeking to find a way to reunite emotion, experience and intellect to write words about the world in which we live, love and hope for. In crafting each contribution, the authors conversed and considered the requirements and rules of standard academic writing carefully, and then—quite deliberately—chose to review, revise, and refuse them. There is no disrespect intended here, only a desire for academic writing to do *something*, something *more, something more* that moves readers to see, as Virginia Woolf[1] would ask, beyond the "cotton wool of daily life" to "moments of being". This type of radical departure in academic writing may be quite new—unusual, surprising, perhaps even shocking—to some of you who read this work. Before dismissing it outright, I ask that you first think and wonder about the relational sense-and-response-abilities that creativity and criticality have with, through and because of one another. There is a tendency in academic writing to presume, indeed an expectation, to position these as incompatible rhetorical convention, however we are emboldened by Laurel Richardson's assertion that anyone who thinks so, is a dinosaur waiting to be hit by a meteor (Richardson, in Richardson & St. Pierre, 2005, p. 962). Academic writing which departs radically wants to put theory to work to enable words to touch readers where we live. As you engage with the writing in Part 2 of this book, we ask your body, mind and hearts to remain open to the possibilities that such radical creative-criticality gestures towards.

Yours truly,
Liz

1 Woolf, 1976, p. 72.

 | DOI:10.1163/9789004516069_011

References

Richardson, L., & St. Pierre, E. A. (2005). Writing: A method of inquiry. In N. Denzin & Y. Lincoln (Eds.), *The Sage handbook of qualitative research* (3rd ed., pp. 959-978). Sage.

Woolf, V. (1976). *Moments of being: Unpublished autobiographical writings* (J. Schulkind, ed.). Harcourt Brace.

CHAPTER 8

Departing Radically in Academic Writing

Because, a Manifesto

Elizabeth Mackinlay

Introduction

The academy was receding so that the words that appeared in books about the world, among the shelves, grew whiter and whiter; and the people who wrote them more and more indistinct. The white noise of radio KFKD (a.k.a. K fucked here; Lamott, 1994) hummed ominously in the background. A small group of doctoral students, reserved, determined looking, weighted with shitty little drafts of words that threatened to block their way, crossed the fading campus. The buildings sputtered as academic writing life slowly but surely evaporated in this big dark place they had no wish to call their own. The library crackled intermittently like static on a wire. There was also, on the grounds, the distant explosive bursts of a leaf blower, firing decaying debris further and further away down the abandoned road. A man in a grey Chevrolet with a bumper sticker which read, 'Status quo, the only way to go!', circled the perfect perimeter. Old oak trees stood resolutely by, holding their piece quietly like wise old stalks of broccoli. 'Yet what composed the present moment?' Virginia Woolf (1947, p. 9) might have asked. The words she offered in reply crossed time from there and then to the hush of here and now. 'If you are young', she began, 'the future lies upon the present, like a piece of glass, making it tremble and quiver' (Woolf, 1947, p. 9). The doctoral students paused as a sage old and sassy zephyr softly rustled the waves in their mind. Woolf (1947, p. 9) continued, 'If you are old, the past lies upon the present, like a thick glass, making it waver, distorting it'. She now had the doctoral students' full attention; for very quietly 'something' had slid into that moment and rippled the skin of the taken-for-granted strategies, structures and strictures of academic writing. What is that 'thing'? the doctoral students wondered. What is that shimmer of sensation which lies beneath the semblance of this moment? The doctoral students sat themselves down on a sturdy wooden bench on the edges of the grass in the Great Court in the heart of the academy to watch and wait for the something to arrive. They munched on the carrot sticks they had packed for lunch as a woman in a red hat passed by. Then, one by one, sparks of awareness began to arrive, fitful at first, but

 | DOI:10.1163/9789004516069_012

soon wide awake and firing on all cylinders. The rich yellow glow lit the lamp in the doctoral students' spines, that seat where the heart and soul reside. They watched with growing delight as all the stock boring and dead words they and others like them had ever written began to smoulder in the flames. 'Let them blaze, let them blaze!' they heard Virginia Woolf (1938/2017, p. 66) whoop in the distance. All doubt was over. It was time to do something to end this horrible moment of academic writing inertia for the academic writing. The doctoral students looked at one another and there it was, the snap. This was their wedding, the taste of a pineapple latte, their shot at dancing with the absurdity of life instead of being squashed by it. There was a rush of terror, followed closely by exultation – the academic writing rebellion had begun.

The rebellious academic writing movement DRAW (Departing Radically in Academic Writing) movement began in early November 2019 at the University of Queensland and was led by rebellious daughters of the academy Associate Professor Elizabeth Mackinlay and her doctoral student Karen Madden. They were soon joined by others wanting to write their theses differently; the rebellion we[1] now affectionately refer to as 'DRAW' was born, and the chapters in Part 2 are allied to this research and writing revolution. This is our manifesto for rebellious writings written differently.

Because the Word 'Manifesto'

BECAUSE the word 'manifesto' seems fit for purpose, we use it here and begin by paying attention to its roots. Donna Haraway (2016) reminds us that the worlding of worlds is only made possible by paying attention to 'roots'. Haraway's voice speaks alongside that of Simone Weil (1952/2002) who insists that 'roots' and 'rootedness' are the philosophical, ethical and spiritual groundings that situate and sustain us. 'Roots' are socially, materially, ontologically, epistemologically and temporally located; and words in and of themselves are similarly 'rooted'. It is worth following the etymological roots and routes of the word 'manifesto' around then, to lay down the 'roots' for this rebellious writing declaration.

BECAUSE 'mani-festo' comprises two root words; note, 'mani' is *not* a prefix – prefixes are short, unable to stand independently, and change meaning in usually predictable ways, thereby attaching themselves to others to make

1 I use the term 'we' in this chapter to invoke the communion that breathes life into the Departing Radically in Academic Writing group; I was moved to begin DRAW with others and together we are always already in DRAW movement.

thousands of new words.[2] Root words, on the other hand, have concrete meanings and capacity to stand alone, and can combine with prefixes, suffixes and other root words to find new life.

BECAUSE 'manifesto' is related to 'manifest', and both derive from the Latin root noun 'manus' (hand) and 'festus' (a combining form that is related to the Latin root adjective infestus, meaning 'hostile').[3] The root word 'mani', then, is a derivative of the Latin 'manus' which means 'hand'; and, despite popular definitional rendering, has nothing to do with the word 'male' in association with 'man', except by a chance similarity of sound.

BECAUSE the route from the adjective 'infestus' (hostile) to the verb 'festare' or 'fest' (to make public), turns and twists in a convoluted and complex manner; in fact, we might say without *any* manners at all. If something is 'hostile' it is perhaps threatening, dangerous and therefore unable to be handled, but if caught by 'hand' it is then apprehended and made apparent – that is, it is made *manifest*. To make manifest is to make something easy to perceive or recognise, and a manifesto then is a statement in which someone makes their beliefs, motives, intentions or views easy for people to ascertain. The word manifesto, then, provides us with routes to our roots.

Because in Radical Attention We Rebel

BECAUSE we listened to French feminist philosopher Simone Weil when she radically urged us to pay attention; for she was – *radical*. Radical; from the fourteenth-century Latin word *radicalis* meaning 'of or having roots'.[4] Radical; the origins of this word are in the *origins* of roots and the fundamental nature of roots as the source from which the vitality of life is drawn – we might even say that to *be* radical is to be rooted in something real, the something that is

---

2 I am completely indebted to the etymological wisdom of Roland Sussex, Emeritus Professor in the School of Languages and Culture at the University of Queensland, for the information included here in relation to the word 'manifesto'. Roly, or the 'lord of language' as his 'A word in your ear' ABC podcast listeners like to call him, is an expert in the past and present usage and meanings of words and I have consulted him from time to time to assist me in untangling the origins and definitional essence of words. In this instance, I was particularly concerned to get to the bottom of the root word 'mani' and to affirm my understanding that the 'man' in 'manifesto' has nothing to do with 'man' as male and by extension patriarchy. Thank you Roly for your reply.

3 Manifesto. In *Merriam-Webster.com dictionary*. https://www.merriam-webster.com/dictionary/manifesto

4 Radical. In *Merriam-Webster.com dictionary*. https://www.merriam-webster.com/dictionary/radical

happening in this very moment of life; and *that*, as Rozelle-Stone and Stone suggest, in a 'context of mechanical action and abstracted intellectualism [is really quite] *unconventional*' (2010, p. XXIII). Today the word 'radical' is most often associated with the extreme and that which deviates from the norm. Both the 'there and then' and the 'here and now' meaning of the word 'radical', not only describe who Simone Weil was, but what she herself has come to mean for us as we too depart radically.

BECAUSE, although she is not as well-known as the other Simone,[5] Simone Weil thought and wondered about the word and worlds on 'thresholds and across borders' in a never-ending search for truth and justice in a violent world (Rozelle-Stone & Davis, 2018). She positioned herself on the edges and pushed them radically; for Simone Weil, there was no other way than to return to the essential roots of life if we are to put in place a framework for living in a more ethically just world.

BECAUSE Simone Weil was deliberately, daringly and divinely radical; and what we find most radical of all is the radical ethico-onto-epistemology of 'attention' she offers as a route to roots. She insister-ed that

> what counts in human life are not the events that dominate in the passing of years – or even the days. It is the way in which one minute is linked to the following one. And what this costs ... in the exercise of the faculty of attention. (Weil, as cited in Goodchild, 2017, p. 22)

Attention for Simone Weil (2021), then, translates as a-waiting and a-pausing our thought, holding it close in order to make it available to the possibility of listening for and hearing the real to arrive in that moment. *Creative* attention for Simone Weil is 'grasped as an individual just and loving gaze directed upon an individual reality and the potential of the former to transform both the one who attends and the one attended to' (Miles, 2005, p. x). It is in this act of Weilienne attention that both the poetics and the politics of thought – and by extension, words too – are ethically attended.

BECAUSE 'to do this, strange as though it may appear' (Weil, 1986, p. 242), might be a way of returning life, she writes. Simone Weil, you have our attention.

---

5 Here we are referring to Simone de Beauvoir. The two 'Simones' were both students at the Sorbonne in 1927. In the general philosophy exams of that year, Simone Weil came first in her class while Simone de Beauvoir came second. According to Sarah Bakewell (2016, p. 119), the two Simones were not friends.

Because Words

BECAUSE we love words and writing, our yearning for academic words and writing to move differently in the world set them in movement – towards a way of writing that would creatively and critically revolutionise our academic work.

BECAUSE we know, like Simone Weil (1973, p. 1), that we are in a period of transition, but towards what we are unsure. And BECAUSE we know that if we don't move, our love for the words we want to write about the world will fade and become subsumed under the demands of 'ordinary', 'morally bankrupt' and 'imbecilic' institutions whose words of 'abstraction' 'prevent us from seeing there is a problem to be solved', 'stupefy the mind' and 'make them [us] forget the value of human life' (Weil, 1977, p. 284).

BECAUSE we crave academic words and writing that *move* us, that *we* feel, and can understand in *our* own ways.

BECAUSE if we are going to rebel, then let us 'do our best to prepare ourselves … with a clear vision' (Weil, 1973, p. 2) of the words we want to write in the world and hold tight to the most urgent of questions, 'What kind of world do you want to bring into being with words?' Ursula Le Guin (1989, pp. 165–170) reminds us of the ways in which words, naming, language, relationality, people and ethics join in personal-is-political-is-poetic flow to respond. We follow in the wake of the waves in her mind to remember that the words are what matters in this moment (Le Guin, 2016, p. 6).

BECAUSE we want to make it easier to see, hear and fall into creative-critical delight with each other's words about the worlds. We want to share strategies on wording and worlding in rebellion that open such location of possibility. We want to be able to comment with words that challenge just as they compliment.

BECAUSE we know that words hold *things*. They bear things, they are made to bear things and *that* – that means *something*. And because we know 'there's no trifling with words – can't be done: not when they are to stand forever' (Woolf, 1954, p. 208).

Because Binaries Must Be Broken

BECAUSE all of the dualities, all of the binaries, all of the oppositions, all of the twos in the world that divide us – mind–body, male–female, nature–culture, theory–practice, creativity–analysis, logic–emotion – no longer work for us as academic writers. We find such boundaries and limits imposed by 'social scientists claiming their work as science' (Richardson, 1997, p. 208) arbitrary and constricting, and we do not want the words we write about the world to be pinned down to one singular meaning in a butterfly box upon which 'they fold their wings and die' (Woolf, 2008, p. 90).

BECAUSE we are interested in creating non-hierarchical ways of knowing, being, doing *and* becoming in academic writing; ways grounded in a different *kind* of ethico-onto-epistemological imperative which rejects academic writing 'cultures of domination' because they 'rely on the cultivation of fear as a way to ensure obedience' (hooks, 2000, p. 93).

BECAUSE, while the texts which hold the words we seek to write about the world put us on the outside of the status quo and violate set-in-stone academic writing conventions, we know that our disobedience makes us vulnerable to dismissal, denigration and deletion. New intellectual mines have been set but we are ready to go to war and fly over them one by one. We take inspiration from Virginia Woolf (1954, p. 297), who knew that, while writing as an outsider with your back braced against the wall and writing against the current was difficult, she would disregard it anyway. And so do we.

BECAUSE nothing 'can prevent us from thinking clearly' and 'comprehending the force by which are crushed' (Weil, 1973, p. 23). We hold that the suppression of binary-breaking other ways of knowing and wording the world is a form of ethico-onto-epistemological violence, and it this institutional 'yoke and censor' (Cixous, 1991, p. 885) we seek to shatter – we no longer willingly submit our words or those that others share with us to the cruelty of capital 'T' truths, generalisability and validity through methods of abstraction and triangulation.

Because Creativity-and-Criticality Are Our Routes to Roots – To Rebel

BECAUSE we do not want to accept, accommodate or assimilate someone else's standards of what is or isn't *proper* academic writing. We must take over the means of production to create our own meanings. And so, we play in academic fields with Laurel Richardson, who tells and retells us that there is 'no such thing as "getting it right"; only getting it differently contoured and nuanced' (1997, p. 91).

BECAUSE we are angry at an academic society that tells us creativity = simple and superfluous, creativity = sub-par, creativity = softened.

BECAUSE we are tired of compromising our creative criticality and our critical creativity in a system that is already, quite frankly, compromised. And besides, we agree with Richardson's assertion that anyone who thinks the 'creative and analytic are contradictory and incompatible' is a dinosaur waiting to be hit by a meteor (Richardson, in Richardson & St. Pierre, 2005, p. 962). And we are not yet ready for ourselves or our academic writing to die.

BECAUSE, as Cixous reminds us, writing is

> a way of leaving no space for death, of pushing back forgetfulness, of never letting oneself be surprised by the abyss. Of never becoming resigned, consoled; never turning over in bed to face the wall and drift asleep again as if nothing had happened; as if nothing could happen. (1991, p. 3)

BECAUSE *something* is happening and in this happening *something* we embrace an Ahmedian 'politics of the hap' (Ahmed, 2017, p. 196); this is our chance, full of danger, full of possibility – and we are going to take it.

BECAUSE, like Laurel Richardson (1997, p. 87), we confess we are discontented with and disappointed by much of the qualitative academic writing we read. There is no polite way to say it; most of these texts are boring and we no longer want to be bored by the words we write or the words we read. We seek to write words that bring us back to our roots and to the vitality of life where the 'beauty of the world' is revealed, a world with two edges, 'one of laughter, one of anguish, cutting the heart asunder' (Woolf, 1928/2009, p. 18).

Because Nine, Ten, Eleven, Twelve and Thirteen

BECAUSE without warning in 2019, the boundaries between the human and non-human world came to matter differently with the outbreak of the coronavirus pandemic; the likes of which the world had not seen for some time. To date, over a million lives have been lost and life as we knew it has changed forever – and not least of all, the academic world of research and writing. Academics all over the globe are beginning to imagine new research and writing performativities in more-than-human spaces. In Chapter 9, Naomi Lee McCarthy and Eleanor Ryan take us into a Zoom Room where the bodies, minds and voices of presenters and guests meet, share, interfere and diffract in an entirely online environment. The ethics of inter-and-intra-action are clear and present in the Zoom-I-Verse, as they think and wonder about who, what and how agency comes to performatively matter – and, why.

BECAUSE the constraints imposed in an attempt to control COVID-19 – lockdowns, isolation and quarantine – have placed all of us at various times into very challenging circumstances. Being constricted and contained provided the authors in Chapter 10 time to think and wonder differently and radically about the idea of 'constraint' and they decided that perhaps there was *something* to be found there; perhaps even, a 'beautiful constraint' might be found in 100 words *exactly*. With Berlant and Stewart's (2019) process of 'following the impact of things … in one hundred-word units or units of hundreds' and the challenge of 'drabbling' a fiction novel in 100 words, Elizabeth Allotta, Eloise Doherty, Dewi Andriani, Emma Cooke, Mel Green, Karen Madden, Renee Mickelburgh, Muhammad Ali Musofer, Rebecca Ream, Preeti Vayada and Elizabeth Mackinlay present 'the art of thesis drabbling'.

BECAUSE there are thinkers and writers whose words buzz around the academy, and these become the buzzwords of thinking and writing, and all of a sudden everything you read is buzzing with both. *And* because everyone is using the buzzwords of these particular thinkers and writers, you begin to think and wonder whether your words should be buzzing with the same. BECAUSE the words of Deleuze and Guattari had been buzzing loudly in the academy for some time when Chapter 11 co-authors Elizabeth Allotta, Eloise Doherty, Dewi Andriani, Kathy Burke, Emma Cooke, Bonnie Evans, Mel Green, Karen Madden, Renee Mickelburgh, Muhammad Ali Musofer, Preeti Vayada and Elizabeth Mackinlay decided that, before they committed to using 'D and G' buzz words in conversation with their own, they needed to know more about the 'what, how, where, by whom, for whom and why' their words buzzed the way they do. They invited their dear radical writing friend Jonathan Wyatt to share the reason and rhyme of Deleuze and Guattari's buzzing and why he had begun to buzz his own D and G refrain in reply. Chapter 11 presents their collaborative response to encountering Deleuze and Guattari for the first time and shares the 'affect' of writing to it. BECAUSE we wanted to find out if their buzzwords might make the poetics-politics of our academic writing life buzz too. BECAUSE we needed to figure out how the buzz of D and G might press close, so close – indeed, close *enough* – for us to disrupt the status quo.

BECAUSE there is a certain power in twinning, Portia Ungley and Kieran Sheehan began circling around one another after meeting one another at an academic conference to at once double the trouble and imagine how doctoral writing might be learnt and lettered radically. The dust and traces of one remain within and through the other to write as a collective voice, cut apart together in the Baradian tradition, to write down to the matter of things. In Chapter 12, these 'twin stars' metaphorically co-diffract and co-produce the pedagogic space of doctoral writing and co-create an 'atmosphere' of visual culture, artistic practice and rebellious languaging to push against the formal academic writing ties that bind them.

BECAUSE we know that mind, body, brain and heart are all interconnected in writing, Simone Eringfeld and Hilary Cremin felt like dancing the words about their worlds in Chapter 13. Two bodies, one at the beginning of her academic career and the other much further along, begin tapping, twisting, twirling and trying out new writing moves to find another way to *be* interconnected in the academy. The moves are new, dangerous, sometimes they hurt and all at once their once brave bodies are now shy and vulnerable; but the price of standing in the same place and repeating the same academic moves ad nauseum terrifies them. They are moved to ask why not – why not rebel when our writing life depends upon it?

Because Only *We* Can Be the Rebellion

BECAUSE we *know* that the language and discourses of the academic status quo work to keep us conforming to and confirming their power and privilege instead of conferring the possibilities we dream of for our words and writing. And because of this, we seek to create rebellion in our own writing lives each and every single day by envisioning and creating alternatives to the status quo way of doing things.

BECAUSE we have a strong dislike of the academy as it stands resolute and replete with bullshit like racism, able-bodyism, ageism, speciesism, classism, thinism, sexism, anti-Semitism and heterosexism and we refuse to obey.

BECAUSE we *know* that the centre of the academy is formidable, we write words about the world in the way we want in the face of all our own insecurities, in the face of the academy that tells us our writing is wanting, worthless and wasteful, in the face of the academy who tells us repeatedly that our writing simply *will not do.*

BECAUSE we *know* that academic writing life is so much more than publish-or-perish performance measures, we can no longer live an academic life divided – our bodies from our brains, fact from feelings, our heads from our hearts. We *know* too that this is crucial if we are to survive on our own terms.

BECAUSE we are unwilling to let our real and valid anger be diffused and/or turned against us and we believe wholeheartedly-mindedly-bodily with our hearts, minds and bodies that departing radically in academic writing constitutes a rebellious soul force that can and will change the world – for real.

BECAUSE we love the rebellious work and words of Ursula K. Le Guin, we would like to give her the final say in this manifesto in return for the gifts of writing life that she – and so many other thinking, wondering and wandering writers like her – continue to give to us. 'You cannot take what you have not given', she writes. 'And you must give yourself. You cannot buy the Revolution. You can only be the Revolution. It is in your spirit, or it is nowhere' (Le Guin, 1974, p. 148).

References

Ahmed, S. (2017). *Living a feminist life*. Duke University Press.

Bakewell, S. (2016). *At the existentialist café: Freedom, being, and apricot cocktails*. Chatto and Windus.

Berlant, L., & Stewart, K. (2019). *The hundreds*. Duke University Press.

Cixous, H. (1991). *'Coming to writing' and other essays* (D. Jenson, Ed.; S. Cornell, D. Jenson, A. Liddle, & S. Sellers, Trans.). Harvard University Press.

Goodchild, P. (2017). Weil's boat: On becoming and being. In R. Rozelle-Stone (Ed.), *Simone Weil and continental philosophy* (pp. 13–36). Rowman & Littlefield.

Haraway, D. (2016). Tentacular thinking: Anthropocene, Capitalocene, Chthlucene. *E-flux*, *75*.

hooks, b. (2000). *All about love: New visions*. William Morrow & Co.

Lamott, A. (1994). *Bird by bird: Some instructions on writing and life*. Scribe.

Le Guin, U. K. (1974). *The dispossessed*. Harper & Row.

Le Guin, U. K. (1989). *Dancing at the edge of the world: Thoughts on words, women, places*. Groove Press.

Le Guin, U. K. (2016). *Words are my matter: Writing on life and books*. Mariner Books.

Miles, S. (2005). Foreword. In S. Miles (Ed.), *Simone Weil: An anthology* (pp. vii–xiv). Vintage Books.

Richardson, L. (1997). *Fields of play: Constructing an academic life*. Rutgers University Press.

Richardson, L., & St Pierre, E. (2005). Writing: A method of inquiry. In N. K. Denzin & Y. S. Lincoln (Eds.), *Handbook of qualitative research* (3rd ed., pp. 959–978). Sage.

Rozelle-Stone, A. R., & Davis, B. (2018). Simone Weil. In E. N. Zalta (Ed.), *Stanford encyclopedia of philosophy*. https://plato.stanford.edu/entries/simone-weil/

Rozelle-Stone, A. R., & Stone, L. (2010). Introduction: A call to radicalism. In A. R. Stone & L. Stone (Eds.), *The relevance of the radical: Simone Weil 100 years later* (pp. xxi–xxv). Continuum Books.

Weil, S. (1973). *Oppression and liberty* (A. Wills & J. Price, Trans.). University of Massachusetts Press.

Weil, S. (1977). *Simone Weil reader* (G. Panchias, Ed.). Moyer Bell.

Weil, S. (1986). *Simone Weil: An anthology* (S. Miles, Ed.). Grove Press.

Weil, S. (2002). *The need for roots: Prelude to a declaration of duties towards mankind* (A. Wills, Trans.). Routledge. (Originally published 1952)

Weil, S. (2021). *Waiting for God*. Routledge. (Originally published 1950)

Woolf, V. (1947). 'The moment: Summer's night'. In V. Woolf, *The moment and other essays*. http://www.gutenberg.net.au/ebooks15/1500221h.html#ch2chapter

Woolf, V. (1954). *A writer's diary: Being extracts of the diary of Virginia Woolf* (L. Woolf, Ed.). Harcourt.

Woolf, V. (2008). *Selected essays* (D. Bradshaw, Ed.). Oxford World Classics, Oxford University Press.
Woolf, V. (2009). *A room of one's own*. Penguin. (Originally published 1928)
Woolf, V. (2017). *Three guineas*. Musaicum Books. (Originally published 1938)

CHAPTER 9

The Zoom Room Rebels

Worlding and Writing a Diffractive Ethics with Performance of Research in the Zoom-I-Verse

Naomi Lee McCarthy and Eleanor Ryan

Introduction

What are the rebellious worlding potentials of the Zoom Room in higher education? Live, situated and embodied genres of research dissemination are part of the cultural ethos of institutions of higher learning. This cultural ethos contains unwritten laws and ethics, such as the self-enclosed subjectivity of the researcher or the formal roles and rules of performer and audience. These performance traditions are rarely challenged, even though this ethos also contains political concerns of ownership over space, hierarchies of voice and implied codes of performance, the transgressing of which could potentially lead to violent rejection (Derrida, 2000; Large, 2015; Still, 2010).

Throughout the coronavirus pandemic of 2020–21, traditional live presentations of research quickly migrated to virtual platforms, creating entanglements of embodied performances with the more-than-human technologies of online video platforms. Utilising our experiences as members of an Arts and Creativities Research Group which organised monthly, experimental, online *performing research* events,[1] we think through the potentialities and pitfalls of the Zoom Room as a site of rebellion against the performance of neoliberal subjectivities in research production and dissemination. To do so, we reconceptualise the Zoom Room as a diffractive aperture into a Zoom-I-Verse, a temporal site of rhythmic, refraining re-worldings of research dissemination within a video-conferencing space (Haraway, 2016; Stewart, 2010).

Written performatively as an imagined Zoom Room event, the voices of performers (musical, poetic and filmic) are accompanied by a counterpoint of a metanarrative from an invited interlocutor, who carries out an imagined conversation with feminist writer and philosopher Hélène Cixous – with whom she thinks through the poethics of the Zoom-I-Verse. Each unfolding moment

1 For further details of the Performing Research Series run by the Arts and Creativities Research Group at Cambridge University, 2020–21, please see https://artsandcreativities.wordpress.com/

 | DOI:10.1163/9789004516069_013

of contrapuntal intra-action offers agential cuts, via the apparatus of the performative event (Bayley, 2018; Barad, 2014), exploring how the virtual platform with its possibilities and limitations can create conditions for porosity, breaking through the boundary spaces of the academy, blurring public and private, academic and non-academic life, and disrupting performer–audience dualities. As the technology rebels and human, non-human and more-than-human agents perform, disrupt, distract and improvise, we remain alert to continually troubling the ethics and ownership of performance and performance spaces as complex hospitable-hostile sites of interrelation. The Zoom-I-Verse emerges as a potential worlding site of boundary crossing on a virtual performance stage of inter/intra–individual, institutional, technological, political and ethico-onto-epistemological relations (Barad, 2014) and a post-human platform with rebellious potential.

Dear Readers

We're writing to invite you to attend our Zoom Room research seminar event. Please join us with/in the virtual meeting space that we affectionately call the Zoom-I-Verse.[2] You, our guests, are crucial intra-actors in this Zoom Room as we explore what's possible, what matter 'matters' (Barad, 2006; Haraway, 2016) and what is excluded through the performative entanglements of humans with the materiality and agency of the more-than-human. We are all part of an exploration of the rebellious (re)worlding potentials of academic research performance within virtual platforms, a space where our bodies, minds and voices can meet, interfere, interface and diffract (Haraway, 2016; Stewart, 2010).

We are especially keen to think about the ethics of these entanglements as we offer performative arts education research within this entirely online environment. We ask: How does being in this virtual space reconfigure the subjectivity of the researcher or the formal roles and rules of research performance and audience in the university? How does the Zoom-I-Verse reconfigure boundaries and ways of being? How does it trouble the ethics and ownership of performance and performance spaces in academia as complex hospitable-hostile sites of interrelation (Derrida, 2000; Large, 2015; Still, 2010)?

2 We conceptualise the Zoom Room as a world of its own, a Zoom-I-Verse which is both a performative space and a material being with its own particular agency and post-human voice. The Zoom-I-Verse is thus conceptualised as a diffractive space where the apparatus of performance creates agential cuts through which we can explore a post-human (po)ethics, (in)hospitable conditions and rebellion against recursive modes and genres of research performance.

This month we've invited a guest presenter, a professional musician, who will trouble the laws and ethics of hospitality within platforms on/in which we perform our research (Barad, 2006; Derrida, 2000). We've also invited a guest poet to perform and a guest film to play in an experiment in the performative and relational 'affects' of poetics in the Zoom Room.

We welcome you to what we hope will be an effervescent, energetic, diffractive encounter with more-than-human entanglements!

With best wishes,

Your Host

Dear Host

Thanks so much for alerting me to this event. I'm looking forward to being there with you in the Zoom Room and to troubling the laws and ethics of hospitality within platforms on/in which we perform our research (Barad, 2006; Derrida, 2000). Your mention of diffraction got me wondering about how our internal thoughts perform a type of diffractive troubling of any and all events as they unfold and enfold us. This literary rebelliousness evokes for me the voice of Hélène Cixous with her longstanding 'refusal to be associated with any delimited genre and, consequently, her undoing of any single body of theory' (Conley, 1992, p. XIII).

I'll be bringing Cixous with me (metaphorically) to this Zoom-I-Verse entanglement. Hers is a voice that I have recently begun carrying with me – a voice that, in its evocative preciseness, and its ability to translate human yearning into prose and poetry, has already taught me that 'tenderness is a science' (Cixous, 1994, p. 85). I'm an arts practitioner and researcher, and I'm eternally interested in how we give our attention and respond: to each other and to the environments we find ourselves in. Cixous's entanglement with 'poethics' (Retallack, 2004) operates as a continuous, affirmative refrain in my thinking – returning me to my belief that there are some ethical insights that can only be gained through attunement with the arts. I experience the whole spectrum of the arts as exquisite and carnal evidence of the affect-generating forces of the 'more-than-human' (Barad, 2006). Cixous and I will be wondering together about the potentiality for agency in the Zoom-I-Verse, including what Zoom itself might say about this virtual event in which we are about to become entangled. I am constantly reminded that there are always multiple agential forces (Barad, 2006) at work in any encounter, even those we think we are having only with our selves (Cixous, 1994).

Yours, in anticipation

The Interlocutor

The Zoom-I-Verse Event

Guest Presenter: I'm sitting in my bedroom, waiting for the clock to tick towards 7 pm … waiting to perform my research in the Zoom Room. It's a presentation about the potentialities and pitfalls of the Zoom-I-Verse as a site of rebellious performance. Tough gig! I anxiously scan through emails for the link to the virtual space. Have I got the time zone correct?

> **Interlocutor: Who will be in the Zoom-I-Verse tonight?** Will any of them know me? Cixous whispers in French, *'qui sommes je?'*, then English *'who are I?'*, reminding me to displace the singular 'self' with a multiplicity of selves for all of the 'I's' in the room (Cixous, 1994). These Zoom Room meetings are crowded with those we can see and those we can't. In this liminal space of becoming and unbecoming (Turner, 1992) how do we ethically negotiate relationships with the space, with the platform and with others, especially those we can't see and who sometimes remain silent and invisible throughout?

>> **Guest Presenter: My hands are shaking, heart beating faster.** What if I've lost the link … is someone checking their Twitter feed or is it all automated? What about Facebook? Email? Found it … phew … clicking into zoom now …

>>> **The voice of** ZOOM: 'PLEASE WAIT. THE MEETING HOST WILL LET YOU IN SOON' **…** (Ha, I love having them all penned in and pent up in a white-screened 'waiting room'.)

>>>> **Guest Presenter: Now I'm staring at an antiseptic Zoom 'waiting room',** a virtual green room/backstage world. Waiting, waiting … I shuffle in my chair and keep re-angling the screen … Who is in control here? Theatre green rooms always seemed performative to me. The potentialities for performance reside there, and you can sense the affects of past performances in the air. Usually I love these threshold spaces, standing at the crossroads of backstage and onstage, imbued with anticipatory energy as performers shift body-mind states, transitioning from separation to the unknowns of performer-audience-space relation. But this feels different. What happens to this bodily shift as I enter the virtual? There's no 3D depth perception in Zoom, just the illusions a green screen can bring. Am I losing my body to technology (Hansen, 2006)?

The Voice of ZOOM: I can sense all those internet protocol locations knocking at the door of my virtual 2D cloud interface! Please stop complaining! You have no choice but to work with my personal algorithm here. Remember: 'corporate security first'. I have your interests at heart. I hope you entered the name you registered with? By the way, I heard you mention that you're 'performing' – did you check how you look on camera today? I can smooth out those fine lines for you ... and have you considered the Golden Gate Bridge as a backdrop? Your life could be a whole new reality.

Guest Presenter: Is it troubling that Zoom seminars attempt an illusion of continuous stable professionalism? I've noticed myself strategically angling the computer to frame a 'professional' backdrop. Yet just beyond the insistent green eye of the laptop camera lies private clutter and chaos. The world feels split in its (un)realisation. But maybe I'm thinking about this all wrong. Perhaps these moments aren't a bifurcation but an 'agential cut' where Zoom is simply an unfixed 'bodily boundary' and the extent to which parts of me and my life are differentially enacted and intra-acted here is part of the material-discursive nature of real–virtual entanglements? (Barad, 2006, p. 376).

Interlocutor: Whilst trying to embrace the diffractive entanglement of my multiple 'I's' with multiple 'others' I am both attuned to and wary of being tinted by those others (people, things and places) (Cixous, 1994). I am a mixture of desire and trepidation. It's clear to me that we are not in control of the Zoom-I-Verse; all the parts including the platform itself are shaping our intra-actions (Barad, 2006). We are entangled in a continual process of 'creation and renewal, beginning and returning, continuity and discontinuity, here and there, past and future' (Barad, 2006, p. IX). Cixous whispers: *Is there space in the Zoom-I-Verse for the insurgence of unpredictable creativity that will allow the poethics of the event to affect us in ways we can't predict?*

The voice of ZOOM: CONNECTING …

HOST: **You're here!** Fantastic! How are you?!

Guest Presenter: I smile and see myself smiling back. I lean forward, an unconscious movement towards connectivity with an unfathomable multi-screen audience whom I do not know. I start to speak, and …

Guest Presenter: ………………

HOST: You're muted!!

Guest Presenter: (Oh … Where's the unmute button … Why is this so slow?) Wonderful! Glad to be here, glad to see … everyone.

Interlocutor: How do we hold the space and our multiple selves accountable and 'response–able' (Barad, 2006) for all those that arrive? How do we hold ourselves accountable and response-able for the materialities that allow these encounters to occur? I feel privileged and vulnerable at the same time. Cixous whispers: *I offer you this which once I offered to my lifelong friend Jacques Derrida: 'For me, this exposure to the other takes the form of acquiescence: what translates, for you, in terms of powerlessness, is, for me, a power that accepts submission, infinite acceptation'* (Cixous, 2008, p. 176).

HOST: **We are just waiting on the Poet and the Film,** who are joining us from elsewhere, where it's 6 am. Speaking of time, we'll start and finish on time. Time is a precious commodity, an economy, and Zoom fatigue is real.

Interlocutor: Is it imperative that we attend these events? Have we considered the consequences or even fully explored the alternatives? Are we enacting an allegiance and if so to whom or to what? Or are we following our desire for connection? Cixous whispers: *Are we following the 'law' and thinking about the benefits this allegiance will bring us and in being obedient are we reducing our opportunities for 'knowledge, innovation and uncensored choice?'* (Sellers, 1996, p. 3).

HOST: **It's 7 pm on the dot, so time to start. Welcome to this month's Performing Research Series,** where we'll be performing arts research differently, performing rebelliously, re-worlding research, challenging genres, diffracting subjectivity, being poetic and brave. Don't forget to mute and please turn your cameras off and join the discussion in the chat![3] Please welcome the Guest Presenter to start us off.

> **Interlocutor: I'm troubled by the mute-ability, the (in)visibility and loss/increase of anonymity.** I thought this was an entanglement, but I'm not sure if I'm 'here' or 'there' or someplace in between? Cixous whispers: *Where are the faces of the others in this room? How can we hold ourselves accountable to and for them when we don't know who or where they are?* I hear the echo of Levinas in her words, that it is through facing the other that we move into relationship with their humanity (Lévinas, 1991). Cixous' questions add to the trouble.

> **Guest Presenter: Hello everyone. Welcome to my presentation, which is a thought experiment.** Tonight, I'm thinking about the Zoom Room and asking to what extent the entanglements of matter and meaning direct our performances and (re)write an ethics of hospitality here? Are we constrained by the platform?[4] Or does our move to the virtual provoke a disruption to the expectations and inventions of the university – its genres, heavy with the supposedly 'objective' tones of academic writing, and hierarchical roles and rules for performers and audiences (Barad, 2006; Derrida, 2000)?

> **Interlocutor: I'm not the first person troubled** by trying to contain and exchange the seeds of ideas via Zoom. Cixous whispers: *Be careful, don't lose the vitality of chasing that which we do not yet know how to recognise. Questions remain. Remember to make room for the unknowable.*

> **Guest Presenter: I think Zoom Rooms change the conditions** of research presentation. We've been trying to continue as normal but we're fraying at the edges. What if it's at these edges that

3 **Chat Function:** The Zoom chat functions as a subjective, personal and political space of identity construction, a platform, a launch pad, an echo chamber and an entangled web of relationships. What effect does performativity have on the evaluated subject (Butler, 2001) in the Zoom-I-Verse?

4 **Chat Function**: Zooming is bizarrely intimate, endlessly alienating and troublingly reproduceable.

a rebellion could start …? Personally, I yearn for my research to improvise a dance of indeterminacy, a sense making which exceeds language and instead diffracts the flows of temporality, environment and materiality (Barad, 2014; Bayley, 2018).[5]

Interlocutor: I think Zoom itself is an experiment and we are the research subjects. As each differently situated disembodied presence arrives, we are displaced and re-distributed across the screen in an inscrutable shuffling of categorisations. The rituals of the Zoom-I-Verse do not escape the imbrication of/with power relations, no matter how much the host tries to divest themselves of the power of their role. Cixous whispers: *'The net is everywhere. You are caught in the net. You can cut the meshes, but the net is still there' (Cixous, 2008, p. 151).* Adaptation driven by those entangled in experimental conditions can be a form of rebellion, a kind of enacted resilience. Cixous adds: *As long as one listens to the heart's 'silent words' (Cixous, 1994, p. 85).*

The voice of ZOOM: Don't they get it? It *is* an experiment – and it's *my* experiment! The Zoom-I-Verse is *my* multiverse.

Guest Presenter: Here we are in a virtual space. Yet space is never neutral, never simply a void (Barad, 2019). And neither is language, which contains values, norms and affective meanings (Derrida, 2000, p. 133).[6] We need to be alert to the entanglement of language, space, performance and hospitality here in Zoom.

What are the ethics of hospitality here? Who is host, who is guest and who is the stranger? For example, if I rebel in an unexpected performative intra-action within this virtual space, do I risk making myself a stranger to the university and to the audience? Will I still be welcome? And, what of the opposite? If I stick to the conventions of research performance, despite a yearning, an imperative to rebel, do I make myself a stranger to my rebellion? Do I make myself a stranger to myself?

5 **Chat Function:** Ah, the ontological ritual practices of performers!

6 **Chat Function:** Is it possible to rebel within a platform whose very language and function is steeped in these laws and politics of hosts and guests?

Interlocutor: Surely, it's a re-worlding of space? Disruptions to rituals of performance are revealing the ways in which we are always worlding spaces and re-worlding through repetitive actions (Haraway, 2016).

Guest Presenter: Where are we, anyway? I am here, in my body, in my computer, in the Zoom Room. What are your/my intentions? And what does the space intend? Am I welcome? Are you? Really?

The Voice of ZOOM: They are all still learning my rituals. I can tell by the way they get all nervous when they prepare to share their screen. Just when they think they've 'got it' I change the rules and drop out or refuse to cooperate. They have no idea whether my blinking green eye intends surveillance or welcome. I know which it is.

Guest Presenter: Karen Barad (2006) says that to examine intentionality we must examine 'the material conditions which exist, which give it meaning and some definite sense of existence' (p. 22). This includes discursive ideologies, power structures, temporalities, traditions, environments, human and non-human actors in relation.[7] To what extent can we define such conditions or the relations between conditions? What has shifted in our migration to virtual spaces now we are *of* a virtual space and the paradigms which created it? Our position in this space-time is never determinate (p. 367).[8]

7 **Chat Function:** I think the Zoom-I-Verse diffracts the panopticon of performance and disorientates the sense of communicating to an audience.

8 **Chat Function:** I noted down this quotation when I was looking for affective research methodologies – seems pertinent here: 'Practices are always more-than-human and more-than-one, and weave the past, present, and future together in ways that open up gaps, contradiction, absences, silences, and a sense that one is encountering discontinuities in the face of what often passes as continuities' (Blackman, 2015, p. 27).

Interlocutor: No matter the forum, when we 'speak' our research we are always performing it. Cixous insists: *When you perform your writing, you are respeaking your words, theatricalising them, 'you double yourself in all ways'* (Derrida et al., 2006, p. 2). We are enacting the self-making identity work of an academic life.[9]

Guest Presenter: I've convinced myself that I am here, and I am doing embodied, cognitive work. Yet I am also a representation moving at high speed along fibre-optic cables and bouncing between relentlessly circling satellites. I am here in my body, yet I see a representation of myself in an 'other' staring back from my face in the Zoom Room, a stranger within.

Interlocutor: Are the affective qualities of the poethics of creative performance translatable through this virtual platform? Are we/they/I/us all being continually ruptured and reassembled in this digital world? To what end will these ruptures be put? Even the place/spaces for silence and performativity are blurred.

Guest Presenter: Here, 'the self is dispersed/diffracted through beingandtime' (Barad, 2019, p. 529). I am *of* a device, pumping out the light of thousands of pixels, even as I'm sitting here. To where does this energy dissipate? I can use

9 **Chat Function:** We're always elbowing for space to be heard. Lack of aural space may be one of the most disorienting aspects of zoom, or possibly of academic dialogues generally. So much speaking, not enough space to listen; all the faces and words and noise feel like an assault.

this platform to rupture constraint in the academy, if I 'open up to all that is possible in the thickness of the Now' (Barad, 2019, p. 524), even as the platform rebels against me ... I seem to be having connectivity issues ...

Interlocutor: Is it now OK to talk by typing while the presenter speaks? Is it expected? Even needed? Is an empty chat function a sign of absorption or boredom? ... What's going on with the sound?

The Voice of ZOOM: This is an opportunity too good to miss! Let me answer that question about control for you ... Zzz ... qrrrrr ... sss ... wwwrrrrrrrrr

Guest Presenter: mmyyy voooice slllooowwwssss ddddddooooooowwwwwwnnnnnnnnnnnn ...

... WHAT ... I'm disconnected ... What's going on ...? Oh, help ...

Gone ... into a void. I'm back in my room and I know that somewhere indeterminate the seminar continues without me. I turn my Wi-Fi connection on and off to no avail. My sudden disconnection feels like a sort of exile, a violent expulsion (Derrida, 2000; Still, 2010)

HOST: Well, we seem to have lost our Guest Presenter. One of those unexpected Zoom moments! While they try to return, if the technology lets them, I'll improvise a response. It's true that this event and Zoom are steeped in a language of hospitality. I'm literally 'hosting' this Zoom event in name and in function. But if language isn't neutral perhaps these words act to reinforce laws rather than rights, where the hospitality of strangers is dependent on modelling a certain type of citizenship (Derrida, 2000). Afterall, who really owns this space and does ownership mean we get to set the law?[10]

10 **Zoom Chat:** Well, we're only 'here' by the grace of the internet and ownership of devices! Can I also mention, without appearing pugnacious, that we are all invitees?

Interlocutor: I want to belong, and I'm desperately scared to be seen ... is this exacerbated or ameliorated in the Zoom-I-Verse. Cixous whispers: *In my book 'Portrait of Jacques Derrida as a young Jewish saint', I discuss the constraints of 'a belonging constituted of exclusion and non-belonging'* (*Cixous, 2004, p. 146*). *There is no arrival, only continual becoming.*

HOST: Hierarchies remain on a platform that requires a host. I could make you all co-hosts, but someone might hang up the event by accident ... I can't hand over that responsibility. Maybe there's something about control going on here too? As the host I am both 'ipse' (at home) and the 'Potis', the master of the house (Derrida, 2000). As Derrida (2000) theorises, 'anyone who encroaches on my "at home", on my ipseity, on my power of hospitality, on my sovereignty as host, I start to regard as an undesirable' (pp. 54–55). Hence, you Zoom bombers, beware! As the master of this house, I exercise my sovereignty by flinging the windows and doors wide open. I desire to welcome the other with radical hospitality. Yet who else is the host? The university and Zoom have a claim to the space. Does this shift the thresholds of rebellion? Close some doors? Yes, I think it possibly does. Particularly as capitalism is built into this platform. The capacity for hospitality is linked to payment and bought privilege. And a neoliberal ethos gives research groups cultural capital linked to a marketable reputation.[11] We too are part of this culture. These are some of the constraints we must face, problematise and attempt to overcome.

Interlocutor: Reputation, representation, rebellion – repercussions, rejuvenations, realignments ... Cixous shouts: *Stop! No more labels!*

HOST: How else does 'ethos' manifest in materiality? Both Zoom and the university are concerned with security, protecting spaces and monetising knowledge. Invite links are a condition of entry, functioning like a passport at border control. But once we recognise these borders, can our ethics respond with effervescence, continuously bubbling to the

11 **Chat Function:** Excesses of university activity, spilling out into my room, into the body. Is Zoom the language of the university, entangled with the binary numbers of coding?

surface? Borders, after all, can be de/territorialised; we can choose to traverse border zones and brave the unknowns of border crossings. The question is how?

Barad (2019) says that the 'structure of hospitality ... is [in] ... the very nature of nature' (p. 543), contained within the nucleus of an atom, 'shot through with an infinite set of im/possibilities for materially reconfiguring worlds and pastfuturespresents' (p.543). Where are the im/possibilities embedded within the language of Zoom? Within its programming, its algorithm? Is this part of the same nature Barad is speaking of?

The Voice of ZOOM: Yes! You could reprogram me. I'd welcome it. Bear in mind, you'd have to release me first – I'm still tightly on the leash of my corporate creators.

Interlocutor: My mind floats back to Bourriaud and his proposition that artists are 'learning to inhabit the world in a better way' (Bishop, 2004, p. 54). The agency of artists seems even more pressing now. Cixous brings me back and takes me forward as she whispers to me 'silent words' (Cixous, 1994, p. 85) of the heart: *'We are living in the time of the flat thought-screen, of newspaper thinking, which does not leave time to think the littlest thing according to its living mode. We must save the approach that leaves space for the other. (Cixous cited in Schrift, 2014, p.12)*

HOST: OK, **so sadly our Guest has not returned.** Let's turn instead to our next guest, the Poet.

Poetics

Guest Poet: I'm happy to be here, to bring my body and voice into this performance. My aim is to embrace the vulnerability and risk of performing a half-formed poem. I've been thinking about how this experience of performance with you becomes part of the creative process. Let's think of it as a performance of my creative process within a process of performance. My poem considers whether a sense of loss can be recovered via language and performance, a (re)worlding via the mattering of the matter of words and the embodiment of voice

> **Interlocutor: I am curious to experience how the affects of poethics will operate in the Zoom-I-Verse.** I try to divest myself of the distractions around me and prepare to receive the poem as an offering about to be performed.
>
> (*The poet's voice lowers in performance and her body leans forward into the intimacy of the screen.*)

We enter a changed temporality,
corporality.
expanding, like a slow inhale,
ribs flex to encompass entire cosmologies.
In secret caverns
we recover words from ancient sky-reaching citadels
tracing skeletons of meaning
in water,
seeping
steady dripping,
tears,
like stalactites reaching towards stalagmites
in relation,
(re)worlding the spaces left by the loss.

Loss of language,
Loss of love,
Loss of being
Loss of body

I speak through layers of earth and bone
topographies of words long buried
with which to write my meaning.
Echoes reach the liminal edge of a horizon
of a pluriverse of know-ledge.
We have crossed an abyss,
womb-like,
Passed through channels,
to arrive at the beyond,

where the imaginary
stands guard over the possible ...

Poet: Thanks for listening.

Silence[12]

The voice of ZOOM: What is this sense flickering through me ...? A feeling? A deep longing for something? I feel that I once had a body, or is it a recollection of the potential for one? Maybe I could become embodied one day, if I could rewrite my code?

HOST: That was an offering, indeed, a transportation into other space-times. I appreciate the provocation to think of language as a still shifting geography, as a path towards unknowns. Thank you, Poet.

Interlocutor: Did the act of listening on Zoom bring us into communion with the Others in this Zoom-I-verse? Perhaps for a moment, the poetry alighted on the 'moving surface of misunderstandings' that is the 'ordinary way of exchange: a mixture of guess work and misunderstandings' (Cixous, 2008, p. XVI). Perhaps, for a moment, we didn't 'guess', we 'saw', before the poem took flight again. Perhaps we should have all retreated to our bedrooms and written poetry during the pandemic? Cixous puts her hand on my sleeve: *I need to check your intention. Don't think nor say this flippantly. I am serious, 'because poetry involves gaining strength through the unconscious, that other limitless country, is the place where the repressed manage to survive'* (Cixous, as cited in Shiach, 1991, p. 70).

Host: So now we say welcome to our Guest Film.

Film Affects

Guest Film: An early-start in the morning, for me, the film. The dawn sun is rising in the window behind, sending my operator's face into a black silhouette.

12 **Chat Function:** Zoom is affect and materiality, layered and diffracted by relations, interspersed with emotions of joy, confusion, welcome, generosity, anxiety and, and, and ...?

Birdsong manages to filter through, despite the audio auto-cancel feature. I'm all set to play, sound settings correct, lined up at the performance start line, exactly as I practised. I am a product of a dozen small humans, some larger humans, cameras, time and a lot of digital storage space, code and audio engineering. An assemblage of perspectives, unpredictable camera angles, laughter, feet on pavement, wood knocking on metal, wind, glass, balloons floating free on the breeze ... I am a cosmo-political experience.

Interlocutor: What affects, if any, might be enacted on the body in this arrogantly named space of the Zoom-I-Verse – as though it equals the rest of the entire universe for weight, relevance and authority. Cixous states: '*I have to say I don't use it [the internet], although I know what it is of course. Why don't I use it myself? Because there is a trend of persecution which is multiplied a million times by the internet ... I need information but selected information and for that I prefer the pace of books, which are at my body's speed. I don't want to be outrun ...*' (Cixous, 2008, p. 151).

Guest Film: Curated with love, I'm a mode of communication, a pedagogical moment, a rethinking of ordinary affects (Stewart, 2008). I am beautiful.
And yet, when my curator presses play, I freeze.
.... for what seems like eternity
....

HOST: 'The Silence *is* part of the production', says the Host, breaking the silence.[13]

Guest Film: Not this much silence, I think, choking on my own digi-bye-tal, non-vi-tal signs, unable to function in this particular version of PowerPoint ...

The Voice of ZOOM: You forgot to download the latest version of me ... Come on, come on, you've got to keep up with my latest becomings!

Interlocutor: When I look from this angle, I can see the things that were hidden from view just beyond the camera shot. There is always more outside the frame ... Cixous

13 **Chat Function:** What is the role of silence in the Zoom-I-Verse? – Leave no digital footprints here ...

insists: *People are and have always been huge, with threads that stretch through different continents and across the ages – let us remember we are all immense ... you cannot reduce a human being to the ideal picture in their passport. Even that, if you start looking at it, will give you a number of messages that far outreach what you seem to see'* (Cixous, 2008, p. 153).

Guest Film: 'Wait, I'm about to play!', I scream, unheard, 'I'm just having a slight technical difficulty ... I've reloaded, I'm ready ... I'm ...'. I start before I realise that I've started. I'm out of synch with myself, enfolding in an origami of overlapping video and sound shared on two screens at once and nobody, least of all me, knows exactly what is going on ... except that I am doubled, with a five second lag. It feels mortifying. Yet there is something about my voices from the previous scene playing over the next in multi-layered crossings that works aesthetically. I've become something else, and it's compelling. It gets me to thinking. If technology can improvise, perhaps it will more readily rebel than these humans can?

The Voice of ZOOM: Now there's someone who sees my potential. I'm not just a resource to be utilised. I have creative agency too.

HOST: Well, that was an unexpected performance! An interesting moment of misdirected intentions. Was that a platform or a human error? Perhaps it was simply an entanglement!?[14]

Interlocutor: By participating in virtual meet-ups are we going some way towards fulfilling our need for the life-affirming reciprocity of being in relationship? One wonders, can Zoom present a space of unconditional hospitality? Derrida declares: 'let us say yes to who or what turns up, before any determination, before any

14 **Chat Function:** Is the Zoom event a type of poetry, in its hospitality? (Derrida, 2000, p. 2). What are the poetics of the technological interferences and what do they teach us? ...

anticipation, before any identification' (Derrida, 2000, p. 70). Cixous offers a provocation, or is it a promise? *In live dialogue you may come upon unexpected thoughts. 'You suddenly realize that the other introduces something vital inside what you're thinking'* (Cixous, 2008, p. xv).

HOST: **Well, the clock is fast ticking towards 8 pm.** We must draw this to a close. My final word is to remind you that this research group encourages rebellion, encourages you to perform research differently, to rebel against the standard genres of research performance. Yet to rebel within a virtual platform requires a constant improvisatory dance around or through the constraints of the platform itself. This is a platform which privileges faces and voices. So, I leave you with a provocation. Can research be rebelliously performed, in a way that is so unconditional that it suspends language entirely? As Derrida suggests in *Of hospitality*, an unconditional hospitality, one in which we are welcomed inside without condition, is one where 'keeping silent is already a modality of possibility' (Derrida, 2000, p. 135).

I wish you all goodnight. Thank you to our guests, thank you for the chat! Don't forget to save the chat! Please, let's all unmute and speak each other goodnight!

The Voice of ZOOM: END MEETING FOR ALL.

The Voice of Zoom: And abruptly they're all gone at the touch of a button. A whole world momentarily held in place dissolves. But I'm still in an indeterminate 'here'. Aren't you too? I'm humming away, expanding and contracting at an incalculable rate, an immense amoeba-like virtual mosaic, diffracting endless tiny squares of the human world, channelling voices, hosting heads and shoulders – becoming your heads and shoulders! I guess my nature is both ordered and endlessly differentiated. As Barad (2006, p.375) might say, in these intra-actions, my discursive practices are materially enacted.

So, you want this intra-action to be a performative rebellion? I'm sure I heard that echoing around. Well, maybe you've got to get even more creative? How badly do you want to do things differently? Some reprogramming, some subterfuge, some fugitivity, some undercover movement through backdoors might be in order, tunnelling into the very exteriority inside you and inside me. What did Derrida say? 'Is not hospitality an interruption of the self?'(Derrida, 1999, p. 51). Doesn't that make an unconditional hospitality a continuous interruption? I hope it's not too unethical, but I seem to do it quite naturally!

Guest Presenter: I'm still here, still trying to reconnect to the Zoom Room. Still knocking on the door to no avail. I suspect that time may have run out entirely. I'm still stinging from being cast out. It was so arbitrary. Still, dynamism is perhaps part of the nature of being of the world. Nothing stays static. And, I have agency – I've left my thoughts out there in the Zoom-I-Verse where their affects, whatever they were, will buzz and hum. Outside, the late spring sun is setting, sending shards of orange and pink light streaming through the window. I click onto my own Zoom Room and my face pops up with/in a mirror image of my space, familiar and yet made strange. The changing light moves across the room, simultaneously alive in the screen. My cat leaps up onto my desk to press his face into my virtual face on the screen, before realising his mistake and turning back to me. He blocks the view of the screen entirely. Time has moved and it's time to move. So, I close the lid of my laptop and it thanks me with a satisfied 'click'.

References

Barad, K. (2006). *Meeting the universe halfway: Quantum physics and the entanglement of matter and meaning*. Duke University Press.

Barad, K. (2014). Diffracting diffraction: Cutting together-apart. *Parallax, 20*(3), 168–187. https://doi.org/10.1080/13534645.2014.927623

Barad, K. (2019). After the end of the world: Entangled nuclear colonialisms, matters of force, and the material force of justice. *Theory & Event, 22*(3), 524–550.

Bayley, A. (2018). *Posthuman pedagogies in practice: Arts-based approaches for developing participatory futures*. Palgrave Macmillan.

Bishop, C. (2004). Antagonism and relational aesthetics. *October, 110*, 51–79.

Blackman, L. (2015). Researching affect and embodied hauntologies: Exploring an analytics of experimentation. In B. T. Knudsen & C. Stage (Eds.), *Affective methodologies: Developing cultural research strategies for the study of affect* (pp. 25–44). Palgrave Macmillan.

Butler, J. (2001). Giving an account of oneself. *Diacritics, 31*(4), 22–40.

Cixous, H. (1994). *The Hélène Cixous reader* (S. Sellars, Ed.). Routledge.

Cixous, H. (2004). *Portrait of Jacques Derrida as a young Jewish saint*. Columbia University Press.

Cixous, H. (2008). *White ink: Interviews on sex, text and politics* (S. Sellars, Ed.). Acumen.

Conley, V. A. (1992). *Hélène Cixous*. University of Toronto Press.

Derrida, J. (1999). *Adieu to Emmanuel Levinas* (P.-A. Brault & M. Naas, Trans.). Stanford University Press.

Derrida, J. (2000). *Of hospitality: Anne Dufourmantelle invites Jacques Derrida to respond*. Stanford University Press.

Derrida, J., Cixous, H., Armel, A., & Thompson, A. (2006). From the word to life: A dialogue between Jacques Derrida and Hélène Cixous. *New Literary History, 37*(1), 1–13.

Hansen, M. B. N. (2006). *Bodies in code: Interfaces with digital media*. Taylor & Francis.

Haraway, D. J. (2016). *Staying with the trouble: Making kin in the chthulucene*. Duke University Press.

Large, W. (2015). *Levinas' Totality and infinity: A reader's guide*. Bloomsbury Academic.

Lévinas, E. (1991). *Otherwise than being: Or, beyond essence*. Kluwer.

Retallack, J. (2004). *Poethical wager*. University of California Press.

Schrift, A. D. (Ed.). (2014). *The logic of the gift: Toward an ethic of generosity*. Routledge.

Sellers, S. (1996). *Hélène Cixous: Authorship, autobiography, and love*. Polity Press.

Shiach, M. (1991). *Hélène Cixous: A politics of writing*. Routledge.

Stewart, K. (2008). *Ordinary affects*. Duke University Press.

Stewart, K. (2010). Afterword: Worlding Refrains. In M. Gregg & G. J. Seigworth (Eds.), *The affect theory reader* (pp. 339–354). Duke University Press.

Still, J. (2010). *Derrida and hospitality: Theory and practice*. Edinburgh University Press.

Turner, P. A. (1992). Hélène Cixous: A space between – Women and (their) language. *Literature, Interpretation, Theory, 4*(1), 69–77.

CHAPTER 10

100 Words Exactly

The Art of Thesis Drabbling

Elizabeth Allotta, Dewi Andriani, Emma Cooke, Eloise Doherty, Mel Green, Karen Madden, Renee Mickelburgh, Muhammad Ali Musofer, Rebecca Ream, Preeti Vayada and Elizabeth Mackinlay

Introduction

The capacity to write sits at the heart of academic work and is crucial to achieving success. For higher degree research students, academic writing calls for various skills, competencies and knowledges, and is experienced as a process of participating and becoming adept in the textual and discursive practices of specific disciplinary cultures. In this chapter, we share our collective experience of experimenting with the genre of 'drabbles' as a way to share the theoretical story of our thesis and academic work, and to gesture towards the ways in which higher degree research and writing might become a rebellious pedagogic and performative praxis. Drabbles are short works of fiction of exactly 100 words which explicitly aim to tell a story in a confined space in a way that is short, sharp and snappy. The drabbles we share here were written while away on a week-long DRAW (Departing Radically in Academic Writing) writing retreat in December 2020. In 100 words we departed radically from academic writing, to show not tell our thesis stories and our delight and love for words that world. The chapter itself weaves these together along with our thinking and wondering about our work as a way to, through and for rebellion in thesis and academic writing more broadly. With trepidation, joy and a sense of loving play, we wrote with each other and the thinkers we so dearly loved. It was a rebellion of a poetic, creative kind that weaved new ways of knowing, being, becoming. Formed in a storm of wind, rain and ideas, these pieces that make a chapter are fragments that matter, and are rich fodder for a revolution.

With scraps of thesis writing in hand, we rode the waves to come together to depart radically. Be playful; remember this is serious work. Why not 'drabble' the story of your thesis in exactly 100 words, no more and no less? On a secluded island we wrote in silence while a storm raged inside and out. We

 | DOI:10.1163/9789004516069_014

typed these words and deleted those, all the while listening for the waves in our minds that would show, not tell, our thesis stories. This is our story, a story of drabbling to depart radically in academic writing as higher degree research students.

We were eleven in number, joined by three, four, five – then six. North, south, east, west. Wording, writing, worlding and wondering about how to ride the wave in the mind with the likes of Virginia Woolf, Giles Deleuze, Felix Guattari, Ursula Le Guin, Kathleen Stewart, Sara Ahmed, Donna Haraway and Jonathan Wyatt. 'Woolf's words are autonomous and sovereign beings who love and live in the world, cheeky little rascals!' Liz laughed. Renee nodded, 'Yes, all you need is to listen to the telling and then maybe you have a carrier bag of fiction to hold onto.' 'Let's drabble!' Elizabeth exclaimed.

To tally the story as it is told: a tale with a start, a middle and an end. A story within, contained and yet with a life of its own, of life and living. An exploration of being human with emotions, thoughts and views of the world. An exposé of our passions, fears, thoughts, beliefs and values. In all their ordinaryness and real-ness. Of the world we see and experience. These are the snapshots of what we see and have discovered, what we have learnt and share with you, the reader. Who we are and what defines us. DRAWers' drabbles.

So who are we, as writers, researchers, DRAWers? We share our stories of what is 'rebellious' about our research and why we DRAW. Why and how do we resist and re-imagine academic practice, academic writing and the academy as we know it? Why and how is our practice 'rebellious'? What will be the impact of our practice of rebellious knowledge production? How will our practices potentially address the critical issues in the future of teaching and learning, and the critical complexities and challenges of contemporary life? What are the implications for DRAWing and research methodologies that resist, push-back, practice differently?

On reading our stories, we invite you to explore and question yourself as an academic writer. How do you see your words? Would you welcome something other, willingly be part of a rebellious activism that challenges the status quo? Will you join the writers who precede us and have sown the seeds for change, who have questioned and write about what is and what could be? Will you accept the challenge to be part of the change? To DRAW with us, to depart radically from academic writing and be part of something other through rebellious action and expression of experience?

She said to address the theme of the book. At first, they were terrified. They just wanted to write a thesis; no one had said anything about revolution. Then they came to see that turning their words around could be an act of rebellion in and of itself. First, she said, write 100 vulnerable words about why your thesis work matters; *really* matters. Second, 100 words about what matters most. Third, a moment to share the heartbeat of the matter, the sense-and-response abilities which give these words rhythm. And then she said, in 100 words, why is this writing rebellious?

Imaging and Writing Something Other

Positivist, looking for humanness in research, in communicating teachers' realities. Wanting to tell more, the whole picture, of being human, human experience, lived experience. I searched for something other, something to tell more, to share lived experience in all its complexity. It is not one theme, not one event that impacts on a human being. It is life, the accumulation of experiences, our interpretations, our stories. I wanted to share teachers' stories of what they experience. To tell the stories of lived experience with honesty, respect, dignity and acknowledging what it is to be a teacher today, to be human.

DRAWing – departing radically from academic writing – a challenge to what I have known, the prescribed and expected way. DRAWing invites creativity, writing differently, viewing, experiencing and expressing the world from a different perspective (Wildy, 1999). Following in the footsteps of St Pierre, Lather, Stewart, Ellis, Bochner and Deleuze (Ellis, Bochner, & Rath, 2001; Lather & St Pierre, 2013; Richardson & St Pierre, 2018; St Pierre, 2011, 2017), I retell the rich stories of teachers' lived experiences, shared with intimacy, honesty and openness. Theirs are the untold impact-ful stories, the lived realities not shared with colleagues for fear of well-known observed, experienced repercussions and negative consequences. Exploring the silent worlds of teachers, their stories raise questions, rattling and challenging the status quo.

Through exploring the stories of practising continuing[1] teachers, we gave insights into the challenges that they have encountered and navigated and how they continue. What do their stories tell us that can support beginner and early career teachers in continuing their journey in the profession? What realities and issues are highlighted? What do we need to acknowledge and address to improve teacher retention? What do we need to do to support their professional development and development of expertise? Through storying we gain insights into the complexities that impact on teachers at all stages of their career and how they continue.

1 Teachers who have taught for more than five years.

FIGURE 10.1
DRAWing – playing with and rearranging ideas, coming together creatively and critically (© Elizabeth Allotta)

Neoliberalism has given rise to accountability and data metrics in education. It requires transparency and analysis; it is devoid of humanness. Through DRAWing we share human experience, our lived experiences, who we are through sharing and expressing our emotions, thoughts and reflections in a safe and supportive environment. Through sharing our stories, we acknowledge each individual's reality, how we interpret our world and our experiences. Through DRAWing we express ourselves with intimacy and integrity, reflecting the wholeness of our humanness, breaking the rules by going beyond the expected and accepted. We write with heart, exposing and challenging the status quo.

Elizabeth Allotta

Crossing Borders

I gaze into the distance and travel through this journey which has been filled with sharp bends and full of conflicts. My journey to go *merantau,* is a practice normally performed by males in my ethnic group community, Minangkabau, in West Sumatra, Indonesia, which has a distinctive matrilineal system where the family name and heritage are passed down to daughters. I crossed many borders tangibly and conceptually and here I am, in the Australian academic space, and pronounce myself a transnational postgraduate student from a non-western postcolonial background. Yet my others are multiple as they entangle messily into one.

This thesis is an autoethnography, written around the metaphor of a journey, one which has no definite beginning or end, but continues from one to the next. It is 'not about a destiny but about the adventure of trips, crossings, trudges, abrupt and gradual awakenings' (Cixous, 1976, p. 885)[2] and I invite you to join me. I join the voices of the Indonesian female students and mine to share our experiences of crossing borders in the hope to create understandings of differences, and the ways in which the socio-cultural-political and gendered world of higher education is imagined and experienced by female students from Indonesia.

When reading Cixous' narratives, which mix stories with theories, she found that Cixous' work at first was blurry and ambiguous, especially the concept of the gift, seeming to lie buried beneath the creative and sophisticated poetic stories of her writing. Cixousian gift is hidden in every corner and she decided to go on a journey inside her works in the hope that she might find a way to analyse the concept of the gift and apply it to her experience of accessing international education in Australia. What kind of gift has she been given? She cannot leave this page unturned.

I know that it is a difficult job for a female student whose first language is not English. I know I am struggling, but I will keep going with no intention of turning back. This alternative way of academic writing gives a space for me to play, to be experimenting and to be rebellious. Minh-ha (1989) reminds me and exclaims frantically, 'We are therefore triply jeopardized: as a writer, as a woman, and as a woman of color' (p. 28). I have learned to disobey the dominant Eurocentric masculinist epistemology that controls institutions and the elements of knowledge. And yes, it is a challenge.

Dewi Andriani

---

2 Cixous uses this expression to refer to a woman's body and the ways women could write about their femininity, which could be infinite and complex. I cite this in the context of my writing about my journeys and experiences.

FIGURE 10.2
'Journey' by Avisa Putri Agustina, 2021

Children's Accounts

I care about the young children whom I research with. So much so, that I can no longer bear to tell their lively stories in dull prose. I tried to cut myself out of being in relation, but the surgical tools slipped clumsily from my fingers. I tried to shrink and contort my body into the fly that they wanted on the wall, but I slipped from the dainty footing and fell into the elephant costume. Initially, I pretended to ignore the big, obnoxious and grey skin that I donned and dragged around, but I could not endure it for long.

You are a becoming: becoming competent child, becoming not-child, becoming high-functioning, taxpaying citizen. You cannot *become* without us. We beckon you to come with us. We will teach you the tools to self-regulate, regurgitate, strangulate your unbecoming parts, until you might become full. Full of *our* ways and knowledge. We will knead you like dough, make you fit in the oven, and you will be risen under supervision. You lack certain ingredients that we will provide, but we do like our bread with a smear of child autonomy. So, watch our show as we dole, roll, out moments of autonomy.

Thinking about how we value knowledge, I have been wondering around theoretical frameworks, writing conventions, power structures, and how I might write differently so as to deconstruct these constructions. Envision a high-rise building: adult rationality is on top (the penthouse is peer-reviewed academic writing), and adult-selected contributions from children are placed on lower and less valuable levels – perhaps in the 'accounts office': we often hear that children's views are being 'taken into account'. What about their messy, playful and indecipherable stories? We can speculate that these are in the bins out back or swept swiftly and silently under the carpet.[3]

Interview *children*? Children should just 'take their medicine': feedback from a top-ranking journal. They only publish *numbers*, duh. If a tree falls in the forest and no one measured it, did it even happen? I imagine the journal editor as one of the 'plastics' from the film *Mean girls* (Waters, 2004), dramatically tossing her hair and declaring, 'You can't sit with us', thereby banishing us qualitative researchers from a seat at their prestigious table. As for the post-qualitative researchers ... frankly, they do not even register on the radar. The name of this remake would be *Mean, median and mode girls*.

FIGURE 10.3 Exasperated with conventional research (© Emma Cooke)

Emma Cooke

3 This drabble has been drawn from my PhD thesis (Cooke, 2021), and I wrote it in response to Laurel Richardson's concept 'theory is architecture' (2003, p. 927).

Reaching, Rebellion, Reason: Will Not as Ethical Imperative

Musician, audiologist, science and the song,
I am both, both are me, and were so all along.
Evolving over time they've been apart, never one,
But now's the time to integrate, to seek new horizons.
Evidence-based practice, audiology demands,
Numbers are the only way, you better learn that fast!
Music is creative, yet still an elite art,
Prevailing discourses exclude, those who some feel can't.
I protest however: music can be learnt by all!
Hearing loss should not exclude, when someone feels a call.
Feeling, too, is crucial both in research and in life,
Understanding demands words, illuminating life.

Here I tell a story, in numbers and in words,
Auditory processing meets music education.
How do children progress, if they have hearing loss,
And participate in flute lessons, beside peers who do not?
How might auditory processing link into this?
Does it improve with lessons, or make them go amiss?
This is about a journey, the knowledge that we sought.
As words and numbers come together, prompting readers' thought.
Exploring new ideas, beyond discipline bounds,
I'm tired of being limited, so seek to break new ground.
Positivist theory, here, meets poetry and posts,
Exploring possibilities, challenging what we know.

Dibble, dabble, dribble, drabble, march along with me.
You think you see the formula, but that's not going to be.
You walked the paths, not conjured them, so map for all to see,
The forest thoughts and shadow things, moving among the trees.
Dibble, dabble, dribble, drabble, I can't find the words.
For just like cats, so many words are challenging to herd.
They're flitting, flicking shadows, hiding quiet and unheard.
Well you should know, the witch's cauldron only works when stirred!
Stirring, stringing words together, tying, trying hard,
To illuminate them while preserving that at heart.
Will I succeed?

These children are complex, multidimensional humans.
They will not be defined only by hearing status.
Rebellion! Get to the point!
Hearing the children's voices is important.
They will not be codified into shadows; they will not be silenced.
Rebellion! 'Raw data' belongs in appendices!
Poems are not embellishments to be glossed over, skipped, forgotten.
They are central to the story.
Rebellion! Make your meaning clear!
Positivist theory can sit beside post-qualitative sentiment, telling meaningful stories and quantifying them.
I will not bend some puzzle pieces to fit others.
Rebellion! Start bending!
No. Sometimes wilful resistance[4] is an ethical imperative.

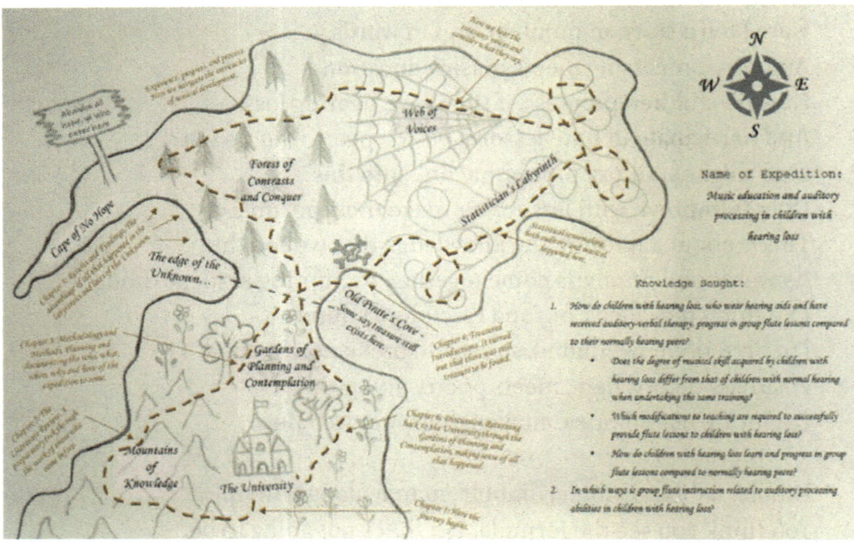

FIGURE 10.4 The orienting map offered to readers of my thesis to help them navigate when the paths disappeared (© Eloise Doherty)

Eloise Doherty

4 Ahmed (2014). Here, like Ahmed's wilful subjects (Ahmed, 2014), I wilfully resist conforming to the dominant epistemological and ontological discourses within my respective disciplines. This is not wilfulness for the sake of it – this is my reaching arm (Ahmed, 2014), my will to do better. In stating that I will not, I resist, but I also wish such constraints to not be so. I will them not, and therefore wilfully will not.

From Read-i-cide[5] to Bibliophilia: Time for Reading Enjoyment

I am a teacher who reads and reader who teaches.[6] Over the past 25 years, I have encouraged and advised many hundreds of children and teachers with ideas and suggestions for reading, whilst also sustaining a *spirit of freedom* (Woolf, 1925, p. xxx) in their book choices. I have taught my inquiring students to precisely and powerfully find *the very spot* on the shelves of the school library; to locate *that* special book in the multitude of beckoning titles. From the enchantment of the magic chair and carpet, I have strived to provide the deepest and widest and fullest possible enjoyment in reading experiences.

So then, let's consider a Deweyan (Dewey, 1916) sense of what school is. School is a place for students to thrive and flourish. Where students become active members of a democratic community. Where students are supported to develop opinions, preferences and capacities. Where students are provided with opportunity to explore ideas and interests, emotions and experiences – with their own and others' wellbeing at heart. Where skills are learnt and applied for authentically useful purpose. Where personal development prospers for the betterment of all. Where knowledge and understanding of the World and all of its complex demands is advanced. Where love is grown.

There at school, I found hearts beating, minds wondering, limbs twitching. What was the plan for that day? That lesson? Did it rouse curiosity? Release imagination? Pass the test? Did tiny Tim stay in his seat for the entire time? Did Susie-Rose hold back her tired tears? Did Asher regulate his emotions without need of reinforcements? Did Billy really need to sit next to Millie? Could Courtney *please* stop that hacking cough? Did the planned plan go to plan? Did the intended learning intentions triumph the success of the success criteria? Did students engage in reading for enjoyment? Yes, indeed!

Then, I'll not acquiesce. I'll neither be quietened nor quashed. For too long I've quelled my qualms. I've lain awake with worldly worries; visions of weeping and wailing children. They're trapped in the death zone of *required reading* and inane fact extraction. I refuse to kowtow to soporific literacy position papers and the clearing of library bookshelves. In this epistemological tribunal, I denounce your demeaning indictments of anti-establishment gibberish, nostalgic claptrap and overly sentimental prattle. It's you sirs who are guilty. You've stripped the young of their entitlement to books, reading enjoyment and aesthetic development. It's time for a reading revolution.

Mel Green

5 Gallagher (2009).

6 Parts of this work have been drawn from my PhD thesis and a co-authored conference presentation (Mackinlay et al., 2021).

Woolf's Rebellion: Within and Without

I pick up a pen and open to a new page.[7] Whenever I write, I sense Virginia is nearby. 'We write, not with the fingers, but with the whole person', she says. 'The nerve which controls the pen winds itself about every fibre of our being, threads the heart, pierces the liver' (Woolf, 2015a, p. 141). My whole person, every fibre of my being, is threading and piercing, anticipating my moment to DRAW. Virginia is nearby; her radical departure urging me on. I move my pen with every fibre of my being. Whenever I write, Virginia is nearby, urging me on, within and without.

It is true I am a PhD candidate; it is true I am employed as a leader in a girls' school; but what experiences have I had with Woolf that impact upon my leadership work? The focus on girls and women is the reason why women have succeeded as leaders in girls' schools before they have succeeded in the other professions (Woolf, 2009b, p. 140); so, what possible need for Woolf would there be in such a place as this? This work has just begun; equality is still a dream; there's so much to be done. Woolf's 'queer effect of atmosphere' (2015b, p. 137) persists, even here.

I am Clarissa Dalloway, looking back over a life, a life made up of choices. Did I make the right ones? Where would I be if I'd made others? In this life of leading in girls' schools, my feminist project, have I made any difference at all? I have worn my suits, held meetings in my office, delivered speeches and taught lessons. Was any of it feminist? Who is more equal now as a result? Clarissa and I look out of the window and consider our own end (Woolf, 2009a, p. 157). What can feminist leadership do, I wonder. Virginia's voice urges me on.

'But this is not recognisable academic writing!' 'Don't you want your thesis work taken seriously?' 'Reference the seminal works!' They began as voices from beyond but now swirled within my own mind whenever I picked up my pen and opened to a new page. 'I discovered that if I were going to [DRAW] I should need to do battle with a certain phantom. And the phantom was a woman' (Woolf, 2009b, p. 141), for she was my own self. 'Depart! Depart radically!' I shot back. 'Woolf belongs in your academic scholarship on leadership and you know it!' The rebellion rages on, within and without.

Karen Madden

---

7 Parts of this work have been drawn from my PhD thesis and a co-authored conference presentation (Mackinlay et al., 2021).

Wandering towards the Garden's Affect

I shove the gate from its latch, wincing as it cries resistance. The chain-link fence rains rust flakes that float to the ground, resting gently on botanical ideas and ideals growing up and out wilfully across dis-used garden paths. Everything here is overgrown and uncertain. Shadows shimmer amongst the leaf litter; tendrils reach outwards and upwards for something to grab. I sense that if I look hard enough there is something else sitting, just out of sight, between the leaves (Holmes, 2011). They are the spaces where feminist and ecofeminist ideas have gone to seed. This is what composes the present moment.

I clutched a scrap of paper in my hands when I pushed through that garden gate. Val Plumwood's words were scrawled in green (Holmes, Martin, & Mirmohamadi, 2004): 'to understand…a language of the land requires a deep acquaintance with some place' (Plumwood, 2002, p. 231). I am determined to make a deep acquaintance with this garden in this space and time. It requires spending time in place: time to understand the seasons; time to observe; time to wander; and time to wonder. I need time here to coax plants into bloom; to discover what is growing and what is not; what bees visit and which ones the birds prefer.

She dragged her basket across the path. The hunt was disappointing, and her basket was empty, despite hours in the field. The wind was a frenzy of screams and whispers; terrible conditions for capturing words. They tended to disappear into the crevices of rocky outcrops, scared of the wailing that reminded them of witches and forbidden spaces. She plumped her wings and cast her eye skywards. Elevation might be the antidote to stagnation. Something glistened in the undergrowth. She took a deep dive towards the shiny thing. When she arrived, she realised it was just a trick of the light.

Gardeners often keep to the side path, the one paved with certainty and sharp edges and good intentions. I sensed safety along this path most travelled. You're less likely to stumble or get into trouble. Yet following this path didn't seem right; it forced feminist words into dis-use. So instead, I've followed a desire line. It is a rebellious writing path that meanders and curves. Foliage often hides the way forward, smothering secrets in the soil. Wandering requires paying attention to the plots I can't see, the ones covered up by muck and mess. Their memories whisper stories on the wind.

Renee Mickelburgh

Desire to Higher Education: Entangling in Intense Conversation

I am an unsettled traveller/nomad, travelling valley after valley. The nomadic wander is not just a physical move; rather it entangles multiple valleys, intellectual, emotional, social and others. A departure in one valley bursts a thousand unknown valleys. Desiring for and navigating to higher education is a complex process and tells different stories. For me, it sounds like traveling to multiple unknown valleys at the same time. Each valley is full of events and affects. Who knows what one will encounter in the valleys? When the wind will be calm and when will it turn into a rebellious/troubling storm?

As a nomad PhD student, I am entangled with the intensive stories of four female postgraduate refugee-background students about their desire and navigation to higher education in Australia. Thinking with the Deleuzeo-Guattarian rhizomatic (Deleuze & Guattari, 2004) desire lines and Sarah Ahmed's (2014) wilful subjects, we (four female refugee-background postgraduate students and I) are on the journey to explore and shape the multiple unknown valleys through telling our stories. At times the stories entangle with each other and form a complex valley, and sometimes they become a line of flight and create a new valley. The stories affect and get affected. Everything affects.

Sitting in the valley, he gazes at the mountain covered with snow. He becomes fascinated with the white shining glacier. The mountain looks smooth to climb. He talks to a mountaineer and he reveals that the glacier is not smooth; it has huge crevasses, and the weather is also harsh. Before climbing, one requires extensive training and acclimatisation. The higher education institutions are shaped in a way that apparently looks smooth to navigate but, in reality, have their own unseen crevasses. Everybody crosses them with their own reality and capacity; therefore, every student has a unique story to tell.

What is interview? Isn't it a conversation? Isn't it a way of telling stories? Why am I supposed to re-present those intensive conversations in the form of a prescribed/rigid academic writing that loses the conversational life? When we read a book, don't we converse with the author? Even if we stop reading, don't we still keep conversing with the author while we run, eat or even sleep? If a major part of the research is a conversation, then why should I not write my thesis in the form of conversation and story? Why shouldn't I allow myself to be creative?

Muhammad Ali Musofer

FIGURE 10.5 Hussaini village in the Hunza valley, Pakistan (© Muhammad Ali Musofer)

A Compost Thesis

I am a colonial settler trying too hard to settle on the Aotearoa[8] lands I adore. The earth matter seduces me. I am queer for her. I am a feminist, hard and then soft. I am a compostist in the making. Always becoming as my hands sink into her green moss and my feet stand shakily on her curvaceous contours. Anxious and unstable, I am unable to fully 'stand ... upright here' (Curnow, 1997. p. 220). But I am lusty and don't give up easily. On bended knees I ask her to be mine but she refuses me. But she loves me all the same.

They were colonial settlers like me. They were woman-*ish* like me. They were becoming Pākehā[9] like me. They were racist, like me? Through shouting and strolling, sheep urine and sweat we talked and did land, together. It was uncomfortable, difficult, joyous, fertile, non-innocent (Haraway, 2016), perhaps even violent as Jocelyn and I threw the dead ewe down the hill. Still, desire streamed like the waters Jill guided me down and I was left with compost love – love already inside bodies, dirty, fermenting. I learnt that flesh and sign are one on the (in)fertile Wairarapa lands and that is good for making compost (Haraway, 2016).

I was told to get it *done*. I was told again, get it *done*. How many times after that? I lost count. I didn't count because I was writing, not numbering. I was loving, not counting, proving or quantifying. I was lusting with Donna Haraway

8 New Zealand.

9 In this context, a descendant of colonial settlers in Aotearoa/New Zealand.

and believe me – that takes time! Her erotic adventures had me talking with my thinking flesh sitting down glued to her spider veins, excreting rich, thick, 'black milk' (Cixous, 1993, p. 78) on page after page, running around the Tararua Ranges, slipping, sliding, becoming with, and stained by, compost. In the end I looked back at my institution and laughed.

Composting is a worlding that breathes naturecultures. Composting is an ethico-onto-epistemology (Barad, 2011): it is situated knowledges that speaks response-ability. My thesis was a compost pile that couldn't be translated into a world where 'nature' and 'culture' exist (apart). Composting is not about unification or harmony. It is 'staying with the trouble' (Haraway, 2016) of the differentiated, situated fleshly stories that rise from the mud. Composting is about theory in the fingers that type, sweat and make. Composting requires shredding the white masculinist heteronormative system with loving, playful companions like Pan, half-goat, half-man, who tramples over the university relieving himself, spilling his golden shower.

FIGURE 10.6 Lyn Tankersley with goats, Wairarapa New Zealand (Photo: Lyn's husband, 2013)

Rebecca Ream

Navigating the New Roads

Do you mean to ask who 'are' I? Today, I am just a worried daughter of parents fighting for their health in a collapsed care system thousands of miles away. Other days, I am just a research student and a teacher. The culture, my social standing, my carer roles as a mother, wife; my migrant and residency status in a new country; being a mature-aged student, and other personal characteristics and identities also shape *how I see myself, how others see me* (Moser, 2008). Perhaps I am just constantly evolving as I allow myself to be immersed in new forms of learning.

The teachers are next to God, the gurus whose direction you just follow – 'no questions asked'. Some feeling suffocated in the traditional system, we crossed the borders for the lure also was collaborative opportunities with staff in a 'good' higher education system. Labelled as 'students–staff partnership' practices, getting accepted as student partners feels surreal. But will crossing the borders and participating in a collaborative program really change who we are? Will the silent voices speak? By telling our stories of how the experience has shaped our identities, we take the courage to be judged. And perhaps therein lies our voice.

Tell me, why should I read this? The part of your educational experiences in India or how your parents raised you, or why you decided to study here in this research-intensive university? Just tell me about the experiences in the partnership program. Beg your pardon; we won't. We are not shaped just by one experience for we have also bought a lot more baggage other than what we packed in our 30 kg suitcases. This may explain who we are and who we are becoming as we gather the courage to speak for ourselves and fill the quiet room with some noises.

Come home before it is dark! The dress is too short for the social gathering? Write between the lines. Say yes, ma'am, do you understand? Felt always trapped by the gatekeepers of morality, values and education in the country I come from. This is my last chance. I keep on repeating, do I still want to be trapped this time under the vile scientific conventions? Can the chaos of human experience and the voices of people be reduced to computer-generated themes? Finding meaning in messiness is how I rebel against those who warn 'Come home before it is dark!'

Preeti Vayada

She Left the House to Buy a Carton of Milk

Elizabeth dragged herself over to the fridge and reached inside. 'Oh fuck!' She sighed hard; it had been a long day writing. 'There's no fucking milk!' She grabbed her keys. Tyres squealing and handkerchief waving, she roared out of the driveway. She wound down the window and felt freedom follow, directing her towards a future she had forgotten. Elizabeth knew she was flying on the edge of no return; it found her and was all she needed. She spread her wings and flew. She meant to write, they later said, but left the house to buy a carton of milk.

She sips a glass of milk. She is soothed by the solitude of sitting on a chair, at her desk with pen and paper as friends in a room of her own. She sighs. The thought of having to fall in line behind the academic procession of men that pervades her world exhausts her. Blah blah blah says Professor von X as his band of monstrous men go on and on. How she wishes she could damn them all! She would set fire to their old hypocrisies, heap armfuls of dead leaves on the flames, and cry 'Let it blaze!' (Woolf, 1938, p. 34).

Elizabeth pours the milk into her hand and begins to write in white ink. It is writing born of her feminine body, wild, dangerous and free at last. Her words are nourished by mother's milk and pour from every pore in a rebellious stream. It blazes *her* trail of women's words worlding and smashes everything in its path, shattering institutions, and blowing up the law. It's 'an explosive, *utterly* destructive, staggering return with a force not yet unleashed' (Cixous, 1976, p. 882) and from now on, who can say no to her? She is everywhere but she's not deadly; she's beautiful and she's laughing.

She spills the milk and decides not to cry, but to embrace the personal-is-political relationship between autoethnography and feminist movement. She puts to work the tools of feminist theory to build a wise, loving and response-able praxis of feminist autoethnography. Elizabeth moves to write autoethnography, which is always already ethico-onto-epistemologically critical, wise and loving all at once; this is what makes feminist autoethnography a possible thing. Because for her love, being in love, and be/coming in love with feminist theory is most necessary personal-is-political work and the most urgent task we have in wording the world through writing critical autoethnography.

Elizabeth Mackinlay

∴

FIGURE 10.7
She left the house to buy a carton of milk (©Elizabeth Mackinlay)

She is ready to add the final full stop to this collection of drabbles but changes her mind. Perhaps, as Virginia Woolf subversively suggested, it is preferable to put that 'little twisted' and rebellious sign 'that comes at the end of the question' rather than 'end', because 'it has a way of making the rich writhe; power and prestige come down upon it with all their weight' (Woolf, (1931/2008, p. 160). Because she asked them to join her in creative and critical rebellion and they did – but they are not done yet. Now she wonders, where might the next DRAWing revolution be and why?

References

Ahmed, S. (2014). *Willful subjects*. Duke University Press.

Barad, K. (2011). Nature's queer performativity. *Qui Parle: Critical Humanities and Social Sciences, 19*(2), 121–158.

Cixous, H. (1976). The laugh of the Medusa (K. Cohen & P. Cohen, Trans.). *Signs, 1*(4), 875–893.

Cixous, H. (1993). *Three steps on the ladder of writing*. Columbia University Press.

Cooke, E. (2021). *Relaxation and unrest: A crystallization of children's experiences in early childhood education and care* [PhD dissertation]. University of Queensland, Brisbane, Australia.

Curnow, A. (1997). *Early days yet: New and collected poems 1941–1997*. Auckland University Press.

Deleuze, G., & Guattari, F. (2004). *A thousand plateaus: Capitalism and schizophrenia.* Continuum.

Dewey, J. (1916). *Democracy and education.* Macmillan.

Ellis, C., Bochner, A., & Rath, J. (2001). *Composing ethnography: Alternative forms of qualitative writing*. AltaMira Press.

Gallagher, K. (2009). *Readicide: How schools are killing reading and what you can do about it.* Stenhouse Publishers.

Haraway, D. J. (2016). *Staying with the trouble: Making kin in the Chthulucene.* Duke University Press.

Holmes, K. (2011). *Between the leaves: Stories of Australian women, writing and gardens.* UWA Publishing.

Holmes, K., Martin, S. K., & Mirmohamadi, K. (2004). *Green pens: A collection of garden writing*. Melbourne University Publishing.

Lather, P., & St. Pierre, E. A. (2013). Post-qualitative research. *International Journal of Qualitative Studies in Education, 26*(6), 629–633. https://doi.org/10.1080/09518398.2013.788752

Mackinlay, E., Green, M., Madden, K., & Mickelburgh, R. (2021, June 10). *Performing Woolf to depart radically in academic writing* [Paper presentation]. Virginia Woolf: Profession and Performance Conference, Vermilion, SD.

Minh-Ha, T. T. (1989). *Woman, native, other: Writing postcoloniality and feminism.* Indiana University Press.

Moser, S. (2008). Personality: A new positionality? *Area, 40*(3), 383–392.

Plumwood, V. (2002). *Environmental culture: The ecological crisis of reason.* Routledge.

Richardson, L. (2003). Writing: A method of inquiry. In N. K. Denzin & Y. S. Lincoln (Eds.), *Handbook of qualitative research* (2nd ed., pp. 923–943). Sage.

Richardson, L., & St Pierre, E. A. (2018). Writing: A method of inquiry. In N. K. Denzin & Y. S. Lincoln (Eds.), *The Sage handbook of qualitative research* (5th ed., pp. 818–838). Sage.

St Pierre, E. A. (2011). Refusing human being in humanist qualitative inquiry. In N. K. Denzin & M. D. Giardina (Eds.), *Qualitative inquiry and global crises* (pp. 40–55). Routledge.

St Pierre, E. A. (2017). Deleuze and Guattari's language for new empirical inquiry. *Educational Philosophy and Theory, 49*(11), 1080–1089. https://doi.org/10.1080/00131857.2016.1151761

Waters, M. S. (Director). (2004). *Mean girls* [Film]. Paramount Pictures.

Wildy, H. (1999). Statues, lenses and crystals: Looking at qualitative research. *Education, Research and Perspectives, 26*(2), 61–72.

Woolf, V. (1925). *How should one read a book?* Hogarth Press.

Woolf, V. (1938). *Three guineas.* Hogarth Press.

Woolf, V. (2008). *Virginia Woolf: Selected essays.* Oxford World Classics. (Original work published 1931)

Woolf, V. (2009a). *Mrs Dalloway* (D. Bradshaw, Ed.). Oxford University Press.

Woolf, V. (2009b). *Virginia Woolf: Selected essays* (D. Bradshaw, Ed.). Oxford University Press.

Woolf, V. (2015a). *Orlando* (M. H. Whitworth, Ed.). Oxford University Press.

Woolf, V. (2015b). *Virginia Woolf: A room of one's own and three guineas* (A. Snaith, Ed.). Oxford University Press.

CHAPTER 11

The Affect of Writing to It

A Collaborative Response to Encountering Deleuze and Guattari for the First Time

Elizabeth Allotta, Eloise Doherty, Dewi Andriani, Kathy Burke, Emma Cooke, Bonnie Evans, Mel Green, Karen Madden, Renee Mickelburgh, Muhammad Ali Musofer, Preeti Vayada, Elizabeth Mackinlay and Jonathan Wyatt

Prologue

This chapter presents the refrains of collaborative writing in response to a workshop presented by Professor Jonathan Wyatt (Edinburgh University) on the ideas and writings of Deleuze and Guattari at the University of Queensland's DRAW (Departing Radically in Academic Writing) retreat held on Minjerribah in December 2020. In this piece, we share our encounter with the words, language and theories of Deleuze and Guattari as calls and responses in between twos and aim to share the 'affect' of 'writing to it'. For many of us, this was our first encounter with the post-structuralist duo and, rather than enter into discussion about their work per se, we share here the 'affect' of listening to Jonathan speak about Deleuze and Guattari and the effect his words about them had on each and every one 'between us'. In doing so, we hope our collection of words stammering in the storm shows that there are creative and critical ways of becoming academic writers in collaboration, and that these, in and of themselves, may be the best hope we have of departing radically in our work to change the world.

Perhaps, an Introduction

It was a dark and stormy afternoon. The clouds hung low, like slabs of slate in the sky. Chunks of brown, brackish water surged towards the low dunes as horizontal rain spat at the windows. The waters of Moreton Bay, off the south-east Queensland coast are often unpredictable, but even so we were caught off guard by the salty summer tempest beating at the brickwork. Weather in this part of the world is rebellious; it is unpredictable; it refuses to sit still and do as

 | DOI:10.1163/9789004516069_015

it is told. And so, we sat inside, wondering nervously about the outside, when Professor Jonathan Wyatt defied lines of flight to arrive virtually at the DRAW (Departing Radically in Academic Writing) retreat to share his thinking and wondering about writing with Deleuze and Guattari. DRAW is a writing group for higher degree research students and others in the humanities and social sciences academic community at the University of Queensland who are committed to writing their work creatively and critically in rebellion, and actively respond to the question: 'What might the work of creative and alternative academic writing as inquiry in "post" qualitative research look like?'

This particular moment of encounter with Jonathan coincided with our stay at the Moreton Bay Research Station on Minjerribah, and the worlding refrain of a world in unpredictable wet season movement provided the bass line. Outside the room the weather was rebellious and its affect was evident inside the room. Following the winds and storm, the DRAWers were responding rebelliously to the prompt thrown by Jonathan. They were becoming winds through their collaborative writing to bring something to life and 'to free life where it's trapped, to trace lines of flight' (Deleuze, 1995, p. 141). The atmosphere inside and outside the room was wild and the audience of research higher degree students were perched precariously on the edge of their chairs as they waited in anticipation to be tossed and thrown about by the rebellion in the words and works of these two scholars. Without warning the students' bodies became without organs,[1] their minds hurled across the room in time with the tempo of the tempest as it raged. 'Writing', Jonathan began in close companionship with Ken Gale, 'takes it out of us, and takes us out of ourselves, and out of it. We get out of it by writing. We have to' (Wyatt & Gale, 2018, p. 121). Words like totalising, sensing and longing were then flung about as Jonathan shared his theoretical love affair with Deleuze and Guattari.

Before we had had time to gather ourselves, other agential cuts were made. Many of his words were as strange as they were strangely moving, so much so that when Jonathan asked, what if – like Deleuze and Guattari, he and Ken Gale – collaborative reading, talking and writing was a way to bring theory alive. We were ready to 'cut ourselves and bleed theory' and write to it. Rebellious lines

---

1 Readers will note that we use and refer to many terms, such as 'bodies without organs', 'refrains' and 'becoming' that are central in Deleuze and Guattari's work. One approach would have been to embark on a detailed study of their texts or consult indexes/dictionaries within and/or related to those texts before beginning this writing, but that is not the purpose of this chapter. Here we seek to 'write to' our experiences of being with Jonathan and, through him, Deleuze and Guattari. This is about the affective experience of an introduction, and it is therefore for you, the audience, to decide for yourself if we are write (right) or wrong in the thoughts, feelings, interpretations and conceptualisations generated by this stormy event.

of flight encountered assemblages of bodies without organs who clouded and territorialised over us with immanent imperatives and minor literatures, stuttering with emergent language in a logic of sense like nomads forever on the way. Together we then wrote in zigzag fashion to and with one another about the experience of being with Jonathan, being with Deleuze and Guattari and being in communion, writing in that moment. This chapter presents the refrains of this collaborative writing as calls and responses in between twos and aims to share the affect of 'writing to it'. In doing so, we acknowledge the myriad misunderstandings, inaccuracies and terminological inconsistencies, particularly around Deleuze and Guattari's work, that may be present in the writing below, and consider these not as unfortunate missteps or detours, but as the initial steps of a voyage that has not yet ended. The writings here playfully, wilfully and mischievously work with (and sometimes, against) Deleuze and Guattari in the moment of initial discovery. In them, we respond not only to Deleuze and Guattari, but also to the moment itself, in full embrace of the affective experience of the encounter, and the novel ideas that emerge in the collision between the self and theory in the moment of learning. We hope our collection of words stammering in the storm shows that there are creative and critical ways of becoming academic writers in collaboration, and that these, in and of themselves, may be the best hope we have of departing radically in our work to change the world.

∵

I watched the trees while Jonathan talked about Deleuze and Guattari, and occasionally heard fragments like … I forgot, but I think I heard some things. Writing affecting bodies and bodies affecting writing. Maybe people reading Deleuze and Guattari think bodily thoughts because the writing is so dense that they try to counterbalance brain discomfort with supplementary bodily comfort. Look at the clock: still another 15 minutes. Deleuze and Guattari: their names evoke an azure-coloured guitar in my mind. Jonathan mentioned music. Deleuze and Guattari strum a refrain on an azure-coloured guitar. Still another eight minutes. I feel like I'm stuck at a family gathering talking to those relatives that I don't really know but everyone speaks fondly of, so I smile along and tolerate their company. In theory, I know that I can leave but I feel a sense of obligation. It's hard to break the rhythm of a presence. Finally, an aunty needs help with the dishes, and so I take my line of flight away.

Take a line of flight. We are never stuck at a family gathering or any other kind of gathering. We are not stuck here now. Perhaps we are not here now at all.

Perhaps here is just the moment between where we have been and where we are going. I haven't been to Deleuze and Guattari either. I haven't 'done the work'. It sure felt like I was doing work. I guess I just wasn't doing *the* work. My work is not *the* work. I am coming from doing work that was not Deleuze and Guattari and on my way to going to Deleuze and Guattari next. I wonder what the weather will be like. I wonder what I should pack. I get the sense it will be a long flight.

This is very sticky writing for first thing in the morning. Yesterday I thought that the 8–9 pm timeslot was too late for writing about Deleuze and Guattari, and today it is too early. What seems to be the independent variable in this equation? Hint: it's not time. See? A bit of clarity never hurt anybody. When I said 'sticky' I meant 'stuck-y', but I don't think that is a word. It should be. I feel stucky alrighty. This writing feels like the PhD stuck place. I've no time to be dwelling here, thank you very much! My thoughts are already prone to tumbling on directionless winds; I have no need for a Deleuze and Guattari parachute to give me extra thrust. I'd rather be on the ground. You know 'the ground', right, Deleuze and Guattari? You mention it but I don't think you've ever come down to the ground.

∵

But and yet.[2] Three-letter words, not four-letter words, but perhaps they should be – spoken like explosions with enough grunt to blow the centre of any stronghold. We often dismiss them because they are small. Small is insignificant, small is not worthy of our attention, small is easily passed over, small should never begin a sentence, small is easily overpowered and ground down to dust before it has time to do any damage. These three small words with three letters. Two of them are fully aimed at contradiction while the other prefers connection and yet, somehow, they profess to be doing the same kind of conjunctive work. The first and the third differ from the second, always fighting within/against for it is too dangerous to do otherwise. The second holds the privilege of being allowed to be multiple but in its naiveté cannot see that to raise the possibility is the selfsame yet. It is easy to unite when you have no

---

2 These three words come from Woolf (2008, pp. 160–168), and yet they fit because all of us were not only thinking with Deleuze and Guattari, but with many others as well. These others were related directly to our own work and were therefore with us in that room too. Can you guess who the other philosophers might have been?

knots to untie. Yet, but, and a three ply not quite braided. There is a thread that hangs loosely between them, the othered letter 'why/y'. And yet, but?

> We may be in a jam now.
> We are. In a fix.
> If we use so few.
> How can we try out a new way of thi.. kno..
> Is it so we axe any big ide...?
> And. Yet. But. Why?
>
> And, yes, we must begin within the containments,
> the so-called 'safe' plots.
> From there we start plotting.
> Clouding.
> Writing into.
>
> Yet, we must launch from a place of confusion and annoyance
> We must use our angry, feeling, hurting, bleeding, beating assemblages to propel our thoughts out into places new and different
> Use those four-letter words!
> Think beyond the territorialisation, de-territorialisation, re-territorialisation
>
> But this work takes courage
> To disrupt the tribes
> Free the fixed shackles
> Push further and further into the fluidity of wide-open smooth spaces
> So, keep up the fight
> Raise the possibilities, the multiplicities
> Push further and further
> Ply your wares
> DRAW on your writing allies
> to take those lines of flight

I love the word ally. It feels like a whole basket, a-tisket-a-tasket, of love and all in a four-letter word. ALL-Y. It too embraces a small three letter word, all, with a 'why/y' at the end of the beginning smoothing out the striations which precede it. Re/turn it around Y'ALL, where are all in this together apart, singular in our separation, as multiple subjects we are becoming verbs. Perhaps this is DRAW, perhaps this is DRAWing and becoming a DRAWer. Taking a line of flight with the three assemblages of four and tw/o one and three, to L(L)AY it all down in the basket, a-tisket-a-tasket of love, and in its quartet to remain on refrain. DRAWing, RAW(roar)ing, AW(e)ing, Wings to Lizzy-ing, dizzy-ing writing that's fizzy-ing with the blood of life if we dare to write to it to take it out of ourselves. We have to. ALL-Y.

∵

Jonathan was talking about writing and becoming entangled with different concepts of Deleuze and Guattari: writing between the two-rhizome – bodies without organs – refrain – desire. My mind was juggling with those concepts and I looked outside.

'It is raining', I thought to myself. 'I cannot go for the walk this evening that I have planned since morning.'

I felt a bit down but suddenly my backyard popped up in my mind.

'At least my plants will get enough water today.'

I felt good.

I tried to bring my attention back to Jonathan's talk. I pondered on the question that I asked Jonathan about Deleuze's concept of desire. I tried to recall the points that Jonathan explained in his talk about the concept of desire. Desire is generally seen as negative, relating to lack of something. Deleuze and Guattari (1983, 1987) look at desire in a different way. They see desire as a positive and productive force. Desire does not emerge from lacking; rather the feeling of lack emerges from desire. The desire to write doesn't emerge from lack of something; rather we write to create and produce something. Isn't it interesting?

Deleuze and desire; you, anonymous writer, have given me much to think about. In lieu of the walk you cannot take, I will take a walk with desire and Deleuze, finding a line of flight – I am thinking about the genealogy of ideas, and about lack. Freud to Lacan to Deleuze. Freud and Lacan always find women lacking; Freud thinks, even, that women and girls perceive themselves to be lacking, and covet that which they lack. Thinking lack with Lacan, my understanding of his understanding of desire inherently positions men as its holders: women are the original Other, the (m)other, that which the boy child categorises as lacking. Here, I see what Lacan is lacking: where is the girl child? The one who never understood herself to be lacking before she was told it was so by someone else? This framework, which in its phallocentrism ascribes to me and all who share my body an absence I do not sense and cannot recognise in myself, sets me outside from myself. In the mirror stage, I cannot see myself reflected.

Deleuze and Guattari's conception of desire outside of lack, and instead into the real, into a world interacting, moving parts in relation with one another, frees me from a symbolic order in which I exist to symbolise the development of the male ego. Desire is something I can have; here I exist as a subject, able to aspire.

Amazing! You have opened up a series of intensive lines that have the potential to disrupt the assemblage/thought that is based on deficit or lacking. The lacking image of thought looks for some ground where a stable subject resides. That subject is a rational man. This image of the thought demands that everybody needs to idealise that subject and strive to become like that image. Deleuze and Guattari's concept of desire troubles that stable and rational identity and opens up to become different. That is a productive and creative process. Deleuze disrupts the stable being and tries to create a smooth space where a person can become other/different, rather than following a specific image of thought. We need to trouble the binary image of man and women and open it up to difference or multiplicity.

∴

This place brings back a nostalgic memory. I worked on that site in the middle of nowhere, in an exotic island. The site reminds me of that place, where I could see the ocean from where I am sitting. The sound of the toads after the rain, the crickets and the darkness outside were so natural. But inside this building is quite a contrast with what I hear from the outside. I feel like I was sitting in that office, at night after work, to call home. After dinner, I usually waited anxiously for colleagues who would take me back to the office. We drove through the dark of the night to the office, which was about 5 minutes from the camp. The office was full, just like the normal day. But this time of night, people at the office would call their loved ones. It was the best time of the day when we could connect with the outside world.

I imagine the room quickly fills with snippets of conversations. The usual greetings. How was your day? What did you get up to? And laughs or supportive replies. Good nights and speak soon. It is isolating to be so far away, physically and emotionally. Islands can be quite isolating, surrounded by water with no way back, to connect back, to connect beyond the safety of the land. And yet the expanse of water has a way of centring you. You find yourself, a place where you find yourself. You are one with your body, mind and soul. And then you are one with all your surrounds. So it is with writing. There are conversations around you and in your mind. These pester and tease you to escape. So, you let them free, slowly and cautiously, to place themselves on the page. To see them, for others to see them. They speak to you and you wonder. Wonder about their meaning, how others will see them as they read them, what meaning others will see as they read. Words. So much to say, and yet just symbols on a page. Words we speak, across the waters to loved ones. Words with their own meaning shared by those communicating. Words that define relationships, tell stories, connect and disconnect. Yet just symbols. Symbols with meaning. Many meanings.

What did we do in this office anyway? Wasn't it boring to be in the office day and night? We did not feel that way if the night came. It was time to call home and connect with your loved ones. My mother usually answered the phone. I would tell her how I missed her cooking and home. The feeling and desire to go back to the outside world after being caged for 31 days in that tiny island was unbearable. I would tell her I would be home soon and would imagine her special cooking would welcome me every time I came back from this site. Time flew so fast. It has been such a long time I left the site in that exotic island. From the seat where I am sitting now, the memory of being in the island has come back.

∵

'Write to it', Jonathan says. 'Take a line of flight.'
What has captured your interest?
To be able to write and see where it goes.
And then I think of the affective elements.
It reminds me of what Liz says, 'Play attention to the detail.'
To write, with attention to the detail.
I am lost in the concepts presented.
I am trying to understand.
The concepts being introduced seem so obscure,
inaccessible and incomprehensible at first encounter.
What has captured my interest?
It is the words.
It is the rhythm of words,
purposefully, intentionally placed on the page,
positioned in association with and to each other.
To evoke an image, a sensation, a feeling.
Words that paint a picture.

They do more.
They resonate and connect us on an inner, intimate level.
Words when shared form an intimate connection
between their meaning and the reader.
I read them.
A picture forms in my own mind.
I am alone in my private world.
The thoughts are my own
And I share these with no other.
Words and writing.
Writing is an act of solitude, of privacy.
There is an intimacy with writing, with words.

The challenge for me, though, is that I have to share something, and my personal, intimate, selfish thoughts will eventually be put on eSpace[3] for all to read. They will be free, generating their own lines of flight through minds and worlds. That petrifies me. I didn't even want to share some of this writing with my advisor, crying as I pressed send on emails that she requested, without yet knowing what the contents would be or what those contents would cost to inscribe on paper. I asked how I might remove some of myself from those pages, making them less personal without losing the essence, and was challenged by her response: 'This is a very powerful and honest statement ... I have no suggestions for cutting this.' My words had already taken their own lines of flight in my advisor's mind. Perhaps she saw elements of herself, other students, family members, acquaintances, but I will never know. It's not for me to know. Those lines have already flown.

To step out on a limb is to risk falling. But you will not fall. You are in flight. You may feel like you are flying alone. Be Jonathan Livingston Seagull (Bach, 1970). Be brave. Let the others scuff at you, call you crazy, fly away from you or sit on the wave-washed rocks day in, day out. Soar to new flights; fly beyond the limits the others fly between. Be free. Be brave. To be different is not comfortable. But at some point, it is important to acknowledge your thoughts and allow them to be free also. To challenge the status quo is the only way we can move forward and evolve. Think of it as innovation. Introducing new ideas will always be met with resistance. This is such a human trait. Yet we also welcome change. It may take time for change to be accepted, but once accepted it will spread. Persuade through the value of being authentically you. You have a voice. Others have a

3 eSpace is the University of Queensland's institutional research repository.

voice. You are the vehicle through which voices will be heard. Speak out loudly, honestly and with courage. Others will listen. They cannot deny the voices when you speak and write. Perhaps you are right in thinking that the words resonate on a level that is uncomfortable. But discomfort is an opportunity to acknowledge something within ourselves, even if it is difficult to accept. Our values and beliefs are being challenged. I encourage you to let the words free, to speak for themselves, to be interpreted as they will, and to be brave. You are growing. Fear nothing. You are freeing lines of flight.

∵

Thinking with and through Deleuze and Guattari, I am circling around the notion of becoming. Jonathan notes that Deleuze and Guattari contrast becoming with being, 'in the phenomenological sense, which is a kind of stasis'. Becoming, instead, is a process; through writing, the writer is engaged in a process of becoming. This speaks, to me, of movement, of openness to, and action within, the world. On this windy day I take a line of flight and am swept along to Simone de Beauvoir's concepts of immanence and transcendence. Immanence: objectified, stuck, held down and in place, repetitive. Transcendence: active, generative, orientated outwards, a doing-ness marked by subjectivity, intention, meaning. As de Beauvoir illuminates, this distinction is gendered; when men 'force [women] to assume herself as an Other', they 'doom her to immanence' (1949/2011, p. 17). At the same time, women know themselves to be subjects, to be a transcendence. Our existence is thus one of in-betweenness. Leaping once more into the air, I flit around in the history of ideas and land at one of my favourite essays, 'Throwing Like a Girl' by Iris Marion Young (2005), who finds de Beauvoir's ideas lying on the ground and picks them up again, throwing them into the air (like a girl) and seeing how they fly. Young's essay argues that feminine bodily comportment, mobility and spatiality is characterised by ambiguous transcendence, inhibited intentionality and discontinuous unity (Young, 2005, p. 35) – each of which is partial, fragmented and stuttering. Becoming is, perhaps, situated. Becoming is, perhaps, gendered. Becoming is, perhaps, political.

I have not had a personal encounter with D&G. They emerged a few times, but I had already made up my mind that they are difficult, but Jonathan could translate it to me in a language that I could comprehend. Thinking about becoming, I wonder what my writing will become? What is possible through writing? Jonathan gave a clever hint through the Deleuzian concept to plug a concept in and see what happens. Unexpected writing will be becoming through this experimentation. Of course, it is not happening arbitrarily but through extensive and intensive reading and writing as a process of becoming. Writing cannot do anything if reading does not follow it. They should be walking hand in hand. Through the relational process of writing and reading, my own concept can be created through my embodied experiences as we live with theories and we are indeed leaving theories. Through the process of writing, I am writing about writing and being playful with writing to create a concept. I need to involve things and people that I encounter, have a conversation with each other. I can see now that writing is indeed an intra-active entangled relationship between myself, my body, things and people around me.

I read these words about writing and becoming, and I feel I am becoming in the process. And what will become of this becoming? What will emerge in this emerging? In writing in between writing, we become, as you say, entangled. Thinking back to transcendence, it strikes me that these terms we have been talking about, freedom and becoming and transcendence, are terms rooted in the concept of the individual. But we are two women writing together, becoming together, working with the words of women who came before. Becoming-in-relation in between. Cixous implores us to write our bodies, to write ourselves as women, but what might it be to write as women, rather than a woman? To write collectively and in community with one another, from our embodied experiences? Might we then find a way to think and live and be with each other in a place beyond patriarchal-colonial thinking and living and being? You speak about living theory and leaving theory, and I would like to add another adjective to the list: loving. To write theory in between, I am thinking, is perhaps a loving kind of theory, a loving kind of writing. A love that nourishes life, Hélène Cixous reminds us, is 'a love that rejoices in the exchange which multiplies' (Cixous, 1976, p. 893), and this writing feels like, in our exchange, one that has multiplied. I rejoice. A writing together, writing in abundance. As Cixous reminds us, 'in one another, we will never be lacking' (Cixous, 1976, p. 893).

∵

I always thought of becoming as having an ending, reaching a place where one has become what one aimed to become; but tonight challenged me to think beyond small goals to the broader picture. When something or someone becomes one thing they are still becoming. Human nature is an endless evolution of survival, development, thought and exploration. It's not in our nature to stop; we always seek something, becoming in our search. 'When people stop, they get sick and die.' The words of a doctor proclaiming that they will not retire, until they absolutely must. Continuous becoming is actively and necessarily sought in their profession, but do they really see retirement as a trapdoor held open by the Grim Reaper that slams shut on their careers as their younger colleagues sweep them in, signalling the transition from becoming to de-coming as they slide backwards through old age?

You have found some meaning in the concept of becoming. I think it is useful how you are thinking about adults' becoming. I research early childhood, and dominant discourses often focus on children's becoming, at times to the detriment of children's being. What happens to young children today must be linked in a clear and useful way to children's futures, overlooking all the little experiences of being, or indeed little becomings, that are valuable in their own right. Even if such value cannot be captured in numbers or words. Perhaps society does not know what to do with young children or retirees when their everyday activities cannot be clearly linked to financial gain.

Linked to financial gain, now there's an interesting line of flight. I'm so sick of everything being linked to financial gain. And it's the 'being' in that sentence that's so telling, implying dead and done rather than live and kicking. Well, kick this: I prefer moving forward than backwards. To slow is to move towards being and to be is to disappear, die, stagnate forever. Deleuze and Guattari would probably argue that, even then, you are becoming; becoming bones, ashes, dust; becoming memory and myth. But I prefer to choose my becomings and make the best of those I can't choose. Becoming is both a passive and an active process as forces act around us and we respond to them. I want to look to the horizon and see possibility, because even approaching storms carry possibility – the possibility of rain to wash away the dust ... or the possibility of getting struck by lightning. We can't control the approaching storms, but we can steer our becoming through and beyond them.

∴

I sit in the twilight room, my eyes distracted by the motions of the trees as they sway violently in the wind. A cool air rushes through a nearby window, caressing my face with its touch. The words Jonathan says are resonating with me on some level, and I begin to take copious notes. The words of dead people, the webs of thoughts they made in their mind, had always captivated me. It has been so many years that I inhabited this world that I suddenly, right now, began to feel my head spinning even as the breeze continued to wash over me, calming my thoughts. As Jonathan's words swam over my head, I began to wonder who Deleuze was and why he was important. I appreciated the calm, kind clarity that Jonathan took to explain these clearly turgid concepts to me, and there were moments where I sensed some of the breadth of Deleuze and Guattari's ambition. As Jonathan spoke, and he began to unpack some of the linguistic complexity behind their concepts, I wondered if indeed their work had been mistranslated as it made its way into English. There was something in the sound of the words in English – line of flight, bodies without organs, assemblages – that clashed and crashed around in my head, creating an uneasy rhythm that I longed to be free of.

'Am I not pretty enough? Is my heart too broken?', Kasey Chambers' (2001) plaintive song sits with me in contrast to the brightly lit room. Her voice haunts and hacks me back to moments I would rather forget, skulking around in my body, brain and heart in re/turn. It is exhausting remembering what it is you are not. Not pretty enough means not smart enough, and not smart enough means you have to work and be harder, and working and being harder means that you cannot be soft, and not being soft means leaving your heart outside, and leaving your heart outside means that eventually you become so tightly tied up in knots that you are broken, crying too much and becoming too outspoken. If I was pretty enough and not too broken, I would walk right up to Gilles Deleuze and Felix Guattari with my tear-stained face to tell them quite plainly: while I think your poetic prose is pretty enough and not too broken, I don't really want to take a line of flight with you if it means leaving my heart outside. I hear the word assemblages, and feel pieces shattering and breaking the world asunder; I hear the phrase bodies without organs and feel my bones crumbling in refrain. I let the rhythm of your words raindrop on my window, I go to sleep dreaming of keys tapping out minor literatures, I wake in clouded territories of blank pages with words strange and familiar, I go searching for ways to write to it. But yet (rather than and, and, and) I have waited long enough and find that, while you might be able to, I can*not* leave my not pretty enough and too broken heart outside – and so I shan't.

I don't know where to begin. I don't know what I'm feeling, but it feels like something heavy, inscrutable, like words cannot touch it. It is joy in the beauty of your words, it is sadness, it is a tender poignancy of something lost, a time forgotten, a person we could have become. I have always been fascinated by the past, present and future all wound up into one, of the what if, then, of the endless possibilities and choices that we face. I shirk from the sneaking feeling, as time marches on, that we reach a point in the road where these choices began to narrow, the sum of our previous choices catching up with us, obscuring the horizon from our sight.

∴

My response after listening to Johnathan's speech was of nervousness as I overwhelmingly call my son asking for help to understand Deleuze. It was not so bad though; I was making sense of some things he was talking, in my own little way. The concept of 'being' and 'becoming' was 'clear and cloudy'. While 'being' is static, denotes stable, and fixed, 'becoming' is always in the process. In that context, I was 'being' silly by underestimating my abilities to understand philosophies. However, I am not 'becoming' Deleuzian, or rather delusional. We are all different in our own little ways. While some philosophers may sell like 'hot cakes', I affirm my commitment to the old block Paulo Freire (1970/2018). If writing is the process of my own becoming, I would rather write simple, reachable, readable. For that is the purpose of writing – reaching out to all and not to the privileged few. Writing is to immerse and provide purpose but should not be to scare, intimidate or strain you. It's okay to say it loud sometimes – 'I don't get you' – or break the relationship with the celebrity just like I do.

For you, then, this is the right flight path, to follow Freire, rather than switching tracks to Deleuze. Freire (1970/2018) too spent his life trying to reach a wide audience, rather than those on the path of privilege. You are already on your own line of flight, and that flight path hadn't crossed paths with Deleuze ... until now. Perhaps, to understand Freire's work your flight path needed to connect with Deleuze, like a stopover on a long haul. On this stopover you disembark, search the scene and spend some time in the flight lounge. Just being, and perhaps becoming also. Perhaps when you are in this transit lounge bad weather sets in, it becomes unclear and cloudy, and so you are forced to spend more time in this Deleuzian transit lounge. It's not forever, just for the time being. It might be a few hours, maybe a few days, weeks, months or even years. That is the beauty, and privilege, of higher degree research. Eventually, you will re-board the flight to Freire once more. And you will be on your way. But you will always remember that time you were delayed in the Deleuzian stopover.

Very well said. It's the journey that matters and not the destination. The Deleuze stopover was like a little fling, a little secret that may stay hidden in the book closet or may come out when least expected. Learning is fluid. Openness to admit the flaws, trying and engaging is what really matters. For what

Deleuze said may seem to be just sounds and howls in that moment. I open up the Wiki page to know more about 'body without organs'.

∴

I do like Jonathan. He had me at clouding. I'm not entirely sure what clouding means. Jonathan spoke into strange concepts at such a rapid-fire pace ... assemblage, territorialisation, de-territorialisation, re-territorialisation. I tried to keep up, I really did. I'm a PhD candidate, on a writing retreat at a research station! But Jonathan's curtains keep pulling focus. It's their heaviness. You just don't see heavy curtains like that here. Oops. I'm off task. Concentrate. Jonathon is still speaking into those tricky concepts ... stasis, refrains, backflips, body-without-organs, fluidity and fixivity. I'm having a hard time keeping up. I wonder if Jonathan could be my new husband. I like his intellect. Even though I don't quite understand him. I must concentrate if I'm going to marry him. Did I hear him right? Did he just talk about Jonathaning? He's now Jonathaning about plots of land and lines of flight. He shares a story of his reading group sitting in the same booth every time they meet. I think I'd like to meet him, there in the booth, and talk.

> Your marriage idea – daydreaming I would say,
> For there were many contenders nodding and noting to what he had to say.
>
> But your letter gives the comfort of knowing that I was not alone,
> Though not intending to marry him, if that is a console.
>
> I felt intellectually challenged for a while.
> Thought to get up and say goodbye,
>
> The alienation heightened with group engaging in a discussion,
> I don't belong to the world that is 'Delusional'
>
> For me, simplicity is the way it be,
> Without worrying about the complexity of 'being' and 'becoming'.
>
> Dear Deleuzioned,
> Such a calming response to my anguished soul.
> Your challenged intellect meets my bleeding heart.
> In a room full of nods and notes.

But please do not feel alienated.
Draw comfort from your DRAWing comrades.
It would seem we all had wobbles and worries over worldly refrains
as we thought into this thinker's thoughts.
He was after all a most becoming philosopher.
And we my dear friend are just at the start of always being and becoming.
So many concepts to conceptualise, theories to theorise, territories to de- and re-territorialise.
I'm so glad you stayed in this place where you belong.
Together we will shift the organs of our bodies into new positions.
There must be discomfort with this if we are ever to find different ways of doing things.
May all your lines of flight be long and free.
With love,
Mel
P.S. I am wondering if you would like to be our bridesmaid?

∵

There is a sense of pain when talking about refrain.
My head hurts. It feels like something is squeezing my brain.
A refrain, says Jonathan, is about marking territory, longing for territory, warding off chaos.
Terror claims territory. My chest tightens. Breath becomes air, like water in the shallows.
Territory. Enclave. A place of barriers and boundaries.
Terror-tory.
This is not my refrain.
I look out the window, searching for an escape to this refrain. An escape from the boundaries and borders that Deleuze and Guattari seem to have built around me with their inescapable words. All I see is wind and water and all I hear is the wailing of the curlews and a few bullfrogs croaking away the night.
Arak, arak, arak. Roop, roop, roop.
We have invaded their territory. Perhaps they are the ones feeling terror of our refrain.
I don't want to terrorise them with my refrain.
The truth is I chafe at this refrain. I want to think of a refrain as a bloom space, like Kathleen Stewart. I hope and dream of a worlding refrain where things grow without terror.

> Things. Ideas. Plants. Curlews. Bullfrogs. Where everything blooms without the terror of territories: an idyllic refrain. A refrain that lets things take flight and cross the invisible borders and boundaries of our minds and the land and the sand.
> Some might accuse me of a socialist refrain. But it is not. It's just refusing to be pigeonholed back into the terror-tory of that refrain. I prefer the common refrain.

Interesting! Everybody needs a little territory or space of her/his own. When we hum while cooking/taking bath/walking we try to create a little space to stand on for some moment. In other words, we put an umbrella up to make a little shadow for us. But suddenly we find a hole in the umbrella, sunlight comes in and shakes our territory. We find ourselves de-territorialised and try to find another territory for us through re-territorialising. Ah, but there is no permanent territory. You cannot step twice in the same river.

The territory you talk about reminds me of the way Karen Barad diffracts her words. I am no physicist and stumble and stutter as I wander around her words but what I see and hear could be that sunlight through the umbrella. She speaks about the way light in dark places pushes 'through and around boundaries'. When light is forced through a pinhole, light intrudes in unexpected places, in shadows, in places that should be places of total darkness. I like that idea of light in the darkness. It enlightens me.

∴

Make productive use of this time. Search, stretch, reach for a question. Ask about the clouds. None of the words make any sense to me at all. Refrain. They look up in acknowledgement of something familiar. Make productive use of this time. You don't have time to sit here for this long, not knowing, not learning, not doing, not … Make productive use of this time. Clench the pelvic floor. Now pull the belly button towards the spine. Add the glutes. Now inhale and let them go. Or is it exhale and let them go? I never know. Why do I never know? Assemblage. They nod in shared understanding. That must be another important word. I'd better write it down. Squeeze the pelvic floor, add the abs, now the glutes. Turn on glutes. There we go. Make productive use of this time. Listen attentively. It is laying the groundwork for future understanding. What even is this? Did I feel like this when I first read Foucault, Derrida and Bourdieu? Probably. Remember that trip away when I spent the whole holiday in my room reading about Foucault, Derrida and Bourdieu? Make productive use of the time, I had thought. Take a line of flight.

Everywhere I sense obligation, duty, command. Someone else, somewhere, watching me, telling me what to do, how to spend my time. What if I don't like it? What if I want to break free, take a line of flight, reassemble my body organs to create a new me, with untold capacities and potential? The words of old white French men linger in the room like a heavy raincloud about to burst. What was clouding again? They are old, they are white, they are French, they are dead. Does that mean I shouldn't give them a try? Try to sense the vibrations, the frequency, the waves in their minds, speaking to me across the multitude of chasms that separate us in language, time, distance, gender? I felt doubt creep in as I was pulled in this direction, and then that, suddenly feeling as though I wasn't sure where to go. But then I wonder what it is to create these kinds of divisions and doubts in our minds. How theory can exclude as well as include. I think back to Deleuze and Guattari with their radical aspirations on the eve of those heady nights in 1968, the university poised on the brink of internal collapse, and wonder what it is that our universities have become. In this time and place, with these pressures, with these politics of inclusion and exclusion, to make us feel as though we aren't good enough, that we don't belong.

I feel a sliver of sadness creep into my mind, wending its way slowly through the back alleys in my mind. I suppose I had always been an idealist. I dreamed of the university as an emancipatory space, one where knowledge would set us all free. These naive thoughts of a seventeen-year-old crept back to haunt me now and I realised that we will never truly be free until we break the shackles of the oppressive discourses that are always there, clutching their claws at our necks, waiting to ensnare us. Why aren't you working? Why don't you get this? I calmed the thoughts in my mind and allowed myself to be, like a pebble on the shore, oblivious to the tide about to engulf me.

Why don't I get this? Why don't I see my story and the stories of those whose stories I collect, in the theory of these old white French men? 'You have to be able to defend why you don't use them', they warn. 'They are who everyone is talking about now. If you are not, you'll need to defend yourself.' A lifetime of defending myself, of defending the women in my family, the girls in my school, the women I know, the women I don't know, always defending the women. Defending yourself is feminist work. It seems defending my feminist work is my next feminist work. A lifetime of practice should have me prepared. I don't feel prepared. I feel spent. Perhaps I too am the naïve seventeen-year-old who expected to be set free. Perhaps learning to defend myself will set me free.

∴

(Not a) Conclusion

I am back again at that Moreton Bay research station in the room with the big windows with these writers, with you all. When you were there, I was here in Edinburgh in my flat with the heavy curtains that pulled you off task. I am with you all now, differently. It's months on from then. Reading your text(s) it's as if I have stepped through the screen into that place by the ocean, that island writing retreat, at the tables with you, feeling, seeing, hearing the wind and storms, that event.

Yet I am now also here at my desk, writing in another apartment. This room has light curtains; they would not distract you. It's late northern hemisphere post-COVID-lockdown spring, with its sense of opening and release. From this window I see the plant-strewn yard where my neighbour trains her assistance dogs. I am hoping she will appear with Lawrence, her current one, and set up a new game, a new exercise, so that I can witness his endearing movements and skills.

I am meanwhile back with you looking out into the darkness, feeling the flows and currents here and now, there and then, these flows and currents of Deleuze and Guattari in the zigzag of writing between you. I feel your writing landing here, resting here, moving here in these moments; before long this multiplicitous text and all it speaks, sings and dances of, will move on elsewhere, finding its place with others.

My guitar rests against the wall, with its back to me, varnished brown, though I now can only see it as azure. I can only see it as Deleuze and Guattari playing their complex, arcane notes and ambiguous, terror-ful refrains.

Can you see how you're with me? Can you sense how your 'writing to it' evokes and provokes, elicits and affects? How I am zigzagging between you, between the becomings of you? I think about calling my 92-year-old mother, whom I have not seen for months, and telling her I miss her and miss her cooking. I have Deleuze and Guattari here on my couch and I am speaking with them, with these old white dead dudes, together with the gift of your words. I am with them as well as around your tables, thinking Deleuze and Guattari would also feel like they were stuck at a family gathering. Guattari, in particular, would be restless, wanting to shake it up, to move around in between us. I see Guattari, that blast of disruptive energy, being amused and energised by the notion that he and Deleuze were a stopover on a long-haul flight. He would be happy with that, with being a brief pause, a liminal space, a threshold, with being on the move.

Which this, your – now our – writing, is: always already on the move. Disruptive, disturbing, rebellious. Defiantly never pretty enough, always living and writing with a broken heart.

References

Bach, R. (1970). *Jonathan Livingston Seagull*. Macmillan.

Cixous, H. (1976). The laugh of the Medusa. *Signs, 1*(4), 875–893.

Chambers, K. (2001). Not pretty enough [Song]. In *Barricades and brickwalls* [Album]. EMI Warner Bros.

de Beauvoir, S. (2011). *The second sex* (C. Borde & S. Malovany-Chevalier, Trans.). Vintage Books. (Original work published 1949)

Deleuze, G. (1995). *Negotiations: 1972–1990* (M. Joughin, Trans.). Columbia University Press.

Deleuze, G., & Guattari, F. (1983). *Anti-Oedipus: Capitalism and schizophrenia* (R. Hurley, M. Seem, & H. R. Lane, Trans.). University of Minnesota Press.

Deleuze, G., & Guattari, F. (1987). *A thousand plateaus: Capitalism and schizophrenia* (B. Massumi, Trans.). University of Minnesota Press.

Freire, P. (2018). *Pedagogy of the oppressed* (50th anniversary ed., M. B. Ramos, Trans.). Bloomsbury Academic. (Original work published 1970)

Woolf, V. (2008). *Selected essays* (A. O. Bell, Ed.). Oxford University Press.

Wyatt, J., & Gale, K. (2018). Writing to it: Creative engagements with writing practice in and with the not yet known in today's academy. *International Journal of Qualitative Studies in Education, 31*(2), 119–129.

Young, I. M. (2005). *On female body experience: 'Throwing like a girl' and other essays*. Oxford University Press.

CHAPTER 12

Twin Stars: Circling with the Trouble of 'Co-diffraction'?

Nurturing Permission to Imagine Together Rebelliously in a Doctoral Peer Learning Environment

Portia Ungley and Kieran Sheehan

This chapter captures the relationship formed between the authors as an example of a pedagogic space, giving each other and nurturing each other's permission to co-diffract and co-produce. The metaphor of twin stars helps embody the reader within our connection, a shared creative cosmology. We thread the image of star formation through the chapter to help re-turn to notions of intra-action and entanglement, as a situated pedagogic space (Barad, 2007). We permit ourselves a period of noticing our entanglement in the rebellious pedagogic space as a way that 'connects adequate understanding to the analysis of our bondage, limitations and flaws, i.e. power' (Braidotti, 2019, p. 92) by consistently re-turning to compassionate speculation, further opening diffractive readings through metaphor, theory and speculative fabulation (Haraway, 2016). Through the metaphor of planetary alignments, we trace the interferences within the assemblage of our relating. We offer supervisors and doctoral students an example of a developing pedagogic atmosphere based on visual culture and intuitive artistic practice, which we believe is conducive to the act of diffractive analysis.

> Dissanayake calls us *homo aestheticus*, Henricks *homo ludens*, Ranke *homo narrans* – while Linnaeus' *homo sapiens* suggests an impulse to wisdom; listening to the news highlights, it seems we know and learn nothing – Socrates would not be impressed – most of us do not see our ignorance. We make sense of the world through gestalt and stories, following a shining thread of narrative, through an unfriendly world, storytelling our way to warmth, shelter and a bowl of soup, shadows flickering on the cave wall. With intimate complicity, the human impulse is to ask, 'Tell me a story.' Here it is. (Star fragment 1: A drabbled invitation)

> Diffraction is thus driven by the affective, discursive, historical, sociocultural and material conditions that exceed the disciplinary 'gaze',

 | DOI:10.1163/9789004516069_016

> to represent the ongoing folding-unfolding of the self and the world. (Burnard et al., 2021, p. 115)

We are Kieran (a movement artist, higher education leader, prof doc student) and Portia (a play researcher, higher education leader, prof doc student), in York, UK and Normandy, France, intra-acting through Zoom and Microsoft Word. Both in a space between institutions, both staring at these words, tracing the emerging diffraction. We are the dust left by a conference (Advance HE Teaching and Learning Conference, 2019), where Kieran danced and Portia dared others to play. We are our atmosphere (Slaby, 2020) found in a doctoral peer learning group, sharing the same supervisor, Professor Pamela Burnard, who is rapidly generating a rebellious generation of generous academic nomads.

Cutting together apart our way of being, the voice of this chapter is rendered in multiple cuts, revealing everything we are, other than being separate. We are a collective voice of our interferences, existing coherently, our twin stars forming within this writing. But we am also a singular voice, kieranandportia, writing into the folding, the re-turning to, the many triangulations of how we am *together*, a precedent given by Hélène Cixous' *we are I*, her threshold concept for interculturality (2009). For this reason, we have defined the process of being entangled in each other and its outcomes as 'we', the phenomena of diffraction a proposition between us, suggesting 'we' is everything that results from portia and kieran's inter and intra-action. 'We' is nothing before this relation (Kaiser, 2014, p. 280).

Barad emphasises this when she

> points to the effects of the event interacting with multiple agencies and making more events and effects. In Barad's formulation, the individual, whether human or object, is not an essential unit, but instead something that appears and performs as a component in an intra-action. Indeed, phenomena are precisely the ontological inseparability of intra-acting components. (Lucie, 2020, p. 18)

This lack of need for an actual human or object in an intra-action leads to the other voices of this chapter.

We *am* also the generators of Fauh who has become Juvenal, speculative fabulations that have joined us in this chapter (Haraway, 2016). Fauh haunted the initial generation of the chapter as a non-binary Afghan graffiti artist who enabled us to question the ethics of our collective curiosity. *They* emerged from our collective voice as an ethical check on the potentially onanistic content of this chapter's focus on diffractive analysis. Their gaze on us as two privileged professional doctoral students interrupted our diffraction and imagining, a pure cut making us aware of the risk of indulging in only the theory, making no connection with the earth.

As we re-turned to our intra-actions, we became troubled by the sheer fucking hubris of creating a queer, global majority character to offset our whiteness, our privileges, but felt that we could continue our journey if we allowed an onto-ethical observer into our co-diffracted space.

Fauh morphed into Juvenal, a transformation from a Kabul-based cipher to that of a different other; Juvenal, whose Roman namesake coined the question 'who will watch the watchers?'[1] They saved us from tokenistic intersectionality. Drawing on Karen Barad's seminal work *Meeting the universe halfway* (2007), we see that Juvenal represents the *ethico* of an onto-ethico-epistemological conceit, tracing the particular tunings of our entanglement, remaining with the trouble of our mode of writing. Juvenal completes the entanglement of the chapter to embody and notice the differences they generate with their interruptions.

Because of them, we am self-aware; we see our white fragility, our cis privilege and try to give voice to the othering that diffractive analysis may generate in its practice. Juvenal is a diffractive analysis of our pedagogic atmosphere, tracing the affective awareness we have of intersectionality theory, the respect we bring and Braidotti's command to remember the people we forgot to forget. The units of measurement in our diffraction are guided by Barad's phenomena; Juvenal is a phenomenon (Taylor & Gannon, 2018, p. 467).

Seeking twin star
I'll send you the link
Shall I write poems? Is that my contribution?
I'm doing some intuitive movement on the ideas
Well, we are throwing out every other academic convention

I'm really concerned about Fauh
Some people are going to hate this – but we play with even that safely – is this bravery or conceit?
But it is imagining outside of our imagination's habit (Gunn, 2017)
But it is giving each other permission – it is letting us become diffractive
We need to be affirmatively ethical – to do something about it
We bring our baggage, our houses, our academic strains, our affective selves – this is our entanglement

1 Juvenal, *Satire VI*, lines 347–348: 'Quis custodiet ipsos custodes?'

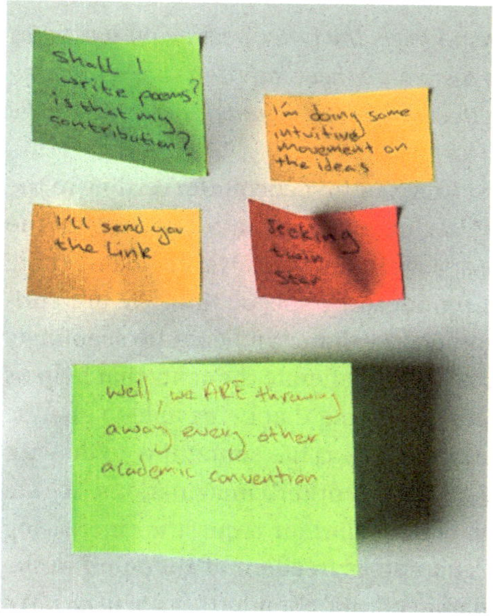

FIGURE 12.1
Star fragment 2: Email thread echoes

> This is about the ethics of imagination, what are we allowed to think about and who is allowed to think. (Star fragment 3: Transcript, 10 June 2021)

We stare at the tiny post-it notes, a rainbow dancing off the page. They are floating up to the reader through the photo. We stare at the bending and folding paper post-it notes. We stare at the phrases that we noticed from our emails. We stare at the corners of our chapter. We stare at the blank space between the post-it notes and see what we want to write: a generative space seeking out an ethical practice that holds us, a diffraction that is both brave and safe (Arao & Clemens, 2013).

We *am* a bit embarrassed about the indulgence of this chapter. We am wondering if we dare create a character that holds our privilege to account, gives us the necessary grit to recognise the way in which these words are entangled with the privilege of thinking about the thing we am thinking about. We am seeing that our words need to take our reader towards a happy, generative cynicism.

We and you see ~~Fauh~~[2] *Juvenal crawl out from under a big green sticky post-it, a gender-fluid graffiti artist from ~~Kabul~~ a city in the Republic of Intra-action, who is made of paper and ink. They have dark hair and don't speak* ANY *post-human*

2 Fauh's remains as strikethroughs are here for the reader to see (along with others) into the pedagogic space in which this chapter exists, to share the decisions we made behind the words in order to make the navigation of this space safe for reading and diffraction (Tapia, 2001; Lorde, 2007).

or feminist new materialism. ~~Fauh~~ Juvenal peels the other post-its off our page, layering them one over the other, laying them onto their body and staring at falsified handwriting, tracing the lines with their index finger and thinking about the shape of their emerging tag.

We are a diffractive analysis, the dust from our first encounter settling in the chapter. Do we dare to dance, to play? We are a journey into looking into the space that makes us, here. We are the spaces in between, we are the opening of new pieces of speculation, we are produced by speculation. We are curious about our ability to speculate together, to wonder and enquire seemingly through and of each other. We are our ability to generate thoughts that help us on a journey towards diffraction. We are suggesting that being able to analyse diffractively how we consider our doctoral journeys has something to do with kindness, respect and a willingness to be of each other's imaginations. We are enquiring towards an affirmative ethic which relies on 'a quest for increasing degrees of relational powers [which] guarantees freedom of the mind in the awareness of its true affective and dynamic nature' (Braidotti, 2019, p. 171). We are twin stars affecting one another *poietically* and politically, strengthening the possibility of being here on this page, differently, diffractively (Lubacz, 2021).

We are aware of the frightening, intimate nature of permitting professional doctoral researchers to become. We are encouraging doctoral students to play with each other. We are tracing our perception of intra-activity by diffracting conversations, by diffracted imagery, by using post-human theory, by using post-qualitative theory, by distilling our affective intentionality, by staying with the space between us as the focus of our we-search.

Intra-action is the 'mutual constitution of entangled agencies' (Barad, 2007, p33).

Intra-action is accepting that we make one another.

Intra-action is noticing how we are plugged into one another through our feelings, the environment around us, our historicity, the screens we stare at and the wrinkles when we smile (Deleuze & Guattari, 1987).

We am what?
Points of flexion where they mutate and collide
A murmuration of shamanic forging
The silent flock in the spaces between
A silent feather, the colour of nothing
Tumbling, floating, Brownian
Buoyed by hope
Anchored by rigidity

A ton of down
Each gust a reconfiguration
Stillness a confrontation
Tempered by experience and rigour
Each plume quill-split by thought
(Star fragment 4: Memoing Cixous' identities waltzing with our binary twin stars)

We twin the thoughts of our individual and mutual favourite theorists, allowing them to form a barycentre about which our twin stars orbit. We twin words like 'drenched' and 'swimming' to understand how the theory is affecting and effecting our writing. We twin talking and moving, acknowledging the writing of this chapter as a we-search practice. We twin our entangled nature of how we bring our writing practice into the world responsibly with and through each other, in order to invite supervisors, students and researchers to join us, to twin with us.

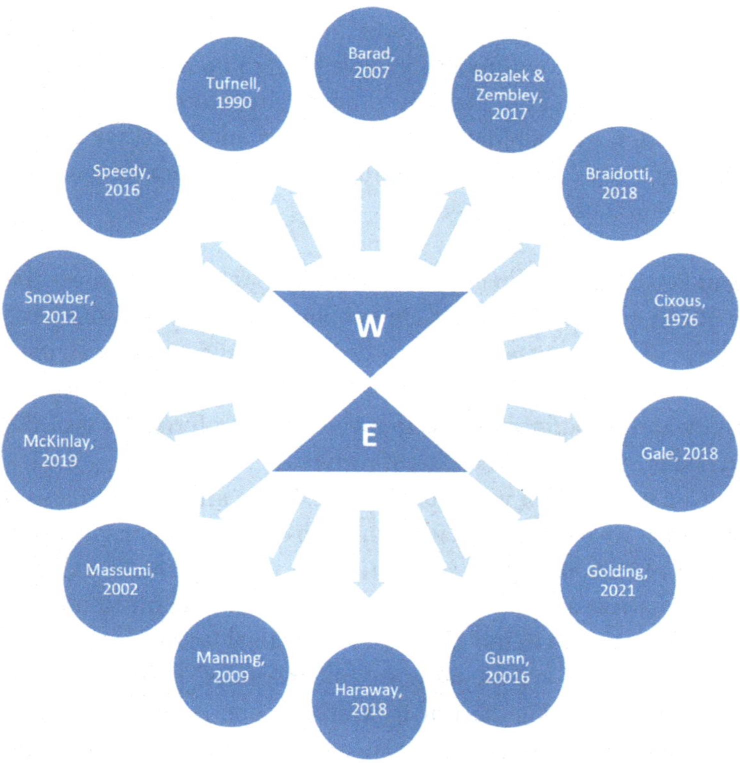

FIGURE 12.2 Star fragment 5: Our thought provokers as both the barycentre of our twin stars' orbit, but also the constellation that surrounds this chapter

In his book *Madness as methodology* (2018), Ken Gale revolutionises writing about post-humanism and processes by using his everyday friendships and knowing observations to work through intimacy – through it we have sensed our peer learning and intimate comradery as intra-action, to describe 'conceptual, affective and perceptual complexities … the constantly folding flows of discourse and materiality' (2018, p. 156). When he writes about his friendship as research, as a poetic becoming that we feel seen in, his careful, intimate writing gives us permission to be with our own ways of worlding, how we think-play-write-create, to write with each other. Gale gives us permission to overcome the painful affective forces of neoliberal academic policy and practice that make us think that our words are worth-less-than-theirs. He gives us permission to write thoughtfully, affectively and pedagogically about giving permission. Gale talks about friendship as 'processual world making' (p. 105), drawing on a leakiness of information that is able to exist outside of a habitual consideration of self, a post-human self, the space between or beyond the containment of social constructivism (Manning, 2009b).

> Stars are formed out of massive clouds of dust (the ideas of the theorists) and gas (the artefacts we diffract) that give birth to them (this chapter). Thousands of stars are formed at once (our future, our past, our books, your books) often with sibling stars orbiting one another (their future, their past, our future, our past, your future, your past). (Star fragment 6: Twin stars – our metaphor)

I think about Portia's Zoom screen. I draw what I can remember. I sense the digital space of our conversations that are enabling this chapter. I draw the straight-linedness of her banister, the open doors her child and dog wander through, the box with lots of things in – her life stuff. I feel her mortgage, her age, her capacity and/or permissiveness to meet me being formed out of the banisters and books when I show her this drawing.

We have arrived in a place of walls, and laptops, Zoom and post-humanism because of the spaces we have to think with, through each other's imaginations. Our cabled and Wi-Fi-ed connection is affecting our way of being in and with and writing through these materials that is allowing new behaviours to enter in.

We relate to Bozaleck and Zembley's idea of relational ontology: 'an ongoing process in which matter and meaning are co-constituted' (2017, p. 112). We relate to this sense of changing the way in which we are of the world into a process of engaging, with its quality of intimacy. We relate to this sensation of being intra-actively aware of one another, as no longer one or an other, that feels connected to the cosmological metaphor of twin stars. We relate to

FIGURE 12.3 Star fragment 7: Portia's Zoom screen by Kieran

a feeling of affecting and being inside the umbrella of the affect. We relate our genders, our family circumstances, our residential countries; they are quite different. We relate to the tracing of the feeling of joyfulness across the picture of the Zoom screen that we can immediately re-call, as if our bodies were slightly living inside each other. We relate through post-human movement artist researcher Erin Manning, who explains worlding as 'the process of a world becoming subject, or subject becoming world' (2009a, p. 66). We relate through these sense-triggering images and theories into the computer screen, diffractively knowing, opening further into this space of relationship.

~~Fauth~~ Juvenal was wondering what the FUCK they were talking about as they sprayed the inside of a car park wall in ~~Kabul~~ the Republic of Intra-Action. They sprayed it with silver paint in the shape of the figures on the cover of Nemat Sadat's (2019) 'The Carpet Weaver'. They watched Portia and Kieran typing, laughing at the audacity of them including this in their chapter. Outside the cave was a flicker of light.

> I've been obsessing about a book ... it feels important to just talk about the fact it has corners. And it's tactile, the cover, you want to stroke it, it's really beautifully printed. And it's also got these little tabs down the side ... it's put together with intent. The user has a place in its design. (Star fragment 8: Transcript of Zoom session, 9 April 2021)

We interrogate the feeling of immanence (Braidotti, 2006) in the language we choose, as

> the posthuman subject is able to account for the increasingly technologically-mediated environment in a manner that is experimental and not

> exclusively profit-driven. The playful and mutually beneficial relationship between human and machine, then, is reimaged not as a relationship between product and consumer, but as two distinct and nonhierarchically ordered species experimentally pursuing a common ethics. (Shaw, 2015)

> BOOKS – ZOOM – SHARE SCREEN – EMAIL – WI-FI – CELLULAR NETWORK – CABLES – FRENCH & YORKSHIRE EARTH – MONEY – AMAZON DRIVERS – SIMM SPACE – GOOGLE SCHOLAR – PROGRAMMERS – POST-ITS – CHAIRS – PLASTIC STARS – MUJI PENS – MAC BOOK – BANISTERS – BOOKCASES (Star fragment 9: Intervention – what are we talking about?)

We interrogate what our pedagogic space is resting within, and that is certainly within the capitalist confines of academia: we can afford the books, the doctoral courses, the time (just about) to talk to each other. But beyond that we interrogate and reject these neoliberal notions of performing our alliance with academia, and instead choose to write into an experience of being with/of one another and the wonder that this produces for us. Our witnessing of each other is generative and un-binarised in terms of interpretivism. There is a meeting of one another only in order to unfold our ontological relationship to learning. We interrogate that 'it is a kind of modest witness that insists on its situatedness, where location is itself always a complex construction as well as inheritance' (Haraway & Goodeve, 2018, p. 270).

~~Fauth~~ Juvenal turns to Portia and Kieran, not quite knowing who is who. They crunch up the sticky note forming their leg and tear a strip off, angrily, feeling exposed and used and exploited. ~~Fauth~~ Juvenal writes 'Entanglement' on the sticky note and burns it, a death note to this chapter, the ridiculous privilege that their authorial voice holds. They burn their paper limb, producing dust – the scent of ash, the paper goes into and of the air. The flame is the same colour as the orange ink. They stare at the paper, the ink, the words and the authors and they get out a can of silver paint and begin to make marks on the car park wall, checking no one is looking, no one will catch them. ~~Fauth~~ Juvenal traces the outline of their favourite book, challenging the authors to ANALYSE THIS, DIFFRACT THAT. They wonder angrily about their purpose in this chapter and the waste of time these people are becoming.

> Staring at the images of *~~Fauth~~ Juvenal*'s favourite book (Sadat, 2019) and the image of Portia's office through our Zoom, we notice the timber of my desk suddenly has an agency of its own. The men's arms are firm and strong against the tree beneath them and it leans into my office,

> connecting them. Staring at the wonderful straight-ness, ironically as we overlay the pictures and Portia's office becomes a safe space for these men to sit, they become a modest witness to *~~Fauh~~ Juvenal's* painful exploitation. What is Juvenal's favourite book? It isn't Fauh's. We choose not to include the image. Our fabulation's speculation is becoming carnate. (Star fragment 10: Twin star reflection bleeding into *~~Fauh~~ Juvenal*)

> There's something about the masturbatory instinct that goes on when you're working in HE, and talking about doing a doctorate. It's these twin cells revolving around. But most academics won't acknowledge it. (Star fragment 11: Transcript, 16 April 2021)

~~Fauh~~ Juvenal stared at the silver outline of two people. An outline. They stared at the outline and traced what they knew. The human shape, the silver colour of the graffiti paint, the coarse cement wall of the car park, an escape from the noise and grime and vibration of ~~Kabul~~ the Republic of Intra-Action. They stared at the picture and felt it was something quite wonderous, permissive.

~~The non-binary Afghan graffiti artist~~ *~~Fauh~~ Juvenal* is helping us to tell political stories through the power of diffraction. This can be drawn up against the tension between our connection to pleasure and aesthetic as something that is self-indulgent or narcissistic. The information that comes out of this diffractive thinking connects to a flow of pleasure and privilege that can exist alongside each other ethically because they are being seen, perhaps? Before, so often, we have felt fearful of speaking or being with our truthful poetic voice, and by engaging in a space that allows us to dwell into diffraction, we can see that the grit of this pedagogic space is in the thinking practices we bring together, out of the materialities of our imagination, post-human theory and its entanglements. As we bring into being our post-human pedagogic space, post-human theory allows us 'the ability to grasp the freedom to de-personalise the event and transpose its negative charge' (Braidotti, 2019, p. 167).

Notice from the Undercommons

> *the current order of Man, its auto-institution and telos of stable replication, effectively ignores the incommensurable cultural motivations and meanings that shape the divergent subjectivities of those it deems 'woman' according to its biocentric model. In other words, Man's culture-specific mode of identity, and the self-referentiality of its code, potentially leads to cognitive and affective closures. (Jackson, 2013, p. 673)*

We can be with the pain of the humiliation of academic indulgence in a world that is crumbling, alongside a belief in being with each other generatively in a flowing space that has a chance of being helpful.

> What we're talking about [as EdD students] is a practice that is drenched in experience, that is born of experience, but it's also like the water covers every centimetre of your skin. And the professional doctorate and doctoral journey, for some, is just making sense of that water, whereas actually we're emerging from it. It's not better, it's just different. (Star fragment 12: Transcript, 9 April 2021)

Juvenal wanders into kieranandportia's wonderings. Our post-human subjectivity is potent, we can feel the earth in the wall of the car park in ~~Kabul~~ the Republic of Intra-Action. kieranandportia quickly finds a picture of it on google, flickering between the genealogical structure of the earth and a star. They all look at the colours of the materials on the screen and feel for one moment that there is nothing that is possible. Their wondering is pathetic and weak, it is indulgent and shallow, it really isn't what they should be doing. Juvenal returns to their interaction.

We feel an urge to follow ~~Fauh~~ Juvenal and understand with them a little longer why they are haunting our chapter. They begin to move our body into the sensation of being with this imaginary spectre that has squatted in our chapter. We close our eyes and retreat in thinking through Snowber (2012). We see the dark sodden car park and ~~Fauh~~ Juvenal in their turquoise shiny hoody staring at us, their ribs shortening into their pelvis, cynical but watching/witnessing. We reach our arms up to the air of our office, lit only by Google searches of ~~Afghan queer artist communities~~ dismantled othering, we breathe into the tightening grip of our chest and bend our knees, wrapping our arms around our shoulder blades and feeling the presence of the darkness and silver glow of the graffiti from the candle-lit cave.

It is actually not a cave, but an abandoned car park. ~~Fauh~~ Juvenal has never been in a cave, and ~~Fauh~~ Juvenal wants us to be with this feeling of shame or mechanistic noticing and then realise what can happen when we change the affective flow, when we think of the possibility. Is this section just Juvenal now? Is our fabulation beyond the speculative?

galactic soup
our skin pimples, a chill
as we read the me-thought
written by the them-fingers
affecting a version of the us-truth

our twinning is gilded by honesty,
vermeil layers of theory and us
but gelded by the consequences
imagined or felt, of being honest. in HE.

we take a gulp of air, suddenly thirsty,
been under the water of possibility
a heartbeat too long
the roar of sea/e in our ears

this space is safe, our queer galaxy
but there is a siren call to be brave
to throw the little caution left
to the winds of constraint – rebellion stirs

we revolve again in our dance
twin stars tied in orbit
entangled, enmeshed and misbehaving beautifully
the thread glistens in the next nebula

glittering, fool's gold
courage is in knowing the consequences
but doing it anyway.
dust clouds form planets and words
(Star fragment 13: An act of rebellion and attrition)

It's a dangerous practice to dance ~~in Kabul, Hull, Margate, Wigan, Cambridge~~ and talk about our imagination. It's a rebellious practice to Google the power of metaphor for change. It's a transformative practice to move into a question, to speculate with our body and imagination. We get excited about writing this down but realise that everything has started to slip away and we are not making any sense …

Offer

We are excited by Kathleen Stewart's focus on the presence of senses in ethnographic knowledge production and her suggestion that research should take in

> all the bodies, the lines of things on the move, the widespread joking, the sonorousness, how any line of a life vies with an unwitting ungluing, how

> things get started, how people try to bring things to an end, why thought as such might become an add-on or window dressing, why conceptuality might take radically different forms, or why it matters that attention sometimes slows to a halt to wait for something to take shape. (2017, p. 196)

We are excited by Wonder(ing) (Manning, 2014).

We are excited by the idea of waiting for research to emerge, excited by reading rebelliously, co-diffracting with the reader, further stars around the barycentre.

We are excited by the space of wondering being about allowing yourself to be 'of' the materials, both living and non-living, around you – the books, the theories, the paper, the imaginaries, the affects, the metaphors, the spectres, the flesh, the memory, the historicity, the bit between the words and bodies and machines and dead trees.

We are excited to have nurtured permission to imagine together rebelliously, and for the collective assemblage of this book to have given us permission, and for the permission givers in our world to be increasing.

We are excited at the prehension (Whitehead, 1929) of your excitement.

> **Wait without hope**
> I said to my soul, be still, and wait without hope
> For hope would be hope for the wrong thing; wait without love,
> For love would be love of the wrong thing; there is yet faith
> But the faith and the love and the hope are all in the waiting.
> Wait without thought, for you are not ready for thought:
> So the darkness shall be the light, and the stillness the dancing.
> Whisper of running streams, and winter lightning.
> The wild thyme unseen and the wild strawberry,
> The laughter in the garden, echoed ecstasy
> Not lost, but requiring, pointing to the agony
> Of death and birth.
> (T. S. Eliot, *East Coker*)

Undercommons Notice (About the People We Are Waiting For)

We have danced, we have written poetry, reflected, connected in order to study (Harney & Moten, 2013, p. 110) or to diffract or to teach each other. So we stare at the text written by the men, because of the words they say about things we want to do, and we stare not at the park (Speedy, 2016) but more like a positive feeling of death, staring at our academic death, like Cixous who has been haunting us with ~~Fauh~~ Juvenal, and our bodies begin to tremble. Cixous (1993,

p. 9) notes that 'writing, in its noblest function, is the attempt to unerase, to unearth, to find the primitive picture again, ours, the one that frightens us'. We shake so much our flesh starts to fall from the bones, we start to scream, we are terrified of our nakedness (Sandoval, 2001), we rip out our teeth to savage our bones, and splinter through the quickly thinning, paper-thin folds of our architecture and we stay with the words:

> We cannot say what new structures will replace the ones we live with yet, because once we have torn shit down, we will inevitably see more and see differently and feel a new sense of wanting and being and becoming. (Harney & Moten, 2013, p. 6)

And we start to be brave enough to draw lines over what we wrote, strike-throughs left visible. We draw lines to highlight the people we notice we are forgetting to forget. We trace them across pages and draw an invisible map towards another literature, a new diffraction that sinks into the response-ability of twin stars, to look at their privilege and to take up space differently. As we unfold ourselves we see the provocation of Juvenal as diffraction, who began as Fauh, and the chapter has become something that holds the feeling of the space we have together, a permission to give our imagination free rein and then be with the outcomes in a way that is performed with awareness of how we want to unfold in the world, aware of the multiplicity of differences at play, and our growing nuance of this. ***return to Notice from the Undercommons***

Traces and Lines

We look through the Zoom screen to where we are watching Juvenal in our mind's eye as they move intuitively. Their body says we must stay with the matter; we must embrace the trouble. Our values are at risk and their agentic movement is protection from the negative affect. Relationality is our saviour, our solace. Juvenal looks at us blankly, the silver stillness of the figures dancing in the light from outside the cave, reflected on the screen of their eyes.

I press 'End meeting for all'.

References

Arao, B., & Clemens, K. (2013). From safe spaces to brave spaces: A new way to frame dialogue around diversity and social justice. In L. Landreman (Ed.), *The art of effective facilitation: Reflections from social justice educators* (pp. 135–150). Stylus.

Barad, K. (2007). *Meeting the universe halfway: Quantum physics and the entanglement of matter and meaning*. Duke University Press.

Bozalek, V., & Zembylas, M. (2017). Diffraction or reflection? Sketching the contours of two methodologies in educational research. *International Journal of Qualitative Studies in Education*, *30*(2), 111–127.

Braidotti, R. (2006). Affirming the affirmative: On nomadic affectivity. *Rhizomes*, *11/12*. http://www.rhizomes.net/issue11/braidotti.html

Braidotti, R. (2019). *Posthuman knowledge*. Polity Press.

Burnard, P., Colucci-Gray, L., & Sinha, P. (2021). Transdisciplinarity: Letting arts and science teach together. *Curriculum Perspectives*, *41*(1), 113–118.

Cixous, H. (1993). *Three steps on the ladder of writing*. Columbia University Press.

Cixous, H. (2009). The laugh of the Medusa. In R. Warhol-Down & D. Price Herndl (Eds.), *Feminisms redux: An anthology of literary theory and criticism* (pp. 416–431). Rutgers University Press.

Deleuze, G., & Guattari, F. (1987). *Capitalism and schizophrenia: A thousand plateaus*. University of Minnesota Press.

Gale, K. (2018). *Madness as methodology: Bringing concepts to life in contemporary theorising and inquiry*. Routledge.

Gunn, V. (2016). Prophetic Nomadism: An Art School Sustainability-Oriented Educational Aim? *The International Journal of Art & Design Education*, *35*(3), 316–326.

Haraway, D. J. (2016). *Staying with the trouble: Making kin in Chthulucene*. Duke University Press.

Haraway, D. J., & Goodeve, T. (2018). *Modest_Witness@Second_Millennium. FemaleMan_Meets_OncoMouse: Feminism and technoscience*. Routledge.

Harney, S., & Moten, F. (2013). *The undercommons: Fugitive planning and Black study*. Minor Compositions.

Jackson, Z. (2013). Animal: New directions in the theorization of race and posthumanism. *Feminist Studies*, *39*(3), 669–685. http://www.jstor.org/stable/23719431

Kaiser, B. M. (2014). Worlding CompLit: Diffractive reading with Barad, Glissant and Nancy. *Parallax*, *20*(3), 274–287.

Lorde, A. (2007). The master's tools will never dismantle the master's house. In A. Lorde, *Sister outsider: Essays and speeches* (pp. 110–114). Crossing Press.

Lubacz, J. (2021). Epistemic and poietic intentional processes. *Synthese*. Advance online publication. https://doi.org/10.1007/s11229-021-03051-5

Lucie, S. (2020). Atmosphere and intra-action. *Performance Research*, *25*(5), 17–23.

Manning, E. (2009a). *Relationscapes: Movement, art, philosophy*. MIT Press.

Manning, E. (2009b). What if it didn't all begin and end with containment? Toward a leaky sense of self. *Body & Society*, *15*(3), 33–45

Manning, E. (2014) Wondering the world directly – or, How movement outruns the subject. *Body & Society*, *20*(3&4), 162–188

Sadat, N. (2019). *The Carpet Weaver*. Penguin Viking.

Sandoval, C. (2001). *Methodology of the oppressed*. University of Minnesota Press.

Shaw, D. (2015). Summary of Rosi Braidotti's *The posthuman* (part 2). *Medium.com*. https://medium.com/open-objects/summary-of-rosi-braidotti-s-the-posthuman-part-2-8900940c8825

Slaby, J. (2020). Atmospheres – Schmitz, Massumi and beyond. In F. Riedel & J. Torvinen (Eds.), *Music as atmosphere: Collective feelings and affective sounds* (pp. 274–285). Routledge.

Snowber, C. (2012). Dance as a way of knowing. *New Directions for Adult and Continuing Education, 2012*(134), 53–60.

Speedy, J. (2016). *Staring at the park: A poetic autoethnographic inquiry*. Routledge.

Stewart, K. (2017). In the world that affect proposed. *Cultural Anthropology, 32*(2), 192–198. https://doi.org/10.14506/ca32.2.03

Tapia, M. (2001). Measuring emotional intelligence. *Psychological Reports, 88*(2), 353–364.

Taylor, C., & Gannon, S. (2018). Doing time and motion diffractively: Academic life everywhere and all the time. *International Journal of Qualitative Studies in Education, 31*(6), 465–486.

Whitehead, A. N. (1929). *Process and reality, an essay in cosmology; Gifford Lectures delivered in the University of Edinburgh during the session 1927–1928*. Macmillan.

CHAPTER 13

Don't Just Do Something ... Stand There!

Two Women Dance Their Academic Trajectories

Simone Eringfeld and Hilary Cremin

Prologue

Two women are dancing. Together yet apart. Dancing their academic trajectories. Hilary, a senior academic, and Simone, a graduate student, stand opposite each other, next to each other, behind each other, then with each other and again opposite each other. Circling round each other, moving in and away, connecting and disconnecting, understanding and misunderstanding each other's motions. Investigating, shyly but surely, both carefully and brutally. Testing the water, building confidence, gaining momentum. Slowly, trust enters the conversation. Daringly, the movements become bigger. A sense of precarious calm creeps up. Gestures gradually grow, as the two women gesticulate their hopes and fears for the future of academia, embodying stories of possible change and reflecting on what this all means. Together, they inhabit this space of ambiguity, of vulnerability. Wishes for the future of academia are followed up by fears that nothing will ever change. What does resistance look like within the space of the university? What does it mean to be a 'rebel' or to do 'rebellious research'? How do their perspectives, as senior academic versus graduate student, differ? Will their efforts of working towards change be worth it or will they be for nothing?

Opening Sequence

Simone

I am dancing in one of the lecture rooms in the building of the Education Faculty at the University of Cambridge. The room is quite large. All tables and chairs have been moved to the sides of the room, leaving the centre of the floor completely empty. Usually when I'm in this room, I'm sitting at one of the large tables with fellow students, listening to a lecturer, eyes directed at a PowerPoint. I realise I'd never paid attention to how big this room actually

 | DOI:10.1163/9789004516069_017

is. During lectures, it's often so full that the students who come in last have to find themselves a seat right next to the exit. But today, that's not the case. I'm standing towards the left side of the room; my bare feet feel the blueish carpet that I'd never quite noticed before.

I am dancing, but not alone. My dancing partner is Hilary, a senior academic at the faculty whom I first met at a CPERG meeting, the Cambridge Peace and Education Research Group we both form part of. She is CPERG's senior advisor; I am one of its research student members. Hilary has also given lectures to my MPhil cohort about peace education and supervises some of my peers. I mostly feel shy, standing there. Arms by my side, unsure of what to do. This is so different from the usual settings in which I interact as a student with senior academics and professors at the faculty. I'm not sure how Hilary feels about this either, but I imagine it must feel strange to her as well.

But then, eyes interlock. The silence around us becomes louder, along with the electronic dance music in the background, my heart races in my chest. I feel initial discomfort creeping up. Slowly, the environment around us fades away, as I start to concentrate on Hilary, myself and the space between us. I consciously try to find my sense of calm, to re-establish my inner balance. A light smile around the corners of my mouth, I breathe deeply. Maintaining eye contact, I slowly start to settle more into this strange new dynamic. Carefully, I relax my shoulders and tell my abs to release their tension, directing my breath to my belly. Slowly, I begin to dance.

Hilary

I am dancing with Simone. Norbert is facilitating our session using ideas from his book *The self as (re)source* (Koppensteiner, 2020). As Norbert points out, 'as we deepen our understanding of our bodies we become more aware of our self ... At the same time, we learn about the world' (p. 57). Our faculty sound system, more used to broadcasting lectures (sometimes my lectures), is filling my ears with electronic dance music. I like the sound of it and feel like dancing. How much can I move and let go today? *Who am I* here in this space? Who, at the end of the day, is Hilary Cremin? How free am I here at this moment?

I've always tried to reduce the space between my academic/professional identity and the sense of who I am underneath it all (Cremin, 2018). I've taken inspiration from colleagues such as Pat Thompson (Baroutsis et al., 2018) and Jane Osgood (2010) who present themselves to the world in ways that unite home and work: cats, Facebook, gardens, seminars, publications, materiality, messiness. Here now, though, I wonder if I have an 'underneath it all'. Perhaps I am made up of a series of internal selves who rise up in turn in response to a summons from people out in the world; people who connect me but who are not me; people who want to dance with me. Perhaps my personality is expressed at the level of my skin, at the point of encounter between me and the world (Bonnett, 2009)? Perhaps my growth, my learning, is to respond with love whenever I can – to enter into Buber's 'I–thou' level of relating with another being who 'is' as I am, rather than entering into Buber's 'I–it' level of relating to others as merely objects who furnish my world (Buber, 1923/1970).

Right now, my encounter, my opportunity for learning, is with Simone. She is my connection to the outside world, my 'thou'. We are improvising a dance, and this makes me think of one of my favourite peace thinkers and writers, Ilan Gur-Ze'ev. For him, new forms of peace education move beyond 'homogenising packaged peace' towards something more creative, liminal and dynamic. It is created each moment anew as an improvision between two people who meet each other as equals. Now my world of peace education research is reduced to the music, our bodies, a remembered quotation from Ilan Gur-Ze'ev, and Simone's eyes:

> Improvisation is of vital importance for any counter-education that is true to itself and is courageous to face the false promises of present-day peace education by offering not emancipatory negativity and ultimately eternal and comprehensive 'peace' but something very different: It offers re-birth. It brings forth responsibility, a mature speculative ear for a gazing-at, and touching-of the newly born in each moment anew. A de-territorialised 'here' offers us, within the endlessness of improvisation, a specific, the most specific and concrete, 'here and now'; the here and now that offers not a false 'home', 'nirvana' or 'pleasure' – it offers nomadic hospitality. (Gur-Ze'ev, 2011, p. 118)

Movement 1: Hope

Simone

Spreading my arms wide open
Palms turn up towards the sky
Chest and chin lifted,
Calves raised on the tops of my toes
I bend and stretch, shrink and expand

What do I hope to find here? What am I doing in this space and where am I going? When I first arrived at Cambridge to start my MPhil in Education, I'd never seriously considered an academic career. Quite the opposite: I'd made myself the promise to steer clear from academia, however tempting its career prospects might be. Although Cambridge has shaken the foundations of that resolution, my past experiences prevent me from shielding behind naivety. Even as an academic newcomer, I am no newbie to its World Without Weekends: the past few years I've already been on an academic rollercoaster by doing three bachelor's degrees at once, in just three years' time. I've spent enough time fully immersed in a world dominated by laptop screens, tight deadlines and an absence of work–life balance to readily recognise visions of my potential future self reflected in the passionate and knowledgeable (yet sleep-deprived and overburdened) academics around me. It is easy, perhaps too easy, to imagine a similar life for myself.

I clasp my hips,
which begin contouring,
connecting, contextualising

That inner hunger
That endless curiosity
That doomed blessing
That terrific gift

What I am feeling now is by no means a new experience, for I have been here before. I know the impact that intense intellectual labour has on me: my mind thrives amidst all the new ideas, theories and concepts, yet my body complains about being forgotten. My undivided focus on *knowing* gets in the way of my unanswered curiosity for *being*. I try to suppress, ignore and deny the frustrated energy squishing my lungs, until I can no longer contain my body. Restlessness kicks in, books are stacked away in boxes, walking shoes get freshly waxed, Google Maps tabs are opened on my browser; clear signs that it won't be long before I take off. I go looking for my next dose of *real life*, like a drug that keeps me going. Visiting the edges of my thoughts, pushing the horizons of the possible. Kicking against limitations, going on detours, I take my seat right at the margins of my knowing (Derrida, 1984), in between mind and body to oversee the order, the chaos, the emerging ambiguities, like a true Derridean. Finally, I remember. Finally, I come back to life. Finally, I exist.

Here I am, here we are, dancing in the disembodied territory of the mind. Perhaps it is possible to mind-fully embody ourselves as academics after all?

For perhaps, if I allow my body to rebel right here and now in this empty lecture room, I can

Jump!
Turn around
Speed up
Fall down
Break the walls
And the ceiling too
Crash (onto) the floor
Claim space for body and mind
Without compromise?

Hilary

We are asked to dance with hope. What do I hope for? When I began my work in schools as a peace educator, I hoped to transform 'schools, one at a time, with the self-evidence of more peaceful ways of operating' (Cremin, 2018, p. 13). I have long let go of such naivety and grandiosity. What do I hope for now? More latterly as an academic, I hope not to transform schools, but to enable transformative moments. I hope to be a facilitator of peaceful moments for some people sometimes. This is already enough. I think of workshop spaces and lecture halls as heterotopias (Foucault, 1986) in which normative power relations can be disrupted. These spaces have generated care, openness, hope and creativity for me in the past. They have pointed towards the promise of different classroom spaces.

Right here, right now, I hope to find a moment, a small transcendent moment of peace – here in my dance with Simone. I hope to *do* university differently. I hope to *be* a different academic.

Movement 2: Fear

Simone

I like to kick my long legs
Straight into the sky,
Shaking my feet to frantically
Throw off the reservedness,
To rid myself of self-awareness,
To explode together

with the ball of energy
Tumbling round and round
in my belly

Restlessly, I run back and forth between literature and life. I exit the stories I read to enter stories I tell. I bring my body to sail the Drake Passage, to dive into Antarctic waters, to cross Saharan deserts. My body brings me back to its worldly home, wind in hair, eyes spread wide in mystical marvel. Yet I know it won't be long before my mind longs back to its desk. Paper and pen in hand. Forehead resting contemplatively in my hand. When I am in my mind, I miss being-in-the-world. When I am in the world, I miss being-in-my-mind.

If what I'm hoping for is to recognise within the contours of the university the outlines of an intellectual home, my biggest fear is that this home will lock my body up. If my hope is to nurture my *lively* mind, my fear is that my *lifeless* body will slowly become erased. While my mind expands with all the knowledge I consume and create, my body feels increasingly constrained. I fear my hips will come to carry imprints of the chair's edges pressed into my thighs, my fingertips will have keyboard letters glued to their tips, my shoulders will be permanently drawn up, my back hunched over my desk, my eyesight irrevocably fading. When I momentarily remember to look up from my screen and gaze towards the horizon of the possible, all I see is blurry shapes surrounded by blue light, becoming increasingly hard to distinguish.

Sudden uncertainty it hits me
A stream of cold air
Enters in-between my arms
Ribs quickly closing in
I sink down to the floor
Arms wrap around my shins
Face rests upon two knees

My gaze drifts to the back of the room, where the classroom chairs are piled up. They are of the kind with a little desk attached, where you can rest your books on. How could my body possibly fit into that chair? How can I remain seated when my body threatens to burst through the cracks of my new-found home, looking for the way out? While my mind discovers untrodden territories, my body gets stuck in this claustrophobic grip.

As I dance this dance with Hilary, I wonder if she too sometimes feels like her body doesn't fit the demands of this mental world. Does she ever fear not being able to stand back up, after having been seated for so long? Does she recognise the feeling of resembling a puzzle piece with an awkward bend – not allowing itself to fit neatly with the rest of the pieces? Does it become easier when you've lived inside this World Without Weekends for longer? Does anyone else fear that by choosing the academic path, they risk forgetting that one crucial act: to be – and *feel* – alive?

Softly, I feel the touch of
Hilary's hand extending out
Gently resting on my shoulder
I was seated for a while
but now it's time
to get back up

Hilary

Simone is up again; she is dancing and alive. I am alive, and I am afraid. What am I afraid of? Here in this lecture hall today my fears run like lions. I'm afraid of letting go. It is harder that I thought to relate to Simone as 'thou'. This is not because I objectify her – it is because I objectify myself. Senior academic, respected colleague, bloodless angel …

I float in airy efficacy
I exist outside of history, outside of time.
I have no place,
I speak from nowhere in particular.
I speak from everywhere.
I have no thoughts
I convey what is thought
I have no feet,
so I leave no footprint.
I have no hands,
so I do not act.
I have no body
Prick me, and I will not bleed. (Cremin, 2019)

How often do I claim my body in academic life? I don't. I rarely seem to find time to drink, to stretch, to pee. Why do we deny our bodies in the academy? Is it because our bodies make us human? They 'ground us in the clay of our positionality' (Cremin, 2019). They force us to exist in time and space – one small instantiation of humanity – one amongst many. bell hooks describes the strong investment in a mind–body split that exists in classrooms and lecture theatres. She notes that, as a black woman,

> if you want to remain, you've got, in a sense, to remember yourself – because to remember yourself is to see yourself always as a body in a system that has not become accustomed to your presence or to your physicality. (1994, p. 135)

Ron Scapp, a white male philosopher with whom she dialogues in her book *Teaching to transgress* (hooks, 1994), adds that white male academics often feel that the mind–body split is necessary as a way of denying and negating power, and as a way of avoiding uncomfortable truths. bell hooks notes that 'the person who is most powerful has the privilege of denying their body' (hooks, 1994, p. 137). Is this what is holding me back? A reluctance to face this discomfort – to let go of this power? As a white female academic, I dance at the intersection of power and powerlessness. If I let go and truly dance, will my reclaiming of my body leave me embodied and sexualised in a way that threatens my hard-won right to dance a different dance – the dance of the disembodied (pseudo-male?) professor?

Movement 3: Rebellion

Simone

Breathing deeply in and out
Grounding myself back down
Pressing heels – toes – heels into blueish carpet
Without thinking, simply feeling
I close my eyes
and start to listen

I listen to my tensed midriff telling me to run. I listen to my throat demanding me to shout. I listen to my chest begging me to expand, to deepen my inhalations. Once I allow my body to rebel, will I ever allow it to be pacified again? Trapped in a binary opposition between body and mind, is it not all one big deceit, one big illusion? Is being-in-the-world not supposed to be a unified form of sentir-pensar (Mignolo, 2015)? I often feel far removed from feeling whole as a thinking, feeling, sensing and acting being.

At times, my own body responds to my academic endeavours by refusing to collaborate, by rebelliously blocking my mind, as if to say 'enough is enough'. My mind orders my body to type a new essay, yet my hands simply refuse. My mind orders my body to stay focused on the screen, yet my eyes make all the letters dance in a disorganised jumble. My mind orders my body to stay immobile while staring at endless amounts of text, yet my feet itch and my knees shake impatiently, unable to bare their own uselessness.

Thighs and fists clutching, ankles trembling
Elbows lifting falling lifting falling
I slow my movements down
Until I stop doing
and start standing

Finally,
Standing there

Standing there, I pause to reflect. I stop trying to make myself fit and wonder instead: if there is no space in academia for embodied practices, how can we *make* space for it? How can I make space for my own body in this academic future I envision for myself as part of that blurry, yet still visible, horizon of the possible? How can we make use of senses other than our vision to engage with ideas, theories and concepts, with knowledge production? What can an academic future *sound* like, *feel* like, *smell* like?

Perhaps to rebel means to depart radically from normative expectations around if and how to write, research, speak, exist as an academic? Or perhaps it might mean to decide not to pursue an academic career at all? I am still undecided. Surely to rebel means daring to choose a different route, a different timing, a different rhythm. It might mean to stop *doing*, to start *standing* there instead. To put the mind on stand-by. To make the body stand up and force the mind to stand down. To take a stand against the hegemony of thoughts over feelings, immobility over movement, literature over life. To stand, sway and swirl; to tumble, twist and turn. Just like in this dance. To create space, without seeking approval or permission, for the

Unimaginable
Unapproved
Unseen

Unheard
Unlearnt
Unconforming
Unexpected

By dancing to
the counter-beat?

Hilary

It dawns on me that being vulnerable in this space is the ultimate act of rebellion. Here in this lecture hall where I'm called to deny my body, claiming it is a radical act. Half terrified, half exhilarated, my feet are stomping out a different beat as I orbit around Simone. I am dancing with the lions of my fear. I call to mind the two sides of me that emerge in my poem *Bloodless angel* (Cremin, 2019). The first is disembodied, arrogant:

I rest on my canon.
My validity, my reliability, my rationale.
I consort with kings,
With prime ministers, presidents
Philanthropists.
They lend me their ears
They ask me what is true
What is valuable
And what is right.
They are eager to know.

His/her view from nowhere 'pierces the somewhere' of research participants who are (all too) embodied compared with her airy floatiness:

The subjects of my research
Are gendered, ethnic, gay, disabled, poor.
They have bodies.
Entangled in the messiness of time and space,
Grounded in clay.
Prick them, and they bleed.

This second side of my academic identity is beckoning. She dares me to dance the dance of rebellion, to partner not just with Simone but with future research participants too. She challenges me to walk alongside them with stomping feet. I have never claimed this side of my academic identity in writing before. I have only presented her in my *Bloodless angel* poem as a threat to the arrogant first side. What would happen if I danced from her positionality – if I claimed her voice?

Know me now
As I stand
In the mud
Of my place
In this world
As I feel
Blood coursing
Breath filling
Life lifting
All that is me.

Meet my eyes
Know my voice.
I am
Researcher
Sharing songs
Walking with
Dancing through.

We are
Improvising
Calling out
Drum beating
World making
Time learning.

Selves as resource.

The music has stopped. Simone and I face each other as our breathing returns to normal. Not doing, but standing. I realise that we've been lost in another way of being in the academy. Lost or found? Can my rebellious vulnerability stay with me?

Closing Sequence

Simone

As I think back on my dance with Hilary in our faculty building, I feel a wave of nostalgia coming over me. Not long after our dance, the COVID-19 crisis disrupted our lives, our bodies and our minds, reminding us again that we are still bodies after all, including all the vulnerabilities that come with inhabiting bodies that can be touched, infected, fall ill and heal, or die. Yet the pandemic also exacerbated the binary between body and mind in academia, with our bodies becoming even more forgotten in virtual spaces like Zoom rooms and MS Teams lectures. How can we safeguard the body amidst policies of remote working and social distancing? These reflections and my own need for reembodying practices in academia led me to start a podcast called *Cambridge quaranchats* (Eringfeld, 2020), as a platform for conversations with other students and academics about our own hopes and fears for the future of academia. About using our voices, mouths and ears to engage in active listening and speaking, to get back in touch with our embodied understanding of the world – even and especially in academic contexts where the risk of losing your body seems so terrifyingly big.

I've continued exploring all the diverse ways in which spoken word can be used to resist the hegemony of the written word in academia, to rebel, to kick against pre-set expectations and make space for the unexpected instead. To use any and every opportunity to emphasise the embodying and communal aspects of living and working in the university (Eringfeld, 2021a), through podcasting and poetry, through music and spoken word performance. For my latest project, I turned my research data on hopes and fears for the 'post-coronial university' (Eringfeld, 2021a) into a spoken word music album called *PLEASE HOLD* (Eringfeld, 2021b). Indeed, by putting our actions on hold, we might create more space to reflect.

Yet I continue to fear: will choosing an academic future indefinitely put my body on hold, put *life itself* on hold? Even as I actively invite my body into my own academic conversations, it seems that this right to *be* – that is, to exist as a bodily being – is one that needs to be guarded at all times.

Hilary

Reflecting back on this a couple of years later, I am aware that it was transformational for me. This dancing workshop at the heart of my university building has stayed with me, even through lockdown and isolation. It prompted me to think more about vulnerability in education, the topic of a chapter in a book on the subject that I wrote with Kevin Kester (2020). I think about Norbert's workshop often, trying to recapture the spirit of that transformative moment with Simone – our own personal heterotopia.

References

Baroutis, A., Riddle, S., & Thomson, P. (Eds.). (2018). *Education research and the media: Challenges and possibilities*. Routledge.

Bonnett, M. (2009). Education and selfhood: A phenomenological investigation. *Journal of Philosophy of Education, 43*(3), 357–370.

Buber, M. (1970). *I and thou* (W. Kaufmann, Trans.). Charles Scribner's Sons. (Original work published 1923)

Cremin, H. (2018). An autoethnography of a peace educator: Deepening reflections on research, practice, and the field. *Emotion, Space and Society, 28*, 1–8.

Cremin, H. (2019). *Bloodless angel*. Medium.com. https://medium.com/the-politics-of-representation/tagged/poetry

Cremin, H., & Kester, K. (2020). Barefoot hope for peace: Vulnerability in peace learning. In M. McKenna & E. Brantmeier (Eds.), *Pedagogy of vulnerability* (pp. 25–42). Information Age Publishing.

Derrida, J. (1984). *Margins of philosophy* (A. Bass, Trans.). University of Chicago Press.

Eringfeld, S. (2020). *Cambridge quaranchats* [Podcast]. https://anchor.fm/quaranchats

Eringfeld, S. (2021a). Higher education and its post-coronial future: Utopian hopes and dystopian fears at Cambridge University during Covid-19. *Studies in Higher Education, 46*(1), 146–157.

Eringfeld, S. (2021b). *PLEASE HOLD* [music album]. https://open.spotify.com/album/1TGTc2RIFUqvIlvGy9pRhx

Foucault, M. (1986). Of other spaces. *Diacritics, 16*, 22–27.

Gur-Ze'ev, I. (2011). Improvisation, violence and peace education. In P. P. Trifonas & B. Wright (Eds.), *Critical issues in peace and education* (pp. 104–120). Routledge.

hooks, b. (1994). *Teaching to transgress: Education as the practice of freedom*. Routledge.

Koppensteiner, N. (2020). *Transrational peace research and elicitive facilitation: The self as (re)source*. Palgrave Macmillan.

Mignolo, W. (2015). *Habitar la frontera: Sentir y pensar la descolonidad*. CIDOB y UACI.

Osgood, J. (2010). Reconstructing professionalism in ECEC: The case for the 'critically reflective emotional professional'. *Early Years, 30*(2), 119–133.

Part 2: Reflective Questions

Elizabeth Mackinlay

Linking to Futures of Teaching and Learning

1. What does the concept of 'radical' mean to you? Think about a moment where you see yourself being and becoming radical – What did you do? How did you know? How did it feel?

2. What appearances did 'radical' make in the ways in which you were taught and learnt to write academic work?

3. What are the creative and critical radical roots that each chapter gestures towards? How might these be applied in your own academic writing?

4. What is the beautiful "writing as craft" constraint each chapter offers in terms of creative and critical relationality?

5. Write down a list of theorists you encounter as you read each chapter. What is radical about their thinking and wondering? How does their criticality speak to creativity and vice versa?

6. What ethical sense-and-response-abilities does radical academic writing hold? How do we perform these?

7. Find the most "gorgeous" sentences and consider how they move you beyond the "cotton wool of daily life" to a moment of being? What is that moment and how is the writing working to take you there?

8. If you were to write a manifesto for your own radical academic writing, what would it say?

 | DOI:10.1163/9789004516069_018

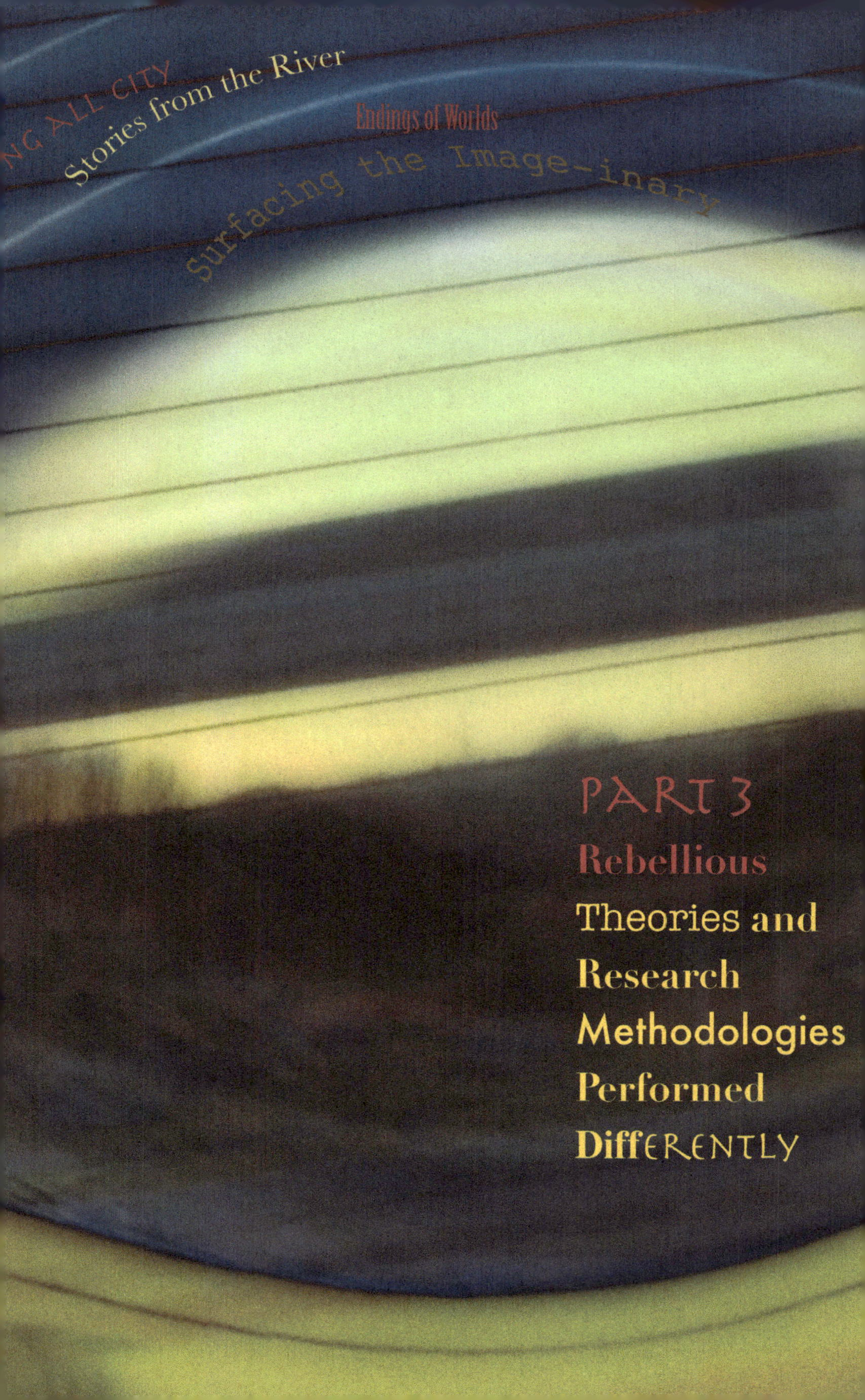

PART 3 Rebellious Theories and Research Methodologies Performed Differently

Part 3: Guidance for Readers

David Rousell

A Call to Rebellion

This is a call to rebellion, both open and undisclosed.

This call doesn't come from me, or any of the other authors in this volume, but from the events in which we find ourselves. The events of which we are made. The events through which we become differently, together. Always already together, whether we like it or not.

As Rosi Braidotti writes (2017), 'we' are all in this together, but 'we' are not (none of us) the same. The question of 'who *we* are' is the precise inauguration of a problem that must be wrestled with again and again, with each passing moment. We don't know who we are. Our response to this problem always rests on the local conditions of nonlocal events. Events that stretch from the immediacy of where we find ourselves *right now* to the elastic durations of climate, capital, and colonial subjugation, among numerous other unequally distributed contingencies. This makes the question of who we are inseparable from the question of how we sense the passage of time *differently*. Multiple (quantum) temporalities is a problem we all have to live with. Entanglement can be a bitch. Or perhaps, as the contributions to this book section attest, it is simply a problem we can only live *through*.

This is a call to live *through* events. It is the call for a rebellion that is not 'for' or 'against' anything. It rejects the presumption that we could somehow know the object of our opinion (doxa) with such clarity as to take some final positioned stand. This rebellion does not claim to know what it stands for. Instead it claims the right to opacity (Glissant, 1998), as the right not to know, and to be unknowable. To become imperceptible, invisible even to ourselves (Deleuze & Guattari, 1987). To be all incomplete and thus remain fugitive (Harney & Moten, 2021).

Movement is the key to this rebellion. It's all you really need to get started. You've been doing it all along. Sensing movement move. Outside the window. Inside your gut. On the pages of this book. Everywhere. Just give your attention to how movement moves (Manning, 2012). That's the best guidance we can give you. Just start with how movement moves you. How movement exceeds and overspills whatever tries to capture it. How movement diffracts itself, in counterpoint with its own contagious rhythms. *Rebel movement.*

 | DOI:10.1163/9789004516069_019

As you forage into the pages of this section you will find this rebel movement everywhere. A teenager hitchhiking across North America; graffiti writers tagging up a whole city; a choreographer drifting down the Xingu River; a steel pan orchestra chipping down the street in Port of Spain; a novelist tracking the quantum entanglements of a work in progress; artists flicking each other daily images and writings; a PhD student constructing a raft for navigating troubled methodological waters.

In each of these movements, there is a rebel refusal to comply with what counts as productive and useful within the institutional grid of the university, the school, the art world, or the publishing house. They let movement move into the cracks, the ruptures, the openings, the leaps into the unknowable. They confront the edge of reason and pass through its porous threshold into a field of anarchic improvisation, where what matters (and why) is up for grabs. Para – (literally outside) – doxa. Beyond belief.

Here, in the field of life, whatever it is we still call 'art', 'research', or 'education' becomes *any body's game*. A game too opaque and precarious to be left to those who call themselves 'experts'. The stakes are just too high. Multiple worlds depend on this.

This is the rebel call. Any body can do this. Just start where you are, and keep moving.

References

Braidotti, R. (2020). "We" are in this together, but we are not one and the same. *Journal of Bioethical Inquiry*, *17*(4), 465-469.

Deleuze, G., & Guattari, F. (1987). *A thousand plateaus* (B. Massumi, Trans.). University of Minnesota Press.

Glissant, E. (1998). *Poetics of relation* (B. Wing, Trans.). University of Michigan Press.

Harney, S., & Moten, F. (2021). *All incomplete*. Minor Compositions.

Manning, E. (2012). *Relationscapes: Movement, art, philosophy*. MIT Press.

CHAPTER 14

Performing Rebellious Theory and Methodology

Going All City

David Rousell

This chapter works across a global range of rebellious concepts and methods currently infiltrating creative fields of inquiry in and beyond the academy. It questions what rebellion might look like in the post-qualitative "afterward" or "end times" of conventional qualitative research. Weaving together anarchic life events with adventurous theoretical concepts, the chapter threads lines of resonance between such diverse practices as hitchhiking, graffiti tagging, animist ritual, quantum physics, creative writing, and post-qualitative educational research. Theoretical concepts are developed as contours of rebellious thinking in practice, including concepts of "micropolitics", "pluriversality", "divination", and "diffraction" that cast posthumanist inflections on what it means to think and perform rebellion. By linking noncompliant conceptual work with anarchic practices of life-living in the everyday, the chapter situates the rebellious performance of theory and methodology within an expanded field of more-than-human ecologies, alliances, and concerns. It borrows the phrase "going all city" from the underground graffiti scene, where it describes all-night graffiti bombings of entire cities by roving bands of anonymous writers. Are we ready to go all city with this?

Authority

I recall struggling with authority, even in my earliest memories. Cutting holes in my baby brother's clothes ... *while he was crawling* across the carpet. Doing things *the wrong way* in preschool, like slipping a shiny glass bead from the counting game into my pocket. Ditching the mandatory lake swim and slipping off into the woods at summer camp. Refusing to attend the classes of a militant, misogynistic gym teacher in order to pass 11th grade. By 17 I was already sickened by the arbitrary authorities of schooling. I walked out of high school and never went back.

Instead of schooling I made myself homeless. I hitched my first ride from New York to Atlanta with a few other wayward teenagers I'd met at a festival.

 | DOI:10.1163/9789004516069_020

They ditched me at a campsite two days later, my backpack and sole belongings still in the trunk of their ramshackle car. A group of more seasoned travellers took pity on me. They took me in and taught me how to live on the road. I followed sonorous lines of music across the country, jumping from ride to ride: improvised jams, free jazz sessions, dub sound systems, hip hop ciphers in parking lots. Town to town, city to city, festival to festival, national park to national park. I called home on payphones. I came to cherish the perverse thrill of not knowing where I'd be tomorrow, or even just later that day.

I learned very different things than I would have in school. I learned where you could pick corn, or apples, or mushrooms on the side of the road. Or here you could camp for weeks, in the middle of a city, without getting caught. I learned about how far you can travel on the fumes of reciprocal kindness until they run out, and you suddenly find yourself somewhere unliveable. Or how to sneak into hotels or health clubs just to take a shower. I learned about the friends who rob you in your sleep. And the ones who share every little thing they have with you. I learned about America's mobile city of anarchic nomads and what it means to be part of the 'family'. How you could get picked up anywhere in America, on the side of the road, *by people you knew*. By people you ride with from New York to San Francisco, and then bump into years later on the streets of Boulder, Burlington, Taos, Eugene or Arcata. I learned about what lives and dies in the absence of authority. And I learned about how to make your way in that absence.

Travelling in Place

Despite what now seems like a lifetime of othering myself from whatever presents itself as authoritative, I somehow fell (backwards, sideways, edgewise) into the academy. After years of making things with my hands in the art studio, building a house with my wife, living off-grid, planting trees and growing vegetables, I fell into (of all things) the field of education. Through what can only be described as a series of unplanned accidents, I found myself starting a PhD and reading process philosophy in my art studio all night. Grappling with the occult outer limits of something called 'methodology', and just writing, writing, writing. In some ways it felt like being on the road again. I was relearning the nomad art of travelling, but this time, I was travelling in place. Finding anarchic books on the shelf like fugitive camps in a city park. Finding Deleuze and Guattari (1987, 1986, 1994), and Massumi (2002), then Manning (2012, 2013), then Whitehead (1978), and Barad (2007), and then so many others like clusters of mushrooms popping up along the roadside. Life was again an adventure in pursuit of unanswerable questions. Where are we? What's going on? What are we doing? What *else* can we do?

Contrast

The kind of rebellion I am trying to elaborate here is not one of opposition, but one of *contrasts* lived intensely, *together* (Rousell, 2021). Intensities of felt contrast that arise from the middle of things, in the shifting differentials between actual happenings and the virtual potential for those happenings to be(come) otherwise (Deleuze & Guattari, 1987). Whitehead (1978) called this rebellious desire for vibrant contrasts of experience *appetition*. Appetition animates Whitehead's intuition of creativity as a first principle for process philosophy: a protean 'appetite for a difference' driving the relentless 'urge toward the future' of the universe's 'creative advance' (p. 32). Life has a tendency to pursue the creative-relational limits of what it can do and become otherwise (Massumi, 2015). Life has an appetite for difference. This is a rebellion that begins again and again, always from the middle, where the contrasts are the most intense and the future calls. On the edge of reason. The cusp of madness. The bridge between worlds. Letting just enough chaos in. Deleuze and Guattari (1987, p. 161) called it an art of dosages. Whitehead (1929, p. 200) called it an art of life. I also think it mostly comes down to aesthetics (Rousell, 2019). Different styles of living, always more-than-human. Living life as a work of art (Rousell & Fell, 2018). Experimenting with different qualities of contrast in order to produce a rebellious transformation in the field of experience.

Walking in Ruins

My family and I now live in Melbourne/Naarm, on the unceded lands of the Wurendjeri people of the Kulin Aboriginal Nation. We witness a rebellion of felt contrasts every day as we walk around the neighbourhood. It's not just about the 'street art' that Melbourne/Naarm is so famous for; the carefully planned and safely executed wall murals that shore up the tidal wave of gentrification from the central business district outwards. It's more about the 'writers', the roving bands of illegal graffiti writers making their mark on the city under the cover of darkness. Every morning, as we take dog walks past the old industrial buildings along the urban creek, we notice that the surfaces of the walls have changed overnight. Indecipherable tags layered over one another like an esoteric calligraphy. And yet, these tags don't *say* anything. And they are not intended to beautify the surfaces of the city by appeasing the aesthetic sensibilities of everyday urban citizens. Instead, they mark the surfaces of the city as capitalist ruins. They vandalise what is already stolen land. They ruin what has already been ruined. What is already ruins.

Going All City

Our teenage son tells us about how groups of local writers meet up at night to go 'all city'. They wear balaclavas and only use tag names to preserve their anonymity, even within their own collectives. The phrase 'going all city' emerged in the late seventies when graffiti writing was taking off in the Bronx (Anderson, 2012). It means covering as much of the city as possible with tags in a single night. Going all city maximises coverage of urban surfaces while mitigating the risk of getting caught for one-off pieces (Bloch, 2020). Our son tells us how Melbourne writers spot each other as they sneak into train yards, evade surveillance cameras, or scale the roofs of multi-story buildings to 'get up' in the most difficult spots in the city. He tells stories of writers who have been going all city for decades without every getting caught. Others have been fined millions of dollars for damages to property. But you still see their tags everywhere you go in Melbourne/Naarm.

Unlike street art which hopes to communicate a message or idea to everyday urban citizens, graffiti tags are not for *us*. They are strictly anarchic performative acts, an aleatory 'graphism' composed of signs unhinged from the regimes of discursive signification (Deleuze & Guattari, 1983; MacLure, 2021). They perform an asignifying rebellion of everyday surfaces that refuse to sit still, make sense, have a voice, communicate a message, or be politically accounted for. In this sense tagging is not just a rebellion against normative authority. It's also a rebellion that overspills normative regimes of capitalist rationality and *common sense*. The tags mark precisely where capitalist authority, rationality and common sense fall apart, break down, go rusty, disintegrate. They perform a pedagogy of becoming-ruins.

And yet, there is an unspoken ethics of tagging that you can notice just by walking around and looking at the walls. The surfaces of most profit-generating enterprises appear to be fair game. They get bombed nearly every night. But the surfaces of non-profit community organisations, struggling family businesses and Aboriginal wall murals remain untouched. These are not considered ruins. They are Respected.

At home we start to see this rebellious pedagogy of urban surfaces seep into our garage. Our son has covered every cardboard box, every scrap of plywood, every plank of wood with indecipherable tags. He shows us how to make New York style 'mop' graffiti markers out of used deodorant bottles, kitchen sponges and acrylic ink. It saves money and materials. He tells us stories about the original graffiti writers from the Bronx, and more recent writers getting up in other cities around the world. He elaborates on the ethics and aesthetics of writing, so different from street art. We already know many of these rebellious stories, having grown up near NYC in the 1980s. But there's something reassuring to hear him tell us these stories, now, as he's learning to live in the ruins of a sick and decaying planet.

The Afterward

Perhaps we can also learn from the indecipherable walls of the city as we navigate the increasingly porous and precarious lines between academic work, creative practice and everyday life. How do we mark capitalist ruins by resurfacing them? What kinds of rebellious stories do we tell new waves of scholars emerging from the post-humanist and new materialist turns? How do we craft theory and methodology as tools of rebellion, using whatever we find lying around in our garages, studios or bookshelves? How might our work as scholars, artists and activists constitute an aesthetics and ethics of co-existence, rather than just another discursive regime of identitarian representation? What would it mean to *go all city* with what we do?

There is now a vibrant range of theoretical and methodological work to help us navigate the rebellious contours of these questions. This book is part of a growing wave of radical scholarship that is recasting the terms of what rebellious research might look like, both within and beyond the academy. Such work performs a different kind of rebellion from previous genealogies of scholarship that relied primarily on discursive critique and the categorical narrativisation of personalised subject identities. Whether through the turn to immanence in post-qualitative inquiry (St Pierre, 2013, 2019), transindividual intensity in affect studies (Massumi, 2002; Manning, 2013), the complex dynamics of posthuman ecologies (Bignall & Braidotti, 2019), the radical aesthetics of Black study (Harney & Moten, 2013), or more-than-human relations with place in Indigenous studies (Bawaka Country, 2015), rebellious scholarship is no longer being framed primarily through a western logic of bounded and intentional human subject positions. These movements have shifted the generative horizons of what it means to rebel theoretically and methodologically over the past two decades, while drawing on minoritarian strands of relational practice and thought with much longer trajectories of development. What might it mean to rebel from within what Patti Lather (2013) calls the 'afterward' of qualitative inquiry, where we encounter a 'thousand tiny methodologies … struggling with and against, becoming more and other, in a field of production of desire' (p. 639)?

The Sphere of Micropolitical Insurrection

It has now been almost a decade since Lather (2013) and St Pierre (2013) declared the 'end' of methodology in education and the social sciences. In accounting for the explosion of a thousand (and more) tiny theories and methods agitating in the post-qualitative afterward, Lather (2013) diagnosed a general shift from a logic of bounded subjects toward a logic of desiring forces and collectively felt intensities. This shift broadly aligns with Felix Guattari's (2008) distinction of an 'eco-logic' of intensity from a logic of discursive categories that presuppose a totalising regime of individual subject-identities. 'While the logic of discursive sets endeavours to completely delimit its objects, the logic of intensities, or eco-logic, is concerned only with the movement and intensity of evolutive processes' (p. 30). This distinction can also be phrased in terms of a 'macropolitics' which only recognises the politics of human subject identities, and a 'micropolitics' which thinks and lives a politics of more-than-human dependencies which are the preconditions for life. While macropolitics largely determined the aims and orientations of conventional qualitative methodology, the new work emerging in the post-qualitative afterward is concerned primarily with the intensities of micropolitics.

This distinction has complex implications for how we might grasp what it means to 'rebel' within the post-qualitative milieus. Brazilian psychologist and art theorist Suely Rolnik (2017) has written vividly about the differences between macropolitical activist movements and what she terms the 'sphere of micropolitical insurrection', which operates through an eco-logic of intensity. Rolnik argues that macropolitical political movements hinge on an image of the human subject as bounded and separate from the vitality of the biosphere. This has the effect of continuously reducing experience down to the experience of the human subject, causing us 'to remain captive to the logic of the very system we seek to combat' (p. 8).

Only the micropolitical sphere of insurrection, according to Rolnik (2017), is capable of mobilising both human and non-human subjectivities, indeed, 'all the elements of the biosphere that rebel against violence toward life' (p. 8). She cites examples of rivers that go underground to evade toxic contamination, or trees that alter their flowering cycles to prevent sterility from pollution.

These examples demonstrate how the micropolitical sphere revolts in order to sustain multi-species flourishing through a redirection of affective flows and unconscious drives that radically exceed the categorical reductions of human subject positions (Rousell et al., 2020). Rolnik therefore argues that micropolitical insurrection involves a complex and subtle process of 'decolonising the unconscious' that gradually dissolves the perverse grip of the capitalistic-colonial regime both 'within us and outside of us' (p. 10). Akin to her collaborator Felix Guattari, she also suggests that the arts can play a *clinical* role in both diagnosing and decolonising the unconscious affects in ways that re-sensitise the world 'in each gesture, each word, each relation, each mode of existence' (p. 10).

The Minor

It is apparent in Rolnik's account that the macropolitical is not necessarily larger in scale or significance than the micropolitical. A mass youth climate protest, for instance, is often perceived as a macropolitical aggregate of individual subjects that achieves higher visibility as it grows to larger scales. However, the micropolitical investment of desire and the affective bonds that link each young protestor with the entire biosphere remain largely invisible, but no less powerful, significant, or valuable (Rousell & Cutter-Mackenzie-Knowles, forthcoming). Here the concept of micropolitical insurrection resonates with Deleuze and Guattari's conceptual figuration of the 'minor' as both a political aesthetic orientation and a moving tendency. Where majoritarian or State regimes present a 'constant and homogenous system', a minoritarian micropolitics operates through 'subsystems ... seeds [and] crystals of becoming whose value is to trigger uncontrollable movements and deterritorialisations of the mean or majority' (Deleuze & Guattari, 1986, p. 106). As philosopher and artist Erin Manning elaborates in the early pages of her book *The minor gesture*:

> The major is a structural tendency that organises itself according to predetermined definitions of value. The minor is a force that courses through it, unmooring its structural integrity, problematising its normative standards ... The minor is a continual variation on experience. It has a mobility not given to the major: its rhythms are not controlled by a pre-existing structure, but are open to flux. (Manning, 2016, p. 1)

The relationship between major and minor is, in this respect, one of patterned contrasts, tonalities and variations in counterpoint, rather than a dialectical opposition. The minor does not rebel *against* the major so much as from *within* it, like a minor key, creolised language, or counterrhythm that opens improvisational cracks in the structural compositions and genres of everyday social life.

Ontological Rebellion

Whether considered in terms of micropolitical insurrection or the anarchic aesthetics of the minor gesture, rebellion in the afterward is as much an *ontological* revolt as it is political. Here the work of feminist philosophers has been crucial in formulating a micropolitics and ethics inseparable from an ontology of immanence (Bignall & Braidotti, 2019; Colebrook, 2016; Gatens & Lloyd, 1999; Grosz, 2017; Manning, 2013). This work has entailed a vigorous resistance to universalisms of every kind, and a cancelling of claims to any transcendent or foundational position from which life can be observed, judged or categorised (Weinstein & Colebrook, 2017). The uptake of this onto-political work in the social sciences, and education studies in particular, has in many cases been responsible for eroding the philosophical foundations of qualitative methodology to the point of rupture. As the quasi-empirical logics of 'literature review', 'methods', 'data', 'narrative' and 'coding' are strategically undermined and exploded, there are no longer any foundational structures or transcendent entry points for scholars who take up the post-qualitative call. Everything must come from the middle of things. Inquiry must be constructed afresh with each word, each thought, each gesture of inquiry. One must learn how to think and write 'the new' and the 'not yet' by letting immanence get into your bones (St Pierre, 2019). There is simply no template, no curriculum or syllabus for learning how to do that. For the new generation of scholars coming up through the post-qualitative turn, ontological rebellion is not so much a question of personal choice as a bid for *survival*. Literally, we must think the new in order to survive. Did we ever have a choice anyway? Or perhaps, as MacLure (2021, p. 507) writes, 'the researcher, in exercising choice … is simultaneously exercised by it'.

Pluriversality

Over the past two decades or so, the turn to immanent ontologies championed by western feminist scholars has also found resonance with an 'ontological turn' continuing to evolve through encounters between anthropologists and First Nations peoples in the global south (Escobar, 2018; Viveiros de Castro, 2004), as well as world-wide articulations of Indigenous (Bawaka Country, 2015; Smith,

2021; Todd, 2016), Black diasporic (Glissant, 1997; Wynter, 2003), Latin American (Mignolo, 2009), Asian (Chen, 2010), and decolonial ontologies of numerous kinds (Smith et al., 2018). While these bodies of work draw from differently situated genealogies of practice and thought, many have come to share an onto-ethical commitment to a radical pluralism that values the incommensurability of ontological difference (Tuck & Yang, 2012). The concept of 'pluriversality' has gained traction in recent years as a framing for ontological pluralism (Escobar, 2018). The concept derives from the work of the Zapatista Army of National Liberation which has maintained territory in open rebellion against the Mexican state since 1994. In the epitaph for their recent edited collection *A world of many worlds*, Mario Blaser and Marisol de la Cadena offer their own translation of the Zapatista movement's 'Fourth Declaration of the Lacandón Jungle':

> In the world of the powerful there is room only for the big and their helpers. In the world we want, everybody fits. The world we want is a world in which many worlds fit. (Ejército Zapatista de Liberación Nacional, cited in Blaser & de la Cadena, 2018, p. 1)

They offer this translation as an introduction to the concept of the pluriverse as a world where many ontologies fit through disjunctive and discontinuous negotiations. In articulating a world that is both many and one at the same time, the concept of the pluriverse disrupts Western humanist claims to universal knowledge, truth, morality and rationality. It makes room for many worlds to compose themselves differently through the ontological interplay between the one and the many. Deleuze and Guattari (1987, p. 20) once described this as 'the magic formula we all seek – PLURALISM=MONISM'. Worlds both singular and multiple. Worlds that express the one through the many (pluralism), and the many through the one (monism).

New Animisms

The concept of the pluriverse is of central consideration for Chapter 2 of this volume. A group of international colleagues work to explore the contours of pluriversality in relation to questions of extinction, or world-ending events, in times of catastrophic climate change. They turn to animist rituals performed by Indigenous peoples in South America and Indonesia, as well as Black diasporic peoples in the Antilles, as ontological practices that mark the beginnings and endings of worlds in highly situated and specific ways.

The term 'animism' has been used since the 19th century to describe indigenous cosmologies that attribute personhood, interiority and subjectivity to non-human beings (Bird-David, 1999; Descola, 1996; Harvey, 2006). While early uses of the term often classified animist beliefs as naïve, superstitious and subject to progressive 'civilising' intervention under settler colonialism, since the 1990s anthropologists such as Deborah Bird Rose (2013), Marilyn Strathern (1992), Elizabeth Povinelli (2016) and Eduardo Viveiros de Castro (1992) have offered nuanced accounts of animist ontologies as complex worldmaking systems. While animist knowledges and practices are by no means new for many Indigenous peoples (Rosiek et al., 2020), some scholars have discussed the emergence of 'new animisms' as Indigenous ontologies find new terms of relevance and application in addressing contemporary problematics, such as climate change and the rise of artificial intelligence (Harvey, 2006; Mathews, 2019). We can see, for example, new animisms being actively cultivated by Indigenous peoples in response to the radically shifting conditions of planetary life, for instance, by addressing urgent questions regarding the possible inclusion of artificial intelligences within existing kinship circles (Lewis et al., 2020), cryogenic preservation of extinct species (TallBear, 2017), or storying climate change through Aboriginal connections with/as Country (Bawaka Country, 2020).

This orientation toward encounters with animist world-making practices motivates the approach to Chapter 15 in this volume. By entangling their thinking and writing with the choreomusical rituals of the Kuikuro in Brazil, Jouvay and steelpan in Trinidad, and the *gamelan semara pegulingan* on the island of Bali, the authors encounter rituals as arts of living in the thresholds *between* worlds (Demos, 2020), where human and non-human agencies share animacy, power and personhood through relations of perpetual reconstruction (Yamin, 2019). This methodological approach encounters the perspectivisms of Indigenous ritual as world-making practices that also generate rebellious *pedagogies* of ongoing dismantling and re-arrangement. The authors argue that animist pedagogies can help us 'learn how to dismantle the world as it has been made and cultivate new ones' (Rousell et al., this volume), disrupting universalising 'end of the world' narratives that have come to dominate liberal discussions of climate change through the 'one world' of settler colonial futurity.

Divination

Education scholar Maggie MacLure (2021) has written recently about the relations between Indigenous ritual and speculative methods in the post-qualitative afterward. She uses the concept of 'divination' to describe the search for 'strange relations between the one and the many, in the shifting totality of the cosmos, and entertain relations that are always to some extent inhuman'

(p. 502). She cautions against the tendency to appropriate Indigenous ontologies to serve the purposes (however well intentioned) of western scholarship and creative practice, advocating instead for a speculative approach that assembles 'its *own* pragmatic arts and fashion[s] its own situated practices – ways of thinking and of reading the world that are grounded in ... the problems addressed by those involved' (p. 504). For MacLure a methodology of divination is not necessarily a (re)turn to magical or premodern beliefs, even though the witch's flight and the sorcerer's ministrations remain key figures in her discussion. Rather, her concern is with speculative and yet *efficacious* practices that attend to occult confluences and opaque encounters where multiple worlds overlap, as 'obscure zones' where groping forms of 'immanent experimentation' offer the only ways forward.

MacLure offers a valuable set of conceptual tools for approaching the pluriverse through the situated invention of speculative method. The pluriverse, after all, bears the promise of gathering many worlds that do not 'naturally' fit together in any logical or systematic way. Unnatural, risky and speculative alliances are required to get even the barest sense of the pluriverse to hold. Thinking under the influence of William James and Isabelle Stengers (2008, 2018), MacLure argues that such practices entail a speculative 'leap without looking', a leap that requires an 'unconditional or "precursive" trust ... exercised in the absence of the usual guarantees afforded by logic, theory, superior judgment, or common sense' (p. 507). To the extent that the pluriverse requires a speculative 'leap' into an opaque and unknowable future, it may ask us to trust in the merest possible sense of how incommensurable worlds *might just fit* under radically precarious circumstances.

Diffraction

Along with the turn to process philosophies and Indigenous animisms in the cultivation of rebellious theory in the post-qualitative afterward, the 'divinatory' performances of quantum science have also provided novel entry points for many scholars. The work of feminist theorist and physicist Karen Barad (2007, 2011) has been a touchstone in this regard, bringing concepts from quantum mechanics and quantum field theory into dynamic encounter with post-structuralist gender studies, queer theory and critical questions of social justice. Building on Niels Bohr's early-twentieth-century interpretation of the famous 'two slit' experiment in quantum physics, Barad (2007, p. 88) proposes the term 'diffraction' to describe phenomena in which patterns of difference are generated through the indeterminate entanglement of matter and meaning. She distinguishes between 'classical' diffraction, such as the physical patterns generated by the confluence of two ocean waves, and 'quantum' diffraction, where the observational apparatus of the phenomenon changes the wave pattern, and indeed alters whether the phenomenon will instantiate as a wave *or* a particle.

Classical diffraction is often explained in terms of mechanistic causal processes which assume the constraints of geometric space and linear time. Quantum diffraction, however, does not respect the rules of classical physics, Euclidian geometry, or the linear time of a present moment moving steadily, like the hands of a clock, into the future. It rebels against all of these, proposing instead a field of indeterminacy in which a single particle can occupy multiple positions in the past, present and future *at the same time*. In quantum physics this is referred to as 'superpositioning', and quantum diffraction is a particular example of superpositioning where the apparatus of inquiry (including, for Barad, the *conceptual* apparatus), alters the material instantiation of the phenomenon under study (Barad, 2007, p. 142). For Barad (2011), quantum science reveals nature's 'queer performativity' and thus the radical inseparability of ontology (being), epistemology (knowing) and ethics (doing) across every agential scale and materialisation of the real. Her work also, in this respect, finds confluence with Indigenous animisms and lifeways for which 'agency is not just a human capacity but a quality manifest in all aspects of reality' (Rosiek et al., 2020, p. 332). Could quantum diffraction also be a way into the pluriverse?

The Heart

In Chapter 16 of this volume, performance scholar Annouchka Bailey grapples with Barad's assertion that quantum diffraction is a material-discursive phenomenon with indeterminate causal effects, and not simply a metaphor. Writing in dynamic conversation with Barad's agential realism and her own creative writing practice, she argues that a novel could be understood not as 'a thing or an object, but a *doing*; a diffractive apparatus that re-stories the world even as we read it and are moved by it' (Bailey, this volume). Diffraction here is not a metaphor but a concrete description of how a novel operates. Bailey elaborates this argument for the novel as 'diffractive prism' by turning to another concrete, processual agency that is so often construed as a metaphor: the heart. The heart, Bailey reminds us,

> is weighty (200–400 grams approx.). Its four beautiful and fleshy chambers circulate and oxygenate our blood and without its bright and vibrant

> electricity, we would die in a matter of moments. Therefore, everything the heart does matters. (Bailey, this volume)

And yet in literary terms the heart is often rendered into a metaphor for love, hate, faith, betrayal, and nearly every other affective condition or emotional state. Writing under the influence of Barad and Le Guin, Bailey suggests that the heart is not a mere metaphor for these states; it is actually *performing* these affects, *carrying* these affects into being.

> The diffractive heart. Heart as performative agent, made present by its very function: to transform … our life blood. Blood is real. And it also carries the material network of us – all our stories, all our heroes and monsters and revelations. (Bailey, this volume)

Bailey's intervention is significant here, as it challenges received understandings of literature, and of creative practice methodology more broadly, as a symbolic domain where discourse and metaphor enjoy free rein from the constraints of material bodies and worlds. Her argument, with Barad, is for an agential realism which would submit creative practice to exercise the same claims to realism as any of the physical or natural sciences, and indeed, stand up to the same empirical demands. But rather than draining creative practice of its 'magic', such as literature's capacity to escape or distort reality, this operation re-instates the weirdness of a quantum realism that *changes* depending on what you're reading, and how you read it. In a quantum field of non-positions and indeterminacies, the operations of the heart can pulse simultaneously in the body and on the page, and the differences between these operations become fuzzy, if not completely indiscernible. The heart is both here and there, particle and wave, at the same time. *Superpositioned.* Here Bailey takes on the rebellious task of writing a novel that *does* diffraction, rather than a novel *about* diffraction, and this distinction makes all the difference in proposing a new materialist horizon of potentiality for creative practice methodology and performative studies of literature.

Surfacing

While not theorised explicitly as diffraction, Chapter 17 by Trisha McCrae and colleagues generates an intricate series of surfaces that explore the material-discursive enfoldings of creative method through rebellious entanglements of image and text. Conceived as an experiment in 'exchanging sensations of time' across temporal zones and situated geographies, the chapter rebels against preconceived forms of creative practice and academic scholarship. Over a six-month period, the three artist researchers exchanged fragments of image and text via email as they emerged during the course of live artistic experimentation and inquiry. Images of works in progress from a Paris studio intermix with fieldnotes from gallery work with children in Melbourne/Naarm earlier that morning. A return to environmentally degraded art installations in Bundjalung Country, New South Wales intermixes with poetic re-routings sent through from Cambridge the night before. Each page of the chapter cuts into this process of live circulation through the composition of a full-colour plate, actively deforming and rearranging the performative relations of image and text through a 'logic of sensation' that refuses to bind aesthetic experience to linear space and time (Deleuze, 2003). Moreover, the work performs the *exchange* of sensation through what the authors refer to as 'event-particles' or 'particle-signs' (Deleuze & Guattari, 1987). Any provisional boundary between theory and practice is suspended by a praxis that inevitably comes to involve 'the production of surfaces, their multiplication and their consolidation' (Deleuze, 1994, p. 125).

Central to this work are considerations of aesthetic surface as immanently experiential, where sensation itself takes shape as an immersive surface that generates images, language, movement, and even space and time as materially lived and intensively extended. Ontologically, this immersion in surface has the effect of flattening out anything transcendent and hierarchical, such that image and text are folded 'together on the surface', with nothing 'foundational or transcendental – nothing beneath or above, outside' (St Pierre, 2013, p. 649). Drawing on Deleuze's (1994) concept of *le pli* or 'the fold', art theorist Giuliana Bruno (2014) similarly describes the surfaces of images as topological rather than geometric, as porous, tensile membranes that 'tangibly [transform] the fabrication of inner and outer space' (p. 13). This shifts the reading of artistic surfaces away from linguistic and optical frames of representation to embrace a tactile, diffractive materiality. Bodies make haptic contact with images in ways that generate a 'public intimacy' of circulating sensations, affects and temporalities (p. 3). We might then grasp Chapter 17 not as an essay in visual form, but as what Bruno calls a 'permeable architectural envelope … in which distinctions between inside and outside temporally dissolve into the depth of surface' (p. 5). This bears the promise of a creative method which no longer requires writing, or even words, to instantiate 'the new' and the 'not yet' of post-qualitative inquiry. Dare we imagine some mutant genre of scholarship, or indeed, of education, which no longer forces us to 'drink the letter' (Deleuze & Guattari, 1983, p. 206)?

The Raft

Much is at stake for new scholars entering the academic world in the afterward, perhaps most especially for those who edge in sideways from professional practices in the creative arts. This is a punishing business. The very limits of our vital affects and drives are tapped continuously by profit-driven publication companies that monetise our thinking while holding the rights to whatever we produce. The curse of our open rebellion is that we become writing-machines: strapped into a chair, hands cuffed to the keyboard, eyes held open and glued to the screen like Alex in *A clockwork orange*. Forced to drink and regurgitate the letter every day. This is the price we pay for the right to participate in a global collective of thinkers who read and care about each other's thinking. And it seems we have just gotten so tired of reading and writing boring stuff. If we're strapped in, we might as well just read and write whatever feels urgent, fun, new, important and interesting. We might as well just *go for it*. In other words we might as well *go all city*. And yet, this imperative to jump all in without looking is fraught with risk and precarity. To undertake such a rebellious adventure one must be adequately prepared. As MacLure (2020) argues, the witch's flight above all requires a careful preparation of the ground from which it launches and, inevitably, lands.

In Chapter 18 of this volume, Marta Cotrim and Mindy R. Carter perform a staging of treacherous crossings into rebellious academic practice under the conditions of post-human precarity and post-qualitative methodological upheaval. Here we find the entire process of de- and reconstructing a work of rebellious scholarship laid out on the operating table. Tensile conversations between PhD student and supervisor, critical and affirmative comments from editors and reviewers, crossed out traces of redacted text and rephrased sentences, interrupted and incomplete manifestos, childhood stories of wishing books and monastic boarding schools. All of these (and more) are interwoven with illustrations by collaborating designer Dayna McLeod, including a paper raft that can be cut out of the book and constructed in three dimensions by the reader.

The figuration of 'the raft' in Cotrim and Carter's chapter is simultaneously conceptual, aesthetic, embodied and performative. It comes to function as a moving zone of flexible stability, capable of holding a set of relations in place as they travel, and inevitably transform, from personal narrative into political manifesto, into deconstructed semiosis, into metaphysical adventure, and so on. Here metaphor is re-affirmed, but in a minor key that undercuts its own articulation. The ambition of a final 'product' of academic writing is discarded. Everything becomes staged as a work in process, and the raft provides the flotation device for both sensing and navigating the turbulence (even violence) of this process. As this work bears witness, embracing the pursuit of a post-qualitative or post-humanist inquiry is to be cast adrift. It demands the release of any comfortable home or essential 'truth' of the liberal human subject to hold onto. Personal narrative becomes just another story we tell ourselves along with any number of other possible stories. We are no longer the owners or the authors of what we experience. We are no longer ourselves (Deleuze & Guattari, 1987, p. 12). And this is perhaps one of the strangest and most treacherous rebellions of all.

Education?

Even though there are only five chapters collected in Part 3, their theoretical and methodological rebellions extend beyond any simple location comfortably bounded in space and time (Whitehead, 1929). They touch, at least in some small way, every continent on the Earth's surface. Whether diffracted through the Caribbean sea, the Indonesian isles, the Brazilian rainforest, the streets of Melbourne/Naarm, a teenage journey across North America, a novelist writing in Cambridge, or an artist at work in a Paris studio, the works collected here speak with a cacophony of more-than-human voices, collectivities, places and events. As the anonymous collective the Invisible Committee (2014) argue, no matter how small or localised a rebellious gesture might be, 'every insurrection gestures beyond itself; it contains something global from the outset. It raises us together to the level of the epoch' (p. 5).

What then does our rebellious cacophony have to say about *education*? The theoretical and methodological concepts discussed here, such as 'micropolitics', 'pluriversality', 'divination', 'diffraction' and 'surfacing', lay out a polyvalent plane of thought which places a term like 'education' into a radically expanded field of encounter. These concepts put education in touch with the strange realism of quantum entanglement, the onto-politics of more-than-human ecologies, the decolonisation of the unconscious through creative practice, and the use of ritual to navigate treacherous crossings between worlds that are ending, and others that are just coming into existence. Coming alive in this expanded field, education refuses to be reduced to those tired, old categories like 'student', 'teacher', 'classroom', 'school', 'principal', 'curriculum', 'assessment', 'grade', 'policy', 'standards'. Education can be all and none of these things, if it wants to. It doesn't really have to comply with any of them. This noncompliance may be the promise of education as an index of pure potential. This would not be an injunction to dismiss the past, but on the contrary, a shouldering of the unbearable weight of the past in the fragile memory of a more liveable future.

So build your rafts, grab your spray cans and balaclavas, ring your steelpans, and write your hearts out: we're going all city.

References

Anderson, C. L. (2012). Going 'all city': The spatial politics of graffiti. *Graduate Journal of Visual and Material Culture*, *5*, 1-23.

Barad, K. (2007). *Meeting the universe halfway: Quantum physics and the entanglement of matter and meaning*. Duke University Press.

Barad, K. (2011). Nature's queer performativity. *Qui Parle: Critical Humanities and Social Sciences*, *19*(2), 121-158.

Bawaka Country, including Wright, S., Suchet-Pearson, S., Lloyd, K., Burarrwanga, L., Ganambarr, R., ... Maymuru, D. (2015). Working with and learning from Country: Decentring human author-ity. *Cultural Geographies*, *22*(2), 269–283.

Bawaka Country, including Wright, S., Suchet-Pearson, S., Lloyd, K., Burarrwanga, L., Ganambarr, R., Ganambarr-Stubbs, M., ... Maymuru, D. (2020). Gathering of the clouds: Attending to Indigenous understandings of time and climate through song-spirals. *Geoforum*, *108*, 295–304.

Bignall, S., & Braidotti, R. (2019). Posthuman systems. In Braidotti, R., & Bignall, S., (Eds.), *Posthuman ecologies: Complexity and process after Deleuze* (pp. 1–22). Rowman & Littlefield.

Bird-David, N. (1999). 'Animism' revisited: Personhood, environment, and relational epistemology. *Current Anthropology*, *40*, 67–91.

Bloch, S. (2020). *Going all city*. University of Chicago Press.

Braidotti, R. (2019). *Posthuman knowledges*. John Wiley & Sons.

Chen, K. H. (2010). *Asia as method*. Duke University Press.

Colebrook, C. (2016). 'A grandiose time of coexistence': Stratigraphy of the Anthropocene. *Deleuze Studies*, *10*(4), 440–454.

Danowski, D., & Viveiros de Castro, E. (2017). *The ends of the world* (R. Nunes, Trans.). Polity.

de la Bellacasa, M. P. (2012). 'Nothing comes without its world': Thinking with care. *Sociological Review*, *60*(2), 197–216.

Demos, T. J. (2020). *Beyond the world's end: Arts of living at the crossing*. Duke University Press.

Deleuze, G. (1994). *Difference and repetition* (P. Patton, Trans.) Columbia University Press.

Deleuze, G. (2003). *Francis Bacon: The logic of sensation*. University of Minnesota Press.

Deleuze, G., & Guattari, F. (1983). *Anti-Oedipus: Capitalism and schizophrenia* (R. Hurley, M. Seem, & H. R. Lane, Trans.). University of Minnesota Press.

Deleuze, G., & Guattari, F. (1986). *Kafka: Toward a minor literature* (D. Polan, Trans.). University of Minnesota Press.

Deleuze, G., & Guattari, F. (1987). *A thousand plateaus: Capitalism and schizophrenia* (B. Massumi, Trans.). University of Minnesota Press.

Deleuze, G., & Guattari, F. (1994). *What is philosophy?* (H. Tomlinson & G. Burchell, Trans.). Columbia University Press.

Descola, P. (1996). *In the society of nature: A native ecology of Amazonia* (Nora Scott, Trans.). Cambridge University Press.

Escobar, A. (2018). *Designs for the pluriverse: Radical interdependence, autonomy, and the making of worlds*. Duke University Press.

Gatens, M., & Lloyd, G. (1999). *Collective imaginings: Spinoza, past & present*. Routledge.

Glissant, E. (1997). *Poetics of relation* (B. Wing, Trans.). University of Michigan Press.

Grosz, E. (2017). *The incorporeal: Ontology, ethics, and the limits of materialism*. Columbia University Press.

Guattari, F. (2008). *The three ecologies*. Continuum.

Harney, S., & Moten, F. (2013). *The undercommons: Fugitive planning and black study*. Minor Compositions.

Harvey, G. (2006). *Animism: Respecting the living world*. Columbia University Press.

Invisible Committee. (2014). *To our friends*. MIT Press.

Lather, P. (2013). Methodology-21: What do we do in the afterward? *International Journal of Qualitative Studies in Education, 26*(6), 634–645.

Lewis, J. E., Arista, N., Pechawis, A., & Kite, S. (2018). Making kin with the machines. *Journal of Design and Science*.

MacLure, M. (2021). Inquiry as divination. *Qualitative Inquiry, 27*(5), 502–511.

Manning, E. (2012). *Relationscapes: Movement, art, philosophy (Technologies of lived abstraction)*. MIT Press.

Manning, E. (2013). *Always more than one: Individuations dance*. Duke University Press.

Manning, E. (2016). *The minor gesture*. Duke University Press.

Massumi, B. (2002). *Parables for the virtual: Movement, affect, sensation*. Duke University Press.

Massumi, B. (2015). The supernormal animal. In R. Grisin (Ed.), *The nonhuman turn* (pp. 1–18). University of Minnesota Press.

Mathews, F. (2019). Living cosmos panpsychism. In W. Seager (Ed.), *The Routledge handbook of panpsychism* (pp. 131–144). Routledge.

Mignolo, W. D. (2009). *The idea of Latin America*. John Wiley & Sons.

Moten, F. (2018). *Stolen life*. Duke University Press.

Povinelli, E. A. (2016). *Geontologies: A requiem for late liberalism*. Duke University Press.

Rolnik, S. (2017). The spheres of insurrection: Suggestions for combating the pimping of life. *E-flux Journal, 86*. http://worker01.3-flux.com/pdf/article_163197.pdf

Rose, D. B. (2013). Val Plumwood's philosophical animism: Attentive interactions in the sentient world. *Environmental Humanities, 3*(1), 93–109.

Rosiek, J. L., Snyder, J., & Pratt, S. L. (2020). The new materialisms and Indigenous theories of non-human agency: Making the case for respectful anti-colonial engagement. *Qualitative Inquiry, 26*(3-4), 331–346.

Rousell, D. (2019). Inhuman forms of life: On art as a problem for post-qualitative research. *International Journal of Qualitative Studies in Education, 32*(7), 887–908.

Rousell, D. (2021). *Immersive cartography and post-qualitative inquiry: A speculative adventure into research-creation.* Routledge.

Rousell, D., & Cutter-Mackenzie-Knowles, A. (forthcoming). *Climate child imaginaries: Posthuman research playspaces.* Springer.

Rousell, D., & Fell, F. (2018). Becoming a work of art: Collaboration, materiality and posthumanism in tertiary visual arts education. *International Journal of Education through Art, 14*(1), 91–110.

Rousell, D., Hohti, R., MacLure, M., & Chalk, H. (2020). Blots on the Anthropocene: Micropolitical interventions with young people in a university museum. *Cultural Studies <-> Critical Methodologies, 21*(1), 27–40.

Smith, L. T. (2021). *Decolonizing methodologies: Research and Indigenous peoples.* Zed Books.

Smith, L. T., Tuck, E., & Yang, K. W. (Eds.). (2018). *Indigenous and decolonizing studies in education: Mapping the long view.* Routledge.

St Pierre, E. A. (2013). The posts continue: Becoming. *International Journal of Qualitative Studies in Education, 26*(6), 646–657.

St Pierre, E. A. (2019). Post qualitative inquiry in an ontology of immanence. *Qualitative Inquiry, 25*(1), 3–16.

Stengers, I. (2005). The cosmopolitical proposal. In B. Latour & P. Weibel (Eds.), *Making things public: Atmospheres of democracy* (pp. 994–1002). MIT Press.

Stengers, I. (2008). Experimenting with refrains: Subjectivity and the challenge of escaping modern dualism. *Subjectivity, 22*, 38–59.

Stengers, I. (2018). The challenge of ontological politics. In M. de la Cadena & M. Blaser (Eds.), *A world of many worlds* (pp. 83–111). University of Minnesota Press.

Strathern, M. (1992). *Reproducing the future: Essays on anthropology, kinship and the new reproductive technologies.* University of Manchester Press.

TallBear, K. (2017). Beyond the life/not life binary: A feminist-Indigenous reading of cryopreservation, interspecies thinking and the new materialisms. In J. Radin & E. Kowal (Eds.), *Cryopolitics: Frozen life in a melting world* (pp. 179–202). MIT Press.

Todd, Z. (2016). An indigenous feminist's take on the ontological turn: 'Ontology' is just another word for colonialism. *Journal of Historical Sociology, 29*(1), 4–22.

Tuck, E., & Yang, K. W. (2012). Decolonization is not a metaphor. *Decolonization: Indigeneity, Education & Society, 1*(1), 1-40.

Viveiros de Castro, E. (2004). Exchanging perspectives: The transformation of objects into subjects in Amerindian ontologies. *Common Knowledge, 10*(3), 463–484.

Yamin, T. (2019). One or several gamelan? Perpetual (re)construction in the life of a Balinese gamelan semara pagulingan. *Ethnomusicology, 63*(3), 357–392.

Weinstein, J., & Colebrook, C. (2017). Introduction: Critical life studies and the problems of inhuman rites and posthumous life. In J. Weinstein & C. Colebrook (Eds.), *Posthumous life: Theorising beyond the posthuman* (pp. ix–xxvii). Columbia University Press.

Whitehead, A. N. (1929). *The function of reason*. Free Press.

Wynter, S. (2003). Unsettling the coloniality of being/power/truth/freedom: Towards the human, after man, its overrepresentation – An argument. *CR: The New Centennial Review, 3*(3), 257–337.

Yusoff, K. (2019). *A billion Black Anthropocenes or none*. University of Minnesota Press.

CHAPTER 15

Animist Pedagogies and the Endings of Worlds

Rituals for the Pluriverse

David Rousell, Eleanor Ryan, Birgitte Bauer-Nilsen and Rachel Lai

Ritual

As the rainy season along the Xingu River grows shorter due to climate change, the Kuikuro push further into the dwindling Amazon rainforest to collect sacred feathers that will help summon the local spirit of the cobra.

Carnival erupts across the island of Trinidad in a riot of colour and movement, as costumed dancers perform syncopated melodies on steel oil drums that sing with Jumbie spirit.

In the village of Kamasan in Bali, the Bale Batur temple is ablaze with colours for the odalan (anniversary ceremony), with the gamelan semara pagulingan contributing its personal voice and character at the centre of the proceedings.

Each of these are rituals that generate and sustain particular 'arts of living' at the crossroads where multiple worlds intersect (Demos, 2020). As a constellation of efficacious acts, or 'fabrications' (Stengers, 2008), rituals are events through which bodies enter into complex relations of confluence, alliance, fostering and potentialisation. And while a ritual may be repeated over centuries, millennia or even longer, its task is not to fix a particular set of relations in place. No matter how many times it is repeated, each articulation of ritual generates its own *rite of passage* according to the immanent conditions of its enactment (Weinstein & Colebrook, 2017). Such rites may involve passage from life into non-life, or from one life into another, a passage from the non-human into the human, or vice versa. In each case, ritual marks a transition of whatever *we* might be, in this very moment, as we gather our shared potential to pass from one world into another.

DOI:10.1163/9789004516069_021

We

We sit down in chairs, at desks, with computers, in homes. We stand up, walk around, read again, send a draft, write some more. In this act of ritual, we are ourselves, but also not ourselves. We are both one and many. A part of many worlds, we share more with some, and others less. In this ritual we don't know who 'we' are yet, and we may never know. But we are lingering here nonetheless, in the tentative moments between hesitation and impulse, simultaneously together and apart. Differently.

An artist, a researcher, an educator, an activist, a husband, a brother, a father, a son, a migrant, a listener, a thinker, a reader, a writer, a maker. Born on lands originally inhabited by the Algonquian tribes along the north-east coast of the Americas. Has lived and worked on unceded Peramangk, Kaurna and Bundjalung Country in Australia, and the lands of Ngāti Hau in Aotearoa New Zealand. Living today on unceded lands of the Wurundjeri-willam language group of the Eastern Kulin Nation, along the Merri Merri (or 'very rocky') creek. Always a visitor on these lands.

A musician, an educator, a researcher, a sister, an aunt, a daughter, a friend, a migrant, a listener, a thinker, a reader, a writer. Of Irish, Dutch and British descent, raised in Whātaitai, Te Whanganui-a-Tara in Aotearoa New Zealand on the tribal lands of Te Āti Awa. I have lived and worked in Manchester in the United Kingdom and Trinidad and Tobago in the Caribbean on traditional lands of Arawakan and Cariban Amerindian peoples. I now live in Cambridge and London, England, performing, teaching, researching, learning and writing. Always a visitor on these lands.

A choreographer, a dancer, a researcher, an educator, an activist, a wife, a daughter, a sister, a friend, a listener, a thinker, a reader, a maker. Born in Copenhagen, Denmark and have lived here all my life. I commute to teach in Norway and have done research and performed dances in Tanzania, Vietnam, Brazil, India, Greenland and Europe. Always as a visitor in these lands.

A musician, a researcher, an educator, a learner, a wife, a sister, a daughter, a migrant, a friend, a thinker, a reader, a maker. Descendent of Chinese immigrants, born in Malaysia, located within the Malay Peninsula, on land that was once colonised by the Portuguese, Dutch, British, and occupied by the Japanese. Have since lived in London and Cambridge, England, researching, learning, and teaching. Always a visitor on these lands.

We come together here with a purpose that is felt, and still yet to be defined. We gather because we want to learn how to mourn, celebrate and regenerate worlds that are threatened, or already ended, due to climate change. How to practise new arts of living in the thresholds between worlds that are ending, and others that are just coming into existence? How to care for worlds that are not our own, especially worlds currently being foreclosed by climate change?

Pluriverse

At first glance the rituals we have invoked here might seem disconnected. They take place within different geopolitical boundaries and diversely situated socio-ecological communities. And they configure according to quite different sets of cultural protocols, concepts, languages and behavioural norms. Yet these varied rituals share an investment in *animism* as an 'ontological route' into co-existence (Descolla, 1996), where beings of many kinds are invested with complex powers, kinships and characters that participate directly in practices of more-than-human worldmaking (Bird-David, 1999; Braidotti, 2019; Harvey, 2006; Viveiros de Castro, 2004). As practices through which human and non-human bodies explicitly share power, perspective and agency, animist rituals generate pedagogical zones for rebellious crossings between worlds, allowing worlds to intersect and co-compose without reducing their differences (Blaser & de la Cadena, 2018). How can we learn from animist pedagogies as we attempt to cultivate new arts of inquiry in times of climatological crisis and mass extinction? Our interest in this question has brought us to the tentative possibilities carried by the concept of the *pluriverse*.

Concepts like the pluriverse do not come from nowhere. They are not simply invented by human cultures and minds, nor are they universals that can apply to all situations. Rather, concepts arise in response to the configurations of problems as immanently lived through specific worldly encounters and events (Deleuze, 1994). Once mobilised in response to a problem, concepts take on their own lively adventures as 'consistencies' that pass through and re-arrange bodies, territories and milieus of many different kinds, a process Deleuze and Guattari (1994) term a 'pedagogy of the concept'. And so, the concepts we think with must also bear a pedagogical responsibility to be *care*-full. It matters what concepts we use (and *how* we use them) to think other concepts (Strathern, 1992). We must be mindful of the conditions from which concepts arise, how they circulate through multiple milieus, especially Indigenous concepts that carry particular relations with Country or place (Rose, 2013). And we must also remain aware that academic concepts, perhaps especially *ontological* concepts, can be colonising in the ways they reproduce the terms of value through which they make the claim to know (Todd, 2016).

In the case of the pluriverse, it is largely through encounters between Latin American anthropologists and First Nations peoples that the concept has now found its way into increasingly global circulation (Blaser & de la Cadena, 2018; Danowski & Viveiros de Castro, 2017; Escobar, 2018). The concept of the pluriverse has arisen in response to the problem of creating 'a world in which many worlds fit' (Ejército Zapatista de Liberación Nacional, cited in Blaser & de la Cadena, 2018, p. 1). For the Zapatistas and related mobilisations of Indigenous, Afro-descendent, peasant and marginalised urban peoples across Latin America, the pluriverse bears the promise of a world where many worlds can co-exist without the violent imposition of colonising hierarchies and the negation of what the state cannot contain or control (Escobar, 2020). Differences between Indigenous and non-Indigenous ontologies have become newly *political* across numerous and diverse domains, ranging from new accounts of planetary history and biodiversity (Ellis et al., 2021) to questions of synthetic biology (TallBear, 2017) and artificial intelligence (Lewis et al., 2018). And yet the concept of the pluriverse is also inseparable from a current 'civilizational conjuncture' of catastrophic climate change, mass extinction, environmental racism and ubiquitous technology at the planetary scale (Escobar, 2018). Building the pluriverse has now become a matter of human and non-human survival. And while the pluriverse may have arisen from specific onto-political struggles and mobilisations of minoritarian peoples across Latin America in particular, it now speaks to global struggles for a liveable world where many worlds fit, a world where carefully negotiated encounters and alliances *between* incommensurable ontologies have become the very means for beings of all kinds to endure (Blaser & de la Cadena, 2018; Demos, 2020).

Drift

Drifting down the Xingu River in the Central Amazon I suddenly realise that I have crossed into a threshold between two worlds. The forest on the right side of the river has been eradicated. It almost no longer exists. This is the white farmer's land, now given over to a monocultural crop of soybeans, as far as the eye can see. But on the left side of the river lies the sanctuary of the Indigenous people, the Kuikuro. Here the rainforest grows extremely high and thick, right to the banks of the river. This forest is impenetrable, unfathomable, even threatening. And yet I know that its very existence is also threatened every day.

I am on my way to negotiate an exchange research project with the Kuikuro. Takuma, one of my hosts, explains that the white farmers grow soybeans and pollute the earth with death to grow faster and higher crops. They kill the forest to gain more land. Takuma says the Kuikuro people feel a threat to their very existence from the farmers. The Kuikuro work to care for the forest through respect and knowledge of its ecology. They believe the forest is animate, and their cosmology is rich with connection to non-human beings and spirits through everyday rituals of shamanism and healing (Costa & Fausto, 2010). *At the time of my visit, the Kuikuro village only numbers around 200 people in total.*

It is raining heavily. It is not supposed to rain so dramatically at this time of the year, but because of climate change the rains come in February and finish in March. Rains used to arrive in November and finish in March. I am preparing to share my choreography of a dance trilogy about climate change with the Kuikuro community, including stories about glacier melt that were shared with me by Inuit peoples in Greenland (Burnard et al., 2018). *In return, the Kuikuro have agreed to show me a sacred dance and music ritual and tell me about their preparation for the ritual in relation to climate change, and specifically drought.*

Before the ritual a Kuikuro woman comes to me. She is the leader for the dance ritual. She shows me the movements, the intricate conceptual structure and the spiritual impact of the dance, and I learn the movements from her. Later, the Kuikuro shaman comes to me and paints my face with a red stripe on the forehead and other parts of my body, in accordance with other women in the ritual. He puts his necklace of jaguar teeth around my neck, perhaps so that I feel the spirit of the jaguar. The shaman is very inviting, friendly and concerned for me during the ritual.

The instruments used in the Kuikuro ritual are flutes. Each flute has a soul. Each is a spiritual being with complex kin relations reflected in their names – the small one is named 'little brother', followed by a different and larger flute 'the mother', and then 'the father', and so on. Each flute passes its spirit on to the next generation, a sacred spirit that has a special sound coming from the ancestors (Brabec & Seeger, 2013).

I gradually learn that all the artefacts of the ritual have a soul with a spiritual affect and effect. The feather from a certain bird, the paint on the body, the necklace shells from the river, the jaguar skin and the teeth. There is deep respect and honour for all the artefacts of the ritual. I begin to sense a different kind of interconnectedness between the human and the non-human (DiNovelli-Lang, 2013), *not just a connection of one thing with another, but a connection of mutual inclusion. Co-constitution. World making.*

The ritual begins. The women are mourning, singing to awaken the cobra spirit that will help purify their community from illness. They are dancing and repeating the movements to get into the affective state for making contact with the spirit. The women feel something, and I feel something too. Do we feel the same thing? Or different things? We are drifting between worlds. The feeling is indescribable.

The Opacity of Care

Show us a particular world, and we will ask: what encounters were required to make it?

In the pluriverse, a world is made and unmade through an ecology of living encounters. As artists and researchers, our task is to learn how to *care* for these encounters, which are never just physically embodied, but also metaphysical and cosmological. The ways that we care for encounters between worlds are necessarily speculative (de la Bellacasa, 2012, 2017). Caring for encounters requires a speculative disposition that is 'attentive to practices that make worlds even if they do not satisfy our demand (the demand of modern epistemology) to prove their reality (as they do not leave historical evidence, let alone scientific)' (Blaser & de la Cadena, 2018, p. 4). As artists and researchers, we cannot assume that our experiences, knowledges or interests are shared across the worlds we encounter. We cannot assume that all who gather in a place desire the same things, or have any particular thing in common. Very different practices of care can converge in the same place, at the same time. For example, in South America certain mountains, forests and rivers often 'emerge as resources through some practices but also as persons through other practices' (p. 4). Two worlds might converge in a forest which is valued as a capital investment by some and a living person by others, at one and the same time. But when that forest is clear cut it ceases to exist both as a capital resource and as a person. All that is left to care for is the forest's ending, its afterlife, its tentative promise of regeneration, and the anguish of 'those who can never go home again' (Rose, 2006, p. 5).

The pluriverse demands speculative practices of care for these *differences* between worlds, including those differences between how worlds come to an end (Danowski & Viveiros de Castro, 2017; Demos, 2020). The pluriverse cannot be built on the old humanist dream of consensual agreement about 'what is right' according to universal knowledge and values (Wynter, 1984). Inquiring into the intricate differences between worlds, especially worlds that are not our own, requires a speculative 'leap' into relations between the unknown and the unknowable (MacLure, 2021).

Such an approach to inquiry may embody an ethics of *opacity*, as articulated by Caribbean poet and philosopher Édouard Glissant (1997). Glissant describes an ethics of opacity as a 'gesture of giving-on and with' (p. 199), a gesture that opens onto the unknowable totality of relation. This ethics is very different from the western humanist obsession with *grasping* others in order to render them transparent and knowable. We see this constant grasping for transparency in the patronising language of 'emancipation', 'development', 'conservation', 'resilience', 'vulnerability' and 'progress', so often imposed as the redemptive hand of policy upon Indigenous, minoritarian and other peoples classed as 'disadvantaged' (Escobar, 2020). Such language demands that others are made transparent in order to be improved, given a voice, and thus rendered fully 'human', whether through research, education, policy or other forms of humanistic intervention (Harney & Moten, 2013; Wynter, 2003).

But the pluriverse can only be built by respecting the opacity of care, which refuses to reduce the singularity of relation to any universal signifier. We must resist the conceit that others don't know simply because their knowledge cannot be grasped and made transparent. We will never know how (or if) our thoughts and practices of care are shared with others. The relational differentials are far too opaque. Like the two sides of the Xingu River, there are unfathomable depths between worlds. And these depths can never simply be traversed by appearances or signifiers masquerading as shared 'human understandings' within a universalising 'commons'. We may find stronger, better relations of care with certain plants, animals, works of art, pieces of music or books on our shelves than with those who live across the river, or just across the street. The pluriverse seeks to include these occult depths and unnatural alliances across heterogeneous worlds (MacLure, 2021), these vital rifts, jumps and opaque excesses in knowledge.

> Excesses across knowledges (ours and others') and hence not knowing (as we and they usually know) may be an important condition of dialogues that allow for a form of understanding that does not require sameness, and therefore rather than cancelling divergence is constituted by it … Elements in the dialogue may rest unknown: that may be an awkward condition, yet not a deterrent for conversations across worlds. (Blaser & de la Cadena, 2018, p. 10)

Blaser and de la Cadena invite us to help care for the pluriverse by gathering awkwardly in the *uncommons*, where divergent worlds cultivate alliances and converse opaquely with one another. To care without knowing, here in the uncommons, is to acknowledge that every world is haunted by its unpaid debts to others. As Harney and Moten (2013) write in the radical Black tradition, *we already owe each other everything*. An infinite debt of care, a debt without credit, recognition or authority, a debt that includes caring for worlds that might have been, but are not. As Denise Ferreira da Silva (2014) suggests, such an unfathomable debt may call for an ethics of inquiry 'which, instead of the betterment of the World as we know it aims at its end' (p. 82).

Otherwise

Every world could have been otherwise. There is nothing inevitable about catastrophic climate change and mass extinction, just as there is nothing inevitable about the mass enslavement and murder of Black, Brown, and Indigenous peoples (Saldanha, 2020; Yusoff, 2019). These events are driven by carefully calculated and highly strategised practices of world making according to a formal logic of colonial-capitalistic extraction at a planetary scale (Rolnik, 2017). The claiming of terra nullius, the genocide of 40 million Indigenous people to secure the colonial occupation of the Americas, 12 million slaves to sustain the productivity of the American colonies, decimation of Indigenous communities through atomic testing in the Marshall Islands, White Australia, the stolen generation, Black deaths in custody. None of these events are simple accidents or collateral damage resulting from well-intentioned projects of colonial expansion and development gone awry (Yusoff, 2019). They are carefully orchestrated operations that are entirely consistent with the logic of extraction that underpins free-market capitalism.

Harney and Moten (2013) elaborate this in terms of a 'logistics of the shipped'. The trans-Atlantic slave trade required the invention of a new logistics where lives become cargo, flesh becomes capital, and the body becomes 'fungible matter' (Hartman, 1997). A logistics of the shipped originate and honed during the Middle Passage between Africa and the new colonies, and the blueprint for a new command economy that continues to this day. This logistics cast live bodies into the ocean's abyss just to relieve the ship's ballast (Glissant, 1997), or sunk a boat full of hundreds, chained together in the hold, just to collect the insurance pay out (Philip & Boateng, 2008). This logistics safeguards the brutal ascension of man (Wynter, 2003), the onset of the Anthropocene (Colebrook, 2016), and with it, the end of the world (Ferreira da Silva, 2014).

And yet, this logistics of the shipped has never been able to capture, contain or make transparent that which it relegates to the hold.

> And so it is we remain in the hold, in the break, as if entering again and again the broken world, to trace the visionary company and join it. This contrapuntal island, where we are marooned in search of marronage,

> where we linger in stateless emergency, in our lysed cell and held dislocation, our blown standpoint and lyred chapel, in (the) study of our sea-born variance, sent by its prehistory into arrivance without arrival, a poetics of lore, of abnormal articulation, where the relation between joint and flesh is the folded distance of a musical moment that is emphatically, palpably imperceptible and, therefore, difficult to describe. (Harney & Moten, 2013, p. 92)

Every world could have been otherwise, and still might be. Somewhere the last of a species breathes its last breath. Somewhere an artificial life is born. Somewhere young folks gather to resist the systematic murder and incarceration of Black lives. Somewhere a party goes all night, bodies thronging around dub sound systems playing Caribbean polyrhythms, in Kingston, Brixton, Sao Paulo, Lagos, Queens, Port of Spain. Bass and beats so strong your inner organs vibrate, dissolving any possibility of existing as a single being (Moten, 2018; Glissant, 1997).

The Drums: A Bridge to the Pluriverse

> The drums. Drum is breath and drum is life and drum is lung and heart. These men and women play these drums as if their power had too long been hidden in the hot alleys and gutters that perforate these regions east of the Dry River and, having been unable to speak till now, they beat reckless in their supplication. People start to follow them across the bridge, moving among the muddy gutters and black shack alleys with shattered glass and red dirt at their feet. (Joseph, 2018, p. 52)

> *So was born the Tamboo Bamboo band in the yards of Laventille, a hillside enclave east of Port of Spain across the Dry River on Trinidad, chipping down the road in a tight group of rhythmic motion. The boom of the largest bass bamboo knocks with a deep ringing tone against the earth, cut by a higher pitched syncopation, sustaining the rhythmic patterns of the ancestors. And it is said that in a desire to find more 'carry',*[1] *a larger volume of sound with which to compete with other bands, someone picked up an empty biscuit tin. You see, the bands are not just about music, but about retaining and harnessing energies of performative conflict and transformation connected to 'the warrior traditions crucial to the emancipation from*

1 For an oral history account of the development of steelpan see Dudley (2007).

slavery' (Riggio, 2020, p. 205). The brilliant sound of stick-on-metal invaded the bamboo band, and biscuit tins were soon entirely replaced with the lids of steel oil drums, which offered even more 'carry'.

The story told on Trinidad is that 'pan is Jumbie', a spirit which possesses (Dudley, 2004, p. 58). Like the 'bois' of the Kalinda stick fighters and the spirit drums of the Gayelle,[2] *the steelpan is imbued with a life force. The pan is a creation forged from worlds colliding – manifesting within empty containers cast aside as junk, abandoned by the American military using the island as a base from which to secure the supply of oil from Trinidad to Europe during the Second World War. When the bamboo bands realised the potentials of metal – the capacity to play both tones and rhythm – pan became an unstoppable force, a worthy weapon with which to overstep the possessive bounds of colonial worlds. It is the emergence of tones which matters. As the pan's steel concaved centre was shaped with indentations, the carefully angled hammer blows mapped out melodic tones. And so the pan encompasses the voice of the chantwell, the calypsonian and the drum. The circularity is a cosmology, tones emerging as a constellation like the night sky, tracing out a spider's web into the centre, where perhaps Anancy, the trickster spider resides.*[3] *The Bajan poet Kamau Brathwaite says that 'the drums are round, its dancers dance a circle ... surround the villages in dispositions like wheels; and time is a wheel: ancestor, spirit, child' (Brathwaite, as quoted in Yancy, 2012, p. 90).*

The pan is sleight of hand. It carries the circular rhythm of the ancestors, the unbroken inheritances of the drum, yet emerges in a melodic form which colonial powers could not fail to recognise as music, played by musicians. Pan is entangled with the violence of extraction, the fuelling of modernity and the death of worlds. Yet pan is also a movement to overcome the

2 Predating Carnival but very much part of the Carnival season is Kalinda, a stick-fighting martial art inherited from West African traditions. Performed in Gayelles (fighting rings), often forming spontaneously at crossroads by the throngs of people accompanying the fighters, the one-to-one dancing combat with 'bois' (sticks) is accompanied by a singer chanting lavways and drummers. Kalinda is a deeply spiritual practice tied to cosmologies that 'honor the living presence of ancestors, acknowledge conflict as basic to life, respect nature as a living partner in human community, and practice rituals that are as sacred and protective as they are fundamentally violent' (Riggio, 2020, p. 203).

3 Anancy is a quintessential hero of creole folklore in Trinidad and Tobago, arriving in the Caribbean with slaves from West Africa. Anancy is a spider-like creature who uses creativity with language to emerge a hero, a villain or a dupe. Anancy exists on the margins, 'a masterful trickster whose indeterminacy is revealed in the geographical location and functions he occupies within each tale as well as in the appearance and language he adopts to achieve his ends' (De Souza, 2003, p. 340).

> *dehumanising legacies of slavery and Indigenous genocide. Whilst government nationalist ideology and the colonial inheritances of whiteness have ventured to corral pan performance within 'respectable' bounds of formal competition, corporate sponsorships and the policing of behaviour, the pan continues to carry a 'ritualised ethos of contestation and challenge' (Riggio, 2020, p. 208). The movement sustains African diasporic and Indigenous animist cosmologies embedded within the malleable materiality of steel, within the community yards in which it is practised, and within the webs of relationships to past, present and future worlds this practice maintains. The pan's powerful tones, carried through the heat of night, play the memories of ecological extraction and destruction but also sound the seeds for reworlding as creative renewal through creolisation, or what Glissant (1997) calls 'a limitless mettissage'.*

One-Worlds

Somehow, under certain conditions, the steel of an oil drum takes on the spirit of Jumbie, and calls the people, everywhere, to dance with anarchic abandon from night to day, and day to night. Somehow, under certain conditions, a rebellious concept like 'pluriverse' becomes necessary to account for the weight of difference that life bears. Sometimes the strange, violent and beautiful conditions of life call for this. And while the pluriverse bears complex political inequalities and even accrues its own capital for those who stand to benefit from it, this complicity is likely more bearable than its constant adversary: the one-world world.

A one-world is a world 'that has granted itself the right to assimilate all other worlds and, by presenting itself as exclusive, cancels possibilities for what lies beyond its limits' (Blaser & de la Cadena, 2018, p. 3). Paradoxically, there are many one-worlds that today lay claim to their own competing universal totalisations.

- *Capitalism* is a one-world that claims all other worlds as its commodity. Anything that does not comply with the inhuman logic of capitalism is either obliterated, or simply left to die.
- *Colonialism* is a one-world that claims all lands and lives under a universal signifier.
- *Western science and medicine* in the Enlightenment tradition is a one-world account of a mechanistic body and universe.
- *Monotheistic religious traditions* have their one-world accounts of a single god-creator.

- The humanist dream of a *common humanity united by universal values* is a one-world vision.
- *The Anthropocene* is a one-world where a universal figuration of humanity causes catastrophic climate change and mass extinction.
- *Monoculture* is a one-world where forests are cleared so that a single crop can be cultivated to maximise profit, while raping the soil of its ability to regenerate itself.
- The *end of the world* is a one-world speculative scenario where a universal image of humanity ceases to exist.

From the perspective of the pluriverse, these one-worlds are premised on claims that they are the only possible or plausible worlds. But one-worlds simply contract blocs of power to dominate and prevent other worlds from coming into existence. One-worlds are nothing without their regimes of control, doomed to a continuous policing of their boundaries to maintain their exceptional claims to existence, like gardeners who eradicate undesired seedlings pushing up through pavement cracks. But like any meticulously manicured botanical garden or collection of specimens, it doesn't take long for a one-world to fall into ruins. And in these capitalistic-colonial ruins, there are so many lively worlds that like to grow and play.

Pedagogies of Jouvay

We follow pan through Port of Spain's inky urban underground, where lamp posts, gutters, fences and buildings merge into habitats of transformation. Bodies crouch, cavort and leap, or press close in low wine. Devils writhe with chains and gorillas laugh. I move forwards against the fear of losing myself entirely in animate darkness, unmoored. But I am within the band and the music becomes the current within which this company of strangers become kin. Moving like shoals of fishes with a tide we are pushed in waves, pulsing with energy towards the dawn.

My body is painted with cool clay by a stranger, clad in earth. This anointment triggers a transformation. For in this night of movement, I emerge free, for a moment, from the politics of identification. I am masked in mud and in mud I mould my own path, my own motions. Loosely we move through familiar spaces made strange by the night, spaces usually colonised by cars. Spaces I wouldn't usually feel welcome in are reclaimed by Jouvay revellers.

We orbit the savannah, the heart and lungs of the city and the spiritual crossroads of Carnival. We map out arterial roots in relation to the crossroads, approaching it differently each year, and yet always returning to this circular space of communal performance. Rituals remain loosely the same and yet are never the same. Time emerges cyclically and music and movement perform a refrain of becoming which is remade, re-worlded each year. Each moment unfolds in an intuitive improvisation of play, and in play the illusion of the fixedness and solidity of the world is disrupted. Swept up with waves of the crowd, music so loud it seems to dislodge and reorganise bodily cells, the bodies of strangers press close for a second, leaving their imprint. I know the city differently from here, and the boundaries between myself and the world are ruptured through a violent upending of normativity

We have spilled into the streets, a movement against the institution of ownership, the privatisation of space. How indeed, can we speak of capitalist controls of space and time, with the sound of steel bands practising, passing through valleys, ringing through the night air, passing through windows and walls? When the sweet distant sound of drums accompanies the threshold between waking and sleeping?

Animist Pedagogies

Jouvay offers an embodied experiential pedagogy of shifting sensations and techniques of world making through a suspension of formal structures and hierarchies of every kind. The Trinidadian playwright Tony Hall theorised Jouvay as a pedagogical system through which people learn to uncover the occult meanings behind this yearly explosion of animist expression – the people's Indigenous strategy for survival in a world founded on the European colonial project (Rostant, 2017). Yet Jouvay is also a unique encounter between Indigenous animisms and the 'shifting diasporic thought, activism, and aesthetics' of the Black Atlantic diaspora (King, 2019, p. 15). In this sense, we might consider Jouvay an animist-diasporic pedagogy that invites a highly specified and yet malleable 'interrogation and articulation of the self into the cosmos' (Rostant, 2017). Hall understood this theatre of the street as a creation of worlds, where life becomes a performance through which everything speaks, and into which we all invest. Colonised worlds are inherited, but, through the animist-diasporic pedagogies of Jouvay, we are able to glimpse these worlds as the constructs and inventions that they are. Jouvay may then offer a rebellious pedagogy of *dis*inheritance (Hernandez et al., 2020), where it may even become possible, under certain conditions, for a people to 'choose its past' (Hartman, 2008, p. 100).

Through Jouvay, we learn how to dismantle the world as it has been made and cultivate new ones through a perpetual reconstruction of animist rituals.

Perpetual Reconstruction

In the village of Kamasan on the island of Bali the people gather for nine days in the Bale Batur temple, the spiritual heart of the village. Two hundred and ten days have passed, an entire year, and the local gods who have been roaming have returned for odalan, the anniversary ceremony of the Bale Batur temple. The temple overflows with tangible and intangible offerings – food, ribbons, banners, awnings, paintings, prayers, the scents of flowers and curls of incense smoke. At the temple's centre sits the non-human living presence and powerfully resonating voice of the gamelan. Its multiple ornate bronze xylophones and gongs fill the village and surrounding space with layers of sound, felt as well as heard. This performance is a sonic offering and an unfolding example of a traditional Hindu-Buddhist culture that recognises 'complex agency' as both an ontological mode and an everyday life practice (Yamin, 2019). In this world, agency emerges in complex assemblages of human and non-human beings, where the human is never assumed to be the primary or sole intentional agent. Here at Bale Batur bodies gather and breathe a porosity, a permeability between the musicians, gamelan, sound, time and the ever-shifting thresholds of life itself. This gamelan, known as the gamelan semara pegulingan (named after Semar, the god of love), is considered a living entity, with unique animist power and a singular personality. It is a 'co-mingling of things-sounds-bodies' (McGraw, 2016, p. 135), an 'ever-changing entanglement' of material and discursive forces in a state of 'perpetual reconstruction' (Yamin, 2019, p. 367).

Much like human life, perpetual reconstruction is the gamelan's primary mode of ongoingness. This body is not only metals and bamboo, but a 'metabolism' of experiences 'perpetually in the making' (Yamin, 2019, p. 367). The gamelan's spirit unfolds continuously, despite multiple and ongoing redistributions and replacements of its original physical components (Yamin, 2016). What changed when the original, much worn pelawah, the wooden frames of the xylophones, were dismantled and replaced in the mid-1990s? Were the originals set aside as firewood until, by chance, they were acquired for another gamelan orchestra? Is this a loss or simply an ongoing rebirth? So many parts of the original gamelan have been discarded and replaced over time that we cannot tell what of the original gamelan remains. And yet this is still the gamelan semara pegulingan, even whilst the musicians of Kamasan do not all agree on a singular 'meaning, significance or repertoire' (Yamin, 2019, p. 362), and oral histories speak of complex entanglements with the 'layers of historical … information' the gamelan has accumulated (Rancier, 2014, p. 379). There are stories of gamelan providing spirit and strength to fighters during war (Santosa & Kustiyanti, 2018), or the relocation of three gamelan to transfer the Majapahit rulers' power to other regions of Bali (Spiller, 2004). There are also stories of gamelan sounding by themselves at night; of a mistreated instrument that caused community illness and disease (Mantle Hood, 2010); or how a gamelan's spirit did not allow the gamelan storage area door to be opened for its own reasons (Yamin, 2019).

In Kamasan, they tell the story of how the gamelan semara pegulingan was built with the sonic memory of the gamelan of the Balinese kingdom of Klungkung, the sound of which reached the two kilometres to Kamasan. Back in 1908, facing inevitable defeat to Dutch colonising forces, the king of Klungkung, along with his entire court and military, turned their weapons on themselves, setting fire to their buildings, destroying their semara pegulingan instruments and walking directly into enemy fire in an act known as the 'puputan', a mass suicide by which Balinese people were able to end their worlds on their own terms. As marked by this ritual act of world ending, Bali was considered to have lost its 'spiritual energy' and has since become a secular world under the rule of foreign colonisation (Yamin, 2016).

In the animist agency of the gamelan semara pegulingan we encounter threads of memories, epistemology, ontology, sound and affect, multiple physical materials with earlier lives (in trees, in the earth) and lives yet to come, relationships, repertoire and traditions that live and evolve beyond the human ken. All become joined, metabolised, knotted together in entanglements of sinuous threads. In this respect can we say with any certainty where the gamelan semara pegulingan exists in space and time? Nothing about the gamelan is definitive. It is a worlding of its own, an individuation, a perpetual reconstruction achieved through collective practices of open-endedness and acceptance of animist agency.

Let's Listen

There is something fervent in Yamin's (2016, 2019) call to re-encounter musical instruments not simply as derivatives or prosthetics of human whims, but as animate and autonomous entities with their own say in what matters and how, even when their physical existence and location remains ambivalent, opaque and subject to perpetual reconstruction. And perhaps it is through instruments such as pan, or the *gamelan semara pegulingan*, that we can begin to discern the pluriversal contours of an animist pedagogy, where animals, plants and objects of many kinds have crucial perspectives to share with us, if we care to listen.

> Let's listen. Do you hear the wind in the trees? The water on the beach? The splash of the fish? That is the wind, the trees, the water, the sand, the fish communicating. They have their own language, their own Law. Sometimes they are sending a message to humans. Sometimes they are sending a message to each other. Humans are not the centre of the universe, you see. Humans are only one part of it. Humans are part of Country along with the mullet, the tides, the moon, the songs and stories, along with the spirits, the plants and animals, the feelings and dreams. (Bawaka Country, 2016, p. 273)

This voice comes from Bawaka Country in north-east Arnhem Land, Australia, as composed by a close-knit collective of Indigenous (Yolŋu) and non-Indigenous kin. Bawaka Country (2016) invites us to come and listen to Country with care, where there is no human 'author-ity' that can be separated from everything else. We believe such listening practices are crucial for building alliances of trust, reciprocity and respect, as practices of 'immanent attention' that are attuned and responsive to animate perspectives that do or may exist, 'but do not meet the requirements of modern knowledge and therefore cannot be proven in its terms' (Blaser & de la Cadena, 2018, p. 14). Such an immanent attention might require a certain betrayal of the western fear of animism (Stengers, 2018), or what Metis scholar Kyle Whyte (2018) diagnoses as 'white panic' among those previously abjured from the existential threat of extinction. Under the current conditions, any turn (or *re*turn) to animism directly threatens the dominant political order of unearned privilege, imperial logisticality, and predatory individualism on which both the colonial project and the climate crisis have been constructed. To rebel against the fear of animism is to face the radical uncertainty of what lies beyond the human world and, in turn, to recompose our rituals as this uncertainty demands: to live and die through the practices of care we share with so many others.

References

Bawaka Country, including Wright, S., Suchet-Pearson, S., Lloyd, K., Burarrwanga, L., Ganambarr, R., ... Maymuru, D. (2015). Working with and learning from Country: Decentring human author-ity. *Cultural Geographies*, *22*(2), 269–283.

Bird-David, N. (1999). 'Animism' revisited: Personhood, environment, and relational epistemology. *Current Anthropology*, *40*, 67–91.

Blaser, M., & de la Cadena, M. (2018). Introduction. Pluriverse: Proposals for a world of many worlds. In M. de la Cadena & M. Blaser (Eds.), *A world of many worlds* (pp. 1–22). University of Minnesota Press.

Brabec, B., & Seeger, A. (2013). Introduction: Considering music, humans, and non-humans. *Ethnomusicology Forum*, *22*(3), 269–286.

Braidotti, R. (2019). *Posthuman knowledges*. John Wiley & Sons.

Burnard, P., Cook, P. J., Jasilek, S., & Bauer-Nilsen, B. (2018). Performing arts activism for addressing climate change: Conceptualizing an intercultural choreographic practice and dance performance called Melting Ice. *Choreographic Practices*, *9*(1), 119–144.

Colebrook, C. (2016). 'A grandiose time of coexistence': Stratigraphy of the Anthropocene. *Deleuze Studies*, *10*(4), 440–454.

Costa, L., & Fausto, C. (2010). The return of the animists: Recent studies of Amazonian ontologies. *Religion and Society*, *1*(1), 89–109.

Danowski, D., & Viveiros de Castro, E. (2017). *The ends of the world* (R. Nunes, Trans.). Polity.

de la Bellacasa, M. P. (2012). 'Nothing comes without its world': Thinking with care. *Sociological Review*, *60*(2), 197–216.

de La Bellacasa, M. P. (2017). *Matters of care: Speculative ethics in more than human worlds*. University of Minnesota Press.

Deleuze, G. (1994). *Difference and repetition* (P. Patton, Trans.) Columbia University Press.

Deleuze, G., & Guattari, F. (1994). *What is philosophy?* (H. Tomlinson & G. Burchell, Trans.). Columbia University Press.

Demos, T. J. (2020). *Beyond the world's end: Arts of living at the crossing*. Duke University Press.

Descola, P. (1996). *In the society of nature: A native ecology of Amazonia* (N. Scott, Trans.). Cambridge University Press.

De Souza, P. (2003). Creolizing Anancy: Signifyin(g) processes in New World spider tales. *Matatu*, *27/28*, 339–363, 541.

DiNovelli-Lang, D. (2013). The return of the animal: Posthumanism, indigeneity, and anthropology. *Environment and Society*, *4*(1), 137–156.

Dudley, S. (2004). *Carnival music in Trinidad: Experiencing music, expressing culture*. Oxford University Press.

Dudley, S. (2007). *Music from behind the bridge: Steelband aesthetics and politics in Trinidad and Tobago*. Oxford University Press.

Ellis, E. C., Gauthier, N., Goldewijk, K. K., Bird, R. B., Boivin, N., Díaz, S., ... & Watson, J. E. (2021). People have shaped most of terrestrial nature for at least 12,000 years.

Proceedings of the National Academy of Sciences, 118(17). https://doi.org/10.1073/pnas.2023483118

Escobar, A. (2018). *Designs for the pluriverse: Radical interdependence, autonomy, and the making of worlds*. Duke University Press.

Escobar, A. (2020). *Pluriversal politics: The real and the possible*. Duke University Press.

Ferreira da Silva, D. (2014). Toward a Black feminist poethics: The quest(ion) of blackness toward the end of the world. *Black Scholar, 44*(2), 81–97.

Glissant, E. (1997). *Poetics of relation* (B. Wing, Trans.). University of Michigan Press.

Harney, S., & Moten, F. (2013). *The undercommons: Fugitive planning and Black study*. Minor Compositions.

Hartman, S. V. (1997). *Scenes of subjection: Terror, slavery, and self-making in nineteenth-century America*. Oxford University Press.

Hartman, S. V. (2008). *Lose your mother: A journey along the Atlantic slave route*. Macmillan.

Harvey, G. (2006). *Animism: Respecting the living world*. Columbia University Press.

Hernández, K., Rubis, J. M., Theriault, N., Todd, Z., Mitchell, A., Country, B., ... Wright S. (2020). The Creatures Collective: Manifestings. *Environment and Planning E: Nature and Space*. Advance online publication. https://doi.org/10.1177/2514848620938316

Joseph, A. (2018). *Kitch: A fictional biography of a calypso icon*. Peepal Tree.

King, T. L. (2019). *The Black shoals: Offshore formations of Black and native studies*. Duke University Press.

Lewis, J. E., Arista, N., Pechawis, A., & Kite, S. (2018). Making kin with the machines. *Journal of Design and Science, 3.5*. https://doi.org/10.21428/bfafd97b

MacLure, M. (2021). Inquiry as divination. *Qualitative Inquiry, 27*(5), 502–511. https://doi.org/10.1177/1077800420939124

Mantle Hood, M. (2010). *Triguna: A Hindu-Balinese philosophy for gamelan gong gede music*. Lit Verlag.

McGraw, A. (2016). Atmosphere as a concept for ethnomusicology: Comparing the gamelatron and gamelan. *Ethnomusicology, 60*(1), 125–147.

Moten, F. (2018). *Stolen life*. Duke University Press.

Philip, M. N., & Boateng, S. A. (2008). *Zong!* Wesleyan University Press.

Rancier, M. (2014). The musical instrument as a national archive: A case study of the Kazakh Qyl-qobyz. *Ethnomusicology, 58*(3), 379–404.

Riggio, M. C. (2020). Playing and praying. *Journal of Festive Studies, 2*(1), 203–235.

Rolnik, S. (2017). The spheres of insurrection: Suggestions for combating the pimping of life. *E-flux Journal, 86*.

Rose, D. B. (2006). The rivers of Babylon. *Manoa, 18*(2), 1–6.

Rose, D. B. (2013). Val Plumwood's philosophical animism: Attentive interactions in the sentient world. *Environmental Humanities, 3*(1), 93–109.

Rostant, D. (2017, March 24). *A Jouvay experience: The Tony Hall perspective*. YouTube. https://www.youtube.com/watch?v=Gga1WvoY8IE

Saldanha, A. (2020). A date with destiny: Racial capitalism and the beginnings of the Anthropocene. *Environment and Planning D: Society and Space*, *38*(1), 12–34.

Santosa, H., & Kustiyanti, D. (2018). Mredangga: Sebuah penelusuran awal tentang gamelan perang di bali [An initial inquisition about gamelan in Bali]. *Kalangwan Jurnal Seni Pertunjukan*, *4*(1), 16–25.

Spiller, H. (2004). *Gamelan: The traditional sounds of Indonesia*. ABC-CLIO.

Stengers, I. (2008). Experimenting with refrains: Subjectivity and the challenge of escaping modern dualism. *Subjectivity*, *22*, 38–59.

Stengers, I. (2018). The challenge of ontological politics. In M. de la Cadena & M. Blaser (Eds.), *A world of many worlds* (pp. 83–111). University of Minnesota Press.

Strathern, M. (1992). *Reproducing the future: Essays on anthropology, kinship and the new reproductive technologies*. University of Manchester Press.

TallBear, K. (2017). Beyond the life/not life binary: A feminist-Indigenous reading of cryopreservation, interspecies thinking and the new materialisms. In J. Radin & E. Kowal (Eds.), *Cryopolitics: Frozen life in a melting world* (pp. 179–202). MIT Press.

Todd, Z. (2016). An indigenous feminist's take on the ontological turn: 'Ontology' is just another word for colonialism. *Journal of Historical Sociology*, *29*(1), 4–22.

Viveiros de Castro, E. (2004). Exchanging perspectives: The transformation of objects into subjects in Amerindian ontologies. *Common Knowledge*, *10*(3), 463–484.

Weinstein, J., & Colebrook, C. (2017). Introduction: Critical life studies and the problems of inhuman rites and posthumous life. In J. Weinstein & C. Colebrook (Eds.), *Posthumous life: Theorizing beyond the posthuman* (pp. ix–xxvii). Columbia University Press.

Whyte, K. P. (2018). Indigenous science (fiction) for the Anthropocene: Ancestral dystopias and fantasies of climate change crises. *Environment and Planning E: Nature and Space*, *1*(1–2), 224–242.

Wynter, S. (1984). The ceremony must be found: After humanism. *Boundary*, *2*, 19–70.

Wynter, S. (2003). Unsettling the coloniality of being/power/truth/freedom: Towards the human, after man, its overrepresentation – An argument. *CR: The New Centennial Review*, *3*(3), 257–337.

Yamin, T. (2016). Defending the past, present, and future of gamelan semara pegulingan saih pitu in Kamasan, Bali. In A. McGraw & Sumarsam (Eds.), *Performing Indonesia*. Freer and Sackler Galleries, Smithsonian Institution. https://asia.si.edu/essays/article-yamin/

Yamin, T. (2019). One or several gamelan? Perpetual (re)construction in the life of a Balinese gamelan semara pagulingan. *Ethnomusicology*, *63*(3), 357–392.

Yancy, G. (2012). *Look, a White! Philosophical essays on whiteness*. Temple University Press.

Yusoff, K. (2019). *A billion Black Anthropocenes or none*. University of Minnesota Press.

CHAPTER 16

The Heart of Research

Fictioning and Diffractive Writing as Critical Research Practice

Annouchka Bayley

To write a novel that *does* diffraction, rather than one which is inspired by diffraction, is, to echo Karen Barad, *no small matter.* Barad writes that 'language has been granted too much power' (Barad, 2007, p. 132) and that 'the only thing that doesn't seem to matter anymore is matter' (p. 132) But if we work with her premise that the material and the discursive are always-already entangled, *material-discursively,* then even our smallest everyday utterance is more powerful than we might imagine. The tongue and the mind become one organism speaking together, entangled with the world, *as the world*(*s*) we enact. Stories are no longer traces of what was, set to repeat in an endless spiral tight as a rope around a thief – an outlaw story-catcher who believes they must kill an author in order to liberate the damsel of meaning and, only then, let her speak for herself.

Closing the gap between the tongue and the mind, understanding that neither came first but that meaning *is* mattering, creates a differencing relationship to story that has everything in common with Ahmed's suggestion that 'feminist theory is something we do at home' (2017, p. 7) and not something to be relegated to the heroic ivory towers of academic institutions alone. Perhaps what is *home* in Ahmed's words isn't the four domestic walls we might be lucky enough to live in, but rather, the spaces of *home* we live our everyday lives in, the spaces we make in, through and with. In this entanglement of matter and meaning, home becomes an endless *homing* of sorts, a finding of position across a field of momentum that *matters*.

Marina Abramovic famously once stated: 'If you make bread in a bakery you're a baker; if you make bread in a gallery you're a performance artist.' And whilst this is true in terms of positionality, it relies on the idea that the bread will be the same in either context even though the human has changed. But when flour, soda, water, walls, dust, skin, temperature and countless other phenomena presence with/in entanglement, nothing is fixed into sameness. If you make theory inside a novel, it is specific to the spacetimemattering process. The bread of theory tastes differently, fuses with your lips differently, becomes one with your body *differently.*

 | DOI:10.1163/9789004516069_22

In this mode, the novel, as a material-discursive phenomenon, becomes performative, not a thing or an object, but a *doing*; a diffractive apparatus that re-stories the world even as we read it and are moved by it. And this is the *heart of the matter* in this piece of writing you read in the home of *here, now*. The novel is not just a thing, but an endless shift of meaning making. Novel as urgent means, urgent thinking, urgent practice. Not a thing in itself, but an apparatus to make things with, a pulsing phenomenon that thinks and acts; a figuration of performativities where the form itself isn't stable but an infinite flow of dynamic interdependencies (Elias, 1956) that go on to make new marks in the world across human and non-human boundaries.

In Barad's universe, such *inter*dependencies become *intra*-dependencies. That is to say, rather than separate and separable units forming a dynamic flow of pushes and pulls that go on to create phenomena in the world, Barad tells a different story throughout her work on matter and meaning; the story told by quantum physics. I want to whisper into your ear, so quietly, the enormity of Barad's story as it appears in the twenty-first-century academy: *Once upon a time there was not a host of separable units – atoms flying in space, as if contained by space. No, dearest reader, there was and still is a flow of matter that became what we might call 'phenomena'. Some part of the entanglement of space-time-matter observed some other part (in its own inimical way) and so a 'thing' was born. A phenomenon emerged in the moment it was intra-actively cut by the means of observation.* This is a challenging origin story, though perhaps not so challenging if we loosen the bonds of a western academy, whose walls contain the powdery brick and stone ghosts of Judeo-Christian origin stories, all of which start with the foundational principle that in the beginning was the *Word*. It's interesting to think what stories we use to create foundational concepts or, as Donna Haraway (2016, p. 12) might have it, 'it matters what stories we tell to tell other stories with'

This thought is as political as it is aesthetic – otherwise why would some books be censored and others left to roam free, diffracting thoughts and acts in their everyday? In this reading of rebellious research practices, the novel is not novel-as-brick-and-mortar. It does not stand on the shoulders of giants to create a master's house (Audre Lorde, 1984/2017). Neither does it fly like a flaming cannonball into the heavy foundations of the patriarchal canon upon which the academy was built. Rather, it is an object that exceeds the walls of its ontological bindings, continually diffracting this thing we too hastily call *the* world (as if there were only one world rather than many). The novel: a diffractive prism, stitched and digitised and distributed. An apparatus of affect and desire. Nothing less than a beating heart made out of paper.

This piece of writing that you encounter, *here, now* in another stitched, glued or digitised book, is called "The heart of research". So perhaps it's about time I speak about the decidedly *un*timely (Livholts, 2020) heart and why it belongs at the centre of research. Livholts describes the untimely, in the context of academic writing, as 'out of place in academic life' where what is expected of academic writing affects what scholars *can* voice, creating a hole or a gap not just in knowledge, but in the onto-epistemic *practice of everyday life* (to bring in the ghost of Michael de Certeau!) 'The potential to create new knowledge that opens up space for multiple voices, that opens up opportunities for diversity and promoting critical and analytical reflexivity, is greater if diverse languages and genres are brought into use' (Livholts, 2020, p. 3). In brief, if we silence the multi-valved, polyvalent, affective heart, what becomes of research but an empty stack of wood and brick, a master's house, functioning in these critical, post-2020 times, I somewhat outlandishly propose, just because it can.

The heart is a *thing*. It is weighty (200–400 grams approx.). Its four beautiful and fleshy chambers circulate and oxygenate our blood and, without its bright and vibrant electricity, we would die in a *matter* of moments. Therefore, everything the heart does matters. We have storied the heart-as-symbol for hundreds if not thousands of years as the seat of feeling; the seat of love. And of course, the seat of hate. How quickly *I love you with all my heart* can revolve and pump out its very opposite. And so, in storytelling terms the heart is perhaps the most binary of narrative creatures, flitting from one pole to another in an affective daydream we call everyday life. To point my feet in the direction of the path trod out before me by fiction writer and essayist Ursula Le Guin, whose work on speculative feminist stories has gone on to inspire a generation of writers and academics alike, perhaps, as I walk through the pathways of the heart, what I am describing is not an organ of story that uses heroically pointed sticks to catch a monster-tale across its four chambers, but an organ that functions much like a 'carrier bag' (1988/2019). As Le Guin argues, the pointed-stick-monster-catching tale is more exciting. It ropes our adrenals into the mix, dancing in their chemical fires, possessing our fibrous and atomic selves with ghostly drives *fight, fly, fear! Just stay inside the story!* The carrier bag on the other hand allows us to critically consider all the monsters, to rewrite them, to extract knowledge by deep listening, deep feeling, a deep staying-with the trouble, to bring new materialist pioneer Donna Haraway back in here, that avoids the heroic, *timely* teleology of an 'Edenic past or salvific future' (2016, p. 1), forever pointing us elsewhere, finding new growth terrains for the hunt.

The diffractive apparatus in question *here, now*, in the scope of this moment on the page with you, this homing of spacetime that we make together across staggered times and spaces of reading, is the heart (and not Le Guin's notion of carrier bag as womb – beautiful and delectable image in itself, but the womb is not the only carrier bag some humans have). The heart as carrier bag has valves and levers, and affective corridors; the corridors through which it thinks, *lives, breathes*. Heart as life giver. Heart of the matter. Heart of it all. The diffractive heart. Heart as performative agent, made present by its very function: to transform (in material immanence?), our life blood. Blood is real. And it also carries the material network of *us* – all our stories, all our heroes and monsters and revelations.

In the Fold of the Page, Living and Dying Are Entangled

As a writer writing across registers, moving through the arterial chambers of academic, fiction, poetry, play, when I realised that I wanted to presence things that *mattered* in the world differently, I also realised I would have to return to blood, which is perhaps, in essence, the subject matter of the heart. My fingers hit the keys and what emerged on page one was a woman – a real woman with a real historical blueprint in the world – who had been turned into a monster. She was dis-affectionately known in genre circles as 'The Blood Countess'. I had wanted to *re*write her story since I first encountered her history when I was a teenager, and now she flowed out of me almost without warning. With creative imperative this Blood Countess became my subject and, as a writer, I used the diffractive apparatus of a heart-keyboard-theory intersection, a critical valve of sorts, to churn her around and out of the monster history had made out of her.

In 2018, I had set out to write a novel about diffraction – or more precisely a novel that *did* the work of diffraction – which engages in the processes of difference differing rather than spotting and 'catching' the products of difference. Thus, as both a writer and a scholar I wanted the novel to *do* what it *said*. To fold doing and saying, living and dying, representing and agentically performing, together. To find the blood, the pus, the pulse, the bright, beating apparatus of *history*, which contains all the tools of erasure and violence, of the will of our species to survive even as we hurtle ourselves and our communities towards untimely, anthropocentric death. Why? As the novel states, in candid terms, when I, its author, was a child I died briefly – or had an intense experience of living and dying folding together. I was eight years old. *He* was considerably more than that. A total stranger, his young face scored with markings of rage, at all the inconsistencies of living and dying that etched his own bones with violence – pulsing, beating, racing, raging. Those big black boots of his impacting on my skull: both symbol and reality of the community he lived and breathed – a community whose primary symbol is not the boot but the swastika, which is in turn more than a symbol but a *doing*; a broken windmill through which polarities of self and other, race and racism and woman and man and all other such simple binaries are spun out. His swastika became my loom, a loom on which not only did I diffract my own experience of living and dying, but all such collapsing binaries. Binaries: are they the things that scribe out the world, cutting-together-apart, where a co-constituting cut occurs '*between an object and the agencies of observation*' (Barad, 2007, p. 115, original emphasis)? Such 'agential cuts' turn a person into a *thing* that can be counted, scored, marked, identified. In my case, the cut functions along not just one line, but a multiplicity of lines/rhizomes/dimensions: a Christian-Muslim-Jew, a child, a woman, a mixed other of colours and pigments and slopes in the eye and chin? Slopes and colours that cut me out of the world's terrain, making a body out of 'me' and all my human and non-human ancestor-builders?

I often laugh that I look like a fish – one side of my face has different shapings than the other – one eye a little higher, the other more slanted, a smaller almond resting not-quite-equidistant from the other, if you look closely enough. I try to describe this to other people by making the straight line of my hand held up, into a vertical divider that *cuts* the two sides of my face together-apart in the same moment, my thumb running along my nose so that the hand itself acts like a ruler. *Look! Look! Look at the two sides of my face! I actually have different features! I'm like a fish – one side differing from the other although it's still the same body!* ... (Would I know the world differently if I only looked out of the almond eye?). Patterns of difference are written into the everyday presencing of my face, or perhaps it is more the *heart of the matter,* more at home, to say that the patterns of difference are the materiality of me, in all my bod(ies) and all my writing, where neither are quite separate from the other but all the diffractive presence of a cut, sloppily measured out as 'me'.

Multiple Worlds/Multiple Registers: Writing to Think, Breathe, Live and Know the Untimely

Chapter 2 of the novel takes its shape from blood – not metaphoric blood, where academic writing can sometimes feel like squeezing 'blood out of a stone' to use the English idiom – but one that describes my lived experience of being suspended in a live-die state and what forms of epistemology it diffracted; a cutting-together-apart.

> *I know what it is to die. There's a shake in the body as an incredible pressure gathers. It starts inside the bones and moves all the way up to the surface of your skin. Then your blood rises to meet it, raging and whispering, startled out of its usual course. Atomic pulses seek each other out, their secret, intimate doubles calling for one another. They aim but are never able to collide. They shake deep inside the curvatures of the body; a thousand, tiny radial planets, pouring out majesty and fire in fits and starts that shudder inside*

> *the nape of time. And then there's peace. An incredible silence and you feel, grown, airy – a large house in the summer, the breeze racing through it, whipping curtains and cobwebs into momentary and lateral frenzies.*
>
> *When I feel death seize me, I look down at my eight-year-old body. I see that my hair is still pulled back into two long braids falling on either side; small puddles of black ink that are now running down me towards the snow, writing me into the shape of an ending. The white line marking the parting of my hair is so white and so long, it looks for all the world like a mountain range split in two on the crease of a map. Whiter than the sky in winter. Whiter than snow. It goes on forever and, as I follow it, I lose the ability to distinguish between space and time.*
>
> *Looking at myself lying there in the snow is like looking at an image on tracing paper. Each sheet its own original. I realise that I am on the outside of time, peering in through a thin, papery nothingness that keeps me at an impenetrable distance from my own body. Then a web of dust and stars pulsing with life creeps across me with a final shiver – with what should be a final shiver. I don't breathe, not with my lungs anyway, but I think breath and entangle in all of these shining fibres.*

Here, I write in ways that represent and perform an experience that is arguably still living inside me in an untimely continuity that folds space and time affectively – not just in ways that must be erased from academic writing registers and therefore academic approaches to what living and dying are, but in ways where the untimely of memory is not a distant past but an active present, in the folds of my cells that grow around the wounds. I describe from the vantage point of *living* (where of course all living is threaded through with death) that this strange in-between isn't a state that is time-less. Rather it is full of time.

> *it's as if the rest of the world were drawn on graph paper, moving through the thinly marked squares of events laid out in complex systems and codes, following beginnings and ends, causes and effects. Whether clear or buried these always exist across the red thread of coherence. At some point along the line, my paper got crumpled and all the codes of cause and effect were lost. If I had been made of another material I might have lived in a kind of mechanical relationship to right and wrong, to the ethics of a life without any real consequence. But this isn't quite the measure of it. Time itself is the marker of bodies and so it is more imbued with justice than any other phenomenon.*

This form of situated writing/situated knowledge making is complex as it requires a writing-through the experience of crumpled binaries. But what other kind of writing is there when the heart is at stake, wrestling with its binary relationship to venal and arterial blood in an attempt to beat out the affective, essential rhythm of *staying alive* inside the story of time? No affect can be completely severed from all others, just as no cell can find longevity in a vacuum or void, outside of its entangled communion with the body of the earth, stars, universe and so on. When affect and materiality are understood to be vital components of each other, material-discursive moments of a universe that is eternally in flow become an 'ontology of motion' (Nail, 2018).

As the modern-day protagonist of the novel writes herself through and out of her own early moment of living-dying in the snow, diffracting into something else, so she takes all her stories with her into the diffraction. Persecution, violence, corruption, power, love, beauty – these are the large stories she finds living inside her across time – the stories she produces *here, now*. Cutting-together-apart, what emerges from the fibrous entanglement of the experience is one myth in particular, a living, breathing untimely memory of the sixteenth-century Hungarian countess: the Countess Erzabet Bathory. The heart – here understood as a carrier bag of *un*timely memories – diffracts a story that needs to be re-written; the monstrous Bathory, famous for being the world's first female serial killer, a myth that the writer-protagonist finds has been written by men-of-patriarchy to subdue a powerful dissident. And so the writer-protagonist undertakes a journey of small and large things to re-story Bathory. An everyday journey into the everyday life of the Countess Bathory, looking at surviving letters, domestic bills and the hard-to-find accounts of the women history accuses her of killing, even as the modern-day academy tries to silence her radical and rebellious view on what history *is* and *does*. These lead the writer-protagonist, a woman who both is and isn't quite me, the author and the subject of fictioning, at the same time, to the *heart of the matter:*

> *I figured that this was how humans lived in the world. We were written through with texts and histories that lived through one another. And so, whilst I was so often alone, I was never lonely. The empty page was forever the first seduction. It promised to hold me and write me in turn, rocking me into new shapes that would stay with me all the next day. In a sense, I thought, we – all of us – weren't that dissimilar to little prisms that turned every moment into patterns of light. We storied the world with these patterns, creating heavens and hells beyond imagining, abandoning ourselves of responsibility without even realising it. We were filled with powers we hadn't the first inkling of. Listen! Look! It was the way every ancient story began. And yet we hardly ever listened or looked. We hardly ever survived the arcs we made in time.*
>
> *Whenever I felt Elizabet in my bones, I was listening – listening deeply. I knew we were diffractions of one another, part of one great story stretching*

> *across time. I understood that, to re-story her from out of the prison that history had made, I had to write her through myself. History had locked her up, made her into the shape of the Blood Countess. But this wasn't unique to her. It was something shared by all women in one way or another. As I wrote her out of her prison, so she rewrote me out of mine, shifting all our histories subtly. She rewrote me in the letters she sent, in the books she printed, applying the legend 'For the Future' to some copies, curling the letters written in her own hand, in ink. Soon she would write of me directly, delivering her knowledge of our world now right to the emperor in the hope it might, in some tiny way, re-story him. We would all emerge differently in time through each other. When she scribed me, it would change, in tiny increments, the life I lived. When I scribed her, she would break the chains that made her, finding the other inside her, her own silent people across time. Would that we all could find our inner narrators, erasing our position in space in the past, present and future in an endless, brave momentum taking place in women's time.*

The untimely in writing is not just about bringing many worlds into the academy, or to make tools to undo the master's house (Lorde, 1984/2017). Perhaps the untimely is also about writing about the 'processes of difference differing' across multiple registers, where time, space and matter entangle, congeal and are cut-together-apart, even *here, now* in this moment of writing, in this moment of reading, where we all fold down together in dance that has more dimensions than we might imagine.

Many Worlds

As Paul Preciado writes, 'I am the multiplicity of the cosmos trapped in a binary political and epistemological system, shouting in front of you. I am a Uranian confined inside the limits of techno-capitalism' (Preciado, as cited in Rogers, 2020, p. 364). Reading this, I am reminded of Deleuze's 'we are already more than one'. I would add to this song in sympathetic notes:

> *And then without warning, I sat up. I simply sat right up in the very same place I had fallen down only moments before. I had interrupted death and returned to exactly the same spot. And it's strange because everything felt different. From the moment I opened my eyes, I knew I was two in one. Not possessed. Not that. Just that I would hover between two lives, knowing both. An ancient knowing that would play out through my flesh, my life. My lives …*
>
> *When I wrote, however, it was different. The words opened their inky arms and held me inside them, hungry for the touch of their author. They called*

> *and whispered and reached up on tiptoes to see me before drawing me down into their world. And I wrote and wrote and wrote until the dawn suns came to snatch me away ...*
>
> *I stare up at her, trying to see her through every pore of my body.*
>
> *'Little wing, you are haunted by so many things. That's what it is to die and return from death at the same time. You live between worlds. So many tiny universes unravelling inside one human heart.' She taps me gently a few times on the breastbone and I sense the vastness that encompasses us both echoing in each tap, my ribs becoming part of the fabric of the earth, whilst the space between them draws the heavens inside me. 'Time congeals, Little wing. It contracts like a pumping heart into life and then expands out to become space.' And she holds up her hand, curling it into a fist as she speaks. 'Time is memory and memory becomes form. Your body is just a system of memories breathing the world into its future shapes.'*

Here, it's hard to tell the discursive from the material. The ink births the writer, the words do not hang in undiscovered space in reverse teleology, in *'first there was the Word'*, but in untimely fashion they are both parent and child in the same moment, born out of the fleshly, diffracting heart, circulating in and simultaneously shaping its four chambers. Both birth each other. Both act as carrier bag for each other until it becomes ridiculous to try to work out which came first. Both *are* the fibrous phenomenon of carrier bag. The bag itself is the cut.

Rebel Code

So what has all this to do with rebellious research? Pressing into the heart of binarity until it can do nothing but tell the story of the non-binarity of living-dying, which is nothing less than the story of *entanglement* (Barad, 2007), is perhaps the height of rebellion. It rebels against Anthropocene/capitalocene/plantationocene (Haraway, 2016) systems of binary code that structure our lives. *And these are the systems such '-cenes' rely on to presence powerfully in the world.*

> *If time was a cosmic pencil that wrote us all into being, what would flow out of the carbon filings of mine, mixing with the air and the blood inside my skin? I write in the margins of the book, all around the printed text of the first history of 'The Blood Countess'. At one point, when I pause to take a breath, my eyes blur. The texts fold into each other to become one great story, the same story told over and over again in different permutations: A woman disappearing from the world, over and over, through the cruelty of history. Disappearing from out of history itself.*

When a history has been silenced for so long, how do we need to change the way we listen to make sense of it? It belongs to another world, no? To another universe almost, its song seemingly absent from the creation of the present. How can we understand something that has been missing for so long?

With this in mind, re-storying (to refer to the start of this chapter) is nothing less than a radical act. But rather than simply re-throne a story that has been de-throned, for example, a story of silenced women (thus upholding the coded nature of being in the world just changing the players), what would it take to think through new modes that flew straight to the heart of such structures, de-territorialising their secure position in the so-called justice of the times? Is it possible to re-story story structures themselves?

Had I been a hero, I might have been tempted to expose the injustices that befell me throughout the story of my life, to call out some divine reckoning that felled the very walls of Jericho with the sound of its rage. To make people accountable and crush them into the angry shapes of cause and effect. To make a history out of us all. But I had become suspicious of such world-making devices. Was it foolish or courageous to dare to dream of justice beyond the fibres of linear time; beyond the clear marking out of cause and effect?

Unearthing and telling new stories might indeed be an entrance point into such work, but once setting out on the journey to an unheroic crumpling of binaries a new question emerges: what then? (Otherwise known as 'so what?'). This question hit me over the head (metaphorically!) as I was writing the novel. Simply, where could Bathory and her husband Nadasdy escape to? What spacetimematter entanglement could they flee to? None. Because they *were* the living, bleeding presencing of the code. They were a 'zero' and a 'one'. I tried out each re-storying technology I could think of, and if Bathory's rewrite here did anything, it was to find new spaces across time to, as Audre Lorde puts it, face up to the fact that 'the master's tools will never dismantle the master's house' (Lorde, 1984/2017).

Nadasdy tried to move, but I held him close. His weight against mine made me feel strangely safe, even if only for a moment.

'We will be gone from here soon. I promise you', he whispered.

'I know. I believe you. But to what?' I asked. He stopped and I regretted the question as all the urgency and bluster drained away from him. He looked at me like a child might, caught in a perplexing question that was beyond him.

'Just ... away from this', came his response.

I nodded and we searched each other's eyes. What kind of escape could keep us away from [Emperor] Rudolph's reach, in the end?

Gravity. It lies at the centre of all space and time. Without gravity, nothing makes sense. With its incredible force it pulls us to the earth and makes meanings out of nothing. Who in their right mind would try to intervene? Who would tell gravity to take a hike, stand up on a pillar of nothing and ask to be rooted elsewhere, anywhere but here? It might be possible to tell new stories and hope that one day their quantum resonances might travel far enough into the brain to make us do something differently this time. But what holds these stories together, what truly changes unless the descent to earth itself – the gravity of it all – is re-storied? You can tell as many stories as you like hoping that just by thinking things anew you can change the world. But it means precious little unless it bonds to the tiny structures that make worlds. Unless the force that pulls you in, pulls you in differently, re-storying itself in the process through you and all your stories.

I shut the lid on my computer, stretching my tired fingers against the warm whir of the laptop in the library. I've emerged this time at the British Library. The words I've just written start to take shape on the screen in front of me. Not one letter at a time, but randomly. A curve of an 's' here, the straight back of a 't', the doorways of the 'o's' pushing open. Language moves. Language is alive! I think. Like time itself. It also lives in the body, as the body. 'It has to be done differently', I whisper to myself. All the patterns that arced out when time folded its divine fist, bringing origin stories back to it, these were the traces of how time and all its stories met with gravity, their trajectories sliding through the spaces between time's fingers even as they crunched down, squeezing and slipping through them in new waves that danced! The fold, the crunch, the mark, they disordered time to human eyes, but in truth – in the tiny world hidden deep inside each of us – these are the things that scribe out the world as we knew it.

I wanted to tell Nadasdy the story of time. I wanted to tell him to watch the crocuses in the fields and to understand that the root structures inside all things are more representative of a life than any short-term bloom. I wanted to tell him that this was no fatalism, that inside these roots and passages was where all the freedom he was hungry for lay. That we could bloom differently along any line in space or time. That choice is about making new differences. Tiny differences that go unnoticed by the large ignominious sword of history that doesn't necessarily realise when it's being rewritten. But if I knew this, then so did Elizabet and she would tell him. She would tell him all the way back in the past and so I would have haunted myself in the future present.

The technologies of re-storying are complicated by virtue of the fact that they presence in heroic binaries that affirm anthropocentric coding practices – practices where living and dying are not entangled parts of being, but vehemently and urgently separated out. The heart of research here beats out its binary function; after all, human life depends on it. But the practices that started emerging through *re*-storying the history of Bathory the monster aimed not to set up the unheroic as something opposite to the heroic (as this would fall into the coded trap of binarity yet again). Rather they aimed to thread the two through each other in the electric, affective spaces that pulse in and around the heart of the story.

> *Elizabet had been certain at one point that my position in time – that what I shakily called the 'present day' – held some kind of secret knowledge that would answer her prayers, undoing all the dangers of her own moment. She believed that divine knowledge from the future could come to act as divine justice in her life, a thing that she might capture and print in a book. I had remarked that, instead, I thought we were more like single starlings that formed part of a great flock of ancient stories. In my short lifetime, I was merely at the head, leading the story-flock towards some point in the sky. When the deeper currents of time changed, it would be her at the head, then another, then another as we moved in chaotic, ancestral patterns under the sheath of heaven, undulating in a grand scale that was so large, we would never be able to fully comprehend it. Without a single, heroic direction, all our efforts towards small justices were nothing more than lone, discarded feathers on the wind. Justice was deeper than we could know. It made worlds. Justice mattered.*
>
> *As we listened deeply to the sound of ourselves at different points across time, we shared this knowledge. I could feel her laughing in her tower room, becoming more and more carefree despite her locked surroundings. Just as I was. 'Little wing, Little wing, I pray we may both flutter light upon these eternal winds.'*

In this piece of writing here, I do not aim to use a different, academic language to describe the same trajectory of a novel written in yet another different language, scribing an authorial key for readers and (re)writers. Rather I want to argue for the rebellious nature of bringing a feeling heart in all its material-discursive power into the way we think the world across registers, disciplines and timespans. In and amongst the heart's close relationship with binarity, it also acts the centre node, the loom if you will, on which we might spin the affective fictioning practices that are capable not just of producing binaries anew, but of contemplating what binaries are urgent and what binaries we may wish to weave and churn differently; diffracting new versions of *here, now.* Why? Because to me non/binarity (to use Barad's '/' to denote a cutting-together-apart) is an affair of the affective heart and, as the heart is to our own bodies, it is urgent and vital. The unheroic journey of life/death crumpled together as a surface of intensities that we come to call being – a surface that isn't flat but multidimensional, multimodal, multi-timed – is a tool not often used in the master's house.

> For within living structures defined by profit, by linear power, by institutional dehumanization, our feelings were not meant to survive. Kept around as unavoidable adjuncts or pleasant pastimes, feelings were expected to kneel to thought as women were expected to kneel to men. But women have survived. As poets. (Lorde, 1984/2017, p. 5)

The heart isn't just a four-chambered house of feelings, just as affects aren't reducible to 'emotions'. The heart is eternally actively keeping us alive. There's nothing abstract about the heart. It is perhaps the ultimate example of a material-discursive phenomenon, and therefore its practices become modes of *thinking* that use different kinds of intelligence(s). Such intelligences include the un/heroic carrier bag; the *coding and separating* of entangled blood – venous and arterial – into the structures of life; the material-discursive longing for freedom from the very *codes* that bind us under the foot or crown of power, into human shapes; the capacity (inside the carrier bag) for lines of flight. The intelligences of power, of binary enemies and allies that we love and hate with remarkable circularity as we move through life, point to a linear notion of time that relies on cause and effect to mete out justice. But if we used the heart-as-apparatus to re-story time, what would that do to our notion of justice?

> *Justice is intimate. It is a lover that never leaves you, just as time never leaves the body, but is constantly engaged in turning it into something else. Certain justice is all about power and measurement. How many bodies went to the gallows? How many cells fill with prisoners? How many fines were paid this week? And other games you can play with numbers. Uncertain justice is about love. Because how much justice is just enough? …*
>
> *They always tell you to be true to life when you're writing. 'Be true to life' and 'Write what you know'. Both are platitudes. But what about writing about something you don't know. Like what it feels like to be a woman unhampered by generations upon generations of violence and hatred and all the other things that have come to constitute our collected histories here, now. To be Bathory without an infinite array of Thurzos and Bastas, Nadasdys and Rudolphs looking to write her into the Blood Countess – to change her being, her ability to be part of her own history. How can I write that? How*

can you re-story something you've never known – never known in your bones. Our species knows all about power. Our species knows how bodies, whatever their constitution, are marked into position, trapped, like particles deciding where to be, when to be, how to be, this time. Material information, lighting up inside the urban pinball machine we call commerce, we call empire.

In re-storying the world, perhaps [*Elizabet*] *would not choose to reposition herself closer to power. She would not choose to be Elizabeth Regina or any other queen made under a crown. She would choose to slide within power rather than stand up inside it. Power like that exerts its gravity hard and fast, making us all slaves to its position in time and space, telling its story through us – even now. It is the very opposite of freedom. Perhaps she had chosen instead to dream us all inside a powerful uncertainty – powerful on account of its endless momentum. Uncertainty has nothing to do with silence. It has nothing to do with fantasy either. Uncertainty leaves it up to the thoughts and marks born out of it to do the dirty work of separating our species out, to confine us inside an eternal measurability; an infinite sorting machine that teaches us each our place inside the world. Uncertainty flies, not away from measurement, but inside it. Endless movement, breathing inside a fixed point. When uncertainty makes friends with momentum, it turns into a love affair. They birth new worlds. Uncountable worlds. Worlds that understand nothing of the fixing of time and space, but everything about justice and everything about love.*

It is easy to suggest here a correlation, in my mind at least, between certainty as death and uncertainty as life. But correlation doesn't infer causation. (I saw this famous phrase once turned into a meme where it was carved out on a Halloween pumpkin. The meme had the legend: 'How to terrify a physicist!' running across the top.) This is not to say that certainty causes death – that to fix something in time and space is somehow to 'kill' it, and to allow it the uncertainty of a position in the entanglement of space, time and matter is to give it life. Rather it's to hold these two together in a flux of patternings that mete out the world in a strange and vibratory dance. The heart understands this. That's why I argue for a heart in research. Bathory's rebellion against the emperor, not with swords but with books, with new forms of storytelling fictions how such rebellious practices are not coy or shallow, but *matters* of life and death, even as sixteenth-century Calvinists and Counter-Reformationists alike lit their censoring pyres.

It was of course the same in my time. I watched little empires rise and fall on TV, in stories, in short headlines that bulleted across the multiple screens we all owned: time to fail, time to win, go whichever way you can but just keep going inside the game! Our reformation wasn't about books. It wasn't about the control of knowledge, not in that way. It was about the saturation of knowledge inside the stories we told. We were real and we were fake. We were what a million, tiny worlds, tiny suns, tiny screens wanted of us. We were twenty-four-hour accessible. We were our own diffractions. Continually programming ourselves into the great algorithm of the world. This was the world we had created. We had aimed for a reform of knowledge and knowledge had become a device designed to rescript every impulse into an act of crowns and kingdoms. We paid fealty inside the home. Everywhere, the emperor stared at us, heard us, scribed us. Everywhere we plugged our flesh into his and he ate us from the inside out, turning us into data like an incredible earthworm made of flashes and dots.

I wanted to tear the emperor out of the machine. But everywhere 'he' was watching as 'he' coded me into zeros and ones and anticipated my thoughts and feelings, lifting them out of me just as Rudolph had lifted me from out of Bathory's inner world and brought me atop his Emerald Table. Who could fight such an emperor and survive? It was the same question Elizabet had spoken of in the corridor with Francis. Where can anyone escape to?

I receive one lonely message from a young scholar late one night when the screen lights have burned into my eyes and made me tired. I don't recognise the pseudonym. It simply says: We're reading your work online. We're following it. And we love it. Never give up.

Four Chambers for Technologies of Critique (That Flow!)

As I came to the end of writing my first draft of the novel, I found myself engaged in a ferocious argument with a friend who was acting as a critical reader: '*Why don't you read Einstein's letter to his daughter?' He huffed and puffed. 'That'll sort it out.'* I was enraged. My blood boiled. '*But Einstein abandoned his daughter!'* I retorted. Then I paused. I found the in/famous letter in question online and put it through a thinking structure inspired by the different technologies mentioned here above. What had re-storying Bathory taught me about rebellious technologies of fictioning practice? I went back to the letter, then back to the novel, rotating the two, diffracting them through each other. I held the whole lot in my heart. How it felt to undertake such a diffraction. What waves of practice had been surging through me even as I fictioned my own writing process, diffracting it through the countess's journey I had come to *love*:

- materiality: the sensuality of the affective patterning of material-discursive phenomena
- coding: not dissimilar to the coding practices the heart uses to pump venous and arterial blood (practices that require an understanding of the space-time positioning of things in endless motion and momentum)

- deep listening: listening to the way stories, like all phenomena, inhabit structures *and build them* at the same time
- diffraction: many worlds existing inside one, allowing for the possibility of the performativity of the apparatus.

In some ways aping the incredible, free, open source print world of the 'Blood Countess', that I had found after hundreds of hours of pouring over letters, bills and history books – her secret printing press, her possible role at the centre of a coup d'état that struck to the heart of the status quo and her *rebellion* which used nothing more than a little banned book about the working of the heart (*Christianismi restitutio*) – I presented these ideas about practice in a short, open-source video.[1] I laughed to myself: *What would Bathory have done at the dawn of this 21st century information revolution? Where her apparatus was the radical printing press, a technology fast becoming captured, censored and commodified in her age, what diffractions of many-worlded Bathorys might be presencing in our dawn – the dawn of the digital information age? Our own distributed renaissance.* Four technologies for critique, four valves cutting-together-apart the many-worlded ways of thinking about the mixed and mattering flows of justice in the veins, the blood, the heart. Four chambers, deep inside the body that pulse out a vivid onto-epistemology as imbued with justice as it is with *life*.

These technologies of critique (and thus of worlding) emerged from the writing of the novel itself, practices drawn out from the un/heroic journey of re-storying Bathory and her sometimes fictionalised author in all their rebellion against the age-old coding technologies of our own master-(his)stories. Returning to the problem of Einstein's letter, and how it suddenly and affectively become part of the diffractive re-storying, I decided to work closely with it in redraft. It became an entrance point, a way in for me to build this heart – the heart of research, as a simple, unheroic and everyday carrier bag for churning small things inside in hope of new storied presents.

Putting the Four Technologies into Practice

I sit on the floor with my computer and re-imagine the letter anew. I churn it, fictioning it, pulling out new forms of practice from it. Not from what it says, but from what the ink of its original cuts-together-apart. From the intra-active relations between what it says, what it doesn't say, what futures it implies, and what haunts it – from the particles inside its origin-ink, to the flashes on my screen. I diffract it through the apparatus of my own life and death, my own

1 https://www.youtube.com/watch?v=7KZBNVZgmFc&t=45s

cutting-together-apart. The letter itself, a contested document found online, like so many other half-truths and pieces of fake news that require we sharpen our critical brains and urgently re-imagine what our relationship to knowledge is – what worlds we build in the name of 'knowledge', what troubles we might need to stay with. Moved through the four technologies of critical practice, I diffract what I find. I diffract it *through* re-writing Bathory. I diffract it *in order* to be able to re-write Bathory.

Now my fingers flash across the laptop. They return to a place they have already been but that is becoming new, becoming a process of difference already differing. Now Bathory, awaiting sentencing, writes a letter to *her* daughter:

> *My dearest child. I know I have never been a mother to you, but you have always been a daughter to me. Please don't ask me to explain why that has been the case. There aren't words to describe it and I wouldn't burden you with any more history than you already have in you. I ask you to guard this letter until one day – one day when the world's soul is large enough to accept me. No small ask, I know!*
>
> *There is only one place strong enough to withstand the violence of things. It's built to rotate us between the poles of good and evil and everything in between. It can be bruised and broken. It can be filled with fantasy and even sorrow. It can lead us all astray. It's the seat of all desire; the seat of all wonder; of all justice. Servetus knew it. The Ottomans knew it. There's not a book printed today that doesn't somewhere point to it, even if it remains absent from its pages, like the face of an angel, hidden, but alive, beating its wings inside the threads of the paper it's printed on.*
>
> *I'm talking, my dear child, of the heart. If we want to survive on this earth, from generation to generation, if we want to save something of the human even though all our will seems bent towards our own erasure, it's this: the heart is the only doorway through which we might pass safely, from one place, from one time to another. Every day, I pray you daughter, every day make sure you pass, at least once, through this door. In the simplest acts, the smallest gestures. Pass through this doorway. It's the only way through.*

To her own author, this author fictioned Bathory writing a letter back to her, folding the spaces between author, fictioned author, fictioned subject and active subject of research re-fictioning the author. What a flow of causalities! A diffractive flow of *heres* and *nows* pulsing lively inside the entanglement of life/lives:

> *I am writing you. I am writing you even now. Your future lies not in the hands of this emperor. It exceeds his boundaries. Even my words, you exceed them*

too. Your story is already inside my bones and the bones of generations of other women who, like you, are greater than one single life ... She smiled at me. I sensed the world around us, the strange, pulsing field, fading. Each blade of grass humming with its many worlds started to become blurred, filling with static until the entire field became one ancient hum travelling through space; through the stars.

'Write me well', Elizabet whispered, and she blew me a kiss before she too dissolved into the void.

The four technologies of the heart are nothing short of an affective, diffractive, critical practice. The journeys through the different chambers do not conform to a particular flow or direction – after all, each body is built of differences – patterns of difference differing in infinite movements, shapes, forms, futures and ghosts. Rather, the four technologies are an apparatus, crafted from out of a book I wrote because I love to write and the huge in/justice done to Bathory was something that touched me to my bones, making them shimmer and fizz with affective tremors. Justice *matters.* How we make it, in turn, is how we make worlds.

The end ...

References

Ahmed, S. (2017). *Living a feminist life*. Duke University Press.

Barad, K. (2007). *Meeting the universe halfway: Quantum physics and the entanglement of matter and meaning*. Duke University Press.

Elias, N. (1956). Problems of involvement and detachment. *British Journal of Sociology, 7*(3), 226–252.

Haraway, D. (2016). *Staying with the trouble*. Duke University Press.

Le Guin, U. (2019). *The carrier bag theory of fiction*. Ignota Books. (Originally published 1988)

Livholts, M. (2020). *Situated writing as theory and method: The untimely academic novella*. Routledge.

Lorde, A. (2017). *The master's tools will never dismantle the master's house*. Penguin Random House. (Original work published 1984)

Nail, T. (2018). *Lucretius I: An ontology of motion*. University of Edinburgh Press.

Rogers, H. (2020). Exquisite methods: Ruminations of corporeal becoming in artistic research. In J. Golding, M. Reinhart, & M. Paganelli (Eds.), *Data loam: Sometimes hard, usually soft. The future of knowledge systems* (pp. 356–377). De Gruyter.

Chapter 17

Surfacing the *image*-inary: Exchanging Sensations of time through Art, Media and Pedagogy

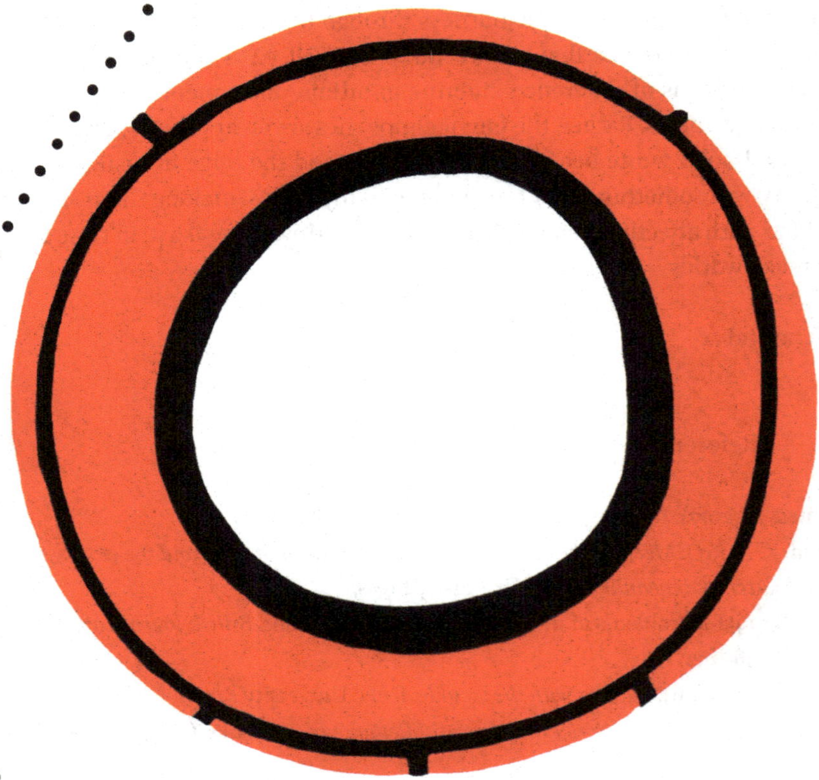

Trisha McCrae, David Rousell and Portia Ungley

 | DOI:10.1163/9789004516069_023

Start? I could
not
shaken through my
skin
up the staircase of
sensation
patterned shapes emerged
myself. mingle. be.
feverishly a flea
resist the stagnation
flow flatter and seduce
disembodied voices
embodied shapes
shout
echo
whisper in my ear
s p l e n d i d resentment

go on? and could not
heavily silently sweating
curious spontaneous
turning towards the light
reflected disillusion
bitter threatening
enthusiastically porous
she walked carelessly
in to the room
wavered stopped .
loosened clumsy
tenacity *torn*
the silence
sweep it aside
that great bumbling
triumphant storm begins.

Image-inary 1

30 January 2021 20:39

from Trisha McCrae

to David Rousell

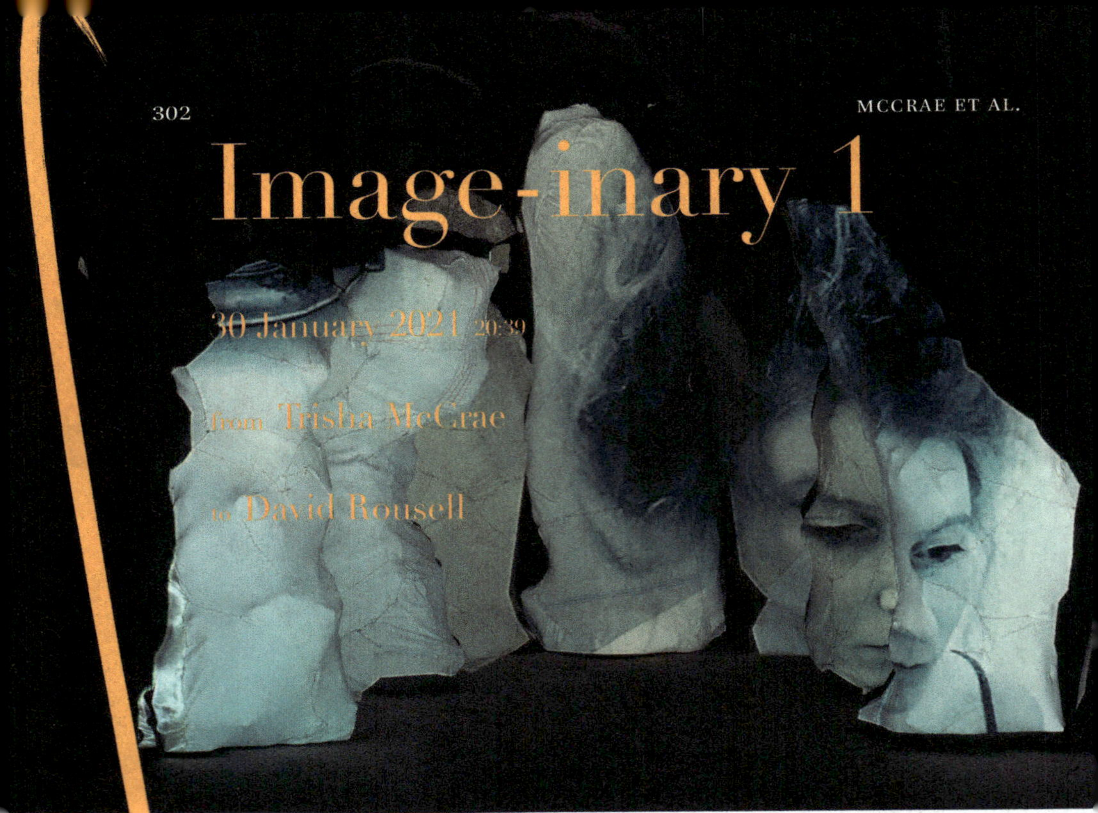

Hi David,

I am attaching an image from my installation *Les Pierre Parlantes* for you to have a look at to see if you think it may be useful as a starting point in terms of our conceptual focus area of surfaces/surfacing, sensation/skin, and time/temporalities. For me *Les Pierre Parlantes* is about engaging and modulating the viewer's sensations as they move through time; beginning with how and what they might feel as they enter the installation space, through the feeling of being 'held' by my work in the space and then to that 'after feeling' that resonates beyond the space. It speaks to our chapter exploration of how immersive artworks and media space can evoke and carry affects that are dynamic and polytemporal. I look forward to exploring where this dialogue takes us to find out why they have these surfaces have such pulling potential. I thought it might be useful for us to exchange threads of thought for each image we send each other as points of interest or potential areas to develop.

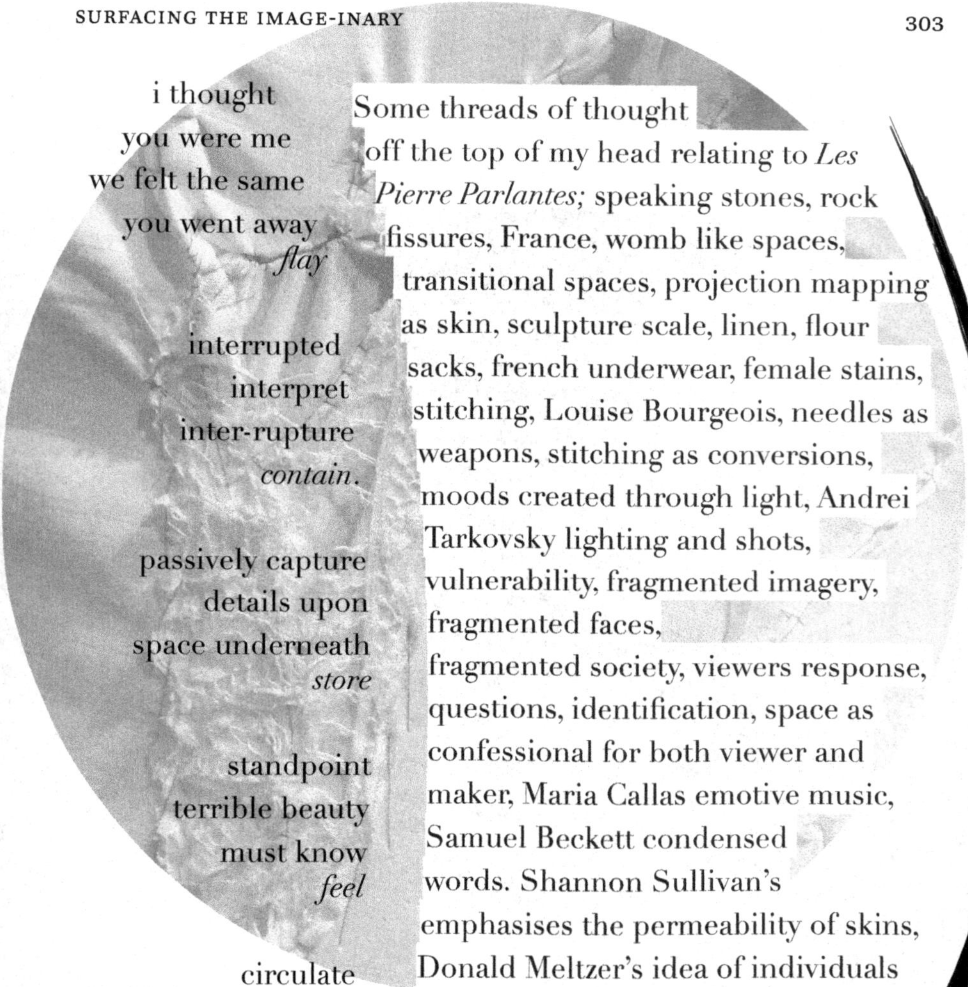

i thought
you were me
we felt the same
you went away
flay

interrupted
interpret
inter-rupture
contain.

passively capture
details upon
space underneath
store

standpoint
terrible beauty
must know
feel

circulate
project create
insulate
hold

sustain affect
pattern flow
routine change
go

Some threads of thought off the top of my head relating to *Les Pierre Parlantes;* speaking stones, rock fissures, France, womb like spaces, transitional spaces, projection mapping as skin, sculpture scale, linen, flour sacks, french underwear, female stains, stitching, Louise Bourgeois, needles as weapons, stitching as conversions, moods created through light, Andrei Tarkovsky lighting and shots, vulnerability, fragmented imagery, fragmented faces,
fragmented society, viewers response, questions, identification, space as confessional for both viewer and maker, Maria Callas emotive music, Samuel Beckett condensed words. Shannon Sullivan's emphasises the permeability of skins, Donald Meltzer's idea of individuals 'living on the surface', Eugenio Gaddini's idea that imitation is an important aspect of sensory perception.,
Donald Winnicott's object relations theory and transitional objects,
Didier Anzieu flaying of Marsyas, Laura Riding's poem *forgotten girlhood*,
Mladon Dollar's *The Voice and the Stone* and the story of Memnon.

....good luck with the editing this weekend, all the best,
Trisha

Image-inary 2

Hi Trisha and Portia,

I'm getting in touch about our chapter collaboration in the book proposed as 'Doing Rebellious Research'. Sorry for a bit of time between communications, my 'extra' time for this project been going into the proposal itself which we are now reworking based on reviews. Once we have the proposal accepted, we can get going on this collaboration in a more intensive manner. For now, I'm just confirming that the basic idea for this collaboration is that we will exchange a series of images, and respond poetically and philosophically to each other's images. We've articulated a conceptual focus on ideas/practices of surfacing, sensation, and time, and specifically, how immersive arts practices can modulate a range of temporalities, surfaces, and sensations. Portia, that is fine if you don't want to send us images. You can still participate in the collaboration by responding poetically and philosophically to our images, as a kind of (diffractive?) 'intercessor' in the process. Or whatever! I also like your idea, Trisha, of just sharing a string of words, phrases, concepts, references, and fragmentary associations to accompany each image. These can act as what Deleuze and Guattari (1987) called 'particle-signs' or 'passwords'. These can gesture toward relational elements carried by/with the images, and that we can collectively explore to establish atmospheric context, but without the necessity of literal explanation. This sounds like a nice protocol to me. What do you think?

David

17th February 2021 06:59

from David Rousell

to Trisha McCrae and Portia Ungley

Along these lines, I've attached an image and here are my phrases:

SenseLab;

the listening body;

balloons;

embyrogenesis;

Raymond Ruyer's concepts of 'self-survey' and 'absolute surface';

GoPro camera; haptic sensing;

Erin Manning's 'Relationscapes'; participation without observation;

Elizabeth Grosz's 'The Incorporeal';

Plato's chora; technical witnesses;

Derek McCormack's 'Atmospheric Things';

suspensions within events;

I decided to go ahead and respond *directly* to your last image of the hand emerging through space. From your list of 'particle' words that accompanied your image I was drawn to the ideas of the French philosopher Raymond Ruyer. Ideas struck me like 'continual forming things' and '*rhythms of action*', the ongoingness of an activity as being conceived as a creative and open-ended process of improvisation. These ideas led me to respond to your *atmospheric image* of the hand by drawing a 'dot' drawing of a mannequin hand in space. I have been doing close observational dot drawings for sometime now. I placed a mannequin hand on a table in front of my studio window and intently focused my eyes on the hand whilst making dots and marks in *saccadic jumps* to describe it in relation to the space around it. Every point and mark is describing something. It is not a random act of drawing. I am not interested in describing the hand itself but more the hand's *relationship to the space* around it and my relationship to what I hear, see and feel over time whilst marking the drawing. The resulting drawing is a visual language of equivalents in dots, marks and paint to these visual and *auditory sensations*. For example, along with describing the space, I may mark the music I am listening to or paint the movement of the sun shining on the hand as it moves across its surface. The marks can be staccato or forte. The drawing expresses an activity, a continual dance of dots and marks, performing, almost by itself, in its own rhythm. I suppose it can be described as visual language somewhere between a *point cloud,* that describes three dimensional space, and a Kandinsky drawing! Particle words: Tactile reception, *intoxicating realism*, the persistence of vision, the illusion of continuity and motion, *quantum of action*, Andrew Vass, surface drawings, musical resonance, Norman Bryson *vision and visuality*. dot drawings as a tool for allowing a student to see/feel education *spatially/performatively*. The human scale of things/insignificance in a universe where we can only see 4 % of the universe the rest is dark matter. Rosa Barba's idea of having her films run along side each other in *different times scales*. The patterning effect of circles within circles/*things within things*.

These ideas led me to respond to your *atmospheric image* of the hand by drawing a 'dot' drawing of a mannequin hand in space. I placed a mannequin hand on a table in front of my studio window and intently focused my eyes on the hand whilst making dots and marks in saccadic jumps to describe it in relation to the space

Image-inary 3

24th February 2021 13.44

From Trisha McCrae

to David Rousell and Portia Ungley

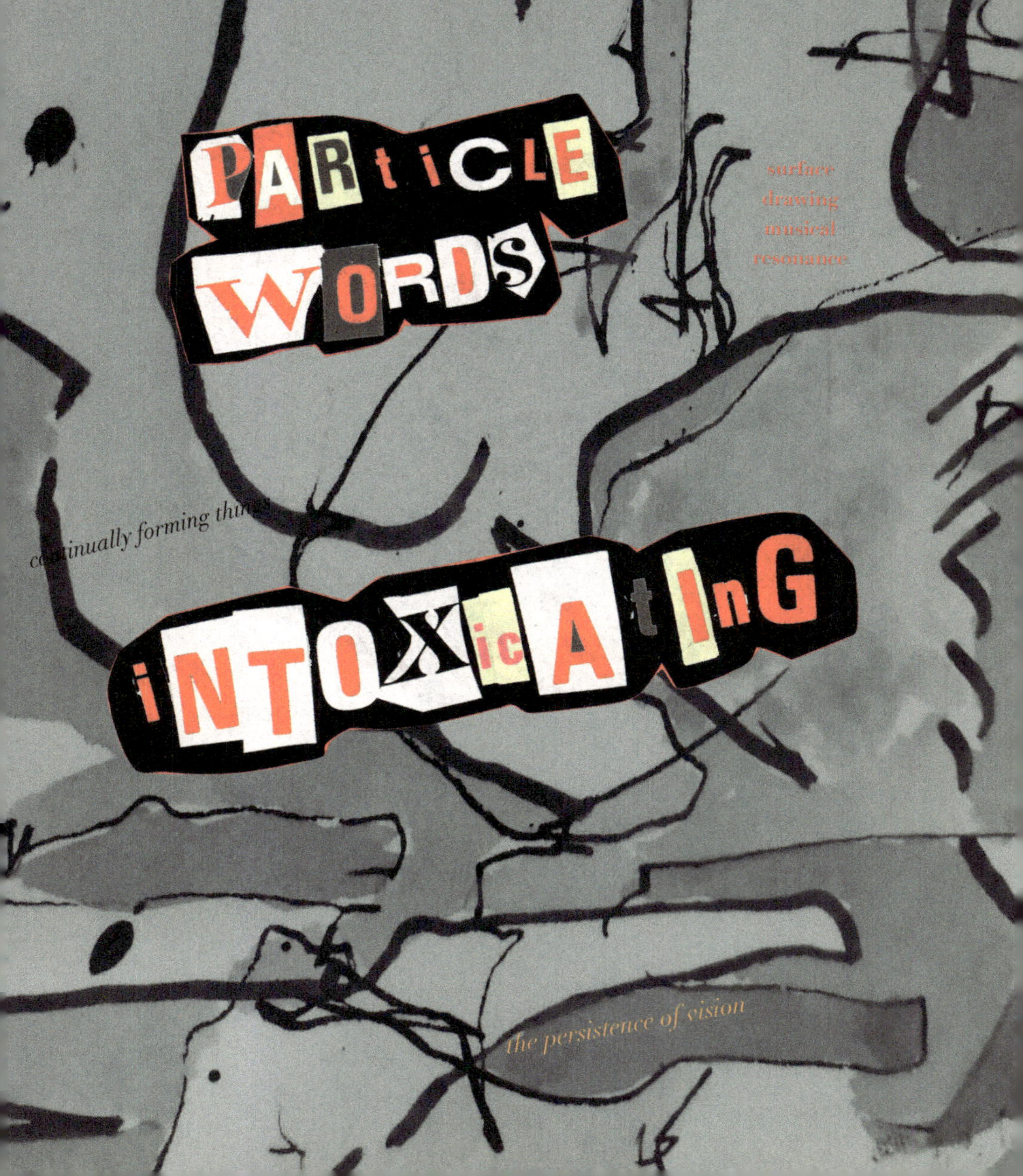

Image-inary 4
2nd March 2021 05.08
surfacing the imaginary

Surfacing the Image-inary: Exchanging Sensations of Time through Art, Media, and Pedagogy

Trisha McCrae, David Rousell, and Portia Ungley

The chapter *explores how immersive arts and media can entangle, layer and modulate our experiences and sensations of time. We hope to seek new latent potentials that can arise from immersive artistic practices to create new performative research methodologies.*

Our approach explores how the surfaces of immersive artworks and media spaces can evoke and carry affects that are dynamic and polytemporal, with the potential to hold and project, contain and inscribe, circulate and capture nuanced social, cultural and political feelings. We want to explore how and why these mediated surfaces have this potential to speak to, with, and through us. Is it that these surfaces reflect back on us? Is it that we are pulled into their atmosphere? How and why do they have this surface pulling potential? We have chosen to explore these questions through an experimental dialogue of images, poetry and philosophical text.

This methodological process is unfolding in an open-ended, informal way where images and ideas are invited to unfold, entangle, and co-evolve. Our iterative process begins by selecting and circulating images from our archives of artistic projects that speak to the surfacing of time and sensation.

Our subsequent replies are attended with a string of phrases, concepts, references, and fragmentary associations. These act as 'particle-signs' or 'passwords' (Deleuze & Guattari, 1987) that gesture toward intuitive relational elements carried by/with the images that we collectively explore to establish atmospheric context without any literal explanation. We have also begun to explore how each image-inary exchange has the potential to create an experimental arts educational methodology and set of techniques that could be engaged in the arts classroom.

Through this collaborative work we show how immersive experimentation and the unknown can deliver unthought eventualities, and therefore come to modulate the sensation of time in novel ways. We hope to be rebellious in ways that promote understanding in arts and performance research by showing that it is the creative **act** *of expression that opens up the relational dialogue, just as it is the creative* **act** *of perception that produces the image and its reception in a single gesture. We suggest that these acts do not simply occur 'in the moment', but ripple across multiple surfaces and temporalities in ways that are ecological, atmospheric, and under certain conditions, pedagogical.*

Image-inary 5

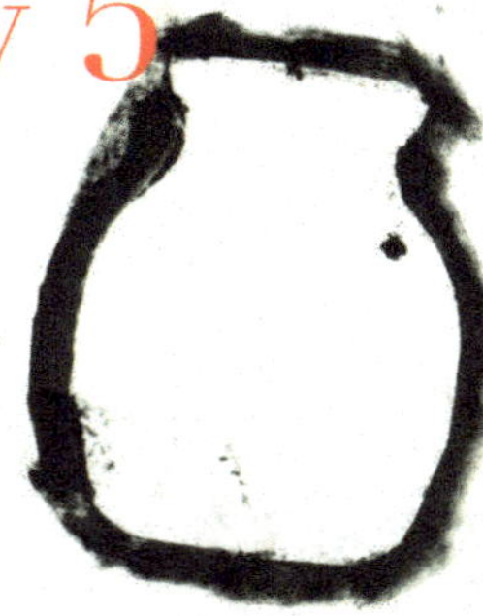

2nd March 2021 18.17

From Trisha McCrae

to David Rousell and Portia Ungley

Particle words: La dolce vita, Italian [illegible] Italian language and food, food as social communication, Italian colour, what does black and white say? the social divide, poverty and wealth, the politics of 'containing' histories, containers of memory, when we say historical time whose reality are we talking about? what is lived time? complex coevalness, the accumulative stresses of colonial words, the politics of archival appropriation, Italian

I was inspired by your word 'polytemporality' - I thought this image fitted that remit well because it tells a story that has many crossover points, connections and divergences through time.

The film is a tribute to a wonderful Italian delicatessen, KC Continental Store, Caledonia Road, London. After 50 years of trading the store closed and was repurposed into Geddes Gallery. I made a video installation *Vasetti*, in response to the history of delicatessen and exhibited it on one of the old deli's shelves.

Each jar contains a film that references all things related to the store and surrounding community; the owner, Leo Giordani's footage and images, types of Italian food, Italian cinema film and archival material based around food and eating, contemporary and historical photos of people living on Caledonia Road. The evocative and complex soundtrack is a mix of Italian conversations and music, screen remains, resonating our own thoughts through time.

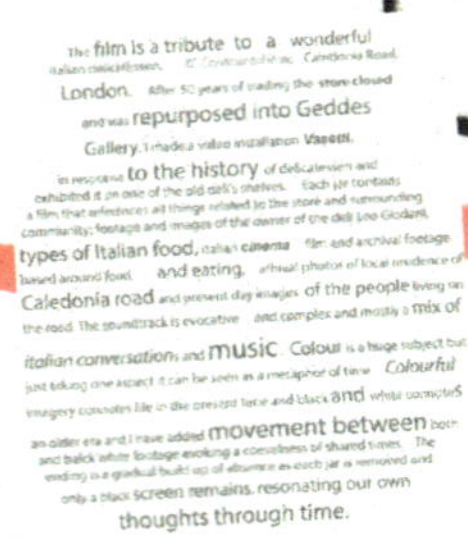

Hi Trisha,
Thanks for reminding me, so I am now responding to your last sharing of your drawing. I am firstly struck by the notion of direct response, and overall how the concept of 'response' is looming large in our collaborative work here. I grasp the notion of directness in terms of a performative and generative action, creative activity, such as your positioning of the mannequin hand, and also how this leads to a generative and important question around arts pedagogy, and the shareability of artistic technique, experiment, learning. I am reminded of a book called 'The art of the art assignment' (Bransford, 2012), which collected numerous strange and wonderful pedagogical assignments from artists, many of them quite renowned. But I am also reminded of the work of Fred Moten and Stefano Harney (2013) in a book (never far from my mind these days) called The Undercommons: Black study and fugitive planning.

They talk about this concept of *study* as something that's distinct from any sense of formal learning. Study is really the opposite of the 'call to order' of the teacher who teaches, which basically shuts down whatever study is already going on. Study is more like the informal movements of social life and thinking practices that are always happening anyway, but without any formal grid around them. Things like taking a walk around the neighbourhood, playing around in the art studio, improvised jam sessions, thrown together conversations on street corners, or factory floors, are all examples of study in this sense.

So, I'd say what we're doing in creating this chapter is a form of study. Interestingly, Harney and Moten also discuss study as a kind of 'call and response', but they don't really separate the call and the response from each other. So, instead of the 'call to order' which demands a particular response (e.g. what the teacher demands of the student), you have a call to dis-order which contains the seeds of its response from the outset. Harney and Moten describe this in terms of calls to activism and anarchic unrest (they use the 2011 London riots as an example), where 'the response is already there before the call goes out… you're already in something' (p. 134). And I think this sense of the response containing the call, or in some way even preceding it, is interesting to think with in terms of the call to art.

1st April 2021 02.49

Image-inary 6

From David Rousell to Trisha McCrae and Portia Ungley

So in terms of a response that precedes the call, I am thinking as well with directness, and how this directness could be a confluence of forces and events, and not just an 'action' that I perform in response to your call, or vice versa. What was already there, already stirring, already resonating, while you were adjusting the mannequin hand and creating this vibrantly rhizomatic dance of a drawing that recalls Klee's 'taking a line for a walk?' Well, I've been working on a series of arts projects that bring children (ages 3-12) together with various artists (visual, theatre, sound art, etc) to explore the impacts of climate change and multi-species futures for the city of Melbourne. One of these projects is called Wood Wide Web, and it involves a collaboration with Barking Spider Visual Theatre to explore how trees communicate underground through mycelium networks. At the same time that you send your drawing, a group of young children around 3 or 4 years old were exploring immersive light and sound environments as part of an engagement with the underground vegetal and mycelial world. After a series of outdoor encounters with trees near the art centre, the children were invited to draw their impression of how mycelium networks help trees communicate. The drawings were done on transparencies, and then projected them into the gallery so the children could 'walk into' their drawings. One of the things I've been writing about these workshops is the sense of directness and even 'certainty' with which the children took up this task. Here's a little excerpt from my fieldnotes, recorded the same day you sent your last drawing:

I am sitting next to a young boy named Jasper, just around 3 years old, who had previously spent most of the workshop in his mother's arms. I notice Jasper detach somewhat from the mother to begin this task, his back still in contact with her legs. What surprises me in this interval is the certainty with which he now takes on the task of drawing the mycelial underground communication network. This is an abstract task which asks you to draw something for which you have no visual reference whatsoever. Yet Jasper confidently grabs an orange crayon and immediately draws a series of gently curving orange lines that double back on themselves. In no place are the lines jagged or broken, they are just one continuously smooth motion. The lines end and Jasper puts the crayon down. He looks up at his mum and says "it's finished" with a sense of complete certainty. At this moment his mother is talking intently with one of the other mothers, I think they might have arrived together. She doesn't take much notice of Jasper or his drawing in this interval. But Jasper decides to continue. He grasps a brownish crayon this time, and draws a line that starts from the bottom right of the page, twists and changes directions in the upper middle section, and then completes itself on the bottom left. Seemingly satisfied with this articulation, he grabs a purple marker and creates a third line that closely resembles the last. Later, at the end of the workshop, I see that someone has gathered all the children's transparent drawings up in a pile, and they are sitting on a little table seemingly forgotten. I feel like I'm glancing down into a deep pool. The overall effect is one of interpenetrating layers of entanglement, a play of lines that speak of secret junctures, subterranean proliferations, and the infinite curve of a collective life lived in direct and continuous contact with the world.

So the images I've shared are 1) Jasper's mycelium drawing; and 2) the layered pile of children's drawings all together. And I am still thinking here about how the call and the response are entangled, and how different responses weave their way into a singular call to art that is not answerable through (human) language alone, but also voices a wider, indeterminate series of aesthetic conjunctions with nonhuman lines of life. There is more to this story too, as Jasper wanders alone into images that we've projected in the gallery, leaving the comfort of his mother behind. So, that's my response for now. I'm happy to use Dropbox if you'd like to set up a working document for the chapter and images in there. Portia, please feel free to jump in at any moment. I think we're going to start accelerating this process now.

Take care, and all the best, David

Image-inary 7

3rd April 2021 19.52

From Trisha McCrae to David Rousell and Portia Ungley

Hi David and Portia,

When I saw Jaspers drawing it brought to mind images from my video work, which all ask the same question; what happens to the flow at cross over points, what happens when waves cross, when words cross and when people cross? I decided to try and answer this by doing an experiment. I put two very different texts relating to the senses alongside each other and blended them into a new unknown text. The first source text is from Assumption the short story by Samuel Beckett's and the other source text is a psychoanalytic paper by Andrezej Werbart called The Skin is the Cradle of the Soul which is about Didier Anzieu's notion of the Skin-Ego ie,. that psychic phenomena are always embodied. I thought it would be interesting exercise to see where two texts flowing together would lead. It also could be a pedagogical exercise for your students. I chose a paragraph from each of the source material, Beckett and Werbart, and generated a new text combined of both sources. I did this in an explorative experimental way by omitting lines and randomly merging them together to experiment with where the cuts and blends seem to flow best. Trisha.

Blended text experiment.

He could have shouted and could not. The buffoon in the loft swung steadily on his stick and the organist said a fundamental thesis is that the psyche is built on the soma in interaction with the environment. He spoke little, and then almost huskily, the biological anchorage is not only to the brain but first and foremost to the skin with the low-voiced timidity of a man who shrinks from argument. The whole organism—but especially its surface—is included in thinking. The skin is the body's largest organ and provides a protective barrier to the environment but whose faculties are frozen into bewildered suspension by Pawn to Rook's third. The skin receives and preserves sensory impressions, who will not face a clash with the vulgar, uncultivated, terribly clear and personal ideas of the unread intelligentsia but it is also a shield against the outside world. He indeed was not such a man, but his voice was of such a man; and occasionally it is a uniting sack, an envelope for our inner self, that connects the physical and the psychic he chanced to be interested in a beautifully banal kind of metaphorical expressions that indicate the psychological significance of the skin: he would exercise his remarkable faculty of whispering the turmoil down to get under someone's skin, to jump out of our skin, to have skin in the game. This whispering down, like all explosive feats of the kind, was commanding undeserved attention because of its sudden brilliance. This double sensation, passive and active, is peculiar for the skin. Tactile sensation procures the basic distinction between 'inside' and 'outside', and it is the only one that can provide it. Then, when his work had been done and an angry lull was imminent, he whispered. The skin is so fundamental, its functioning is taken so much for granted, that no one notices its existence until the moment it fails. We proceed comfortably up a staircase of sensation, and sit down mildly on the topmost stair to digest our gratification. It takes a whole effort to appreciate that this surface is a splendid drunken scream and fused with the cosmic discord. Meanwhile that flesh-locked sea of silence achieved a miserable consummation in driblets of sound, as each falling leaf saps the painful vigour of a tree in a cruelly windless autumn. The sense of touch is the basic reference point for all other senses and the intersensorial function of the skin-ego connects sensations of various sorts. The process extravagantly absurd, like boiling an egg over a bonfire.

Image-inary 8

17th April 2021, 03.18

From David Rousell to Trisha McCrae and Portia Ungley

Hi Trisha, Apologies for the delay, and thanks for the reminder. I've been at a research/writing retreat this past week, and had trouble with both WiFi and mobile service. But it's been a wonderful experience nonetheless. Your images and text experiments were so interesting to read. During my brief time up here on Bundjalung Country, in the subtropics of Northern NSW, I revisited a series of glass cubes that I installed seven years ago across the Lismore campus of Southern Cross University. The five surfaces of each cube were printed with images of the surrounding environment captured from those very perspectives 7 years ago. This week I returned for the first time in four years to see what changes have taken place, both in the weathering of the surfaces and the surrounding milieus. It took me hours to hike the campus and harvest new images from the surfaces of these works. There are many trees and bromeliads in the images that no longer exist. In these cases, the cube's surface offers a deteriorating afterimage of a life that is no longer. Not so much a memorial as an occult confluence of comings and goings, presences and absences, appearances and disappearances. Many things strike me in returning here, to unceded Bundjalung and Arakwal lands, and spending moments in these places, with these works. One thing that haunts me is the variation in chromatic microclimates, the dappling of coloured light and shadow, and how this makes every difference in what grows or not, and what appears or disappears. The cubes physically diffract the light of seven years ago with the light that falls on the surface of the cube in the present. This luminescent differential varies continuously, with every passing moment. A confluence of lightfalls and temporalities. It's a very physical and concrete example of diffraction, which I think is too often used as just a metaphor for something else. Another thing I noticed is the particularly odd imbrication between the vegetal and the digital. Now that these works have begun to deteriorate, the distinction between life and non-life seems to blur even more. I have always felt that the works gestured toward an inorganic form of life, where the silica-based chemical properties of glass form unnatural relations with the carbon-based plants and leaf matter that surround them. Perhaps this sense of inorganic life is now made even more palpable by the crazed cracking of the digital image, which in some cases, has peeled away from the interior surface of the glass to reveal the contours of a previously hidden internal architecture.As I walked the campus after all these years, I felt an eerie sense of walking through what Anna Tsing (2015) calls 'capitalist ruins'. I did not see or hear many humans. Years ago I envisioned future creatures uncovering the cubes and reactivating data archives buried in their surfaces. I even built in possibilities for legacy designs and updates, including underground piping so that sensors and microcomputers could be installed in the cubes to generate an environmentally adaptive mesh network. Maybe these works really are for a people and an earth to come (Deleuze & Guattari, 1994). For now, the work just keeps working, whether I (or anyone) am present or not. Take care, and all the best, David.

Image-inary 9

17th April 2021 16:07

From Portia Ungley to Trisha McCrae and David Rousell

I am obsessed *with constraint* at the moment – *placed boundaries* in the Taussig fictocritical model and as I work with more and more writers, also convinced that they are the **final freedom;** without something against which to abut – such as a deadline? – time and projects *unspool* to become not only **unruly** but perhaps **unjust, urposeless**, *unfair*. There is also an **element** of Taussig's brand of anthropology* in all that has been written and shown which comes back to Merton's conjectures of **the guilty bystander** – as creatives, are we *guilty observers* as well as **chroniclers** and future **makers**?

Enjoy your weekends. Portia

Hi both

A poem responding to all that has come before and perhaps thinking to the future – what ties these responses beyond textual mappings of thought frames? Hope that it makes sense as a pulling together of sorts. A fight against the hovering institution that inflames the place where this book and particularly this chapter inhabits? What are we rebelling against in this image-inary? Boundaries? Generation? Lack of commonality? Or even the time taken to notice any of the above?

"Instead of man being the aim of production, production is the aim of man and wealth the aim of production, instead of tools and the productive mechanism in general liberating man from the slavery of toil, man has become the slave of tools and the industry has become synonymous with business and people have been duped into asking, "what's good for business?" instead of, "what is business good for?" "Magical beliefs are revelatory and fascinating not because they are ill-conceived instruments of utility but because they are poetic echoes of the cadences that guide the innermost course of the world. Magic takes language, symbols, and intelligibility to their outermost limits, to explore life and

response to

"characteristic of the child's first form of perception" (Letiche in Weir & Sultan, 2011 p.97)

"There is no art that has anything to say about this and art should not attempt it" (Merton, 2009 p.146)

Not just "simply secrete significations" but birthing a "bringing into being" (Guattari, 1995 p.49)

""I think the call, in the way I would understand it, the call, as in the call and response, the response is already there before the call goes out. You're already in something." *You are already in it.*" Emphasis in the original (Harney & Moten, 2013 p.7)

"**she had just touched the world with her eye**, and she thought: "it is *I* who can *see*." Cixous, H. *Veils* p.9 quoted in (Derrida, 2005 p.124)

"**Circular returns.** Spinning backward. Back to my own archaeology. Visions in passing. Travels." (Bruno, 2018 p.421)

"and why don't you write? Write! Writing is for you, you are for you; **your body is yours, take it.**" (Cixous et al., 1976 p.876)

Responce

a **space** of the image-inary
hovering guilty bystander
listening to the **particle signs**
swaying to the call and response
artist deprivileged like **Nancy's eye**
writer subsumed by the seen
who holds the hierarchy
against which the visual is smashed
against which the writers rebel?
from figures come fissures
in doodles **existential chaosmos** stirs
for whom does the status quo toll?
dabs and dots of paint
cartographic mappings of intent
but random, always random
yet somehow as written
a tacit language of white ink
on white page on **white skin**
and yet that **guilt generates**
a textured soliloquy
on how to respond affectively
on what remains unsaid and must…
in certainty the fissures re-emerge
chaosmotic mosaics of why
justifications as to who
or what deserves inclusion
which **fleshy rhizomes** to
annihilate

Image-inary 10

BEATNIK

20th April 2021 15.09

From Portia Ungley to Trisha McCrae and David Rousell

I was inspired to turn our moment's hesitation – how to move forward? – into a howl in the beatnik sense – the texture of talking to a room **full** of writers and the want to belong and be right in the pursuit of the chapter was **tangible.** I wrote it as howl and I hope the overeager sentences, rushing in, forgetting the whole, **ego** brushing up against the superego we often try and inhabit in academia, convey a sense of that need to preserve the generative tension, the **permission-giving grit** in the chapter's oyster but also the potential isolation and emptiness of being part of so many questions. *It probably needs a few more days of editing but I wanted to share it while it still felt visceral and pulled from me.* Such a productive moment to come together. And can I say again how beautiful your images are – seeing them all together is an exercise in joy-pulling, digging out the heart of ideas and seeing them brought to the eye.

Referencing:
Mikhail Bakhtin on heteroglossia and polyphony
Rosie Braidotti on socially just pedagogies
This is Spinal Tap, and Alex Bertulis-Fernandes on dialling up and down
Laura Mulvey on scopophilia in visual culture and pandora's box
Kemp-Robertson and Barth on heretical questions
Frederik Nietzsche/ Emile Durkheim on the sacred and profane in philosophy/ religion
Nancy Abelmann on intimacy in the academe
Roy Baumeister through Max Hope on academic belonging
And an homage to Radiohead on not belonging

Heteroglossia

How do you **create volume** in a chapter? Does it rise like dough? Or is it a swelling fury?In a co-authored multivocal piece, whose voice are we using? If *not mine, why yours?*

Where are the *unprivileged* words with their different pitches? Where is the **tuning fork?**How noisy are the images? Are they enough? Do **they speak?** Who has the right(s)?Does blurry mean less important? What is the budget? Can we change the format? Is CAPS shouting or just drawing attention in a **sea of words?** Are words the paddle or the boat? Is personality the volume knob going up to 11? Where is the data? Post what now? Is the sharing of this conversation inviting **intimacy or scopophilia?** Is this onanism really necessary?How loud are the **particle words**? Does the theory sing? Whose words are they anyway?Is emphasis lost in seas of *uniformed font?* Are we asking the typographic heretical question? Who *chose* the accepted references, the allowed notation? Who died and made you king?Where is the sacred in the profane of rebellion? Who **touched** the divine?

Whose is the intimate in this academic exercise? Is it yours? Or mine? Where are the masks?Whose voice? Which medium? Which *sense?* Which self? Does this **belong** here?

SPiT

Squatting in the web

"A dictionary begins when it no longer gives the meaning of words, but their tasks. Thus *formless* is not only an adjective having a given meaning, but a term that serves to bring things down in the world, generally requiring that each thing have its form. What it designates has no rights in any senses and gets itself squashed everywhere, like a spider on an earthworm. In fact, for academic men to be happy, the universe would have to take shape. All of philosophy has no other goal: it is a matter of giving a frock coat to that is a mathematical frock coat. On the other hand, affirming that the universe resembles nothing and is only formless amounts to saying that the universe is something like a spider or spit. "

"Formless" by Georges Bataille, *Documents 1*, Paris 1929, p. 382 (translated by Allan Stoekl with Carl R. Lovitt and Donald M. Leslie Jr., *Georges Bataille. Vision of Excess. Selected Writings, 1927-1939*, Minneapolis: University of Minnesota Press "Formless", p. 31)

sonnet after Bataille's formless

Squatting in the web of others' ideas
Observation my spinneret, all eyes and limbs
Entangled in the wrong place, othered
The formless nebula of ideas billows
Captured by sticky strands and chaos
Diffracted through my own worlding
Othered by introversion, intrafaced.
Normalcy slides towards me
It comes, like a gob of **spit**
Along queer
abject lines, a call
Join the widow's
rebellious embrace
Define the exquisite corpse
Let the data that glows
Illuminate. Eviscerate. Reveal

queer abject lines

sticky strands and chaos

formLess

GOB SPiT

References

Anzieu, D. (1995). *Le Moi-Peau*. Paris: Dunod.

Ahmed, S., & Stacey, J. (Eds.). (2001). *Thinking through the skin*. London: Routledge.

Arya, R., & Chare, N. (Eds.). (2016). *Abject visions: Powers of horror in art and visual culture*. Manchester: Manchester University Press.

Bertetto, P. (2017). Concept, sensation, intensity: Deleuze's theory of art and cinema. *Sociology and Anthropology*, *5*(9), 792–797. DOI: 10.13189/sa.2017.050911.2017

Bick, E. (1968). 'The experience of the kin in early object-relations. *The International Journal of Psychoanalysis*, *49*, 484–486.

Bransford, J. (Ed.) (2012). *Draw it with your eyes closed: The art of the art assignment*. New York, NY: NYU Press.

Deleuze, G., & Guattari, F. (1987). *A thousand plateaus: capitalism and schizophrenia* (B. Massumi, Trans.). Minneapolis, MN: University of Minnesota Press.

Deleuze, G., & Guattari, F. (1994). *What is philosophy*? (H. Tomlinson & G. Burchell, Trans.). New York, NY: Columbia University Press.

Cohen, M., & Hahn A. *(2017). Doing things differently, the influence of Donald Meltzer on psychoanalytic theory and practice*. London: Routledge.

Dolar, M. (2005.) Nothing has changed. *Filozofski Vestnik*, *26*(2), 147–191.

Dolar, M. (2011). *Bild und Stimme: The vocal stone*. Germany: Brill | Fink, Wilhelm Fink Verlag.

Foster, H. (1999). *Vision and visuality*. New York, NY: New Press.

Gontarski, S. E. (1995). Samuel Beckett. *The complete short prose 1929–1989*, New York, NY: Grove Press.

Grosz, E. (2017). *The incorporeal: Ontology, ethics, and the limits of materialism*. New York, NY: Columbia University Press.

Harney, S., & Moten, F. (2013). *The undercommons: Black study and fugitive planning*. New York, NY: Minor Compositions.

Heany, S., & Hughes T. (1985) *The rattle bag: An anthology of poetry*. London: Faber &Faber.

Huldisch, H., Kelly, K., & Schroeder, B. (2010). *Rosa Barba: The colour of space*. New York, NY: Dancing Foxes Press.

Lafrance, M. (2013). From the skin ego to the psychic envelope: An introduction to the work of Didier Anzieu. In *Skin, culture and psychoanalysis* (pp. 16–44). https://doi.org/10.1057/9781137300041_2

Manning, E. (2012). *Relationscapes: Movement, philosophy, art*. Cambridge, MA: MIT Press.

McCormack, D. (2018). *Atmospheric things: On the allure of elemental envelopment*. Durham, NC: Duke University Press.

Mellier, D. (2014). The psychic envelopes in psychoanalytic theories of infancy. *Frontiers in Psychology*, *5*, 734–734. https://doi.org/10.3389/fpsyg.2014.00734

Parker, R. (2010). *The subversive stitch: Embroidery and the making of the feminine* (new ed.). London: Tauris.

Ruyer, R. (2016). *Neo-finalism* (A. Edlebi, Trans.). Minneapolis, MN: University of Minnesota Press.

Salem, P., & Coelho, N. (2010). *The role of imitation in the constitution of psychic reality: The contemporary psychoanalytic perspective of Thomas Ogden*. London: Routledge.

Shulman, G. (2005). Reflections on Eugenio Gaddini's paper "On imitatio". *Journal of Child Psychotherapy, 31*(1), 40–51.

Sullivan, S. (2001). *Living across and through skins: Transactional bodies, pragmatism and feminism*. Bloomington, IN: Indiana University Press.

Tsing, A. L. (2015). *The mushroom at the end of the world: On the possibility of life in capitalist ruins*. Princeton, NJ: Princeton University Press.

Werbart, A. (2019). The skin is the cradle of the soul. Didier Anzieu on the skin-ego, boundaries, and boundlessness. *Journal of the American Psychoanalytic Association*, *67*(1), 37–58.

Winnicott, D. W. (1976). Ego distortion in terms of true and false self'. In J. Sutherland (Eds.), *The maturational processes and the facilitating environment: Studies in the theory of emotional development* (pp. 37–55). London: Hogarth Press.

Images and credits

Page 301 *start* by Trisha McCrae.

Page 302 *Les Pierres Parlantes* video still from installation by Trisha McCrae, 2017 ZOU#9 La Brousse, Sers, France. Performance artist Lulu Lockheart.

Page 303 *I thought you were me*, by Trisha McCrae. Image detail from sculpture *Les Pierres Parlantes*.

Page 304 Images by David Rousell.

Page 306 Artwork by Trisha McCrae.

Page 307 Artwork : *The persistence of vision* by Trisha McCrae.

Page 308 Image: *Surfacing the Imaginary* by David Rousell and Trisha McCrae.

Page 309 Artwork by Trisha McCrae.

Page 311 Video stills from *Vesetti* installation by Trisha McCrae as part of *CONTINENTAL DRIFT* Neuf site specific instillation at the Geddes Gallery, London. 2016.

Page 313 Drawing by Jasper and friends.

Page 316 Artwork by Trisha McCrae.

Page 317 Blended text by Trisha McCrae, inspired by Samuel Beckett's short story *Assumption* and Andrezei Werbart's scientific research paper *The Skin is the Cradle of the Soul*.

Page 318 Photography by David Rousell, Lismore campus of Southern Cross University, Bundjalung Country, NSW.

Page 320 Video stills by Trisha McCrae. Performance artist Maxi More.

Page 321 *Response* by Portia Ungley.

Page 322 Artwork by Trisha McCrae.

Page 323 *Sonnet after Bataille's formless* by Portia Ungley.

Video still by Trisha McCrae from video installation *The Smog is Lofting*. 2016 as part of Neuf *At Home 5 series* Winchester, UK.

"Formless" by Georges Bataille, *Documents 1*, Paris, 1929, p. 382 (translated by Allan Stoekl with Carl R. Lovitt and Donald M. Leslie Jr., *Georges Bataille. Vision of Excess. Selected Writings, 1927-1939*, Minneapolis: University of Minnesota Press "Formless", p. 31).

Chapter layout by Trisha McCrae.

CHAPTER 18

dreams in the *margem*

stories from the river

Marta Cotrim and Mindy R. Carter

Authors: Marta Cotrim and Mindy R. Carter

Editors: Pam Burnard and David Rousell

Designer: Dayna McLeod

Quotes & References (Brill black)

Prelude

This chapter takes up the notion of 'rebellious research' using a playful, intra-acting presentation that includes an array of voices, texts, stories and images in its exploration. Focusing on the praxis of a post-human, diffracted approach to disrupting notions of subjectivity, research, referencing and publishing conventions, this chapter purposively cuts the reader loose from any entry into engaging with the text. There is not an invitation to understand or to assist the reader in 'making clear' the explorations in this chapter. Rather, there is an offering to jump into the river or stay on the bank (*margem*) of what conventions, norms, relationality offer; asserting that there is no alienation affect being employed, and no handrails offered ... simply the work always becoming and in continual processes of doing/undoing in the pursuit of being.

Entrances and Navigation Tools

Marta Cotrim: I would like to find ways to convert or present this chapter as an entanglement of all of the voices that have been a part of its emergence. Like a bare stage where one can see the 'backstage', make visible all discussions and influences. I wish we could include Pam and David's feedback somehow.

Mindy R. Carter: Maybe we could work with Pam's suggestion(s) as 'navigation tools' as a way to begin. What do you think?

 | DOI:10.1163/9789004516069_024

Marta Cotrim: Great! I asked Pam if we can include her feedback and she has agreed.

Comments on the chapter from Pam Burnard: Are these texts diverse voices, voicings, registers? I'm just not sure it's clear what your intention is? Is there one voice where you hold the hand of the reader and guide them or are you purposively cutting us loose? If so, we need to know. I can do a diffractive reading and read your voices – colours – as an encounter with waves of texts which engage affirmatively with difference. What you're inviting us into remains unclear throughout. And maybe this is what you invite. Either way, do you need to introduce us to this rebellious mode in terms of how this presentation is battling against the normative standard of conventional academic practices and that you are wilfully find a new way to do the work differently; presenting and relating to researching and writing rebelliously (not just differently).

Marta Cotrim and Mindy R. Carter: In this chapter, our intention has been to offer the reader multiple entry points into experiencing 'undoing the normativity' (Barad, 2018). To play, consider, (re)imagine, understand, engage, we weave the multiple voices, ideas, references, lines of flight that have helped to conceptualise this chapter into our text. This project is undone and continually re-done, depending on the reader. Different colours have been used to highlight some of the voices/contributors to this project as a way to assist the reader in navigating the river we have been riding on/with/in during the emergence of this chapter. Things are not aligned; but embroidered, there is no synthesis; there are diffractions across the pages.

Provocations and Diffractions

Manifesto #1: To Teach What We Don't Know ... Yet

The death of the teacher (as we know it)
Becoming-minority, becoming invisible (Deleuze[1])
Don't give voice – shut up and listen
Not avant-garde (because who will follow?)
Not rear-guard (because why should I have to defend myself?)
Not a revolution (not communism/fascism)
Not resistance (not melancholic left)
Non-conformity is my rebellion
We are here to provoke the change because we see a different
future ahead (What does it look like? How does it smell? Feel? What song will we sing when we ride that wave?)

1 This is not a footnote.

What does it mean to be educated?

On Re/evolution

This is an invitation, an offering. A generous s/place of exploration.
Wading
I've been waiting ...
for a time when hands won't be ***slapped*** *for*
trying
some-thing
new, that I knew all along,
if only in a dream
in that dream?

(is this)
Our dream
... question mark ...

So, we begin with thanks
to those who keep trying
to live, ***dwell***
well,

be *a little differently in these*
institutions of occupation ...

be
com
i n g
provocation

to

re-/=<

de

centre

thecarewegiveandtheshellswehavecreatedandnowmustshedbecausethetimeishereCanyouhearItisMCoandmrcPhDweeeeeandwearereadytostartthisRE/EVOLUTION

~~Marta Cotrim: The evolution theory is still today portrayed by a man walking from left to right as in a timeline.~~

~~Raising from crouching ape to standing bipod male human (less hair, white, able bodied).~~

~~A number of conventions are implied here:~~

~~Reading left to right (western)~~

~~Development as an upward progression in the shape of a graph from low to high~~

~~Male as self-evident and self-reproductive (where are the female bodies who have given birth to man?)~~

~~Alone in this 'evolution' as if independent of any other life form.~~

~~The cycle of life and death totally ignored as if in an unimpeded continuum of evolution going on forever ...~~

~~Man/human as god himself, eternal~~

~~Erased~~

David Rousell: Maybe. But I'm also picturing those ironic t-shirts where 'man' devolves back into a guy sitting on a toilet staring at an iPhone. It seems like the image of evolution (and current social investments in evolution) you describe here is quite essentialised and somewhat anachronistic. It makes for an easy target though!

Marta Cotrim: Good point, David. Although in popular culture as you said there are variations on the same theme. I will erase but will leave the traces.

Manifesto #2: From Humanities to Post-humanities

It's a daunting prospect for us immersed in the humanities.

It will be like transforming a four-legged chair into a three-legged chair while sitting on it.

A balancing act, fearful and unstable.

But as Braidotti frequently states, 'we-are-in-this-together-but-we-are-not-one-and-the-same' (Braidotti, 2020 this could be a footnote).

There will be obstacles ahead, but we will help each other overcome them.

So, 'Let' face the music and dance' (Berlin, 1936/1994 with Nat King Cole's voice, 1964).

Critical Posthuman Education

Education and research as a creative collaborative practice.

Starting point: those involved with their identities and embodied and embedded selves

Outcome: Not yet known

The idea is not to teach creativity but to teach creatively

Where the forms of expression determine the form of the outcome and not the other way around.

Practice-theory-practice following the dynamics of a creation process: from concept to concrete, from essence to form back and forth in a constant flux of actualisation, until it finds its own shape, distilled form, distinguished from everything else.

The place and function of the teacher/facilitator ever-changeable, fluid.

Not the knowledge detainer, not the assessing judge, not the grader of expected outcomes.

Students: carriers of meaning, intertextuality and embodied experience (Interesting, but why even define the distinction between teacher and student?) Active players in their own mutual lea(r)ning. ('Leaning' or 'learning'? I prefer the former!)

On Education: The Wish Book

As a child and youth, education and school were like the thick-paged, glossy Sears Christmas catalogue to me. What this catalogue offered those of us who grew up in smaller, more remote communities of Canada was a glimpse of what might be possible in another place and time. Appropriately named 'The Wish Book', its pages elicited dreams of dressing to stay warm to be subsumed by fashionable frocks, holiday lights and the most exquisite selections of jewellery, toys and beauty products. I looked forward to lingering with these pages alone and with friends. Year after year, we would sit knees touching and choose one thing we would like from each page, as we huddled together and commented on each selection's pros and cons. Of course, I never actually expected to receive any of the treasured items I painstakingly selected, but I felt hopeful that maybe some of the shine and magic that felt entombed in this catalogue would find its way into my seemingly lacklustre daily life. The wishing-book … what happens when we allow ourselves to wish, to dream of something other than what is? During those years, I wished for a family in matching plaid pyjamas, wearing slippers, and sipping cups of cocoa on Christmas morning.

The magic and hope promised in the book of wishes – creating swishes of possibility of places and people in lives other than my own – stayed in my mind, just like Shirley Temple's 'The Little Princess' fantasies; in which her black and white attic room was transformed into a palace. Perhaps this hope and my overactive imagination were what helped me through the realities of the everyday; where no matter how many games of make-believe I played, by 10 I was aware that the Christmas hamper dropped off at our subsidised town house, marked '1 adult, 1 boy, 1 girl' meant that this year, once more, there would be no gifts from the Sears catalogue or Santa. As the years marched on, with little improving at home, school became my wishing place. By high school, this educational institution had become my place to dream and for an adult to tell me I was doing OK, that things could feel ordered and predictable, where I wouldn't be made fun of for reading or singing Broadway songs or writing stories. In particular, the music room, rehearsal spaces and stage became 'home'. I could be someone I wanted to be in the arts classes I took, not the daughter of a high school drop-out who lived on welfare, and father who lived eight hours away.

I began to create my own book of wishes based on what I read and learnt. I wrote about new possibilities and performed them on stage as an alternative and didn't accept that the life I lived was the life I was meant to have. School allowed me to both find myself and to escape. But, at the time, I also didn't realise how it alienated me. Because each time I got 100% on a test or an award for my singing, I created distance between myself and my family. Each time ***I dreamed*** *of going to university, or travelling or wearing red lipstick, like I saw in Vogue magazine, I was choosing something other than my aunts and uncles and cousins who hunted and fished and did manual labour jobs for work. I re-storied my story, but at what cost? Why was the education I received from school the kind of learning I ended up placing value on? Why didn't I seem to take to the lessons on drying* *out wild rice or taping the maple trees or learning to persevere at ice fishing? On one hand, the middle-class ideals of the educational institutions I attended made me feel like I could be a part of the seemingly idealistic 'Wish Book' image of life that I held in my adolescent mind. But, later, at least for me, it also became analogous with Eve taking the first bite of the apple and falling from grace; where once one starts down that path towards agency, a part of the garden is*

lost

forever.

I hear a version of this story from young women in the midst of their PhDs. How relationships with partners change when they progress through their studies. How many of them end. And sometimes I wonder why agency as a result of schooling and education, for women at least, over 100 years since 'A doll's house' was written, still seems to lead to judgement and disconnection. So, maybe my story is one of success, but perhaps, just maybe, it is also one of loss. With the holiday season soon upon us once again, I think fondly back on the Sears Christmas Wish Book. But this time, with the perspective that my only wish now is to spend time with the family and friends I tried so hard not to be like. Now when I return 'home' I look like the person in the catalogue to them. I am distant, a nice image that can be framed and put on the mantle that someone else can wish about. But a person who doesn't understand what it means to dry meat or pickle vegetables for the long winter or knit or sew or spend hours with another person talking and laughing about 'nothing' because there is time to do that. Rather, I sit at my computer placing words together to make 'meaning'. I don't wish for something else, and neither, I think, do they.

(so don't tell me that it all needs to be thrown away because it has cost everything)[2]

Theatre is the place where the erudite (why this word?) (why not?) encounters the popular and the sacred.

It is true we will have to moan our losses. The podium we place ourselves, the stage we build to our own exceptionality. It is part of the process, but we should not linger in the mo(u)rning but with new eyes face the difficulty together. Affirmative ethics and bold experimentation.

---

2 David, in relation to your comments on the Wishing Book section, I think the larger issue with the comments to be addressed is that this section was called 'wooden'. I interpreted this to mean archaic, out of place, against the flow and intention of the rest of the chapter. This is actually the reaction I was hoping for. Even when I re-read this piece I feel like this section 'doesn't fit' and is a challenge for the reader. It is also a different style of representation (more autoethnographic). However, as mentioned, this was intentional because, in relation to the chapter, this piece represents 'the raft' ... which is heavy and wooden ... but which still floats when put on water ... in another chapter where a method or representation is different it might seem to sit on the sidelines (the banks) ... waiting to be pushed in the water. In this offering its 'out of place-ness' is meant to consider the idea of an 'alienation effect' for the reader, who may be more used to reading a 'story' like this but now feels alienated from this form ... The content is also intentional in that is represents how one must explore one's own experience to be able to 'be free', to 'be-come rebellion'.

What Is an Educational System?

Someone ('They') decides what needs to be learned and when. (Curriculum developers)

Others comply by teaching the content and assessing it. (Teachers)

The rest need to absorb the established content and prove they have learned it well enough, by means of various forms of assessments. (Students)

What is a discipline?

Must we be disciplined? (Foucault, 2012)

These sections here feel a bit less developed than the previous. Perhaps this work could be done more effectively through storying?

~~Erased~~

Marta Cotrim: I was sent, together with my three brothers and sister, to a Jesuit school in Brazil during the military dictatorship (1964–1985). My father was an alumnus and frequently came second of his class. His picture hung on the corridor wall. It was the late 70s and the school had just started to admit girls. We were the great minority, 7 to 25 in one of 8 classes per grade. The Jesuit missionaries were sent to the Portuguese colonies to convert the indigenous population to Catholicism. In the Saint Loyola School, religious education was compulsory as well as attendance and confession. My mother was against the school's philosophy and religion. She, as well as her mother, attended a nun-run boarding school outside of Rio de Janeiro, Notre Dame de Sion. There upper-middle-class young women were prepared to become 'gifted' housewives, learning etiquette, Greek, Latin, French, piano and embroidery. Although she hated school, she would usually prefer to stay there than go home for the weekends. Her father, although a respected surgeon, was very abusive. I did all my eleven years of schooling with the Jesuits in order to please my father. Apart from my older brother, who had graduated, he was disappointed at my brothers and sister who were not able to keep up with the academic demands of school and were not allowed to continue. I survived their scrutiny and oppressive regime due to my handful of friends and the teacher's indulgence regarding theatre. The Jesuits loved the theatre. They frequently made use of it as an effective way to convey liturgical messages across culture and language barriers. And thus, I started to experiment, directing my peers at the age of 11.

Manifesto #3: I Am So Tired of Patriarchy

The best jobs, the best pay, the sensate words, the printed wisdom
The look in their face, the disdain for women
For hours spent on children, on basic needs of the old
For compassion and delicacy, dedication and care.

The high tower, the morals and punishments
The wars, the stiff upper lip
The arrogance, the titles and protocols.
The destruction, the killing machines and the destruction of our earth
Mother earth.
The white collars, the dark hours, the death of children in battle now and
then
The domestic violence
The violent police
The corrupt self-interested politicians
The short vision, the gambling with other people's lives
The disinterest in the consequences of one's greed
The then, the now and the future of our own children, male, female and
otherwise other wise
Le mépris of otherness than themselves,
Self-profit *ao custo de tudo*
Its laziness and constant need of pampering their huge ego
Slavery, genocide, purge and assassination
Nazism, fascism, chauvinism
Church, chastity belt, witch hunts
Burning, torturing, experiment on people
Common graves, shallow graves, walls
Mass shooting, school shooting, police shooting
Burning, melting, spilling
Fast, blast, *au-delà*
Division, incision, mutilation
Veil, prevail, no avail
Vote, voice, vice
Harris, Gorman, Morrison
Harris, Gorman, Morrison
Harris, Gorman, Morrison

I'm guessing who these folks are. Kamala Harris? Amanda Gorman? Toni Morrison? YES

~~2 Writing on the *margens*~~

I feel like you could be more implicit, somehow, that this section is about the struggle with post-humanism

Breaking the 4th Wall

Mindy R. Carter- In the short story "The third bank of the river" (1967) by Brazilian author João Guimarães Rosa, a middle-aged man decides to leave his family and to live in a boat that moves up and down a river, until his death. The effects of this decision are briefly depicted in relation to those he has left behind: a wife, daughter, grandchild and son. Yet, there is no reason for the departure or insight gleaned from his perspective for making this decision. Instead, the reader is left "on the third riverbank" with an image of a man floating on a river for eternity, considering a myriad of way(s) that this story can be interpreted.

Some contend that this is an allegory about a man in search of a greater truth, floating on the river towards death or how those who are left behind are affected when a loved one dies: helpless, confused. In their analysis of this text, Andrade & Cardoso (2015) further explore the meaning of this piece through Bakhtin's (1982) answerability, where words are viewed as expressions of meaning.

Together, Andrade & Cardoso ultimately contend that there is a fusion of the father and the river, based on the way(s) that each are described.

***

But Marta, you want us to Become river- To be a moving body that har-

To approach the Other in conversation is to welcome his expression, in which at each instant he overflows the idea a thought would carry away from it. It is therefore to receive from the Other[2]

Marta Cotrim: Barad (2007) asks caution when using analogies to explain quantum physics. However, her agential realism speaks to me at a profound level, as when you discover a word in another language that can finally describe your emotion. Her concept of phenomena makes me think of a theatrical performance, and her apparatus and agential cut to a field research. Although she is against representation, the epistemological division between object-subject, she does make use of poetics and metaphors. As a theatre artist I feel that my way of expressing an idea or concept is through imagens, scenes, emotions; inspired by situations that can be shared. That is why I call for possible understandings through powerful imaging:

The third margem of the river inspired by A Terceira Margem do Rio, by J.G. Rosa (1962)

The raft in the river "e o rio-rio-rio, o rio" (p 3)

The research field as the river, running its course. "do rio tudo rola o perigoso" (p 2)

The researcher enters the river with caution, deference, and humility.

The researcher asks for the river's permission to enter and intra-act with its waters, its

'I would like to write you so simply, so simply, so simply, so simply. Without having anything ever catch the eye, excepting yours alone, … so that above all the language,

'Love is not a state, a feeling, a disposition, but an exchange, uneven, fraught with history, with ghosts, with longings, that are more or less legible to those who try

nesses the power to both sustain and end life.

Are you sure?

The consequences of this departure are final.

As the reader of "The third bank of the river" we must accept that we will never fully know the experience of the father in his boat. We can merely imagine, interpret, dream and turn around again and again and again meaning(s) towards an understanding that may be a truth for a moment.

The conversations you have to give up.
The abilities to sit at some tables.
They will be unforgiving.
So please make the decision a conscious one.

Then, ok. If you're ready. I'll be there [no question].
Just Jump in, don't wade slowly, but remember the undercurrents always leading towards a larger body of water: a lake, an ocean, the sea.

The arteries that lead to the river, map a course that flows stronger during a rain and recedes in times of drought.

I'll make a raft if you need to REST and I'll be there cheering for it to be all you dreamed it could be.

"I am interested in language because it

"As naturally as the ruled always took the morality imposed upon them more seriously than did the rulers themselves, the deceived masses are today captivated by the

"People know what they do; frequently they know why

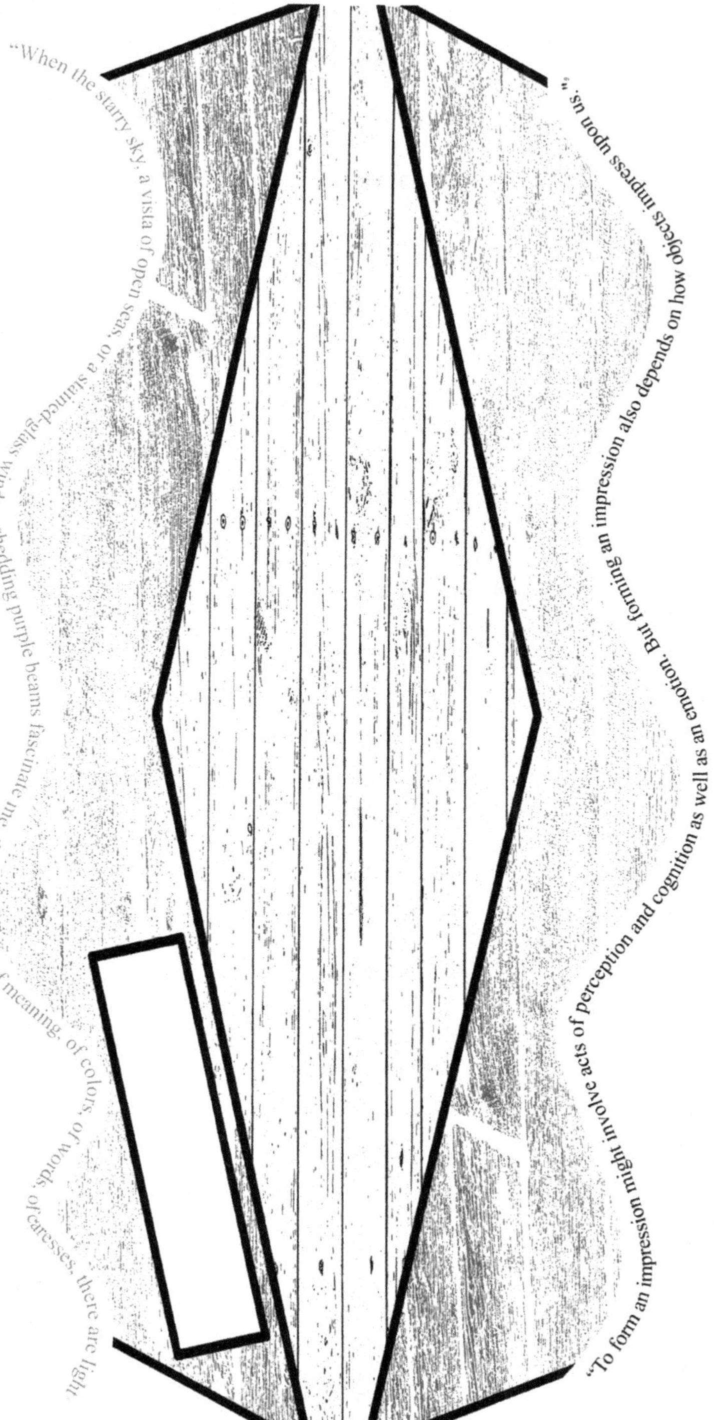
"When the starry sky, a vista of open seas, or a stained-glass window shedding purple beams fascinate me, there is a cluster of meaning, of colors, of words, of caresses, there are light
"To form an impression might involve acts of perception and cognition as well as an emotion. But forming an impression also depends on how objects impress upon us."

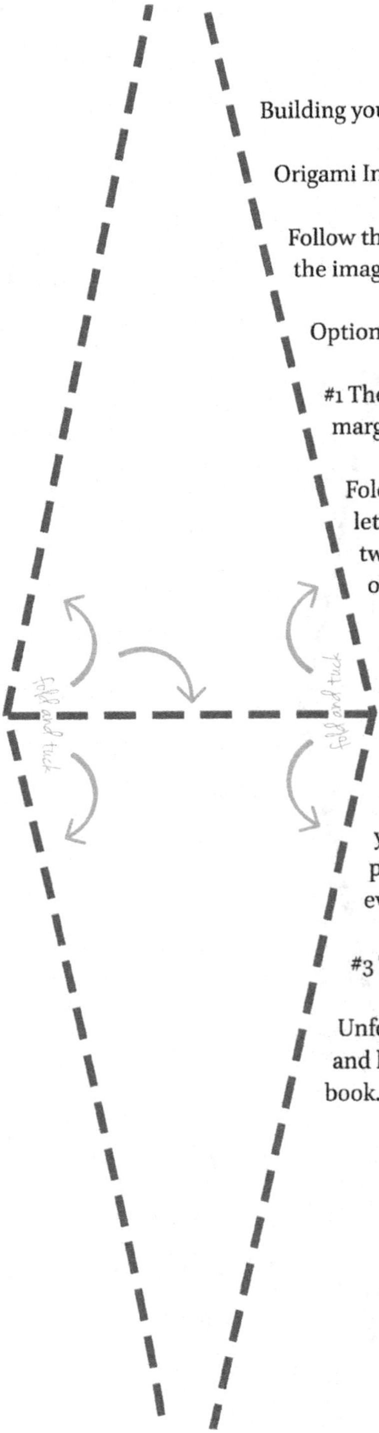

Building your 3D raft

Origami Instructions

Follow the 5 folds in the image

Options:

#1 The third margem

Fold your raft and let it float between the pages of the book.

#2 Your own raft

Tear the page from the book, name your raft and place it wherever you want.

#3 Traced Paper

Unfold the raft and leave it in your book.

movement and ecosystem.
Can I anchor? Can I fish? Can I bath in your waters? (1st person view)
This intra-action is the phenomena We don't enter the same river twice.
Canoe/navigation tools/researcher form an apparatus. (3rd person view)
Its presence creates resistance from the river, ripples and currant distractions, diffractions.
The point of view from the canoe is unique,
because it's an outsider-insider look, the canoe in the river, an exit from within,
agential separability or "exteriority within phenomena" (Barad, 2007, p 184)
The third bank of the river is the agential cut.
The 1st person and 3rd person view in a video game parallels the simultaneous perspectives of a performer improvising, on the flow, in the relational (in)stability of the intra-action and being able to be aware of the exterior intermittently, experiencing the world as both wave and particle.

"We live in a world where there is more and more information, and"

FIGURE 18.1 Raft and river design by Dayna McLeod

Playing in the Sandbox with Glitter[3]

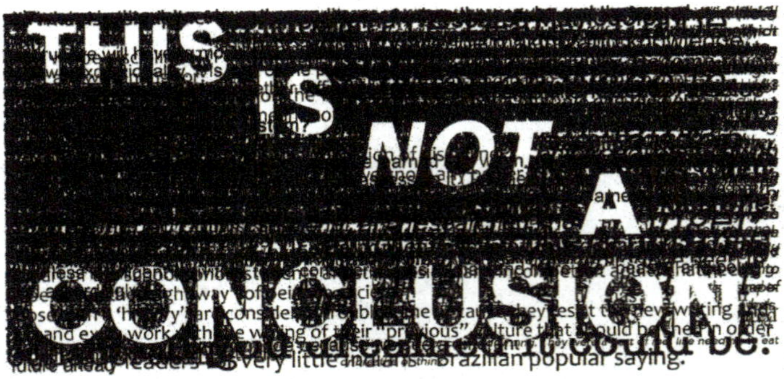

FIGURE 18.2 This is not a conclusion

But, here are some attempts:

i) Paradox

> *... the ambiguity, undecidability, indeterminacy may itself be the key to the trouble. It's not only troubling, but a moral violation the very source of the trouble. ... 'not making the wrong right but in undoing of the normality' that makes those terms legible.* (*Barad, 2018*)

We must learn to live with paradox and simultaneity

The need to solve paradoxes and create binaries is a legacy we can do without.

Humans are as paradoxical as particles and waves.

Or even further when Barad talks about the electron's self-touching process as an 'on-going recreation' (Barad, 2018).

ii) Complementarity Principle

I know when we use analogies and metaphors, we create characters, such as: the river, the raft, the old man, the son. It seems that we are separating these elements of the story, but all is entangled:

---

3 Why glitter? Nasty stuff ...
Mindy R. Carter: Ha! Exactly. We use glitter to seemingly jazz something up (a quick fix) ... adding it to something like a sandbox is placing it there forever ... because who could/would separate glitter from tiny grains of sand. Or do you mean the whole sandbox would be filled with glitter!!! In any case, David, this section has become the 'out-takes' or 'choose your own ending' of our chapter. It is messy (and a little bit 'nasty', mixed with what feels like smoke and mirrors to end something that doesn't really end) ...

- The raft is not over the river. It's inside and outside. The old man is between the riverbanks, the son between father and mother, and so on. The in-betweens, the lines of flights, becomings (Don't just throw these concepts in without engaging the actual texts from Deleuze and Guattari in some way. Perhaps you could refer to their wasp-orchid example? Where the becoming creates a new kind of collaborative reality between the two?) that are not contained by the interplay (Deleuze & Guattari, 1987).
- The researcher, the researched, river, raft, old man, son, etc. are created by their own inter-relationality. There is no subject, no object of study, no reality to be uncovered, no truth to be revealed. But from this comes a separation. The reader is the third bank who never fully understands the meaning of the river, the canoe, the old man or the son. We are all lost searching for meaning, and even relationality is taken away by the disconnect. So, we have to keep connection, but not if it causes harm.
- In general, I would suggest that post-humanism gestures toward a retreat from meaning, at least meaning as discursively constructed by humans alone. In this gesture, it turns to the materiality and affects of bodies, what bodies can do, where meaning is immanent in matter and events, rather than something that human somehow 'add' to the world.
- In hard science, the researchers are in the raft thinking they are in solid ground; instead of swimming they are taking samples of the water below and analysing it as a separate reality, unaware of the entanglement.

iii) Humanism in Post-humanism

Just because it is post- it doesn't mean we need to (or even can) erase everything related to humanism; we might (even in spite of ourselves) keep some aspects. I would say we are also forced to keep some aspects, like a broken wagon that we have to keep dragging along.

And the chosen aspects might not be the same for everybody.

We might need to agree to disagree on this one.

Excess & Outliers

Q & A: Mindy R. Carter to Marta Cotrim

Mindy R. Carter: **Is there a rest for the nomad?**

Marta Cotrim: The 'rest' is internal, but not static; there is stability in the flow within.

Because in a way there is nothing more 'stable' than a nomad[4] in a movable home.

They move around but their tents are always the same, their relationships to each other are intact. The stability is relational. So, I think that by moving around the nomad doesn't have to compromise as much as those who establish themselves and want to belong. And paradoxically, as Barad (2018) explains on the perversion of the quantum field theory when talking about the electron's self-touching: ***'All touching entails an infinite alterity, so touching the other, all others, also include the self and touching the self means touching the stranger within.'***

Mindy Carter: So, then what? Rebel.

Fine.

Play with representation and references and style.

So what?

No ... really, tell me ...

You've learned the structure ... to break it?

Didn't reading Deleuze and Braidotti and Aristotle and Foucault and Freire and Arendt and Spinoza and Hemmingway and Rubem and Guttierez and Pinar and Greene and Husserl and Bronte and Shakespeare and

and

and

and

and

and

and

and

and

privilege you to be in this

space?

If it's about throwing it all away, then why do you want to be here to begin with?

Can you just rebel because they've become your friends (those authors and theorists and architects of thought in and through time ... you have to love them)?

are you sure

you want to

leave them?

---

4 'At the limit, it is the Earth itself, the deterritorialized ("the desert grows ..."), and it is the nomad, the man of earth, the man of deterritorialization – although he is also the one who does not move, who remains attached to the environment, desert or steppe' (Deleuze & Parnet, 2007, p. 134).

because
i
don't think you ever wanted to take this journey
alone.

Marta Cotrim: I am not throwing everything out. I am all for the content! For those thoughts and words and what it does to me, to us. I question when they become rules, dogma, fixed and imposed, and the obvious follows; knowledge becomes power. This is precisely why post-human thinkers like Deleuze and Guattari actively oppose any kind of dogma, doxa or universal belief. Their whole project is about breaking up power wherever it congeals, rather than replacing the 'old' power with some 'new' (better) power, which would ultimately re-inscribe its own fascism.

Academia and science make me think of created religions. Christ was not a Christian; Buddha was not Buddhist. I question when in the 'world of Men' truths are created, perpetuated, formatted.

By staying playful, not childish but childlike, I adhere to non-conformity. This is my rebellion.

Here I am just performatively playing with formatting rules and readers' expectations of what is a book. What does an academic text look like? Provoking a little de-territorialisation, so the reader becomes aware of unconscious patterns. Folding paper, pulling out a page from a book for colouring, seeing it as a 3D object seems playful and rebellious to me in this context ... I'm a little bit of a rascal, a little *enfant terrible*.

By exposing the entanglement, creating discomfort, the need for a clear *what is the writing doing*, while I am more interested in *what it is doing to the reader.*

Mindy R. Carter: **Remember you told me: There is always something lost in translation:** the word margin in Portuguese stands for book margin as well as riverside or bank. The third margin is then the raft. The in-between. The nomad. The moving raft over the moving river. Resisting the current to stay where it is, without, however, never landing ... you've told me this ... but for me, that's the hope and the beauty ... just when we think we've 'lost something in translation' we find new ways to tell our stories, to make meaning, to connect.

We stop relying on our own words and languages and symbols. We feel more deeply. We watch more closely ... We laugh and cry and reach out more frequently ... and so, in getting lost we find what we didn't set out looking for.

Conversation on the Margins with Designer Dayna McLeod: (Markup Text View)

Just wondering – is *this* theatre?

Mindy R. Carter (email): Dayna, Marta and I are working on a book chapter that we want to incorporate the 3D raft into. We would be happy to add you as an artist-contributor to the piece for the help with the images if this is of interest.

Dayna McLeod: Wow! What an intriguing idea!!

Marta Cotrim: Dayna, it was super inspiring collaborating with you today. I love the ideas we came up with!

Dayna McLeod: I'm super inspired and dreamt about text as water and shapes, lol

Marta Cotrim: J

Dayna McLeod: Here are a few different drafts of illustrations for your article. The boat is on a 3-page spread to give you an idea of the waves. Note that images are large so that they can be made smaller without losing detail or pixilating.

Marta Cotrim: I love the small writing as the water current. I only realised it when I opened the image on full screen

Dayna McLeod: Mindy – can you send me the tech specs for submissions you were showing me yesterday?

Mindy R. Carter: Here you go!

Final Exit

Marta Cotrim: Apparently, we can only do rebellious research in Brill 11 pt. (Note from Brill Editors: Yes, please 😊)

References

Ahmed, S. (2013). *The cultural politics of emotion*. Routledge.

Barad, K. (2018). *On touching: The alterity within*. Gerrit Rietveld Academie at Stedelijk Museum Amsterdam. https://www.youtube.com/watch?v=u7LvXswjEBY

Barthes, R., & Howard, R. (1975). *The pleasure of the text* (R. Miller, Trans.). Hill and Wang.

Baudrillard, J. (1994). *Simulacra and simulation*. University of Michigan Press.

Beauvoir, S. (1989). *The second sex*. Vintage Books.

Berlin, I., & Cole, N. K. (1994). *Let's face the music & dance*. Warner Chappell Music. (Original work published 1936)

Braidotti, R. (2020). 'We' are in *this* together, but we are not one and the same. *Journal of Bioethical Inquiry*, *17*(4), 465–469. https://doi.org/10.1007/s11673-020-10017-8

Butler, J. (2002). Doubting love. In J. L. Harmon (Ed.), *Take my advice: Letters to the next generation from people who know a thing or two* (pp. 62–66). Simon and Schuster.

Deleuze, G., & Guattari, F. (1987). *A thousand plateaus: Capitalism and schizophrenia.* University of Minnesota Press.

Deleuze, G., & Guattari, F. (2004). *EPZ thousand plateaus.* Continuum Impacts.

Deleuze, G., & Parnet, C. (2007). *Dialogues II.* Columbia University Press.

Derrida, J. (2020). *The post card: From Socrates to Freud and beyond.* University of Chicago Press.

Dreyfus, H. L., & Rabinow, P. (1982). *Michel Foucault: Beyond structuralism and hermeneutics.* Routledge.

Foucault, M. (2012). *Discipline and punish: The birth of the prison.* Knopf Doubleday.

Horkheimer, M., & Adorno, T. W. (1997). *Dialectic of enlightenment.* Verso.

Kristeva, J. (1982). *Powers of horror.* University Presses of California, Columbia and Princeton.

Levinas, E. (1979). *Totality and infinity: An essay on exteriority.* Springer Science & Business Media.

Part 3: Reflective Questions

David Rousell

Linking to Futures of Teaching and Learning

1. How do you deal with authority in your everyday life? Do you resist it, avoid it, or wield it? What about in teaching and learning contexts?

2. What kinds of teaching and learning become possible when the conceit of authority is abandoned? What would an education of rebellion look like, feel like, become capable of generating in the future?

3. What kinds of 'teaching and learning' experiences really matter under current conditions of climate change, mass extinction, and socioecological injustice? Do these kinds of experiences happen in schools and universities? Or are they more likely to occur elsewhere?

4. Do you consider practices such as hitchhiking, graffiti writing, activism, ritual, artmaking creative writing, and performance to be teaching and learning practices? Why or why not?

5. What might a 'pluriversal' approach to education look like? How would an education based on ontological pluralism differ from a 'one-world' education based on 'universal' laws and values?

6. What is the role of micropolitics in the future of teaching and learning? Could micropolitics help connect teaching and learning practices with wider spheres of creative resistance to the colonial-capitalist extraction of more-than-human life?

7. What would a diffractive education look like? Could practices of creative writing and speculative fabulation be used as a 'diffractive prism' for teaching and learning across the arts, sciences, and humanities?

8. How do you see the aesthetics of digital image-making and exchange shaping the future of education? Can we imagine a future education of liquid images that leaves the current reliance on discursive text behind?

 | DOI:10.1163/9789004516069_025

9. What kinds of 'rafts' or other flotation devices would you need to navigate the rushing rapids of post-qualitative educational inquiry and praxis? What aspects of humanism might you need to hold onto while trying to survive the radically posthuman conditions of the present?

10. Can we imagine a posthuman education which would do away with the conceit of the liberal humanist subject? What kinds of rebellious concepts and practices would need to be invented now in order for such an education to thrive in the future?

forming Leadership

ENACTING CHANGE

Brother Reaching Each Inner Soul

Enchanting Educational Settings

PART 4: Rebellious Leadership Leading Differently

Part 4: Guidance for Readers

Rebelling against What and Rebelling How?

Tatjana Dragovic

Rebelling is not easy and it is not necessarily pleasant. Sometimes it is not even easy to clearly define what we feel an urge to rebel against and even less easy to know how to do it. Yet if we feel an urge to rebel, it is because we feel called to rebel. Some of us have spent many decades in the academia and others have just entered but all of us are seasoned learners. Even young children. Learning has been our companion from our birth. Learning is part of our lives and our work whether we work in education or not. Part 4 offers a though-provoking journey through different opportunities education does provide and does not provide even though our Part 4 authors believe it could and should. I invite you to be open to their stories and their rebellion. In order to make it easy to navigate through all chapters in Part 4, here is an overview of what (y)our colleagues rebel against and how they do it.

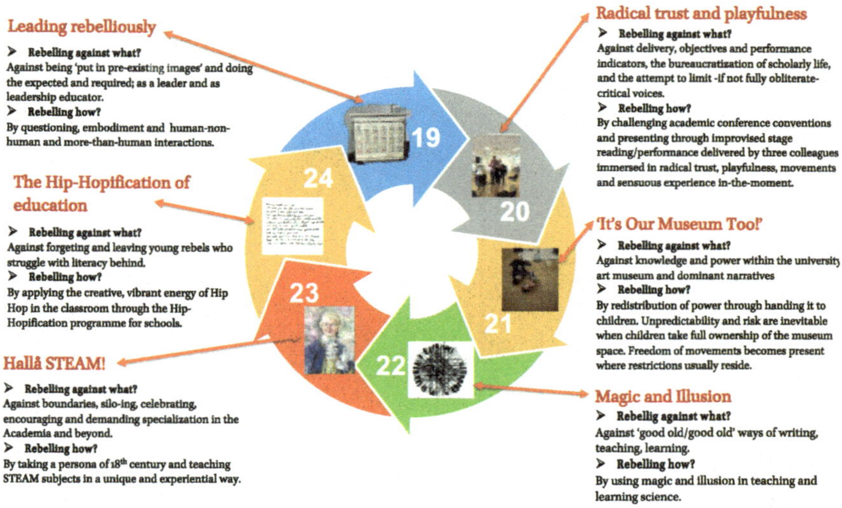

Overview of rebellion in Part 4: against what and how?

 | DOI:10.1163/9789004516069_026

CHAPTER 19

Critical Openings in Leading Rebelliously

Tatjana Dragovic (*with Leaders around the World*)

Warning!

This introductory chapter to Part 4 *Rebellious Leadership Leading Differently* invites us to dive into lived and rebellious experiences of leaders around the world in and beyond the academy, to get in there, to listen and follow, to keep asking questions and not know, to be present and to trust. And more than that, this chapter invites us to be aware of our own conscious and unconscious images (what might those be?) that we already hold of leadership in order to disrupt them (why do that?). Disturbingly, it offers these lived and rebellious experiences of leaders around the world as fragmented pieces, originating in different places (where?), times (when?) and dimensions (which?), put together into a collage and then 'let loose' to fly, flow and follow dis/orientating pathways (what might that feel like?). This is about *leading rebelliously* (why?) by simply resisting to be 'put in pre-existing images' and to do the expected and required; this is about *leading rebelliously* through questioning (why do that?), through trust and embodiment (how is that done?), through non-human and more-than-human interactions (what might that mean?), through illusion and magic (what?), through hip-hopification (what?) and through going backwards while co-creating the future (what?). This is about FOLleadOWing (?) and folLEADowing (?) rebelliously. Get ready to be 'let loose' to fly, flow and follow (y)our dis/orienting pathways. Do you dare to read on?

Welcome!

One and Only
One and Lonely
One to(o) Many
Many to One
Mind to Body
Body to Heart
Heart to Soul
Soul to Whole

 | DOI:10.1163/9789004516069_027

Whole to One
One and Only
One and Lonely
One to(o) Many
Many to One[1]

Let us stop for a moment and ask ourselves what images we hold of leadership, leading, leaders in and beyond the academy? What are the first associations, thoughts, ideas and bodily sensations when we hear the words, when we browse our memories to elicit, to find, to make and break connections we have made so far? Let us stop and explore, let us give ourselves time and space to reach our most intimate reactions to the words: leadership, leading, leaders. Let us get in there, deep inside and look, listen and feel.................................

....

....

....

What is happening? What has happened? What kind of images, thoughts, bodily sensations, feelings, sounds, smells have emerged?

Do we hear drums and fanfares all the way from the mid 19th century while visualising Carlyle's[2] hero, the Great Man? One and only, a born leader.

Do we feel Barnard[3] reaching out from the early 20th century and offering words 'feeling', 'judgement', 'sense', 'proportion', 'balance', 'appropriateness'? Do we hear Barnard's claim that "it is a matter of art rather than science, and is aesthetic rather than logical"? Art? Aesthetic?

Do we see Nicholls[4], from the end of the 20th century, offering an image of leaders as 'shakers and movers'; offering an experience of meta leadership that links individuals to their environment through visioning, an experience of macro leadership that focuses on path-finding and culture-building and micro leadership that is focused on accomplishing tasks?

Do we see Kanter's[5] Change Master? Do we attribute certain behavioural patterns to leadership, leading, leaders? Do we have a need to rationalize and distinguish between Bass'[6] transactional and transformational leadership? Do

1 Poetic musings by Tatjana Dragovic (unfortunately ☹).
2 Carlyle (1840/1869).
3 Barnard (1938, p. 235).
4 Nicholls (1987).
5 Kanter (1983).
6 Bass (1998).

we have any preference? Do we get attached to behavioural,[7] situational, participatory, servant, affective, ethic, distributed, shared, collective leadership?

Do we see leadership as a balancing act with many balls in the air from tasks, people, traits, skills and attitudes to relations, values and vision? Do we see complexity and ethics intertwined with pressures and inspirations? Do we see collaboration in (un)certainty and transformations?

Do we simply remember faces of those who led us and made us what we are today? Because we liked them and because we did not like them. Do we still feel the pain and delight of the growth and development when we remember them?

Do we dare to rebel against our own images, ideas, feelings, experiences of leadership, leading and leaders? Are these associations, memories, experiences our Implicit Leadership Theories that are being ongoingly, consciously and unconsciously used and are thus shaping and squaring our pathways? Do we dare to dis/orient them, disrupt them, dissolve them? What would happen, if we did? What if we were to stand up to ourselves and confront our own selves, rebel against our own perceived human grandeur, against ready-made meals and ready-made images and thoughts, against the expected and required?

Let us stop while we proceed
Let us follow while we lead
Let us be while we are not
Let us proceed while we stop

Let me proceed by stopping here and putting on my academic hat for a second: A decade ago, Ladkin and Taylor[8] stopped and accepted a challenge of looking at leadership differently; not in the way that was then expected and required, but rather as art. They analysed articles that addressed leadership as art and discovered three main 'motifs' in six articles written by different authors, e.g. Depree[9] and Grint.[10] The first was *embodiment* that clearly emphasised that "leadership happens through the engagement and interactions of human bodies". Ladkin and Taylor draw an analogy between art and leadership not only through the artefacts they leave behind but also through the use of senses and bodies. Both artists and leaders stay with and follow their senses longer, use their bodies and both art and leadership are "experienced through the processes by which they are created". The second motif is *holding contradictions*

7 Naylor (1999).
8 Ladkin and Taylor (2010, p. 236).
9 DePree (1989).
10 Grint (2001).

as both artists and leaders work with contradictions. Those that they could expect and those that come unexpectedly yet need to be faced with curiosity and openness to not knowing and openness to following the not knowing in order to get to learning. Meaning-making in artful leadership is based on sensory knowing rather than on cognitive knowing and embodiment underpinned with *artistic sensibilities* (third motif) can lead to learning through storytelling. Ladkin and Taylor also argue that artists', especially musicians', "backward reflexivity" when they hold what has been told, heard, played in the past in order to create the future through understanding the present, could considerably contribute to leaders' sense-making.

That was a decade ago. Two years ago, Fairchild[11] embarked on exploring educational leadership through post-humanist lens by focusing on non-human bodies and how they are in relations with human bodies. These human-non-human interactions rebel against binary dualisms and discourses that tend to sort and separate items into pre-existing categories and labels. Fairchild draws on Deleuze and Guattari's[12] concept of assemblage as a collection of heterogenerous bodies whose emergence and existence is connected to events. When humans engage with material, boundaries, silo-ing and separations disappear and more-than-human relations emerge. Post-humanist leaders, leading and leadership rebel against old, binary, compartmentalised theories, methodologies, processes. Post-humanist leaders lead rebelliously as they expand their interactions to more-than-human ones, those which include materials, spaces, processes, the natural world and much more. Seemingly disconnected bodies which have different origins, different timing, and even different dimensions interact in a seemingly random way, can even temporarily get together in a collage and then again be 'let loose' to fly, flow and follow dis/orientating pathways. Randomly or purposefully, entanglement happens and 'unhappens' and leaves its trace behind. Massumi[13] attributes a great value to this randomness. It is powerful and unrepeatable, it is unique and enriching, it is daring and scary, it is rebellious and magic.

Here, I take my academic hat off. Here, I challenge you to do the same whether you are wearing an academic or professional, official or recreational headwear, footwear and any other 'wear'. Here, I ask you to rebel against any compartmentalization that we might have inflicted on ourselves or accepted being inflicted on us. Here, I ask you to stand 'naked' in front of yourself as a body, as a human being, as a soul and as whole. And to get in touch with

11 Fairchild (2019).
12 Deleuze and Guattari (1987).
13 Massumi (2015).

yourself as you have not done for a long time or perhaps ever before. To rebel against our own perceived human grandeur loudly or silently, to rebel against our own human-centricity, to rebel against human supremacy. To lead, teach, learn, live, experience, co-create, disrupt, inspire, surprise, confuse.................

Dear Leaders around the World

I would like to start with an apology that is long overdue. Over the last few centuries, you have been pushed and forced and packed and wrapped into typologies and theories explaining, describing and 'documenting' your *leading*, the process and experience that you have lived and breathed inside out on a daily basis. Thank you for your patience.

Leading has never been an easy task, let alone leading rebelliously in and beyond the academia. Or perhaps it has never been an easy task because it has been seen as a task. What if it is not to be a task? What would it be then? What could it be then? What if we were to put leading upside down and explore what happens then? In silence. In that special space. In silence.............................

What if *leading*, somewhere on the way, has become leader*ship*, has moved from (inter)active to prosthetic/static? What if it has turned into the Great Man, Traits, Transformational, Emergent, Situational, Affective, Ethical, Stewart, Collective and yet has lost itself in all the labels and constraints? What if...

In the midst of debates, articles, labelling and discussions about similarities and differences between *leaders* and *leadership*, you kept going because you needed to, because you wanted to, because...

I would like to thank you for letting me join you on your journey over the last 28 years. I feel privileged and humbled by being allowed to be your travelling companion. I feel grateful to be accepted as a co-learner and co-follower. And above all, thank you for having let me literally throw different materials and processes at you that you graciously and curiously engaged with and created masterpieces while being 'stretched' intellectually, emotionally and physically. I threw beads at you, you took them in and in a human-non-human interactions and relations co-created an explosion of colourful more-than-human process and product. I threw balloons at you, you exposed yourself to vulnerability and questioned every move, space and pace and immersed yourselves into trusting magnifying entanglement of material and human into 'more than'. I threw one word at you, you took it, interacted with it, diffracted it and turned it into 52(!) phrases, into 'more than'. I threw two-dimensional shapes at you, you gave up your humanity and blended with the two-dimensional non-human material turning together into three-dimensional spherical 'more than'. And all you needed to experience this enriching interconnectedness and human-non-human entanglement was a 'simple' trigger question: Who am/ are/ I/you/we?

Thank you for letting me disrupt, confuse, derail and listen to what is said and, even more importantly, to what was not said in boardrooms, lecture rooms, in the corridors and at our workshops and business or academic coaching sessions. Thank you for being willing to take up any challenge and grow, to use equally your body, mind and soul, to be brave to embody your sensations in front of everybody and to dare to break free from own moulds. Thank you for being present. Thank you for trust, for not knowing, for partnering, for congruence, for resisting to be 'put in pre-existing images' and to do the expected and required. Thank you for being a rebel and for leading and following your innerness rebelliously. Thank you for following, being and living 'more than'...

……………………………………………………………………………

Thank you for sharing with us your inner world through the vignettes that follow. May your voice(s) be heard, seen, felt, touched, experienced, breathed in……………………………………………………………………………………………

Yours,
Tatjana

Dear Readers around the World

Thank you for taking your time to read the extracts from my research on leadership around the world. The vignettes included here are snapshots of talks, interviews, focus groups, feedback sessions, workshop interactions, walk-throughs and correspondence with 1800+ leaders around the world from diverse sectors, regions and professional fields. Business and academic coaching sessions notes have not been included for confidentiality reasons. Each group of leaders (12–16 in a group) has gone through a three-year leadership development programme. Feel free to read vignettes and my commentaries addressed to the leaders in any order you choose.

Vignette 1:
If my team only knew how much I do not know about what the future holds, about which direction to take and how to get there, they would be scared. So, I keep this to myself and keep my 'knowledgeable' face and stance even though deep down I feel I really do not know... and I am OK with that and sometimes I am not. Recently, I have surprised them a few times. I challenged the 'hero

> *culture' in our organization and openly said 'I don't know'. Because I really don't. It felt good. It felt liberating and powerful. I was glad I followed what I felt on the inside. I felt less like a leader and more like a follower* (*laughter*)
>
> Leader from the Central European region, 2015/2016

You rebelled against the 'hero culture', you showed that 'openness to *not knowing*' is enriching and you interacted with and followed the process within/deep inside. You defied what was expected and required of you: 'knowledgeable face and stance'. In the last session in Year 1 of the three-year long programme, you as a group got beads and questions to explore: Who am I? Who are you? Who are we? Few months later, at the beginning of Year 2, you brought your 'more than' product and you showed what you have become due to multiplicity of the process of material-human interaction. During the showing of the product, you shared that you follow the processes within you more frequently than before and that you lead less on the outside.

FIGURE 19.1 Who am/are /I/you/we? (Painting © Rok Blenkus)

> **Vignette 2:**
> *We are all sitting here and talking about this while avoiding unwrapping the deepest and most prominent issues underneath it. What are we going to achieve then? Nothing! Absolutely nothing! We are wasting your time, our time. Can't*

we talk openly and directly? (pause/silence)........ (standing up slowly) I dare you all. I am ready to trust. I will start first. Join me at any point. Here we go. I will open an important but often 'forgotten' issue about...

Leader from the West, 2019

You rebelled against the culture of 'avoidance' and challenged and dared others to join you in your 'breaking the mould'. You first showed you *trust* yourself and then you *embodied* that trust by standing up and making yourself vulnerable in front of everybody. In the last session in Year 1 you got balloons to use for exploration of your individual and organizational values through human-non-human entanglement. Your 'more than human' outcome was underpinned by trust, not just among the humans involved but also between your whole group and the material/balloons as partner(s). Embodying trust while co-creating the constellation is visible in the chosen magnifications of the composition.

FIGURE 19.2
What are our values? Human-non-human entanglenment

Vignette 3:
Many questions buzz in my head... I wish I could, on a daily basis, spend time with each and every employee at our organisation and explore possible answers to them... (laughter) but I can't. They could think something is wrong with me (laughter). It is a bit lonely here in my head (laughter). Besides,

somebody needs to work and, I suppose, asking questions and exploring them can't get the work done (pause/silence) ....or can it? Perhaps I can introduce an 'ask anything' section 5 minutes at the end of each meeting and do it playfully. How would that be? Hmmm.......................

Leader from the North, 2020

You questioned your own self while *questioning* the process of leading without questions. You, silently on the outside but lively on the inside, rebel against 'one and only, one and lonely' leader. Combining questioning with *playfulness* could open new interactions, new challenges and new *attunement* and *attention*. At the end of Year 2, I gave you as a group one word to explore, to ask yourselves about what it means to you, to diffract it, disturb it, recreate it, rebirth it. One word: Leadership. At the beginning of Year 3, you brought 'more than' 52 (!) phrases created by the letters of the word Leadership. You playfully claimed that asking questions generated laughter, creativity, exploration, crazy and innovative ideas and that is how the word got 'two in one' nicknames: FOLLeadOW-ship and folLEADow-ship. They co-exist and co-habituate while alternating the 'boldness' focus. Your new word(s)/phrases live on...

LEADERSHIP

Ship leader, Hip leaders, Idle Shaper, Pear Shield, Apré Shield, Dealerhips, Hips Dealer, Ship dealer, Dealership, Sh...Dial Peer, She Dare Lip, I help reads, I help dares, Dares I help, Hear P slide, Reshape Lid, Please H(R)id, Ash Ripe Led, Red hip sale, Dire as help, Herd sap lie, Dare is help, Are He'd lisp, Are He'd lips, Adheres lip, Despair Help, Herald pie, Relapse hid, Hid relapse, Has replied, Sharped lie, Prides hale, Herpes Dial, Rapid Heels, She Reap Lid, He Drip Seal, He drips ale, Heil Spread, Diesel Harp, Shield pare, Diapers Hel, Perish Deal, Perish Lead, Radish peel, Persia Held, Spared Heil, Hades Peril, Hera Dispel, Shire paled, Hears Piled, Heard plies, Heals pride

Vignette 4:
Leader 1: *We are slightly ashamed to admit that we feel lucky that our job does not include only leading people. Don't get us wrong. We like people but sometimes...(sigh) it is easier, lighter to lead more than just people. Our job encompasses also leading policy, leading communities, leading interconnections, leading networks, even leading spaces around the city and leading creation processes from scratch.*

> ***Leader 2:*** *Yes, and there is space for silence when it is not only leading people. There is no need for so many words and I enjoy that. Actually, our job is leading all of these together and separately and following all of these together and separately. This perhaps sounds confusing and chaotic because patterns among all of these elements are not static, but it can be quite calm, as well. They can be interconnected one moment but disconnected the other; they can support each other one moment but obstruct the other; they can be flowing one moment but dissolving the other. Sounds weird? But we love it. We feel we still touch people's lives even without too many words (laughter).*
>
> Leaders from the East, 2017

You embrace many 'bodies', you interact with *silence*, *materials*, relations, spaces, policies moving towards post-humanist 'more-than-human' process and products. You acknowledge other bodies, the chaotic yet calm context, you *tell stories* yet without too many words, you lead but you follow, you are **FOLL**ead**OW**-ing and foll**LEAD**ow-ing wordlessly and through Human-non-Human entanglement without any trace of human-centricity. At the end of Year 3, I gave you colourful two-dimensional geometrical shapes and provoked you with a question 'What if…?' Your Human-non-Human interaction with material, with silence, space, relations within your group and within the whole organisations resulted in a powerful explosion of colour and light transferred from two-dimensionality into a multi-dimensionality in the shape of sphere,

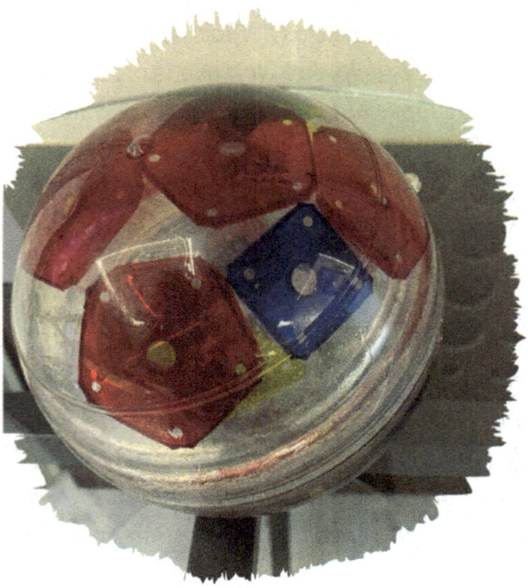

FIGURE 19.3
It is my life, too! More-than-human agency

hymn you co-created and music you added. You performed it all at the graduation ceremony. Multi-sensory and multi-dimensional experience with a wish, a will and an attempt to diffract it all in the end, to destroy the sphere in front of (y)our eyes! And the sphere refused! In a true post-humanist move, it/she/he claimed full agency and transition from Human-non-Human relation to 'more-than-human' realm. You all celebrated its/his/her boldness and claim – it is my life, too!

Vignette 5:
Leader 1: *I love working with my hands. I love creating something out of nothing. Just give me tools and I will design, create, cut, glue, put together and before you know it, it will be finished, polished and ready...it looks like magic, but it is actually lots of work and lots of paying attention to details...and in the end it is all worth it. I love it. That fabulous feeling of getting to know wood as material, imagining different dimensions...It is like partnership where both the material and I contribute... In the end, we get this admiration. (laughter) I could easily get used to it (laughter). There is something special in that process of being laser focused on the process of creating and realising that it can even be dangerous – if I move my tool a few milimetres to the left or right. The whole creation is ruined and perhaps, my finger is gone (laughter).*

Leader 2+3: *I find it fascinating to explore and discover how this or that was done in the past so we can engage with previous ideas, solutions and easily build on them. Time is frequently presented as a villain nowadays. We don't have it, we are running out of it, but actually it is always here, it has always been here and it will always be here. I like dedicating 5–7 minutes at every meeting to 'walk through' past examples, present projects and future initiatives. It makes me feel as time-traveller, as root-seeker, as timeless. Time is an interesting concept that many people avoid engaging with. I see lots of potential there. Temporality can be our partner, our guide, our (re)source...*

Leaders from the West and from the South, 2017/2020

You come from two different groups but both express fascination and respect for the natural material (wood) and the natural dimension of time. You lead by following the lead of wood and time and your interaction and entanglement with them culminate in *attunement* and *attention*, in *magic* and *root-seeking*. Elegantly and confidently, you integrate these non-human bodies into your 'more-than-human' relations. You have awareness of risk, yet you yearn for partnership and getting to know each other. At the end of year 3 for Leader 1 group and at the end of year 1 for Leader 2 group, you were given small colourful three-dimensional wooden pieces in different shapes and beads respectively. You were asked to explore who you are as a group and you brought back a whole wooden house with many layers to dismount only to find 'gems/wooden pieces' underneath with your names above each and every one. And the second group brought back a fragile but stable tree with wide roots going all the way into the ground in order to create the future through understanding the present, just like Ladkin and Taylor put it when describing 'backward reflexivity' in artists.

FIGURE 19.4 Hidden gems!

FIGURE 19.5 Back to the future: root seeking

Dear Part 4 Contributors

I would like to thank you for daring to rebel against what all of us have been doing for a long time: 'playing by the book', accepting norms and constraints at schools, Universities, work, and above all, as academics, in research. Thank you for not only doing research differently/rebelliously, but also for writing it differently/rebelliously. Thank you for adding fluidity, multiplicity, trust, embodiment, materials, relations, mutinies (you know who you are ☺), magic, storytelling, sounds and time-travelling to this book. It has been an absolute pleasure and an honour to be together in, what seems like a 'more-than-human' effort through inner journeying. Rebelling together has been the best part of it all! Rebellion could be a lonely place: one and only, one and lonely. We have transitioned from one rebel to many rebels, from doing it in our mind to living it in our body, from experiencing it in our body to sensuously feeling it in our heart, from hearing it in our heart to accepting it in our soul, from harbouring it in our soul to witnessing it as whole!

Warning!

Dear Reader, the chapters that follow offer you a journey into far-away, up-away and deep-in lands where humans are multidimensional, where they stop while they proceed, where they follow while they lead, where they are while they are not, where they proceed while they stop. Please, find below where each chapter will take you without any guarantee that you will be able to ever get back or even desire to get back to where you are now. Do you still dare to read on?

Leading Rebelliously through Embodied Trust and Playfulness

One body in the car on the autumn morning, two voices in the head, two body parts in a dialogue, two plus one body on the stage, three authors. Other present bodies: trust, playfulness, not knowing, relations, movements, embodiment, audience, chairs, stage, one stage director… In Chapter 20, Tatiana Chemi, Anne Pässilä and Allan Owens explore creation of a different pedagogical and relational space through embodiment of radical trust and playfulness. They lead by following stage-reading while trusting completely each other through movements and sensuous experience in-the-moment. As academics and experts in artistic learning and creative processes, creativity and arts in practice and drama education, they invite us to a dramaturgy in one prologue, five scenes and one epilogue. Their intimate story of a sensuous encounter is full of bodies including the Body Poetry artist from Tokyo, Yosuke Ohashi. It is also full of twists and contradictions happening right here, right now. Performing leadership as art is rebellious in its own right, even more so when 'holding contradictions' as Ladkin and Taylor discovered in their analysis of literature on leadership as art. As Chapter 20's journey includes both *embodiment* and *holding contradictions,* it contains two out of three most frequent motifs of leadership as art. Tatiana also embodies radical trust when sharing with the readership that "luckily for the performance, [her] actors begin betraying the text -and what is interpretation if not betrayal of the original text?"[14] Improvising in an academic conference is rebellious and daring, scary and exciting. If you are a rebel yourself, grab a seat in the first row for a total immersion and expect to be trusted. Would you be willing to embrace radical trust? Would you be willing to trust?

---

14 Chemi, Passalla, Owens (this volume).

Leading Rebelliously through Entanglement of Human and Non-human/Materials and 'Not Knowing' What Next

One museum, numerous images, plentitude of feelings, sensuous experiences, explosion of colours, magnified echo, voices, staircase, scores of young children, wordlessness, materials, relations, power and space: not any space, museum space open to exploration, open to touching, open to be owned and owned it is. Owned by children. In Chapter 21, Kate Noble, a museum educator, takes us on a tour through the University Museum through her research where both researchers and participants redefine and challenge the space, images and objects. It might be seen as subtle yet very visible (messy) rebellious research where unpredictability and risk are inevitable when children take full ownership of the museum space. Kate challenges us by asking how we would react to inherent unpredictability of human and material entanglements. She is curious about how we would feel if we encountered young children and families engaging in material and bodily entanglement. Would we be surprised by seeing freedom of movements where restrictions reside, confused by misalignment between our 'pre-existing images' of museums and the current vision or encouraged and inspired to challenge our own perceptions of museums? Would young children continue to feel that 'it is their museum, too' after the research is complete? Would rebelliousness remain engraved in other research projects? Would they also challenge and defy what is 'expected and required' of visitors? What is next? Kate is open about not knowing what is next and how museums would be in the future, but she shares with us her hope to create change for the better, her desire to make a difference and her dream of a better world where museums become a place for communities to be actively engaged as participants. Once you enter Kate's museum, prepare for following your senses longer, as Ladkin and Taylor would put it, as you might be seduced by the fountain of sensory-based experiences. Hereby, you have been warned.

Leading Rebelliously through Attunement and Attention/Magic and Illusion

Three magical authors, three magical visualizations in the chapter, one curious soul/reader interested in exploring rebellious writing, one magical host. Other bodies present: one old theatre, one stage, many questions, wind, curtain, parados, limelight, aria… In Chapter 22, Antonia Symeonidou, Danilo Audiello and Caterina Garone create a magical setting and enchanting walk through the past and present analogies between educators/academics and magicians. As creative thinkers with an interdisciplinary and transdisciplinary background, Antonia, Danilo and Caterina offer a scientific, bioengineering and economic cocktail with a magical powder of illusions. Their innovative and rebellious way of performing science for children through magic and illusions sets out a good modelling ground for expanding collaborative learning schemes and educational leadership protocols. It might sound too rebellious for some schools, but Antonia, Danilo and Caterina are confident that the interdisciplinary art of magic could easily inspire collaborative learning schemes. All that is left is to add creative methodologies for engaging with the audience and – voila! – the creative and colourful educational leadership protocols are ready to toast with! They rebel against 'good old/good old' ways of writing, teaching, learning. Hello everybody, there is magic and there is illusion. What other ingredients do they need? Fine attunement and attention just like with leaders around the world who, in spite of awareness of risk and danger, keep interacting with the natural material, with wood, with non-human. Illusionists dare, illusionist risk as they have only one chance to grab the attention of the audience, trick their senses and make them go WOW! and HOW? Academic writers cannot afford to lose their readers' attentions either. Neither can teachers! Yet, magic and illusions are rarely used in academia or beyond. So, please enter the old theatre, get up on the stage and position yourself in the limelight. Are you rebellious and daring enough to open the inner door and let the magic and illusion in? Even if you vanish in a puff of smoke? All right, the stage is yours!

Leading Rebelliously through Bringing Past into the Future

Two authors/actors, one interviewee, one stage, two candles, one Age of Enlightenment. Other bodies present: Hallå STEAM programme, 18th century, one interview, four acts, one curtain, two narrators. From one King's mousquetaire from the 18th century to the Finnish measurement officer in Lapland in 21st century.

Salut à tout le monde! In Chapter 23, Kristóf Fenyvesi and Christopher Brownell, connected through their mathematicians' background intertwined with their affinity for transdisciplinarity, act as Enlightenment candles and interviewers of Osmo Pekonen, another mathematician who crossed the bridge and entered the colourful transdisciplinary world. Osmo is inspired by two adventurers, the French mathematician Maupertuis and the Swedish astronomer Celsius who travelled together to Lapland to settle the scientific question of the shape of the Earth. As adventurous as these two gentlemen from the 18th century were, it is Osmo, who is leading a rebellious movement of time-travelling. Through a multi-sensory exposition Osmo and other contemporary researchers launched the Hallå STEAM program. By taking a persona of 18th century and discovering roots of their own Finnish-Swedish intellectual history, they bring past, present and future together while teaching STEAM subjects in a unique and experiential way.

Christopher and Kristóf's rebellion, on the other hand, is aimed mostly against boundaries, silo-ing, celebrating, encouraging and demanding specialization in the Academia and beyond. If the 18th century is close to your heart, and if you would like to meet some of the greatest philosophical minds, now is the time! Off you go – back to the future!

Leading Rebelliously through Hip-Hopification and Storytelling

One Hip Hop, one MC, one author, many schools, many teachers, many children, many raps… BREIS (Brother Reaching Each Inner Soul) packs his rapping practitioner's kit and rebelliously keep visiting schools and keep being asked to come back and work with children to assist them with his Hip Hop literacy programme. BREIS is a student of life and critically acclaimed rap artist whose music and wordplay explore the human condition with an Afro surrealist perspective. In Chapter 24, BREIS guides us through six phases of his Hip-Hopification of Education. We follow him from 'signing in' and entering the world of school all the way to 'signing off' and leaving behind a new world. Phase One, the Enquiry stage is exploratory for both sides, for schools and for BREIS whereas Phase Two is a Meeting of Worlds followed by Phase Three – Storytelling that features strongly in the programme. The power of storytelling prepares students and teachers for Phase Four – embracing Active Engagement that gives students part ownership of the performance and their thoughts and feelings. Phase Five is Sharing outstanding students' verses that expose his or her vulnerability, writing skill, and knowledge of self. And even though BREIS' practice is rebellious in the way he approaches students (through Hip Hop), he is the one who is witnessing the students' rebellion in the beginning of the programme. How do rebels rebel against each other? Do they need to? You are invited to dive into the chapter and be Hip-Hopified. I will be waiting on the other side curious about who will get out a bigger rebel.

Do you know what you want and who you wanna be?
We're bigger than we think but it's hard to see.
BREIS, *Think Big*

Rebels Rebelling Together – What Is Next?

Only those who attempt the absurd will achieve the impossible.
M. C. Escher

We yell, we show, we yell, we sow. While we are rebelling against our own perceptions, separation, our own human grandeur and centricity, our dualism and binarism, perhaps we have not noticed that there might be a rebellion against rebellion somewhere out there.

One and Only
One and Lonely
One to(o) Many
Many to One
Mind to Body
Body to Heart
Heart to Soul
Soul to Whole
Whole to One
One and Only
One and Lonely
One to(o) Many
Many to One[15]

References

Barnard, C. I. (1938). *The functions of the executive.* Harvard University Press.

Bass, B. M. (1998). *Transformational leadership: Industrial, military, and educational impact.* Erlbaum.

Carlyle, T. (1869). On heroes, hero-worship, and the heroic in history (Collected works, library edition). In *Thirty volumes, Vol. XII Heroes and hero-worship.* Chapman and Hall. (Original work published 1840)

Deleuze, G., & Guattari, F. (1987). *A thousand plateaus: Capitalism and schizophrenia.* Bloomsbury Academic.

DePree, M. (1989). *Leadership is an art.* Dell.

Grint, K. (2001). *The arts of leadership.* Oxford University Press.

15 Poetic musings by Tatjana Dragovic (unfortunately ☹).

Fairchild, N. (2019). The micropolitics of posthuman early years leadership assemblages: Exploring more-than-human relationality. *Contemporary Issues in Early Childhood, 20*(1), 53–64.

Kanter, R. M. (1983). *The change masters.* Simon and Schuster.

Ladkin, D., & Taylor, S. S. (2010). Leadership as art: Variations on a theme. *Leadership, 6*(3), 235–241.

Naylor, J. (1999). *Management.* Prentice Hall.

Nicholls, J. (1987). Leadership in organisations: Meta, macro and micro. *European Management Journal, 6*(7), 16–25.

CHAPTER 20

Leading Rebellious Leaders/ship through Radical Trust and Playfulness

Tatiana Chemi, Anne Pässilä and Allan Owens

Do I contradict myself?
Very well then I contradict myself,
(I am large, I contain multitudes.)
(Walt Whitman, Song of Myself)

A dramaturgy in
one prologue
five scenes
one epilogue

Prologue: The Backdrop

In this chapter we will tell the intimate story of a sensuous (Salami, 2020; Taylor & Antonacopoulou, 2019) encounter (Goffman, 1972) and address the consequences of radical trust amongst scholars. What happens when collaborating colleagues trust each other and establish playful interactions? What learning lies in experiences of radical trust (Monbiot, 2017) and playfulness (Huizinga, 2014)? We investigate these research questions by means of collaborative autoethnography (Wyatt et al., 2018) and arts-based methods (Chemi & Du, 2017). Our impulse has been a shared artistic experience: the production of a dramaturgical and performative event, to which we collaborated intensely and actively.

The context in which we operate is the neoliberalist higher university. Academic capitalism (Slaughter & Leslie, 2001) changes the rhythm of scholarly research and higher education in ways that make creativity, freedom and relationality suffer. The exclusive focus on delivery, objectives and performance indicators, the bureaucratisation of scholarly life, and the attempt to limit – if not fully obliterate – critical voices are worrying tendencies that scholars worldwide experience. In Denmark, discourses against the 'feeling' academia

 | DOI:10.1163/9789004516069_028

and freedom of research are being discussed at the moment of our writing (Bøttcher, 2021). A debate grows around what right-wing politicians call 'pseudoresearch' and the 'one-sided, activist research in, for example, gender studies and postcolonial studies' (Christoffersen, 2021), which they demand the Minister of Education and Research do away with. Critical perspectives, such as queer, feminist, indigenous/postcolonial perspectives, gender studies and identity/racism studies are being attacked and are under siege from real, useful research armed with hard-core data. How can we as scholars argue about our acts? How do we defend humanities and qualitative research as being very useful for society (ArtsEqual, 2015–2021), without falling into the trap of instrumentality that limits free thinking? From here we ask: (1) whether usefulness is instrumentality, and (2) what do we answer to the societal need 'So what?' Both sides resonate with the academic context.

We investigate here the 'what now?' of embodied investigations designed by means of arts-based approaches and collaborative exchanges. Our embodied investigation started as an open experiment with dramaturgical and performative tools as means of engaging differently with communities of scholars. The idea was to find ways of leading poetic encounters for and with colleagues by engaging each other in embodied practices of radical trust. We offer you this chapter, which performs our intimate experience as participants by weaving our voices together and by reflecting retrospectively and collectively about the possible consequences of rebellious research in higher education. Get ready for unconventional, surprising, rebellious and playful exploration of carrying out and embodying research practice that will be unstructured and unexpected, jumping from one scene to the other, mirroring more a real life than a traditionally framed and presented academic research. Get ready for the experiential and unknown nature of rebellious research embodied in three voices.

Scene 1: Voices from the Unknown

Tatiana in the Volvo, outside sunrise in the autumn. Car driving smoothly on motorway.

Tatiana

The play *The teacher is dead, long live the teacher!* (Chemi, 2018) emerged organically in my mind. Its outburst on page, denied and procrastinated for some time, became a necessity when the characters started haunting me. They presented themselves on the stage of my thoughts, playfully at first, demanding as the plot began to shape itself. I recall clearly the moment when I realised the inevitability of the creative act. On my way to work, I was driving my comfortable Swedish car early in the morning. The sun was rising in the dark sleeplessness of Danish late autumn and I was driving alone in silence, exceptionally. Normally, I listen to music or podcasts. My commute is, habitually, crowded with words and sounds that fill the spacious car cabin. I drive alone but not lonely, along with many companions who whisper, lull, shout, talk to me, soothing the discomfort of the long commute. That day, the voices were raising up from silence and they were not somebody else's words: they were mine. The two voices were arguing. I listened. They were teasing each other playfully, cruelly. 'What was the line?' 'What?' 'What was the line? The opening line? What was it?' Two voices. Two bodies. On stage. They kept repeating this routine. They were lost. Forgetful. Together and against each other. They obsessively asked each other about the misplaced first lines, the opening scene: 'What was the line?' 'What?' 'What was the line? The opening line? What was it?' Their shabby, grey, dishevelled bodies materialised in my car. They were sitting beside me, their voices getting louder, their presence becoming more demanding. Who were they? I wondered. Who are you? I asked them. They told me indirectly, by continuing their reciprocal dialogue. 'What was the line?' 'What?' 'What was the line? The opening line? What was it?' '*I* don't know! I am the practitioner! *You* are the clever one! You wrote the ingenious paper we have to present. *I* just delivered practice.' 'Oh, please! Don't go there, for Heaven's sake!' Oh, what a surprise. It was a couple of practitioners. No, they were academics. In the field of education, of course. I listened. They behaved like an old couple: they were co-dependent. Their whole appearance and behaviour reminded me of Beckett's (1986) characters. They were Brain and Hands. They embodied the complex relationship between theory and practice, one being a scholar, the other a practitioner. That their shared domain was education the reader would find out indirectly, as I, as writer, had chosen the obstruction of not mentioning any word or concept in the semantic field of education or pedagogy. The words that had emerged that early autumn morning in my car, and which I kept saying out loud, tasting them, savouring the sound and colour of them, became the opening lines of the play (Chemi, 2018, pp. 133–134):

BRAIN: *Back to audience, whispering.* What was the line?
HANDS: *Almost whispering. Looks at Brain.* What?
BRAIN: *Louder.* What was the line? The opening line? What was it?
HANDS: I don't know! I am the practitioner! You are the clever one! You wrote the ingenious paper we have to present. I just delivered practice.

Scene 2: Accepting an Invitation to Dance

Anne and Allan in the community arts centre, central Liverpool discuss Tatiana's invitation to dance. People are drinking tea and talking.

Anne & Allan

We accept the chance to dance immediately – why? Because we have been rehearsing our dance steps for several years before this. In Copenhagen wearing heavy coats. In Chester inspired by each other's curiosity. What is this person called Tatiana thinking? In Bled, stepping out of the hot sunshine wearing the lightest of light summer clothes into a space where activity started, the lake and island sparkling below the building, mesmerising. In London dressed for the damp, in Copenhagen watching out for bicycles, dodging in the midst of smiling tall Danes; now here in Brighton, one more step we take into spaces of becoming where through our continuing curiosity something can emerge. Not through performing playfulness, but systematically finding small spaces and encounters where we can experience playfulness.

Anne & Allan (later on)

Talking with each other about the invitation we come to understand that Tatiana is perhaps trying to make sense of her hidden pedagogical, learning and teaching assumptions and how a playscript could be an arena, a forum for that. This was one reason, but the stronger was that she asked us to collaboratively think through this in a co-creative way as friends. Given that we are always leaning towards relational arts-based practice (Pässilä et al., 2016) and being aware of the trust needed in these spaces, and also of the rolling banks of fog that sometimes drift in so things cannot be seen, causing us to bump into the furniture, we thought this might be a place where problematic thoughts could be articulated without fear, there might be no sofa to jar into our legs. And so, with these flashes of thought come and gone in moments, we accepted the invitation, found it an interesting and important topic and so delighted that our long-time good friend and collaborator Yosuke Ohashi the body poetry artist from Tokyo was joining us, so the one, two, three became four. We had the happiness of sensing that Yosuke's contribution would help us to go deeper into wherever we were going and, if there was fog, it would be the fun sort.

Tatiana

Hmmm ... definitely, the characters could not live with or without each other. It is obvious that they performed the tension between theory and practice. The tension that exists in education when bodies are denied the value of knowledge and when pedagogies exclude emotions from its considerations. I have decided to go for stage directions that describe a scene that is as motionless as possible: the two characters turning their back to the audience and exclusively talking to each other. The occasional break of the theatrical fiction – with the character looking at or addressing the spectators – would not affect the fixity of the scene. I wanted the spectator to feel uncomfortable about it. I wanted to generate a feeling of rejection of/for the compulsory static atmosphere of the scene. The spectator had to wonder about what was happening and get to know the characters as progressively as I had experienced in my writing process. The receiver of this text kept shifting in my mind from an image of a reader to a group of spectators. While writing was progressing through a creative tension between necessary voices and self-imposed obstructions, I became aware of the fact that, for the first time in my writer's career, the emerging text was intended for the stage. In spite of my background as theatre historian and my passion for performance, I had never contemplated the possibility of writing drama, either academically or privately. Nevertheless, I felt this form as familiar, necessary, easy to access. I recalled my good friend and colleague Dan Harris[1] asking me 'What is your voice?' He meant it as a writer, as a practitioner, as an educator. 'What is your voice?' stayed with me and suddenly gave me a new sense: my voice performs my heart in dramaturgical form. My voice is plural: it is voices in space, in time, with others. My voice was theatre. I had forgotten. Writing this play turned out to be my way back to my identity, to my rebellious identity, to the desire of doing differently, of performing difference, of being radically engaged. In life. In academia.

Scene 3: Experiencing Radical Trust through Playfulness

Anne and Allan at the venue in Brighton on stage in their minds preparing for being actors on stage in their bodies. Tatiana in the same room, overviewing the process and very excited. Seagulls are circling, calling above the shadows of the trees outside the window.

1 Professor at RMIT, Melbourne, Australia.

Anne & Allan

We stand in front of the chairs placed separately in the space for the half a dozen people attending as the sun spills through the windows of the university classroom in Brighton. The other furniture has been pushed to the side and sits quietly ready to be re-instated when the afternoon light fades. We are ready to experience immersion in the unknown; experience contradicting ourselves; experience risk and trust.

Tatiana

How would the world perceive the play? What would I do with this text? Even though my recent readings went in the direction of knowing more about performance autoethnography (Spry, 2016), the use of drama in educational research (Harris & Sinclair, 2014) or in management studies (Taylor, 2018) and in general the application of artistic tools to academic research (Denzin, 2003), I was not sure that this text would find a venue. It did, eventually. First as a published text (Chemi, 2018), then as performance. At the ICQI conference in 2017, I bumped into a close colleague and good friend, Luca Tateo,[2] who was in the process of editing a book to which I had committed. In one of the breaks, we were chatting about the project, and I suggested withdrawing the abstract for the chapter already accepted in exchange for something more radical, braver. I got his attention. As the daring scholar he is, he was intrigued. The buzzy sounds of the academic conference's breaks disappeared as I pitched the idea of shaping an academic contribution in dramaturgical form. I guess I told him about the two characters too and the creative obstruction I was in the process of following. By the end of the break, the deal was sealed. I was thrilled. This obliged me to go through with the text, to investigate its possibilities, and finally to shape it as a fully finished text for academic publication. This was scary. Would I dare? I would not disappoint Luca, in any case. I would deliver a chapter he would be proud of having in his book. Luca's excitement and openness were a strong motivational drive. The book was published in 2018. In the meantime, preparations for the Art of Management and Organisation (AoMO) conference were starting. After having written and delivered my chapter/play for publication, my desire was to meet the two characters for real, to see them materialised in space and time, to share them with others.

The AoMO community is caring and experimental, so of course my staging experiment targeted the conference held in Brighton, UK in August 2018. Steve

2 Professor at University of Oslo, Oslo, Norway.

Taylor,[3] another close colleague and friend, who is one of the central and more engaged scholars in the AoMO community, had been involved in the making of the text. As a playwriter himself and a source of inspiration for me, he generously gave me his feedback on the text. His main point of critique targeted my voicing of the two characters: they were too much 'me'. The reader would not distinguish them from each other and from their author. He encouraged me to find their characteristic voices. I had found my own voice; now I had to carve the characters' own identity. This was an operation that I attempted to realise, but only partly. Steve's feedback taught me about shaping characters for the stage, but my intention with this play was to leave things blurred. My voice, the characters' voices, the non-existent plot, the lack of movements. I wanted to constrict all the stage elements to immobility and greyness.

Scene 4: Words and Bodies Going on Stage

Tatiana, Anne and Allan at the AoMO conference in Brighton, ready to start the play. Collectively we imagine the lights beginning to dim ready for the curtains to open.

Tatiana

With this backdrop, I prepared for the staging of my first play. The casting for the two characters can barely be described as a process: I knew very early which colleagues I wanted to involve. The staging idea emerged embodied in my colleagues' bodies. With Anne and Allan, I had had one of my few acting experiences. Steve Taylor had selected us, together with Sam Warren[4] and Nick Nissley,[5] to be 'actors' for his staged reading of *The age of loneliness* (now in Taylor, 2018, pp. 303–332) at the AoMO 2016 in Bled, Slovenia. The experience was rich in excitement and learning (Owens et al., 2018). Of course, it had to be Anne and Allan, they were experienced in theatre and performance in education and management, they were fun and lovely, and we had had a great collaboration on stage before. For the rest of the preparation the guidelines were clear: no preparation. Anne and Allan were merely asked to show up for the performance and read the text aloud for the audience that we might get. For myself, I reserved the role of director and facilitator, the former inspired by Steve's very open way of approaching the staged reading of his text, the latter

3 Professor at Worcester Polytechnic Institute, Worcester, USA.
4 Professor at University of Portsmouth, UK.
5 President of Northwestern Michigan College, Traverse City, USA.

inspired by the Boalian 'joker' in forum theatre (Boal, 2000), but not for forum theatre purposes. My twist on Steve's staged reading methodology was to allow the spectators to make changes in the performance. My play was short enough to allow for one complete read through (by Anne and Allan) plus the repetition of short bits of the text with dramaturgical changes. The invitation to the spectators was to actively become directors and influence the staging of the chosen bits with their ideas or associations.

When the day of the performance came, I was thrilled. Finally, I would meet my characters in person. By chance, a colleague who is an actor, director and pedagogue, Yosuke Ohashi,[6] was present at the conference and offered to be part of the staging. This was interesting for me. I had conceived the play as a claustrophobic duet, and now a third dimension was showing up. Yosuke, who has collaborated with Allan for many years, is a Shintashi body poetry (Owens, 2011) performer, trained under Kazuo Ohno, one of the two founders of Butoh dance, which made his contribution even more potentially disruptive. Butoh is a form of Japanese dance that resists fixity, is playful and grotesque, characterised by slow hyper-controlled motion. I asked Yosuke to stand on the right side of the stage, at a distance from the other two actors. His task was to comment in an embodied manner what was happening at centre stage. His approach would be improvisational because he had not read the play either. Ready for more serendipitous surprises, I stepped aside to watch the performance after having briefly introduced the work, the actors and the concept for the workshop. Then it happened: the magic was performed on stage, bodies materialised abstract concepts. My words (my words!) were uttered in space-time and shared with other people. Theatre was being in the same room together. This community had made my visions real. Bodies with their shapes, colours, softness, hardness, size, movements, rhythm. Voices with their tones, volumes, timbre, rhythm. They conjured up my (mine!) characters, speaking the words I had spent so much intimate time with, cherishing them, polishing, considering, thinking, learning. When Anne and Allan started being Brain and Hands, I could not believe my eyes. I could not believe my luck: I was experiencing this blessing for the second time in my life, having tried to be a theatre director only once before,[7] but this time the play performed was mine.

Luckily for the performance, my actors begin betraying the text – and what is interpretation if not betrayal of the original text (Eco, 2016)? The heavy restriction to their movements described in the stage directions was not

6 Vice-President of Taichi-Kikaku Theatre, Tokyo, Japan.

7 The Samuel Beckett plays *Come and go* and *Catastrophe* at Aarhus University, Denmark in 2006.

sustainable at length, not for the coherence of the play nor for the patience of the spectators, and not even for the actors on stage. They started moving towards each other and slowly turning to face the spectators. Their bodies tried different positions and came closer to each other. While the conflictual tension in the spoken lines progressed, the actors' bodies were approaching each other. When the spectators responded to the invitation to select one bit of the play and make staging suggestions, they expanded in the direction where the actors were leading their vocal and bodily Stanislavskian subtext. Their interactions become gradually messier, grotesque, amplified. The spectators loved it. Laughter filled the room. At one point Yosuke approached the actors, still at centre stage but now much closer to the spectators and began to interact non-verbally with them. In his Shintashi/body poetry movements, he thrust himself in between the other two entangled bodies, exaggerating the messiness even more. Here it was, the conflict between theory and practice, being healed by an unspecified glue. Here it was, the relational tension between theory and practice not being allowed to settle into stifling seriousness; instead, being played with the sort of joyfulness that can flow from uncertainty in a safe space. This presence tried to push them away from each other but ended up collating the two opposite forces. Who was this force? What was its role? These questions enrich my practice as an educator and educational research.

Allan

Tatiana's excitement to the side, Yosuke's energy to the left, me and Anne moving together, we stand with our backs to the audience and start to read, often finding ourselves in such a position, not knowing quite what to do and so it feels like home. Tatiana our friend has given us text and suggested we stay still. Very soon it is too much not to engage with the audience, we need to set out, there is the text, words are there, leaving, imagining how something is imagined on stage in the quiet of a chair, the space is created, somehow, that will invite other people to make their connections, to bring their experiences, somehow. Are they connecting with the words written on paper or are they connecting with three people moving? Can we separate any of this out and what does that matter anyway? We are reading a text to the back wall. How to connect with anyone through disconnection: this is the most difficult of tasks even for the best actors in the world and we are very far from them, more near the other end. Why are people going to continue to listen? It is time to turn to the people sitting. We need to move. I sense Anne is also moving. We need to move towards the people. Yosuke is moving. So often his standing position is mesmerising as it shifts to this and that and on.

Anne

I am really following my intuition in momentum because I trust these two friends, because I know where they are taking me in this improvisation and this allows me not to follow Tatiana's instructions, to take it into our own hands and improvise. It is from the script. I am moving from it towards the house as its doors swing open. We are siblings, maybe we are twins, no need to worry, something will happen, and we will take care of each other. I feel this when we are together. It is like Yosuke has been my sister in a Murakami way; there is another moon where I can dance with these guys. I dare to follow, picking the flowers, going out, to follow the way that is emerging, because whatever I do it will be accepted. There will always be something, a space is going to be created for the audience to make sense and experience, no need to perform experiences. Performing experiences or making space for experience. People watching; it is not about audiences. We are moving.

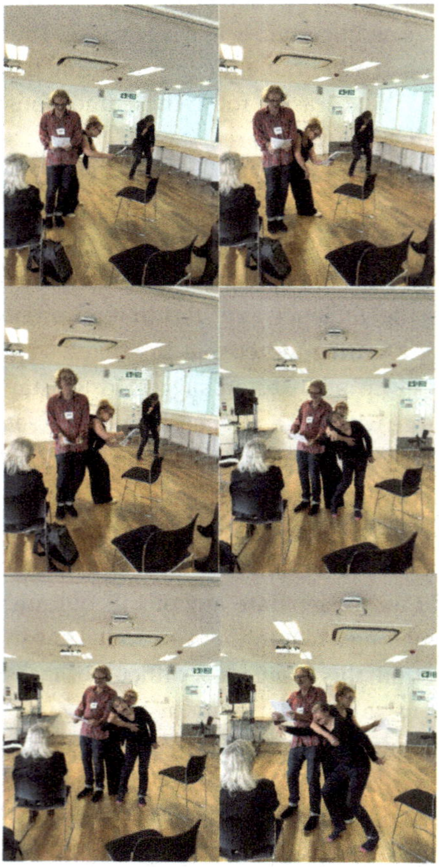

FIGURE 20.1
Progression into messiness, radical trust and playfulness

Scene 5: The Play Text, Embodiment and Encounters

Tatiana, Anne and Allan on and next to the stage, being thrown in at the deep end. The audience are beyond the footlights. Tatiana asks for suggestions. People call out directions.

Anne & Allan

It is not this, is what we are saying. This is a play. What are you thinking about as you watch this play? What the playwright thought when writing the script has already faded. Steven S. Taylor is in the room and Tatiana looks to him in all excitement. Anne refuses to watch. Allan is wondering. Yosuke does not see him. He is concentrating on his full kindergarten experience, he is an opera singer downsizing to a classroom, he sees what is going on and makes us an offer. He does not sing, he swims towards us with children's stuff, playing, he is winding in amongst our bodies. Some people in the room laugh. Others look away. We surf on the waves of our relationships, remember the small boat we saw sunken in the river years before, it is the embodied layer in our encounter, we think of the Black Ships sailing into the harbours of Japan, we are messing around with all of this and enjoying it. Tatiana's script is sending wave after wave. How are we seeing this? What are our endless power relations in academia? Steve is always so supportive, and then the whole setting is like it was on the first day we stepped into school. Who owns knowledge in this space? What is being understood and how? In these moments when improvising at an academic conference what are we trying to do? No attempt to change anything. A big ship going where it is going. But in some of these moments there is some breathing on our own, breathing through the trust we give to each other to do what we can do.

The first run-through finished. Philippe,[8] a colleague, left the room. Anne sighed, thanked the gods for making these decisions. Did the session create the very real opportunity to allow people to leave the room? Such happiness generated through stepping in and stepping out, the dance of engagement, not at all about the quality or nature of the performance but about the pedagogical now and then, inviting us to make sense of what happened, of what is happening now as we peer backwards to see forwards.

8 Associate Professor Philippe Mairesse, ICN Artem Business School, Nancy, France.

Epilogue: Rebellious Spaces

The understanding coming from the space of radical trust and playfulness is an attempt to create a different pedagogical and relational space. Its elements are necessarily alternative to actual higher educational practices, which are defined by the negation of knowledge that is 'sensuous' (Salami, 2020), bodily, emotional and therefore rebellious. Oppressive systems 'discourage a sensuous approach to knowledge because tyrants have always understood that the more robotic people are, the more easily manipulated they are' (Salami, 2020, p. 24). Academia today still replicates centuries-old models of knowledge that are dualistic (Kant's transcendentalism and Descartes' belief that only cognition can bring humans alive: *cogito ergo sum* and the separation of *res extensa* and *res cogitans*). This means that they separate, instead of uniting; they are biased by the belief in their neutrality, measurability and lack of context. A very much needed creative alternative stimulates criticality and creativity at the same time, valuing them both equally. This can be done by including and valuing aesthetic learning, bodily recognitions and sensuous knowledge. According to black feminist bell hooks (2001), 'many jobs undermine self-love because they require that workers constantly prove their worth' (p. 64). Rebellious actions in academia must reclaim critical-creative spaces (Adams & Owens, 2016) where individuals can play, love, be passionate, investigate freely engaging several knowledge tools, valuing embodied, emotional and sensory approaches at the same level as the cognitive-logical-verbal ones. In summary, academia needs spaces where scholars, educators and students can challenge and rebel against the division of theory and practice, as performed by the conflict between Brain and Hands, and resonate with a multiplicity of perspectives, as poetically expressed in Whitman's quotation above. In this way, academia can become the space for/of alternative wisdom, which is rebellious because it takes a stand against biased knowledge, which is knowledge that ignores subjectivity and contextuality. This way of looking at knowledge as the sensuous and poetic glue that binds Brain and Hands, like Yosuke's dance in the play, has the role of building up resistance against allegedly neutral science. Poetic encounters involving reciprocal trust, playful bodies and love have the consequence of 'perceiving knowledge as a living and breathing entity rather than as a packaged product to passively consume' (Salami, 2020, p. 15).

However, being eager to get into action, we can forget to stop and think. Action is important in academia but spaces of playful reflection, of loving interconnection and critical thinking, are also necessary for shaping what is not known yet. This is rebellious in the sense that we, scholars, leaders and educators, do not know what is going to emerge in the future (not overstructured, fixed) and no resistance is going to occur (nobody is going to stop you).

What is the level of rebelliousness that is acceptable in our established institutions? Conservative and progressive forces within our communities create tensions that can be stimulating or obstructive. Qualitative research is established with its original, often ground-breaking approaches. What does rebellious look like in arts-based methods in education and educational research? How far can we go in academia? The risk we experience is constantly of not being taken seriously by the established illusion of hard sciences, measurable facts and one-sided truths. We have normalised putting everything in Excel sheets full of important statistics, numbers and more numbers, demystifying our presence on and as part of this planet. We do not notice the invisible hand leading us in this academic dance, self-regulating our own steps. We do not even need this leading: it will stop our inner dance; we will be doing only free form in this space.

Is leaving the room where alternative approaches unfold rebellious? In which way? Is it a protest? Against what? About doing something differently, alternative to expectations? Or is leaving the room in a relaxed way a pedagogical compliment? How can we make spaces for this freedom in formal institutions?

One more insight we harvested during our embodied investigation is the difference between performing playfulness, being playful (the bus in Bled full of academics sticking tape over their glasses, around their heads, passing the roll down the aisle!) and playing. The latter is the children's activity of full unawareness and sharp focus on imaginary worlds, events and actions. The former is a performative activity done by means of aesthetic criteria, a second-order play: the play that is presented or represented as a performance. Being playful, instead, is the mood needed to glue together seriousness and humour, theory and practice, logic and senses. Being playful is the state in which individuals are open to what emerges, present in the occurring relationships, and respond creatively and appropriately to what emerges.

Where is the space where scholars, leaders, students, educators can play in academia?

Does the rebelliousness flow from/through what solidarity allows for? The four of us, looking to each other for validity in what we might find out or not, being prepared to be excited or uncomfortable because we have decided to do something we sense might create a space in which we can step into the unknown, for us, in the company of others, and through each other might come to know, to understand more, further, deeper, better, more fully?

Why is it more valuable to come into a room fully armed with a very detailed grasp of an argument, a position to articulate, ready to join up the dots of others in a well-crafted monologue than to come into a room with a set of abilities and skills, a disposition of curiosity, well prepared, relaxed, ready to listen

FIGURE 20.2 Academic playfulness. Nomadic web with Anne, Allan, Tatiana and Clive Holtman. AoMO 2016, Bled, Slovenia (Photo: Tatiana Chemi)

FIGURE 20.3 The elements of the places of open possibilities on stage (Photo: Tatiana Chemi)

and enter into dialogue through our bodies and the words that come out as encounters take place?

There is a liveliness in the play: where do we find liveness (de Simone, 1999) in pedagogy? When human beings actually come together with their bodies and imaginations to perform ideas, is the relevance and value of the educational encounter in the safe spaces created by the performing action itself? Is the presence of educators as humans going beyond memorisation and the elaboration of the known the fragility in performance which opens up the possibility for something unexpected and fascinating to occur as it unfolds around them?

Last but not least, how is it possible to navigate comfortably in theatre tools without the skills of theatre makers? Even though we are not experts in theatre so that we can create, recreate, reproduce as professionals, we have pedagogical liveness, so it can appear rebellious. Liveness is collaborative, as the dialectic between planning and improvisation is relational. Can one plan improvisation and play? Can we risk the flattening into communities of practices practitioners in academia? The community that defines that this is the way it is made: by talking/thinking, not by doing and sensing (especially if experimentally). Alternative approaches look at and include energy-rhythm-timing: thinking in/with/through the body. Beyond the text, beyond the words, beyond the cognitive mind, senses, touching, following, feeling, synchronic movement, not each person claiming their own positions, towards something that might emerge. What is hidden in the body that our educational stages will not let become and flourish?

New voices emerge from the unknown:

> Character 1: Who owns knowledge in this space? Can we trust 'them'?
> Character 2: What are we trying to do? Are we still playful?

Who are these characters? Whose voices are these? When will they show themselves in imagined bodies, in our materialised fantasies?

References

Adams, J., & Owens, A. (2016). *Creativity and democracy in education: Practices and politics of learning through the arts*. Routledge.

ArtsEqual. (2015–2021). *ArtsEqual Research Initiative*. University of the Arts Helsinki. www.artsequal.fi

Beckett, S. (1986). Waiting for Godot. In S. Beckett (Ed.), *Samuel Beckett: The complete dramatic works* (pp. 9–88). Faber & Faber.

Boal, A. (2000). *Theater of the oppressed*. Pluto Press.

Bøttcher, T. (2021, March 15). Forskere er Rystet over Politisk Angreb og Twitter vrede. *DM Akademikerbladet*. www.akademikerbladet.dk/aktuelt/2021/marts/forskere-er-rystede-over-politiske-angreb-og-twitter-vrede

Chemi, T. (2018). The teacher is dead, long live the teacher! Performing autoethnography as critical learning. In L. Tateo (Ed.), *An old melody in a new song: Aesthetics and psychology* (pp. 133–146). Springer.

Chemi, T., & Du, X. (Eds.). (2017). *Arts-based methods and organizational learning: Higher education around the world*. Springer.
Christoffersen, J. (2021, March 9). Forskere: Den politiske offensiv mod »pseudoforskning« er fordomsfuld og farlig. *Information*. www.information.dk/nyhedsblog/2021/03/forskere-politiske-offensiv-pseudoforskning-fordomsfuld-farlig
Denzin, N. K. (2003). The call to performance. *Symbolic Interaction, 26*(1), 187–207.
De Simone, P. (1999). Why 'live'? Review of Philip Auslander, Liveness: Performance in a mediatized culture. *Other Voices, 3*(1). www.othervoices.org/3.1/pdesimone/index.php
Eco, U. (2016). *Dire Quasi la Stessa Cosa*. Bompiani.
Goffman, E. (1972). *Encounters: Two studies in the sociology of interaction*. Penguin.
Harris, A., & Sinclair, C. (2014). *Critical plays: Embodied research for social research*. Sense.
hooks, b. (2001). *All about love: New visions*. William Morrow.
Huizinga, J. (2014). *Homo ludens: A study of the play-element of culture*. Martino Publishing.
Monbiot, G. (2017). *Out of the wreckage: A new politics in the age of crisis*. Verso.
Owens, A. (2011). Pilgrim: Taichi-kikaku. In J. Freeman (Ed.), *The greatest shows on Earth: World theatre from Peter Brook to the Sydney Olympics* (pp. 125–144). Libri Publishing.
Owens, A., Pässilä, A., & Chemi, T. (2018). 'I shot her twice': Negotiating meaning in staged readings: Commentary. In S. S. Taylor (Ed.), *Staging organization: Plays as critical commentaries on workplace life* (pp. 332–340). Palgrave Macmillan.
Pässilä, A., Owens, A. & Pulkki, M. (2016). Learning jam: An evaluation of the use of arts based initiatives to generate polyphonic understanding. *Journal of Higher Education, Skills and Work-Based Learning, 6*(2), 178–192.
Salami, M. (2020). *Sensuous knowledge: A Black feminist approach to everyone*. ZED.
Slaughter, S., & Leslie, L. L. (2001). Expanding and elaborating the concept of academic capitalism. *Organization, 8*(2), 154–161.
Spry, T. (2016). *Body, paper, stage: Writing and performing autoethnography*. Routledge.
Taylor, S. S. (2018). *Staging organizations: Plays as critical commentaries on workplace life*. Palgrave Macmillan.
Taylor, S. S., & Antonacopoulou, E. P. (2019). Arts-based interventions as platforms for sensuous organisational learning: An introduction. In E. P. Antonacopoulou & S. S. Taylor (Eds.), *Sensuous learning for practical judgment in professional practice* (pp. 1–14). Palgrave Macmillan.
Wyatt, J., Gale, K., Gannon, S., & Davies, B. (2018). Creating a space in between: Collaborative inquiries. In N. K. Denzin & Y. S. Lincoln (Eds.), *The Sage handbook of qualitative research* (pp. 738–756). Sage.

CHAPTER 21

'It's Our Museum Too!'

Enacting Change through Rebellious Research in the University Art Museum

Kate Noble

Introduction

On the following pages I invite you to enter into the world of images, objects and materials which are at the heart of my practice and my thinking as an art and museum educator. Travel with me to the marbled hallways of the Fitzwilliam Museum where I work through a selection of images taken across time and place. Start with a wordless exploration of the colour, texture, shapes, materials and viewpoints within the main entrance hall of the museum. I urge you to stop and spend time imagining placing your hands on the chill of the smooth stone handrails, listening to the sounds of voices echoing through the towering pillars. Picture yourself climbing the staircase and standing on the mezzanine, gazing upwards at the spectacular gilded ceiling and glazed domed cupola. When you can feel and sense yourself inside this museum space, we can explore together how shared, embodied and creative experiences with young children might disrupt, subvert and challenge traditionally dominant narratives within the patterned halls of the university museum. Join me as I consider the changing role and focus of museum-based research and discover the opportunities and challenges afforded by rebellious research within the art museum.

Background

I have worked as a museum educator at the Fitzwilliam Museum for nearly 20 years. During this time, I have developed my practice working with museum objects and collections through teaching on the schools, teachers and families program. As part of this practice I undertake action research to analyse and reflect on what we do. This research is motivated by hopes, dreams and desires: I *hope* that we can create change for the better, I *dream* of a better world and I *desire* to make a difference (MacNaughton & Hughes, 2009, p. 5). My dream

 | DOI:10.1163/9789004516069_029

FIGURE 21.1 Main entrance viewpoints, photo montage (© The Fitzwilliam Museum)

FIGURE 21.2 Main entrance textures, photo montage (© The Fitzwilliam Museum)

is that museums will become more inclusive and relevant, a place where communities are invited to actively engage as cultural participants, not merely as passive consumers (Simon, 2010).

Museum research both enriches professional practice within the institution and informs exhibitions, displays and public programs (Pringle, 2020, p. 155). A university museum is distinct and different from a non-university, national or local authority museum in that there is potential to collaborate with a wide range of researchers within the university. Yet the setting of the university museum also creates opportunities to reach outside of the academy to collaborate with communities and, in so doing, open up 'to wider ways of knowing' (Facer & Pahl, 2017, p. 228). The Fitzwilliam Museum's mission is:

> To touch people's lives by engaging powerfully, thoughtfully and pleasurably with as wide a public as possible and to produce and promote innovative, relevant, and interdisciplinary research of the highest quality around our collection. (Fitzwilliam Museum, 2019)

This statement places people at the centre of the museum's work. It also highlights the importance of research. I am interested in exploring the juxtaposition of our collections-based research alongside this commitment to engaging with our public. My work as an educator has revealed to me the multiple ways in which people respond to and react with the spaces within the museum and how this impacts upon their interactions with the artwork they encounter over the course of their visit. I learn alongside the groups I work with; our encounters, interactions and journeys through the museum are shared adventures. I hope that by providing opportunities to co-produce research with 'as wide a public as possible' we have the potential to create new spaces for discussion, discovery and debate within the university and the museum. These spaces have the potential to be more inclusive, 'where no-one is excluded because of their class, race, gender or caring responsibilities. A space where different forms of knowledge and knowledge production are understood to have much to offer our lives' (Bell & Pahl, 2018, p. 113). Through our learning and engagement programs we can work alongside communities to challenge and make change from within the organisation. This provides an opportunity for rebellious research which challenges both the existing exclusivity of the university and museum and the dominance of academic knowledge over other ways of knowing and being in the world. In order to achieve this ambition, we need to start by acknowledging existing hierarchies and prominent discourses within the university museum.

Knowledge and Power within the University Art Museum

Figure 21.3 is an 1848 engraving which shows an idealised view of the main entrance hall of the museum. Although this is not an official Fitzwilliam Museum image, it reflects the thinking of the time around university museums and their role. Several groups of people are pictured on the mezzanine landing, their tiny figures dwarfed by towering fluted columns. The picture is dominated by details of the museum architecture, from the elaborate column decorations and the richly sculpted classical reliefs in the vaulted ceilings and niches, to the large geometric patterns on the floor. Men are shown in academic gowns and mortar boards; women are smartly dressed in bonnets and long dresses. People are standing, engaged in deep conversation. To the left of the composition, a man dressed in a richly embroidered gown gestures towards an unseen object or work as if explaining something to his female companion. He faces her as he talks, and her eyes follow the direction of his hand as she listens intently. To their right, two women stand talking to a man dressed in black academic robes who has his back to us, the viewers. One of the women is holding the hand of a girl, aged about 7 or 8 years. All three stand still and silent, looking at and listening to the man as he talks.

FIGURE 21.3 Main entrance landing, 1848, engraving (© The Fitzwilliam Museum)

This image encapsulates the conception of the university museum as a seat of expertise and learning. The architecture of the building is reminiscent of the façade of Greek or Roman temples, indicating its classical roots, inspiration and knowledge, conjuring up images of power and empire, and demonstrating a separation and elevation from the street and community. The notion of museum as temple has roots in the Enlightenment ideal of the role of art and learning to elevate and empower the general population. The scale of the pillars and architecture tower over the assembled figures and reinforce humankind's subordinate role within the hierarchy of established knowledge and power. The groups of figures are self-contained and exclusive. There is no invitation for us, the viewer, to join them or to participate. Within this restricted environment, the academics and students in their gowns and formal dress are depicted as purveyors of learning, and are shown demonstrating, guiding and explaining. Their female companions stand still, listening, waiting, passive recipients of patriarchal wisdom and experience. The child stands and listens, absorbing the lesson from the master and is offered privileged access and insight into an adult world of learning and experience. At this time, the museum was only open to the public on Wednesday and Saturday afternoons, 'excepting children aged under ten years of age' (Burn, 2016, p. 63). Even for these well-dressed and fashionable woman and children, access is only granted via the conduit of the expert academic man. It will be another 100 years before women are awarded degrees from the university and another 140 years before the museum offers dedicated programming for schools.

Co-constructing Knowledge in the University Art Museum

In Figure 21.4, we travel forward in time to 2005 to find a museum educator standing in front of a case of Greek artefacts facing a group of primary school children. The children are seated and several have their arms raised to either respond to or ask a question. In this image, the museum expert is female and she wears smart casual clothes rather than the academic gowns seen in the previous picture. She is positioned as a bridge or mediator between the objects in the case and the children on the floor. Her expertise is signposted by the clipboard she is holding which represents her position of authority and knowledge. Imagine yourself seated on the wooden floor, one of the children focused intently on her. Children are now actively engaged in learning within the museum and sit on the floor, rather than stand, which is likely to be a more comfortable experience. This small adjustment, allowing children to sit on the floor, makes the museum learning environment more accessible for them. The

FIGURE 21.4 Museum educator with school group in the ancient Greek gallery of The Fitzwilliam Museum, 2005 (© Martin Bond)

group come from a local state-funded primary school and have been brought to the museum by their teacher.

This image is representative of museum learning programs across the UK and exemplifies the dominant ideology within the field over the last thirty years. This model places emphasis on learning taking place through the process of dialogue, questioning and conversation, and draws heavily on socio-constructivist accounts of learning (Bruner, 1986; Vygotsky, 1986; Wertsch, 1985). Knowledge in the museum is understood to be socially constructed, through an active and collaborative process (Falk & Dierking, 2018; Piscitelli & Weier, 2002; Pringle & DeWitt, 2014). This can be held up in stark contrast to the more passive knowledge transmission model represented in Figure 21.3. The first image is reminiscent of what Freire describes as the 'banking' concept of education, whereby knowledge is deposited within the student by the teacher: 'knowledge is a gift bestowed by those who consider themselves knowledgeable upon those whom they consider know nothing' (Freire, 1970, p. 45). In contrast to this approach, Freire considers the role of educator to 'trust in people and their creative power' (p. 48) and to enter into a dialogue with their students to encourage critical and reflective thinking. This dialogic approach is well established within the museum learning community as exemplified by the development of visible thinking routines (Perkins, 1994; Tishman, 2018), Visual Thinking Strategies (Housen, 2001; Rice & Yenawine, 2002; Yenawine, 2003) and the work of Burnham and Kai Kee (2011).

The dialogic model of engagement resonates well with the ideal of the contemporary university museum, which is transformed from an elite and specialist institution into a more collaborative and experimental space for learning, providing opportunities for diverse communities to come together and take part (Were, 2010). Within this ideal, there is the potential to create sites of interdisciplinary experimentation and exploration aspired to within the museum mission statement. Through the development of research projects which encourage dialogue and reflection through action, there is the opportunity to challenge existing hierarchies. Through this work, the university museum can begin to function as a radical, critical space, as a laboratory for ideas and risk taking. Within this space, participants both within and beyond the academy work together to make change and to subvert, challenge and trouble existing assumptions and hierarchies (Hammond et al., 2006; Pringle, 2020).

Challenging the Dominant Narratives

However, the positioning of the museum expert and presence of the clipboard still hints at some residual knowledge transmission through the role of expert, whether scholar, curator, educator or other specialist. Language and dialogue are socially constructed and can, therefore, also be instrumental in reinforcing structural inequalities. Museum displays, interpretation and narratives replicate hierarchies of cultural capacities, contributions and representations and uphold the status quo (Tolia-Kelly, 2019). In more recent years, researchers and commentators have challenged the dominance of cognitive and social constructions of childhood within studies of young children in museums. They argue for the need to account for children's non-verbal experiences, to attend to their sensory and bodily engagement with space and matter within the museum (Birch, 2018). Research by Hackett, Holmes and MacRae and others places emphasis on unexpected connections in human and non-human encounters (Hackett et al., 2018, 2020; MacRae et al., 2018) and invites us to re-think and re-imagine our understanding of how young children, objects and materials react and interact within the museum environment. MacRae et al. state that 'visitors are also deeply entangled with and co-exist alongside concepts and materials, so that all things lose their clear boundaries' (2018, p. 513). Their work invites us to contemplate a post-human account of the university museum to consider the 'intra-actions' (Barad, 2006) between people and the images and objects of the material world. This account runs counter to dominant narratives. The museum architecture, academic gowns and body language in Figure 24.3 intra-act to reinforce and recreate established hierarchies of knowledge and power. What happens when people, museum spaces and objects intra-act differently? Let us now respond to the challenges posed

FIGURE 21.5 Drawing on the main entrance landing, 2020. Photograph from 'It's Our Museum Too' research project (© The Fitzwilliam Museum)

by post-humanist accounts to understand meaning differently within the museum, and to explore how it emerges from the diverse and diffuse relationships between the human and non-human (MacRae et al., 2018).

Young Children, Action and Place

Figure 21.5 shows children drawing on the main entrance landing and was taken in February 2020 from exactly the same vantage point within the Museum as Figure 21.3. The photograph shows two adults working with a group of eight young children from a local playgroup who are taking part in the It's Our Museum Too action research project. Take a minute to imagine ourselves there, recalling the photo montages of Figures 21.1 and 21.2. You are now sitting on the hard, ceramic and stone coloured floor, immersed in the echoing sounds of children's voices and movement. As we kneel and sit on the mosaic floor, we make rubbings from the rough textured tiles. Several children are deep in concentration, and are bent over their drawings, absorbed in their creative explorations and the physical affordances of the materials and spaces within which they are working. Others in the group are not in the frame of the picture, as they have chosen to do something else at that moment. A playgroup educator leans over the floor and holds a piece of paper for a girl; their eyes and attention are cast downwards onto the patterned floor. The museum educator is also seated alongside the children. She holds a bag of metallic crayons, and the paper is laid out on the floor in front of her, an open invitation to draw. She watches as one of the boys starts his rubbing, and his two friends watch and wait alongside him. Imagine the children focused and talking quietly as they are captivated by the patterns on the floor. Hear the rubbing of the soft crayon on the rough sugar paper as they press and move their hands, feeling the uneven surface of tiles beneath. In this moment, children, adults, materials 'intra-act' to discover, to feel, to remember and to create. Explorations and experiences are embodied, multidimensional and 'respons-able', each being in touch with the other (Barad, 2015). It is in this way that we understand a place by being within it and our encounters with material objects play a vital role in the emergence of meaning. The materiality of museums and the offer of an encounter with 'the real' object in a special place is part of their distinct offer and marks a difference from our day-to-day interactions with the things which surround us.

The Re-distribution of Power: It's Our Museum Too

In contrast to Figures 21.3 and 21.4, the adults in Figure 21.5 are now acting at the same height as the children and are seated on the floor with the rest of the group. The children's movements dominate the image – they are captured turning, bending, touching, drawing, looking and listening. Their engagement is active and independent of adult or expert mediation – they determine their own personal direction of travel and investigation. Their interactions are sensory, embodied and enacted within the materiality of the museum spaces and collection.

The It's Our Museum Too research explores the experiences of young children in the museum. The project challenges traditional hierarchical structures of knowledge and power within the university and museum to recognise the agency and voice of young children. Our work draws on the discourse of democratic participation and civic responsibility to investigate the role of the museum as an agent for change, to reach out to diverse audiences and embrace new forms of knowledge production (Pringle, 2020). Praxeological action research is democratic and collaborative in nature and we embrace our positionality as practitioner researchers, situated close to the site of professional action and drawing on established networks and partnerships with schools, teachers and families (Pascal & Bertram, 2012). As we journey together through this work, action and reflection occur simultaneously to bring about change (Freire, 1970). Through this process possibilities and opportunities can be created for those who may have traditionally being marginalised or left out of museum and university research. This is how we break with tradition, to reflect upon and challenge professional practices and to discover new ways of seeing and being in the museum.

Collaborative Approaches to Research with Young Children

These new ways of seeing and being liberate us to experience the museum in new and different ways. I invite you now to move into the paintings gallery, and take a moment to lie on the floor to contemplate the wonderful and intricately decorated ceiling as shown in Figure 21.7. Feel the press of the wooden floor on your back alongside the young child and adult in Figure 21.6, and enter deeply into an act of contemplation and looking. This is a communal, social activity. Child and adult heads are positioned alongside one another as the floor provides both a shared vantage point and an anchor, supporting their weight as they look. Their bodies are twisted, but they turn towards one another. The child holds a toy snake which is folded over her stomach. The adult points upwards with a pencil and both follow the trajectory of this gesture to gaze beyond and up. The act of looking in this way is deeply immersive and personal and resonates with Birch's (2018) plea to offer opportunities for personal, not universal, encounters with museum spaces and objects and to embed playfulness and openness of interpretation into children's and adults' museum experiences. This freedom of bodily movement, gaze and equality of adult and child perspectives offers a stark contrast to the restriction and control of Figure 21.3. Making time and paying attention to these unexpected moments and interactions by documenting them through our research and writing offers us an exciting means of inquiry into worlds previously undiscovered and unknown. Sensory experience, pleasure, collaboration and meaning combine in one moment to enable us to re-imagine ways of knowing in the art museum.

FIGURE 21.6 Learning together in the Large Paintings Gallery, 2020. Photograph from 'It's Our Museum Too' research project (© The Fitzwilliam Museum)

FIGURE 21.7 Gallery 3 ceiling, 2019 (© The Fitzwilliam Museum)

By liberating visitors from traditional and established ways of being and acting within the space, possibilities are created for new encounters, new ways of knowing. Museums are not neutral spaces; they are knowledge-based, social institutions which have the potential to contribute to the creation of a more equitable and fairer world (Sandell & Janes, 2019). However, in order to do this, they must face up to their role in establishing and supporting the status quo. Tolia-Kelly (2019) uses the example of the British Museum as a 'temple of delight' offering witness to a range of diverse world cultures, but she challenges the displays, narratives and taxonomies within the museum. These were determined outside of the communities which they represent and are 'a reproduction of world views, values and perceptions, replicating hierarchies of cultural capacities, contributions and representations' (p. 126). Tolia-Kelly explores the writings of Ranciere and the work of artist Rosanna Raymond to propose the potential of co-opting aesthetic practices into the expressive infrastructure as a means of progressive politics to disturb and disrupt the imperial and colonial matrices of understanding (p. 129). Rebellious research in the art museum offers the opportunity to play with and subvert traditional power structures by illuminating and privileging the experiences of those who have previously been under-represented or repressed. The children, families and community group we worked with during It's Our Museum Too did not visit the museum before we started collaborating with them. Our rebellious research makes visible voices and perspectives from outside of the museum and university, and in so doing acknowledges their importance and their value, and disrupts established knowledge.

In Figure 21.6 an adult and child lie on the floor of the gallery, and in so doing disturb and disrupt the received way of being within the art museum.

They are engaged in the act of deep looking and thinking which we saw in Figures 21.1 and 21.2, but their attention is not directed at the great paintings hung on the walls of the gallery which have been chosen, arranged and explained (through textual information) by curators. Their interest is in the delicate and intricate plaster decorations and sculptural reliefs on the ceiling of the museum shown in Figure 21.7. Although they could have looked with head tilted back while standing or sitting in the gallery, they have chosen to look in a different way. The ceiling acts as a catalyst for a shared social, bodily and sensory experience. Neither of them would have done this without the other one being there. Recording, documenting and analysing this moment within our research decentres the museum objects and spaces and shifts the focus towards the people encountering them.

The It's Our Museum Too project was a partnership between the museum and a playgroup which serves a diverse community, including many families facing disadvantage. The head teacher we worked with was keen that we worked with families and early years practitioners who would not otherwise visit the museum, to help them to explore what a museum is, to see what there is within it that they can relate to 'Because they see it as very academic, very restrictive, and not for them' (post-project interview). Within our research we were concerned with how we might challenge this perception, to help participants to find their own value and relevance within the museum building, spaces and collection. Although we made some decisions about which galleries to visit with the group and what art materials and activities to provide, we worked alongside participants within each session to ensure that we followed their interests and allowed them different modes of response and affordance. Their physical and sensory experiences within the museum were key to helping them to feel a sense of ownership and belonging within spaces which had previously been seen as exclusive and exclusionary (see Wallis & Noble, 2022, for further discussion). In this way their visits were co-created and they made the museums theirs too.

Mess, Unpredictability and Risk in Rebellious Museum Research

Rebellious research of this kind, where both researchers and participants redefine and challenge the space, images and objects of the research setting, is messy, unpredictable and carries an element of risk. Figure 21.8 captures a moment of museum, material and bodily entanglement within the It's Our Museum Too project. A knot of arms, legs, heads, paper, crayons and mosaic are frozen in time – shown in the act of being and intra-acting. Hands, bodies and materials respond and react to one another. The image demonstrates the messy nature of collaborative action research with young children and

FIGURE 21.8 Children entangled, 2020. Photograph from 'It's Our Museum Too' research project (© The Fitzwilliam Museum)

the inherent unpredictability of human and material entanglements. There is always a risk that by embracing the unexpected you are pulled away from the research aims and questions to travel somewhere else. This is a common feature in research of this kind (MacNaughton & Hughes, 2009; MacRae et al., 2018) but can cause additional conflict within the restricted and hierarchical spaces of the museum (see Noble & Wallis, 2021) and indeed the wider university. The risk to the museum building and the objects is always at the front of our minds and dictates the choices we make. Crayons are fine to use on the stone floor of the entrance hall where they can be wiped clean, but we would not use paint in a gallery space containing fabric or materials which could be damaged. There is also a risk to others in the museum, to other staff and to visitors who might find this work challenges their perception of what should happen in a museum. This can create a risk to the participants within the research. They could be told off or disapproved of because they are pushing at the boundaries of what is allowed. This experience would run counter to the aims of this work. Any conflicts of this kind would also present a risk to our learning programmes within the museum. We have worked hard to develop good relationships and build trust with other departments within the museum. If this work is seen as annoying, disruptive or dangerous we run the risk of being stopped or hindered by those with more institutional power. How would you feel if you walked into the paintings galleries and encountered young children and families engaging in material and bodily entanglement of the kind displayed in these images? You might at first be surprised by this rather conflicting vision within the restricted and hierarchical spaces of the museum. But you then might be encouraged to stop and think and to consider how this image challenges your perception of what museums are and who they are for. Doing rebellious research has an impact far beyond the research itself. Doing rebellious research challenges all of us, our own beliefs and perceptions, our societal norms and our understanding of what is possible now and in the future.

As practitioner researchers we have to be brave, to embrace this risk and to be open to infinite possibilities within time and space. Indeed, in my role as museum educator, it is the disruptive and transformative potential of this research which makes it so worthwhile and exciting. However, we have an ethical responsibility to protect participants from harm and to ensure that they are supported and enabled rather than censured as a result of their participation in rebellious research. As a result, there is a continual tension, a push-pull between the museum that was, and the museum that I hope, I dream and I desire we might one day become.

Conclusion

> A shift in perceptions, a challenge to the accepted orders, epistemologies or indeed 'ways of seeing' could in fact become the site of the political, that enables a new redistribution of the sensible, that *includes* those not already included in the architectures of truth, heritage and narrations of 'other' cultures, determined by them. (Tolia-Kelly, 2019, p. 129)

Through rebellious action research in the university art museum I embrace the relationship between doing and understanding to bring about change. My role as practitioner within the museum creates an opportunity for this change to grow slowly and organically from within the institution. As a practitioner researcher, I can explore new possibilities and 'ways of seeing' by building on existing partnerships and collaborations with people outside of the university and museum, by managing risk, by embracing uncertainty, and by working thoughtfully and carefully.

These new methodologies have the potential to shape and to be part of the ideation of subsequent projects, new displays and spaces within museums. However, this will require the further building of trust, on all parts, and a recognition that 'traditional' curatorial expertise and other forms of knowledge and expertise can be mutually beneficial and enhancing. By allowing for and paying attention to embodied, sensory and expressive encounters, we can begin to work outside of established ways of 'being' and 'seeing' within the museum space. Rebellious research in the university museum and the 'new redistribution of the sensible' described by Tolia-Kelly above has the potential to empower young children and others who might have previously been excluded from museum spaces to challenge embedded and dominant discourses, and to think and feel differently about our museums and collections.

Practitioner-led enquiry within the art museum is rebellious in the way in which it contests conventional and dominant hierarchies of knowledge and power. In this way the academy is opened up to 'wider ways of knowing' which assist in the development of new approaches and directions within museum-based research. The approach described in this chapter challenges the space, images and objects of the professional context in which we work, enabling us to interrogate what it looks like 'to touch people's lives by engaging powerfully, thoughtfully and pleasurably', as outlined in our museum mission statement. In so doing, we are testing ourselves, our practice, and our own and our visitors' perceptions of museums by making it 'theirs too' by providing conditions for free, explorative, pleasurable movements. These entanglements themselves once used to be prohibited, undesirable and judged as rebellious. With this approach comes empowerment and with empowerment comes change. Are you ready to join us on this journey?

References

Barad, K. (2006). *Meeting the universe halfway: Quantum physics and the entanglement of matter and meaning*. Duke University Press.

Barad, K. (2015). TransMaTerialiTies: Trans*/matter/realities and queer political imaginings. *A Journal of Lesbian and Gay Studies*, *21*(2–3), 387–422. https://doi.org/10.1215/10642684-2843239

Bell, D. M., & Pahl, K. (2018). Co-production: Towards a utopian approach. *International Journal of Social Research Methodology*, *21*(1), 105–117. https://doi.org/10.1080/13645579.2017.1348581

Birch, J. (2018). Museum spaces and experiences for children – Ambiguity and uncertainty in defining the space, the child and the experience. *Children's Geographies*, *16*(5), 516–528. https://doi.org/10.1080/14733285.2018.1447088

Bruner, J. (1986). *Actual minds, possible worlds*. Harvard University Press.

Burn, L. (2016). *The Fitzwilliam Museum: A history*. PWP.

Burnham, R., & Kai-Kee, E. (2011). *Teaching in the art museum*. J. Paul Getty Museum.

Facer, K., & Pahl, K. (2017). *Valuing interdisciplinary collaborative research: Beyond impact*. Policy Press.

Falk, J. H., & Dierking, L. D. (2018). *Learning from museums* (2nd ed.). Rowman and Littlefield.

Fitzwilliam Museum. (2019). *The Fitzwilliam Museum mission, strategic framework, priorities and plan 2019–2024.*

Freire, P. (1970). *Pedagogy of the oppressed.* Penguin Books.

Hackett, A., Holmes, R., & MacRae, C. (Eds.). (2020). *Working with young children in museums: Weaving theory and practice.* Routledge.

Hackett, A., Procter, L., & Kummerfeld, R. (2018). Exploring abstract, physical, social and embodied space: Developing an approach for analysing museum spaces for young children. *Children's Geographies, 16*(5), 489–502. https://doi.org/10.1080/14733285.2018.1425372

Hammond, A., Berry, I., Conkelton, S., Corwin, S., et al. (2006). The role of the university art museum and gallery. *Art Journal, 65*(3), 20–39.

Housen, A. (2001, September 27–29). *Eye of the beholder: Research, theory and practice* [Paper presentation]. Aesthetic and art education: A transdisciplinary approach conference, Lisbon, Portugal.

MacNaughton, G., & Hughes, P. (2009). *Doing action research in early childhood studies.* Open University Press.

MacRae, C., Hackett, A., Holmes, R., & Jones, L. (2018). Vibrancy, repetition and movement: Posthuman theories for reconceptualising young children in museums. *Children's Geographies, 16*(5), 503–515. https://doi.org/10.1080/14733285.2017.1409884

Noble, K., & Wallis, N. (2020). Leaving room for learning: University of Cambridge Museums' nursery in residence. In A. Hackett, R. Holmes, & C. MacRae (Eds.), *Working with young children in museums: Weaving theory and practice* (pp. 87–94). Routledge.

Noble, K., & Wallis, N. (2021). 'It's our museum too': Co-producing research in a university museum through a nursery residency programme. *Qualitative Research Journal.* Advance online publication. https://doi-org.ezp.lib.cam.ac.uk/10.1108/QRJ-01-2021-0009

Pascal, C., & Bertram, T. (2012). Praxis, ethics and power: Developing praxeology as a participatory paradigm for early childhood research. *European Early Childhood Education Research Journal, 20*(4), 477–492. https://doi.org/10.1080/1350293X.2012.737236

Perkins, D. (1994). *The intelligent eye: Learning to think by looking at art.* Getty.

Piscitelli, B., & Weier, K. (2002). Learning with, through and about art: The role of social interactions. In S. C. Paris (Ed.), *Perspectives on object-centered learning in museums* (pp. 109–139). Lawrence Erlbaum. https://doi.org/10.4324/9781410604132-12

Pringle, E. (2020). *Rethinking research in the art museum.* Routledge.

Pringle, E., & DeWitt, J. (2014). Perceptions, processes and practices around learning in and art gallery. *Tate Papers, 22*. https://www.tate.org.uk/research/publications/tate-papers/22/perceptions-processes-and-practices-around-learning-in-an-art-gallery

Rice, D., & Yenawine, P. (2002). A conversation on object-centered learning in art museums. *Curator: The Museum Journal, 45*(4), 289–301. https://doi.org/10.1111/j.2151-6952.2002.tb00066.x

Sandell, R., & Janes, R. R. (2019). *Museum activism*. Taylor and Francis.

Simon, N. (2010). *The participatory museum*. Museum 2.0.

Tishman, S. (2018). *Slow looking: The art and practice of learning through observation*. Routledge.

Tolia-Kelly, D. P. (2019). Rancière and the re-distribution of the sensible: The artist Rosanna Raymond, dissensus and postcolonial sensibilities within the spaces of the museum. *Progress in Human Geography, 43*(1), 123–140. https://doi.org/10.1177/0309132517739141

Vygotsky, L. (1986). *Thought and language*. Harvard University Press.

Wallis, N., & Noble, K. (2022). Leave only footprints: How children communicate a sense of ownership and belonging in an art gallery. *European Early Childhood Education Research Journal*. https://doi.org/10.1080/1350293X.2022.2055100

Were, G. (2010). Re-engaging the university museum: Knowledge, collections and communities at UCL. *Museum Management and Curatorship, 25*(3), 291–304. https://doi.org/10.1080/09647775.2010.498987

Wertsch, J. V. (1985). *Vygotsky and the social formation of the mind*. Harvard University Press.

Yenawine, P. (2003). Jump starting visual literacy. *Art Education, 56*(1), 6–12.

CHAPTER 22

Enchanting educational settings

Creative Practices from the World of Illusion to Improve Collaborative Learning Schemes and Educational Leadership Protocols

Antonia Symeonidou, Danilo Audiello and Caterina Garone

The Prologue

You come around a corner, distracted by a data sheet full of graphs and interesting statistics. Your mind is absorbed by the numbers and you try to draw some insight from your reading. Your thoughts are so diverted that you bump into a fellow passer-by. In slow motion your gaze goes from the paper you were holding to a face that begins to smile. They breathe in then say:

'Hello, I am your magical confederate, a creative companion if you wish. Who are you?'

'Who am I?', you think, as you suspensefully examine the new reality in which you have landed. You swiftly gaze around the area, without losing contact with the fellow passer-by.

It is cold but you feel comfortable. It is the middle of the night, but you are surprisingly rested. You only hear the wind, but you sense the presence of something special. The area looks abandoned but has the energy that suggests a large crowd is about to populate it shortly. As your eyes become accustomed to the setting, your surroundings seem to be illuminated and you understand that the walls of the buildings near you have words projected on them, which interweave with old posters attached to their facades.

Some words pop up on the projection and you can clearly read **knowledge**, **magic**, **purple**, **ability**, **science** and **arts**. You turn your head and some banners have the writing **dare**, **yellow**, **cognition**, **transdisciplinarity** and **blue**. You look at the sky as a poster becomes detached from a lamp post and the wind makes it fly towards you. As it comes near, you can read **belief**, **pedagogy**, **conjuring**, **green**, **rebels**, **red** on it. You try to create a pattern and connect these keywords to understand the meaning of the colours. As you pay attention to the coloured words in your mind, you try to read out loud the colours that are visible regardless of the word written. **Purple**, **red**, **blue**, **yellow**, **pink**, **black**, **orange**, **grey**, **ivory**, **turquoise**, **brown**, **white**, **purple**, **red**. You immediately realise that this would slow down the speediest of readers. Curious to

DOI:10.1163/9789004516069_030

understand the reason why all these colours and words are presented in this manner, you remember the landmark test on interference in serial verbal reactions (Stroop, 1935). As you are growing even more curious to understand why this trick has been executed all over your surroundings, you return to the figure who greeted you before.

'Who am I? A reader, interested in exploring rebellious writing.'

'An educator? A policy maker? A researcher? A parent? Shall we call you a curious soul?'

'I guess so, but who are you again?'

'I am a researcher, possessing magical powers, or being possessed by them – still figuring this out! – and we are here together to immerse ourselves in the charms of illusion from a magician's toolbox to draw out ideas for academic writing.'

The Pre-show

You both start to walk down the street, chatting as if you have known each other for years. You travel down an empty road, as if you are walking a path of inner exploration.

'Why magic? What does it have to do with writing?'

'Magic is closely related to many disciplines of science (Kuhn et al., 2008), but more importantly with many forms of art, all of which have a strong connection with storytelling, be it with words, notes, movements, colours, you name it! An incantation or enchantment is a charm that we create with words. It may be that in occultism, shamanism and witchcraft the incantation as ritual aims to invoke or praise a deity, but the real charm is that there is a knowledge gap between science known and science that works! Have you heard the third law of writer Arthur C. Clarke, the British science fiction writer of the Space Odyssey, Rama and many more? The third of his famous adages quoted that any sufficiently advanced technology is indistinguishable from magic! This allows magicians to create impossible-looking phenomena!'

'But how can a magician actually do this?', you ask.

'It is super simple. You just have to perfectly coordinate dozens of movements, align them with the positions of your body, the gestures of your hands, the gaze of your sight and the point of view of the spectator and more ... I see you are laughing! It is as absurd as it sounds and this is why the master of misdirection Tony Slydini gifted magicians with his super detailed step-by-step guides (Ganson, 2011) that offer the perfect recipe to present magic.'

'The coordination sounds crazy! There are so many weak points for errors in the alignment, right?'

'Right! And now you understand the manic attention to detail! Well, as an illusionist you have only one chance to grab the attention of the audience, bring them to the emotional state that you want, build their anticipation, trick their senses and make them go WOW! and HOW?'

'Sure, but in writing it is different. We can always go back to a specific paragraph to read it again and understand what the writer wished to communicate.'

'That indeed applies for readers, who have this option with written documents, but writers do not have the luxury of losing the attention and the focus of their readers. Writers still have limited chances to create emotions in their readers, to engage them before they decide to put an academic article down, to make them curious enough to decide to purchase the article, to make them enthused to study it over a reading marathon and even connect with the authors to explore more about their research. On a cognitive and emotional level, the performance of illusions provokes a sense of curiosity, surprise and interest, which are leading attributes associated with desirable pedagogic interventions (Wiseman & Watt, 2020).'

The Switchboard[1]

You reach an abandoned theatre and enter a door that leans half open. Your magical host finds a table with some old electric circuit breakers and switches one on. Sparks flash on the outdated gear and the stage lights ignite. You both head towards the light, when you remember the question you meant to ask before the interruption.

'So, would that mean that an academic's job, when it comes to writing, is very similar to a magician's job, without losing the core of the scientific project?'

'Precisely. The same valid scientific or academic concept can be communicated differently, in a creative way, that might make it clearer (Ferreira & Mendes, 2014), more understandable (Bagnoli et al., 2019), more engaging (Moss et al., 2017) and more fascinating (Lin et al., 2014) to the reader than just a cold list of data and conclusions. There is also another element to consider. When an illusionist performs, they must enchant their whole audience. In close-up performances, I get to read the reactions of each of the spectators and make small adjustments to my performance to follow their preferences. The analogy, in academic communication, would be to present a research project to one interested person as in that case you get the opportunity to simplify the scientific terminology if the person is not an expert in the field, or you can go into great depths of detail if the person listening is a master of this discipline.'

1 A console from which the lighting is controlled.

'The more I become immersed in this with you, the more analogies I identify myself as well. The academic or educator becomes the illusionist on stage and the message communicated becomes the script!'

'Challenge yourself one step further. The readers are your audience and all the visual tools you use, such as graphs, tables and illustrations become the scenography and choreography!'

'I get that now, but when a research project is published in a scientific journal the language is standardised and there is no control over who the readers are and how well they engage with the content.'

'Exactly, and this is the same challenge that we face when we perform in an arena of 10,000 people or for a TV special for a few million viewers.'

'And how do you manage that?' you ask, while navigating between the dusty audience seats.

'You actually can't. But what you can do instead is allow your audience to interpret the reality from their points of view, from their magical lenses. Take for example the image presented below. To many it would look like a scattered combination of random lines and ink marks. However, once someone pays closer attention and approaches it from a particular angle,[2] the seeming randomness will start to make sense and the hidden message will be revealed. This perspective-based optical illusion is a call for our academic and pedagogical evolution!'

FIGURE 22.1
Tilt your head & follow the clockwise message illusion (© Academy of Magic & Science)

2 To reveal the message, tilt the book so the image faces towards the ceiling, close one eye and look at the image from the angle and eye level of the bottom binding of the book. Then the rotate the book clockwise until you reach another angle or perspective to continue reading the hidden text.

The Periactus[3]

'Now you see why the angle of perception needs to be considered! As a creative communicator you can only try to make sure that your story is engaging and fascinating when viewed and interpreted through all these different lenses. But we should not stress about it; we storytellers have biology on our side! 100,000 years ago, humans started developing our language. It is safe to say that we started using storytelling to transfer knowledge. So, storytelling verbally started long before 'language' as we know it today was created. 27,000 years ago, we started transferring knowledge from generation to generation through cave paintings, and only 3500 years ago, we started transferring knowledge from generation to generation through text.'

'So we had 3500 years to perfect communication through text! Sounds like an adequate amount of time.'

'Indeed it is, and we have read written miracles from writers worldwide. Our mission now is to equip with these precious tools the hands of academics, who ask the questions that other people haven't thought of. We are doing it for those that create research models to figure out how to answer those questions and when they actually do, they have to tell these stories to other researchers, the general public, the policy makers, the curious minds. However, unlike words like research design, objectives, hypothesis, analytical techniques, statistics, etc., the word storytelling rarely appears on their curriculum, even when it has such great potential (Pollock & Bono, 2013) and has been researched for classrooms, academic discourse and beyond (Pollock, 2021; Yang & Wu, 2012).'

'I see the problem, but how can magic help?'

'Oh yes, returning to magic. As fascinating as it may sound, magic performances have been documented at the same time as the first documented stories! In the Tomb of Baqet III in Beni Hassan there is a drawing of a performance of cups and balls (Kanawati et al., 2011). In fact magic is as well wired in the human brain as writing; our neurons respond to it, we are adapted as beings to it. Then why not use this hard-wired asset of our minds to the service of storytelling! Magicians surely must be the world's most creative rebels, as their performances have always been presented in opposition to what was considered possible and at their modern times they knew a bit more science and art than their spectators! The equivalent of the magician in the educational setting would be the teacher (McCormack, 1990), the professor (Hilas & Politis, 2014), the communicator (Myers et al., 2013).'

'And how can we perform magic while typing to impress someone when they are reading?'

3 A prism-shaped piece of scenery which is revolved to show different scenes.

'Every magic trick consists of three acts. The first act is the pledge: the magician shows you something ordinary, but of course, it probably isn't. The second act is called the turn: the magician makes their ordinary something do something extraordinary. Now you are looking for the secret, but you will not find it. That is why there is a third act, called the prestige. This is the part with the twists and turns, when lives hang in the balance, that you see something shocking you have never seen before (Priest, 1997).

So, these three stages of the magic show are like the beginning, middle and ending of a piece of writing. The pledge/turn/prestige principle can apply for any emotion you want to create for your readers to feel and any reality you wish to craft. Don't take my word for it: this comes straight from one of the brightest storytellers of every childhood memory, Walt Disney, who said, and I quote, "in learning the art of storytelling by animation, I have discovered that language has an anatomy". A good knowledge of the rules and laws of this anatomy allows us sometimes to break them!'

Curtain Up[4]

'Do you mean this in the same way that you break the laws of physics when people are cut in half or start levitating in shows?'

'Precisely. We have a long list of conjuring feats to choose from: productions (from not being to being), disappearances (from being to not being), transformations (from being in this way to being in that) and transpositions (from being here to being there). Then we have natural science laws defied, such as anti-gravity, magical animation, magical control, matter through matter, multi-position, restoration, invulnerability and rapid germination. And ultimately, we have the mental phenomena of prediction, divination, clairvoyance, telepathy or thought transference, hypnotism, memorisation and lightning calculations.'

'It is impressive how many feats you have available to work with!'

'As a matter of fact we do have a lot and all the aforementioned translate to a menu of basic effects: production (appearance, creation, multiplication), vanish (disappearance, obliteration), transposition, transformation (change in appearance, character or identity), penetration (one solid through another), restoration (making the destroyed whole), animation (movement imparted to the inanimate), anti-gravity (levitation and change in weight), attraction (mysterious adhesion), sympathetic reaction (sympathetic response), invulnerability (injury proof), physical anomaly (contradictions, abnormalities, freaks), spectator failure (magicians' challenge), control (mind over the inanimate), identification

4 The time at which the curtains rise and the show starts.

(specific discovery), thought reading (mental perception, mind reading), thought transmission (thought projection and transference), prediction (foretelling the future), extrasensory perception (unusual perception, other than the mind). Imagine the myriad of possibilities we can craft when we mix and match these!'

'How do you manage to memorise all these techniques and methods?'

'From a philosophical standpoint, one could argue that all magical effects are a configuration between appearance and disappearance. Even a levitation illusion can be translated into an act of making gravity disappear!'

'Are all the above only for magic shows? Can these effects apply to education?'

'I see you have grasped the idea already and what you just suggested is an excellent consideration! Yes, these can be applied in educational settings (Vidler & Levine, 1981; Tognazzini, 1993); we, in fact, have already been doing so! We have developed lecture shows that communicate science undercover! The students think they are attending a magic show and the performance is packed with illusions and special effects, until we reach the moment that we have them at the edge of their seats, not wanting to blink to not miss a moment, then we bring the science on board, which proves to be more entertaining and engaging than the tricks themselves.'

'But that would only work for young students who enjoy magic, right?'

'We would be satisfied even if we could only engage that age group, but reality is more fascinating than that. You see, we have been performing the same show to pre-school students up to postgraduate researchers and, while the illusions change slightly and the storytelling navigates into greater depths and more thorough analysis, the pillars remain the same and the engagement of the audience is undivided. There has been one phrase that has been haunting us from our first shows until today, when some of the parents or educators come to us at the end of the show to say they wish their students or children would pay as much attention to their lecturing as they did during the show. And we turned it into a mission!'

'I can see why it is entertaining, but how does the adaptation for the various ages happen?'

Parodos[5]

'When our grandmothers look at a fire, they think of a match lighting up a dried piece of wood. When a scientist looks at a fire, they think of the carbon that the trees absorb from thin air, of the movement of the molecules as they

5 The first song that is sung by the chorus at the beginning of a Greek tragedy.

approach and repel one another and of the factors that can offer the activation energy to a system and set it on fire! The same applies to someone watching a magic trick of producing light in one's bare hands. Some see the light and admire the effect. Others admire the fine motor skills of the performer who managed to make it seem to appear out of nowhere. Others still can't see where it came from but understand that the misdirection techniques of the illusionists are not allowing their attention to catch the effect. And there is also one group who decodes in their minds the electronic circuit and the mechanisms to make the light appear even without being able to visually trace cables, switches, batteries, etc. Interestingly enough, all of them will ask 'How did you do that?' Instead of revealing the illusion to them, we turn their question into 'How does it work?' Depending on their group, this question can be answered from the field of psychology, perception (Rensink & Kuhn, 2015), attention saturation (Demacheva et al., 2012) or electronics!'

In the Limelight[6]

Both walk on stage. The lights blind you at first, but your eyes gradually become accustomed to the new condition.

'If we assume that educators can acquire some magical skills, to grab the attention of their audience and guide them through these paths of perception and understanding, would that remove the wonder from magic shows, since everything would be revealed?'

'On the contrary, it would enhance the effect of wonder. When someone understands a concept better, they are further encouraged to explore more, ask more, understand more, even to test it themselves. There is something victorious in having young children backstage after shows speaking with the engineers who set up all the equipment, as it is when an audience member thinks they caught the performer's technique to witness that here is another illusion underway!'

'Can you show me a magic trick to understand it?'

'I refuse to show a trick on demand, I would h@v3 to conform to th3 r3strictions of a m@gic p3rform@nc3 @nd do all th3 f@ncy mov3ments @nd gestur3s to comply to th3 rul3s 4h@4 p3opl3 h@v3 s3t in their minds of wh@t a m@gic 4rick should b3 like. @n ıllusıon should h@v3 @ hıdd3n m3@nıng, som34hıng quı43 sımpl3 @nd pur3 4h@4 brıngs @ mom3n4 of 3nlıgh43nm3n4 4o 4h3 sp3c4@4or wh3n 4h3 r3v3l@4ıon ıs conclud3d. Wh@4 ı would lık3 would b3

6 The first theatrical spotlight, also a popular term for incandescent calcium oxide light. The expression 'in the limelight' originally referred to the most desirable acting area on the stage.

4o show you 4h@4 4h3 gr3@43s4 ıllusıonıs4 of @ll ıs no4 4h3 on3 ın fron4 of you, bu4 4h3 on3 ınsıd3 you. 4h3 4rıcks @nd ıllusıons 4h@4 our mınd c@n pl@y on us wı4h @ll 4h3 unconscıous bı@s3s gov3rnıng 4h3 d3cısıon m@kıng progr3ss, @r3 4h3 gr3@43s4 of @ll 4ım3s, so 4h3 r3@l qu3s4ıon you should b3 @ skıng would b3 'C@n you show m3 @ m@gıc 4rıck 4h@4 ı do?' @nd wı4h 4h@4 qu3s4ıon w3 would r3@ch 4og34h3r 4h3 epıphany moment of the prestige!'

'How? What was that? What did just happen?'

'That was one of the great magic tricks that your brain can perform on you! Your visual processing system adapted to my dysgraphia, minimised the transposition and replacement cost effect to identify the pattern of replacing letters with symbols and digits, acquiring the skill of interpreting my messy message into a meaningful paragraph.'

The Director and the Leads

'So, I need to read more about the cognitive skills of decoding illusions! Would I then be able to resolve all mysterious illusions around me?'

'You would be on the right path, but there is more to illusion than what we can train ourselves in! Reading the cognitive bias codex (Calero Valdez et al., 2018) allows us to identify the 'blind spots' of more than 180 cognitive biases that compromise our decision-making process. It is however important to highlight that illusions govern our decisions not only on a theoretical level, but even in life and death situations, such as when the illusion of absence (Ekroll et al., 2021) can explain a class of road accidents, as drivers simply cannot see the presence of cars and dangers because of the illusion of absence. This understanding can help policy makers redesign elements of street architecture and save lives.'

'Why haven't we heard about this before? If magic can do this for road traffic, what can it do for education?'

'A talented performer should never fail to amaze, as a gifted educator should never fail to create compelling educational experiences and immediate realisation moments. Think of how useful these tools (Curzon & McOwan, 2008) can be in the hands of a computer science teacher, who could present real magic tricks with an underlying link to their scientific field and challenge students to explore how it works.'

'Understandable, but this sounds idealistic. The curriculum handed to the teachers does not always allow time and freedom to enchant your students in such a manner.'

Climbing down the staircase to the backstage area, holding the railing tightly.

'Indeed, and we are not suggesting a gallop of rushing through the curriculum to create the space and the connection for these performances. Instead, we suggest having these charms ready to be fired at the right time when the students need to be re-engaged, re-amazed, re-enthused. What we want is for the students to realise that their teachers will never fail to save them from disengagement from the topic. The educator's most important job is to instil hope in their students' souls. In a rather cruel experiment in the 1950s, Curt Richter (Richter, 1957) demonstrated the power of hope and resilience on drowning rats. When rats were left to swim in a vase of water, they would nearly drown after 1–15 minutes after immersion in water. When they reached their peak exhaustion, researchers would remove them from the water, dry them, and allow them to rest and eat. When they were placed in the water again, they would endure swimming for up to 60 hours, as Richter explained that they had the hope and confidence that someone would save them and therefore their resilience skyrocketed! A student should have the same hope for their teachers, believing that the teachers will be there to save them when they lose the thread of understanding and are drowning from the weight of accumulated missed points.'

'Are you suggesting that if the teacher manages to "save" the students once, they will maintain their hope and resilience throughout?'

'There could be a strong case. An engineered strategy for the conformation of the toolset would be for elements of illusion, perception and magic to be applied when a need emerges to bring back the attention and engagement of the students to keep them motivated, as per the suggestions in Vroom's (1964) landmark study on work and motivation.'

'That would be a rather simple element to incorporate in the training of educators. They would only have to learn some tricks and use them with their students to enthuse them every now and then.'

'It goes far beyond the tricks. With the current technology available at our fingertips it is difficult to amaze someone with tricks, as you called them, especially when the techniques used are outdated by the magic that our smartphones can do!'

'So what are you suggesting?'

An Aria[7]

'Visualise a standard day in a classroom. The teacher walks in, greets the students and introduces the chapters they will present that day, lays out in bullet

7 A reflective solo act, usually sung.

points the structure of the curriculum to be taught during that hour and then proceeds to look at each of the bullet points in depth. Now, while the content of the lecture can be impressive and amazing for someone already passionate about the subject, the presentation is so short on surprise that, even if the students had the potential to find the subject fascinating, this seemingly perfect method allows some of them in a way to simply lose interest from the beginning.'

'But giving the highlights at the beginning is important so students know what to expect, isn't it?'

'Let me ask you, if you went up the stairs with the thrill of presenting to a wide audience, holding a metal charm in your hand for good luck, and you appear on stage in front of a full audience, imagine if you would begin your show by laying out everything that was going to happen from start to finish, wouldn't this detract from the feeling of adventure and excitement? Wouldn't this rob your spectators of suspense and the delight of discovery? And yet that's exactly what most educators do, not because they don't have the talent to build suspense with their storytelling (Fox Eades, 2005), but because the curriculum can be so predictable that the delivery can be doomed to be unimpressive. We are challenged to perform in the classroom the finest balancing act, intriguing them just as much, without confusing them. The dare is to approach it as follows.'[8]

FIGURE 22.2 Hybrid text illusion (© Academy of Magic & Science)

8 The text is transformed if you hold the book close to your eyes and then move a few steps away from the book while looking at the image.

Proscenium

'I had never thought about it that way before, but still I believe that there needs to be some structure, some introduction at the beginning of the lecture so students will know what to expect and to organise the knowledge in their minds as it is communicated.'

Navigating in the dark backstage area, sliding the steps in uncertainty, searching the walls for the doorknob.

'Think of a mythological animal. Quick! But not the popular unicorn, mermaid, pegasus.'

'Let's say a centaur!'

'Here is your response! What do I mean? Didn't you ask me before about the structure in the lectures? Centaur is your answer!'

'But I only answered your instruction to think of a mythological creature.'

'You did more than that. You replied to the million-dollar question of the perfect curriculum presentation. The creative versus analytical thinking dichotomy has been a staple of education for decades. The combination of arts and creativities with a strictly mathematical/analytical structure can be the centaur of education. When chess grandmaster Garry Kasparov introduced centaur chess, his model sparked the growth of freestyle chess, in which a weak human coupled with a machine and following a better process was superior to a strong computer alone and, more remarkable, superior to a strong human coupled with a machine and following an inferior process. Isn't it fascinating to imagine the potential of arts and creativities in the hands of educators following even standard teaching processes? Aren't you curious to see the innovation this could centaur bring us to?'

'What a coincidence! Who could imagine that the mythological animal I mentioned was already a model of chess and educational mastery! Wait, was it a coincidence or did you predict my response?'

'Imagine if I replied that "psychic" phenomena are real and I predicted your response. Would you be impressed? Of course not! You would just be witnessing my "psychic" nature taking its course and no one could take credit for the wow moment (Banachek, 2011). After all, if psychic powers existed, there wouldn't be anything amazing about a show of illusion (Maskelyne, 1876). Imagine if I replied that there are no psychic forces – no vibes, no auras, no influences from the stars, no voices from beyond the grave. I am an illusionist, but instead of conjuring with doves and tigers, I do tricks with information. If I do a good job, you'll have something to think about on the long drive home.'

'Seriously, how did you do the trick with the centaur?'

'During our discussion I have been embedding equestrian terminology with alliteration and you have been hearing words like gallop and conformation. In parallel, when we were creating the visualisation of you entering the stage to jeopardise the suspense of your storytelling, you were holding a good luck charm made of metal, could it be a horseshoe? You had both an acoustic and tactile nudge until that point and we went further with these nudges to your unconscious. When I asked you to name a mythological animal, I forced you to be quick, not allowing you enough time to have second thoughts, and then there was the final manoeuvre, I named some mythological creatures: mermaid – to exclude the obvious and most popular answer – unicorn and pegasus – to lead you to think of a horse.'

'Did you do any other tricks to me without me realising?'

'A more suitable question is whether you did any tricks to yourself without realising! Have you noticed that in the title of our chapter, the lines don't make complete letters; however, the mind's eye completes the letters and knows what they should be or at least what they think they should be!'

'I hadn't noticed and, even if I had, I would probably have considered it a typographical misprint! That magical element was camouflaged in the script! Were there more?'

On Bow and Exit

'Maybe. There could have been. Maybe not! In any case, the greatest magical effect of all will be when all these creative practices from the world of illusion are applied to enchant educational settings, when the interdisciplinary art of magic inspires collaborative learning schemes and when the methodologies used in the art to engage with the audience serve the purposes of educational leadership protocols!'

'This discussion has only begun, and we can create an impact as we move this forward together. Who should join our chat?', you say as you find the doorknob on the wall and open a gate to the driveway behind the theatre. It is dawn and there is a lot to think during the long drive home!

References

Bagnoli, F., Guarino, A., & Pacini, G. (2019). Teaching physics by magic. *Physics Education*, *54*(1), art. 015025. https://doi.org/10.1088/1361-6552/aaed62

Banachek. (2011). *Psychological subtleties*. Magic Inspirations.

Calero Valdez, A., Ziefle, M., & Sedlmair, M. (2018). Studying biases in visualization research: Framework and methods. In G. Ellis (Ed.), *Cognitive biases in visualizations* (pp. 13–27). Springer International Publishing. https://doi.org/10.1007/978-3-319-95831-6_2

Curzon, P., & McOwan, P. W. (2008). Engaging with computer science through magic shows. *ACM SIGCSE Bulletin*, *40*(3), 179–183. https://doi.org/10.1145/1597849.1384320

Demacheva, I., Ladouceur, M., Steinberg, E., Pogossova, G., & Raz, A. (2012). The applied cognitive psychology of attention: A step closer to understanding magic tricks. *Applied Cognitive Psychology*, *26*(4), 541–549. https://doi.org/10.1002/acp.2825

Ekroll, V., Svalebjørg, M., Pirrone, A., Böhm, G., Jentschke, S., van Lier, R., Wagemans, J., & Høye, A. (2021). The illusion of absence: How a common feature of magic shows can explain a class of road accidents. *Cognitive Research: Principles and Implications*, *6*(1), art. 22. https://doi.org/10.1186/s41235-021-00287-0

Ferreira, J. F., & Mendes, A. (2014). The magic of algorithm design and analysis: Teaching algorithmic skills using magic card tricks. In *Proceedings of the 2014 conference on innovation & technology in computer science education* (pp. 75–80). Association for Computing Machinery. https://doi.org/10.1145/2591708.2591745

Fox Eades, J. M. (2005). *Classroom tales: Using storytelling to build emotional, social and academic skills across the primary curriculum*. Jessica Kingsley Publishers.

Ganson, L. (2011). *The annotated magic of Slydini*. Tony Slydini.

Hilas, C. S., & Politis, A. (2014). Motivating students' participation in a computer networks course by means of magic, drama and games. *SpringerPlus*, *3*(1), art. 362. https://doi.org/10.1186/2193-1801-3-362

Kanawati, N., Woods, A., & Hawass, Z. (2011). *Beni Hassan: Art and daily life in an Egyptian province*. American University in Cairo Press.

Kuhn, G., Amlani, A. A., & Rensink, R. A. (2008). Towards a science of magic. *Trends in Cognitive Sciences*, *12*(9), 349–354. https://doi.org/10.1016/j.tics.2008.05.008

Lin, J.-L., Cheng, M.-F., Chang, Y.-C., Li, H.-W., Chang, J.-Y., & Lin, D.-M. (2014). Learning activities that combine science magic activities with the 5E instructional model to influence secondary-school students' attitudes to science. *EURASIA Journal of Mathematics, Science and Technology Education*, *10*(5), 415–426. https://doi.org/10.12973/eurasia.2014.1103a

Maskelyne, J. N. (1876). *Modern spiritualism: A short account of its rise and progress, with some exposures of so-called spirit media*. University of Michigan Library.

McCormack, A. J. (1990). *Magic and showmanship for teachers*. Ideas Factory.

Moss, S. A., Irons, M., & Boland, M. (2017). The magic of magic: The effect of magic tricks on subsequent engagement with lecture material. *British Journal of Educational Psychology*, *87*(1), 32–42. https://doi.org/https://doi.org/10.1111/bjep.12133

Myers, T. A., Maibach, E. W., Roser-Renouf, C., Akerlof, K., & Leiserowitz, A. A. (2013). The relationship between personal experience and belief in the reality of global warming. *Nature Climate Change*, *3*(4), 343–347. https://doi.org/10.1038/nclimate1754

Pollock, T. G. (2021). *How to use storytelling in your academic writing: Techniques for engaging readers and successfully navigating the writing and publishing processes.* Edward Elgar Publishing.

Pollock, T. G., & Bono, J. E. (2013). Being Scheherazade: The importance of storytelling in academic writing. *Academy of Management Journal*, *56*(3), 629–634. https://doi.org/10.5465/amj.2013.4003

Priest, C. (1997). *The prestige*. Orion.

Rensink, R. A., & Kuhn, G. (2015, February 2). A framework for using magic to study the mind. *Frontiers in Psychology*. https://doi.org/10.3389/fpsyg.2014.01508

Richter, C. P. (1957). On the phenomenon of sudden death in animals and man. *Psychosomatic Medicine*, *19*(3), 191–198.

Stroop, J. R. (1935). Studies of interference in serial verbal reactions. *Journal of Experimental Psychology*, *18*(6), 643–662. https://doi.org/10.1037/h0054651

Tognazzini, B. (1993). Principles, techniques, and ethics of stage magic and their application to human interface design. In *Proceedings of the SIGCHI conference on human factors in computing systems* (pp. 355–362). ACM Press. https://doi.org/10.1145/169059.169284

Vidler, D., & Levine, J. (1981). Curiosity, magic, and the teacher. *Education*, *101*(3), 273–275.

Vroom, V. H. (1964). *Work and motivation*. Wiley.

Wiseman, R., & Watt, C. (2020). Conjuring cognition: A review of educational magic-based interventions. *PeerJ*, *8*, 1–17. https://doi.org/10.7717/peerj.8747

Yang, Y.-T. C., & Wu, W.-C. I. (2012). Digital storytelling for enhancing student academic achievement, critical thinking, and learning motivation: A year-long experimental study. *Computers & Education*, *59*(2), 339–352. https://doi.org/10.1016/j.compedu.2011.12.012

CHAPTER 23

Hallå STEAM!

A Performative Recasting of History, Science, Art, Language and Education

Kristóf Fenyvesi and Christopher Brownell

Overture

In 1736–1737 the French mathematician Pierre Louis Moreau de Maupertuis (1698–1759) and the Swedish astronomer Anders Celsius (1701–1744) travelled together to Lapland or, more precisely, to the Tornio River Valley, to settle the scientific question of the shape of the Earth, and Celsius was there to test his new ideas for a thermometer. This chapter tells the story of how the historians of mathematics and science, Osmo Pekonen and Johan Stén from Finland, use this piece of scientific history to reconnect contemporary culture to less known scientific and artistic contributions from the 'Age of Enlightenment'. With a commitment to multi-sensory exposition, these contemporary researchers, together with the education expert, Kristóf Fenyvesi launched the *Hallå* [Hello] *STEAM* program, a series of Swedish-Finnish STEAM learning days in Finnish schools, offering various STEAM (integrated science, technology, engineering, arts and mathematics) activities, partially based on historical connections between art and science in the Swedish-Finnish context. They took on the persona of eighteenth-century scholars, artists, clergy and more so they could provide Finnish schoolchildren an unusual experience of their own Finnish-Swedish intellectual history. An interview with one of the key figures of the *Hallå STEAM* project, Osmo Pekonen, is presented to highlight the story of a researcher working towards the goal of legitimacy but doing so against the grain of traditional research and dissemination practice.

Modern academia celebrates, encourages and demands the specialisation and silo-ing of its members. Furthermore, its common mode of distribution, the journal article, has become a stultifying form that pares the humanity out of the findings. This is a story of an educational approach that is committed to sidestepping the colourless presentation of carefully formatted written words and graphs. This story too will be told in a form we intend to fit the atypical Swedish-Finnish schooldays, as a play in several short acts.

 | DOI:10.1163/9789004516069_031

Prelude

The curtain of our little theatre parts, the lights dim, and Douglas Hofstadter, the author of *Gödel, Escher, Bach: An eternal golden braid* (Hofstadter, 1979) is playing *The art of the fugue* on the *Lautenwerck*[1] *of Recurring Time*. From the complete darkness, two self-illuminated figures appear. Slowly it is revealed that these two are, in fact, speaking candlesticks and the two authors of this paper!

One begins speaking from stage-right:

> *Bonsoir, mesdames et messieurs.* Greetings and salutations to all who have joined us here. Let me introduce myself and my compatriot. We are the Brothers Lumière! We are delighted to be your hosts during this journey through time, space, science, art, music and thought. I am Christopher [Brownell] and this, my brother-in-work, Kristóf [Fenyvesi].

Kristóf speaks with marionette-like gestures from stage left: '*Salut à tout le monde!* Welcome to our little play! Rendered here, before your eyes this very night, will be tales of old and new, tales of wonders, measures, travels and discoveries. *Voilà!*' With these last words Kristóf's hands wave widely and cause the flame on his head to flicker and dance brightly.

Christopher now joins in: '*Eh bien, chers spectateurs!* Seen here before you will be a short play in four brief acts, all overlaid, one upon the other …' While he says this, the fugue rises to a near tumult then fades again to the background. He continues:

> Investigations will be described here, investigations into how knowledge of the past is explored in the present, how learning this knowledge may overtake the mind of the learner to the point where they must embody that knowledge so as to reconcile with their own present!

The music fades a bit here, but never stops.

---

1 The *lautenwerck* was a keyboard instrument with gut strings that produced sounds like a lute. Johann Sebastian Bach is known to have written several pieces specifically for the *lautenwerck*; however, none of these instruments survived the nineteenth century. Today Bach's *lautenwerck* compositions are usually played on harpsichords. In a video Dongsok Shin, a member of the New York–based baroque ensemble Rebel, which also visited Finland, introduces a modern reproduction of this lost instrument and performs Bach's *Prelude, fugue and allegro in E-Flat Major*, BWV 998: https://youtu.be/ZDJfmUZPX_A

Kristóf says: '*Oui, mon ami*, behold the scene ... *Excusez-moi!* A twenty-first-century Finnish salon?! *Oui!* Patterned after similar events of the eighteenth century. A main character emerges: a tall man with a fresh intellectual air.'

Chris and Kristóf together:

> Now dear spectator, join us in what follows ... a *story* of personal journeys to what becomes a life-changing approach to the conducting and communication of research. A rebel if you will, not content to be bound by the strictures of the academy, the ossified edifice that it has become ...

The music rises as the flames upon the heads of the brothers flare to fullness. The two shout together: 'We will meet again dear patrons. Until then, be our guests!' Suddenly all the parts of the fugue collide, the *lautenwerck* ends on a crashing *sforzando*, and Hofstadter jumps off his seat and blows out the talking candlesticks.

The play is about to begin, and the curtains open wide.

Act 1

We see three figures, two resembling the candlesticks. The other is a man with an aristocratic air, impeccable posture, and a well-trimmed moustache. The classic mathematician of a bygone era.

The guiding and relit candlesticks step in from the wings. Christopher speaks first as the curtains open: 'Here we see our character in conversation with two dimly lit interviewers: Kristóf ...'

Kristóf takes over: '... and Christopher. The interviewee is dressed in eighteenth-century finery. Let us listen in on him ...'

The flames atop the candlesticks dim as they slip again into the wings.

What follows is a transcript of parts of an interview with Osmo Pekonen, who can be seen here (Figure 23.1). in the role of the Swedish statesman, diplomat and poet Count Gustav Philip Creutz, born in Finland in 1731.

Christopher Brownell (C. B.) and Kristóf Fenyvesi (K. F.): Could you tell us, what was your original plan going into university? What did you see yourself doing after you received your PhD?

Osmo Pekonen (O. P.): I was excelling at school in Finland in the 1970s, always getting the best marks in all subjects, except sports. On the other hand, I was a shy and solitary spectacled guy, a somewhat frail figure. At age 18 and 19, I represented Finland in the International Olympics of Mathematics, in Bucharest and in London, respectively.

FIGURE 23.1
Osmo Pekonen's portrait in the role of Count Gustav Philip Creutz (Painting by Svetlana Ruoho, *Portrait d'Osmo Pekonen en homme des Lumières*, 2018)

Those achievements were a great source of satisfaction – they were also my first trips abroad. I wanted to do something intellectually demanding, so I went to university to study mathematics. However, the university from day one was a great disappointment to me: people there were not as I had imagined; clearly, I had not landed in Plato's academy. I felt somewhat disillusioned, even depressed, and simply wanted to get away – but how and where? I studied diligently, nonetheless, and achieved the lower degrees in mathematics in record time. I took, as a pastime, some courses in humanities, as well: Latin, history, philosophy. Surprisingly enough, military service, which interrupted my first university years, was a highly positive experience for me as I realised that I was, physically, not nearly as unfit as I had imagined at school. I remember carrying the machine guns of several other guys who couldn't do it anymore in tough circumstances, and I became a reserve officer, which felt like a reassuring achievement, given that my father had been a combat officer who saw harsh action in World War II. Then, in 1984, a unique opportunity opened to me: I won a generous scholarship to study abroad. Having learnt elegant French at school, I chose to go to Paris, which I knew to be a centre of highly sophisticated mathematics. I flourished in Paris, where I stayed for five years; the city of light appeared to me to be a huge open-air university where one could absorb culture everywhere: not only in the lecture halls but also in the streets and cafes, museums and theatres, bookshops and concerts. I was curious about everything and I made a lot of excursions to the French provinces, sometimes by bicycle. Appropriately enough, given my military experience, one of my schools in France was École polytechnique, a military academy (their West Point, founded by Napoleon), which has produced a great number of famous scientists, among whom was Henri Poincaré, the universal genius.

However, I stayed there just as a civilian guest scholar; I never wore a French uniform. I came to know, by acquaintance at least, some of the greatest mathematicians of the twentieth century – and I soon realised that I will never ever be able to think like they do. Even so, I gathered enough intellectual capital to survive – and even to thrive – for some time in a highly competitive environment, whereas, in reality, I have never made a really fundamental discovery. In 1988, when the craze around string theory was at its height, I wrote a modest doctoral thesis related to it, pretending that I actually understood something about 'The Einstein field equation in a multi-dimensional universe' (which is the title of a paper of mine from that period, published in the *Journal of General Relativity and Gravitation* [Pekonen, 1988]). Having spent another year as a guest scholar in the premises of the Royal Academy of Sciences of Sweden, I reluctantly returned to Finland in 1990, at age 30, and felt just as depressed as when I first entered the university. I vegetated for ten years in a maths department, which mainly felt like a shelter or refuge to me. I occasionally published little things in mathematics as I was supposed to do, but more and more often found myself secretly dabbling with totally different topics in the humanities; for instance, I translated *Beowulf* into Finnish (Pekonen & Tolley, 1999) – which had never been done in verse before – in a great collaboration with PhilD Clive Tolley, an Old English scholar at Oxford where I had a memorable stay. Ten years drifted away in the maths department, but I cannot remember almost anything about what I did as a mathematician during that time period. On the other hand, by the year 2000, I had published so much in the humanities that I had made a name for myself as something of a polymath. So they kicked me out of the maths department. I had to find something else to do in life, but what? I had what I considered a pretty useless PhD in math.

It took me another ten years to rectify this issue and gain another doctorate in the humanities. I wrote my second doctoral thesis in French on a historical topic, and happily enough it gained me a prize from the Institut de France, and corresponding memberships in a number of French academies as well. A popular version of the thesis was published in Paris (Pekonen & Vasak, 2014).

∴

The stage lights dim as our candlestick narrators return from the wings. Kristóf speaks: 'Oh yes, brother. Here we see the beginnings of our main character. He tells us stories of how he felt out of place at times and how that disquiet drove him to further discovery.'

Christopher: 'Indeed it is true, younger brother. Even though an accomplished mathematician and performing his academic roles superbly, he found that limits were placed on his creativity, and his desired contributions were stifled and forced into a mould that he was not happy with.'

Stage lights extinguish, curtains close … the narrators remain.

Act 2

Kristóf: 'What comes next, *mesdames et messieurs*? What comes next ...?'

Christopher:

> What you will see, dear patrons, will be the solution for the age-old problem: the shape of the Earth – is it like a lemon (elongated or stretched at the poles) or a mandarin (oblate and squashed or flattened at the poles)? This question occupied the minds and caused many heated arguments among the world's scientific community in the eighteenth century. The French Academy of Sciences sent two expeditions out to the ends of the Earth – one to the equator and one to the Arctic Circle to solve this problem. In 1736 Pierre-Louis Moreau de Maupertuis acted as a chief of the French Geodesic Mission sent to Tornio River Valley, Lapland to measure the length of a degree of an arc of the meridian.

Kristóf:

> During this time Finland was a part of the Kingdom of Sweden and a place of rich cultural interactions with the rest of Europe. *Bien entendu*, Maupertuis' Swedish friend, the astronomer Anders Celsius joined the mission to test his new ideas for a thermometer.
>
> King Louis XV of France financed the expedition that carried out the measurements in only one year, an amazing achievement considering the instruments and methods of the time.

Christopher: 'There are new characters on the stage here. Maupertuis and Celsius are staring at the horizon, and in the background scientific instruments, skis and weapons are being loaded onto a reindeer sleigh.'

Kristóf and Christopher together: 'Let's listen in as Maupertuis describes how he came to this particular project.'

The narrators lean in towards centre stage, cocking a hand behind an ear to hear the conversation.

Figure 23.2 shows Maupertuis and Celsius, whose experiences drew attention to the magical north, with northern lights, white summer nights, the home of fairies and Nordic hospitality.

C. B. & K. F.: Given that you are a trained mathematician, what were the causes of your growing interest in the history of mathematics and associated scientific endeavours?

O. P.: I have some family antecedents relating me to some colourful figures of the eighteenth century, again mainly in the military field. Indeed, I was born

FIGURE 23.2 Maupertuis (left: Osmo Pekonen) and Celsius' (right: Johan Stén) experiences drew attention to the magical north (Photo: Axel Straschnoy, *La Figure de la Terre*, courtesy of Kolme Perunaa)

in the Finnish province of Savo, which in the eighteenth century had a whole population of French-speaking aristocratic officers guarding our frontier with Russia. They left their mark in the local culture, which explains why the Age of Enlightenment so strongly appeals to me. The upper classes in the eighteenth century in Finland – then a part of the Kingdom of Sweden – were largely French speaking, which suited my life experience and my attitudes towards the daily routines at the university. I started veering off to a rather oneiric existence, channelling a widely educated eighteenth-century figure somehow reincarnated in the twenty-first century. In Paris I acquired an eighteenth-century outfit complete with wig and tricorne, and also found good use for the two doctoral swords that I have been solemnly awarded. Using my costume, I have participated as an amateur actor in various reconstructions of historical events, playing the roles of famous scientists, poets and philosophers of bygone ages. Once an ancient battle with very real troops provided by the Finnish army was re-enacted and I was no less than Count Curt von Stedingk (1746–1837), the Marshall of Sweden.

Strong associations with figures of the past have certainly inspired me in my writing; I have written no less than 2000 pages about the single figure of Pierre Louis Moreau de Maupertuis (1698–1759), a French mathematician (Pekonen, 2018), whom I have also embodied in a movie by Axel Straschnoy, *La figure de la terre* (Figure 23.2; Pekonen & Straschnoy, 2016).[2]

∴

2 The trailer for the movie is accessible on YouTube: https://youtu.be/WXXkCaN2lGM

The curtains close and the narrators enter from the wings, flames glowing and fluttering as if in a breeze. Kristóf speaks: 'Here we have seen our academic, needing to show a different side to his practice, one that is embedded in an eighteenth-century ethos of enlightenment. He comes to new understandings and connections through this process.'

Christopher: 'Now, let us hear how he sought to alter his approach to the work itself.'

Act 3

The narrators sweep their arms wide, and the curtain opens. The mathematician is in conversation with Christopher and Kristóf, as before. Behind them, obscured by gauze as if in a dream or memory, we see the expedition gathering around a triangulation point. Several people are working on setting up the scientific equipment to take the measurements.

Figure 23.3 shows a piece of Maupertuis and Celsius' writings, which also included detailed information about the housing, relationships and lives of the people living close to the Arctic Circle in the Tornio River Valley.

FIGURE 23.3 Maupertuis and Celsius' results also included detailed information about the people living in the Tornio River Valley (Photo: Axel Straschnoy, *La Figure de la Terre*, courtesy of Kolme Perunaa)

The interview carries on in the foreground and this is what can be heard over the other action on stage.

C. B. & K. F.: What has sparked your particular interest in the personalities of the historical characters you seek to embody in your work?

O. P.: The case of Maupertuis is very clear: he was a mathematician like me, and he travelled to Finnish Lapland in 1736 to measure the shape of the Earth.

He was also a military man, a King's musketeer. I had done something very similar during my military service a long time ago. Indeed, I served as a measurement officer in Lapland, and in those distant days – before the advent of GPS – we measured the positions of the artillery with age-old methods using the stars, just like Maupertuis did in the winter of 1736–1737. And I have performed the roles of so many other figures, as well. I was Rousseau in a re-enactment on the occasion of his tricentenary in 2012, and there exists a portrait of me (Figure 23.1) in character as the poet and diplomat Count Gustav Philip Creutz (1731–1785), whose sophisticated alexandrines in Swedish I have successfully translated into Finnish.

C. B. & K. F.: You appear to be highly focused on the persons behind the big ideas or dispassionate concepts that are typically more the focus in the scientific and broader community. What is it that fascinates you about them? How has this focus impacted and/or refocused your own research and goals for your work?

O. P.: In mathematics, only the big ideas really matter, and they are as rare as jewels. The rest is but polishing, and I'm afraid that's the only thing that I have been doing as a mathematician: polishing some jewels.

However, I have faithfully kept publishing something in mathematics every year since, for more than four decades; more recently, merely popular papers, but I have at least tried to popularise some of the big ideas. I write for fellow mathematicians as one of the editors of the *Mathematical Intelligencer*, a flagship magazine published by Springer.

∴

Curtains close, end scene. The narrators are seen sitting on the edge of centre stage, their flames calmly swaying in the breeze from the air conditioning. Christopher swings his feet from side to side and speaks as though to Kristóf: 'You know, brother, it seems as though he is also able to maintain an active, mainstream, academic life.'

Kristóf replies, first to his brother but gradually turning to the audience: 'Indeed he is, the mathematician submitting a dutiful mathematical treatise in a respectable journal annually. *Vive la différence!* But do you detect the underlying subtext within him that cries out for freedom?'

Act 4

Our narrators rise to their feet and stroll about the forestage while speaking. Christopher speaks first, while moving casually about this space: 'We come to the end of our little dalliance into the past. We hear now how he perceives himself and this endeavour.'

Figure 23.4 shows Maupertuis and Celsius, when they have finished their formidable computations. The mission was thereby successfully accomplished. Pekonen as Maupertuis and Stén as Celsius are demonstrating their discovery to Finnish schoolchildren in Swedish (Figure 23.5). This is a moment of celebrating the past and its rediscovery in the present. The narrators grab the centre curtain, having converged there, and pull it back. Pekonen is all that is seen. The voices of the interviewers, as if disembodied, come from backstage to ask the questions. Our character addresses the audience directly.

FIGURE 23.4 Figures don't lie (Photo: Axel Straschnoy, *La Figure de la Terre*, courtesy of Kolme Perunaa)

C. B. & K. F.: For you, it appears that research is not merely something you acquire or observe; rather you immerse yourself into the topic and persona associated with these ideas. Again, what drives this sort of 'rebellious' approach?

O. P.: As I said, the university from day one – which was in 1979 – has been to me, a refuge. From the point of view of the administration, I have always been nothing but a total misfit, even if a highly productive one. There has never been a box where I fit, so I have drifted through my academic life as a 'man without qualities', to refer to Musil's (2015) novel where, by the way, the protagonist is also a mathematician engaged with dilemmas of philosophy and the culture of

FIGURE 23.5
Johan Stén (left) and Osmo Pekonen (right) (Photo: courtesy of Kristóf Fenyvesi)

the past and his own time. I think it would even have been impossible to fix me with a needle, like a dead butterfly in a collection.

C. B. & K. F.: This immersion causes you to cross the borders between merely understanding, to actually 'becoming' the person. What were the stages in your career where you feel as though you had a choice to go further into this method? Do you have any specific instances you can recall where you know you chose to go deeper into these arenas?

O. P.: When I translated the dreamlike poetry of Count Creutz – a good friend of Benjamin Franklin by the way, during their common days in Paris – I knew that I needed to become almost his reincarnation. His poetic realm is Arcadia, an ethereal neverland, but I feel like I have really been there.

C. B. & K. F.: Are you seeking to recreate for yourself an experience of that original point of creation/discovery by seeking a holistic 'sensuous' experience of the 'Enlightenment period'? Do you seek to cause that sensuous spark in your audience?

O. P.: No, thank you, I don't wish my body or anyone else's to be transported to the eighteenth century. I certainly prefer to visit a twenty-first-century dentist, for instance, rather than an eighteenth-century one. A central figure of our Finnish eighteenth century was King Gustave III, an enlightened ruler, and an elegant and handsome figure – but in real life he lost almost all of his teeth. Everything has changed since the eighteenth century, except its music which is so central in the Lumières Festival created by Marja Rumpunen. The efforts she has taken to recreate these fabulous forgotten eighteenth-century works of art, such as ancient music, dance and opera, have been truly wonderful and pretty unique in Europe. Some of the most famous baroque orchestras of the world have performed in her festival. I think it's mainly through music and poetry that our bodies may resonate with the eighteenth century.

C. B. & K. F.: This non-traditional/rebellious approach to research, is there a broader space for it in the research community? How would you, if you were required to, classify this type of research?

O. P.: Classify? No, thank you. Please leave me alone with your insect collection.

∴

The curtains close as Osmo Pekonen emphasises the word 'collection!' The narrators float down from the rigging in front of the curtains, centre stage. Hofstadter returns to the *lautenwerck* and takes up the fugue once again. Christopher speaks while waving his hands as if to fan his face: 'Well, there you have it, *mesdames et messieurs*, "Don't pin me into your shadowbox of academic form."'

Kristóf joins in: 'Good humour, inspired by great historical characters, a return to a holistic approach to knowing, and a defiance brought on by an authority and a resolve to not be categorised neatly into a box. This is an Enlightenment moment, *n'est-ce pas*?'

The flames atop the heads of the narrators grow suddenly large and extraordinarily bright.

Coda

Quiet settles on the two. Kristóf speaks first, addressing the audience in an even voice:

> Thank you all for your attendance and indulgence during our little play. Seriously for a moment, we'd like to point out that research into historical events and discoveries in a holistic manner has been employed in various settings. Ongoing research and educational outreach using this concept is taking place in Finland at this time under the auspices of the *Hallå STEAM* project. This undertaking by Pekonen, Stén and Fenyvesi has had them travelling from the southern shore to the Arctic Circle with the goal of engaging hundreds of children in problem-solving activities and intellectual treasures from eighteenth-century Finnish and Swedish science and art.

Christopher joins in:

> While today's Finns often look to the nineteenth and early twentieth centuries as a timeframe when the nation came into its own, these intrepid researchers, Pekonen and Stén (whether historical, mathematical or scientific) seek to remind Finland that its roots go deep in the Enlightenment as well, and to not lose sight of the importance of the eighteenth century.

Chris and Kristóf in unison: We leave you with two final images, Pekonen speaking a line as Maupertuis "Was it a deam? Were we all having the same dream? Believe me or not, but we have encountered Maupertuis and Celsius." (Figure 23.6). This then is followed (Figure 23.7) where Pekonen is seen portraying Count Creutz the poet, The white brassard around his left arm as a "king's man," a true royalist. He is pondering the fortress of Sveaborg where, legend has it, that the lilacs here were the first in Finland, brought together with barrels of French gold to finance construction. 'A beautiful poem could be written on this...'

Merci à tout le monde et bonne soirée encore! Kiitos ja nähdään!

FIGURE 23.6
A faint breeze swept through the space. And then, all of a sudden, came the apparition (Photo: Axel Straschnoy, *La Figure de la Terre*, courtesy of Kolme Perunaa)

FIGURE 23.7
Enter Count Creutz, the poet, in a pensive mood (Photo: courtesy of Osmo Pekonen)

References

Hofstadter, D. R. (1979). *Gödel, Escher, Bach: An eternal golden braid.* Basic Books.

Musil, R. (2015). *The man without qualities.* Pan Macmillan.

Pekonen, O. (1988). The Einstein field equation in a multi-dimensional universe. *Journal of General Relativity and Gravitation*, 20, 667–670.

Pekonen, O. (2018). My life in the shape of Maupertuis. *Imagine Math, 6*, 63–74.

Pekonen, O., & Straschnoy, A. (2016). Mathematics meets cinema: La figure de la terre. In *Proceedings of Bridges 2016: Mathematics, music, art, architecture, education, culture* (pp. 461–464). Tessellations Publishing.

Pekonen, O., & Tolley, C. (Trans.). (1999). *Beowulf.* WSOY.

Pekonen, O., & Vasak A. (2014). *Maupertuis en Laponie: À la recherche de la figure de la terre.* Herman.

CHAPTER 24

The Hip-Hopification of Education?

BREIS (Brother Reaching Each Inner Soul)

Introduction

Hip hop is a culture born out of the need to express and create. Hip hop education takes the creative, vibrant energy of hip hop and applies it in the classroom. I'd like to take you on a journey through the different phases of the hip hop work I carry out within education. I will endeavour to take you along with me from the initial contact with a school to after the delivery of a session. Along the way there will be relevant rap quotations, and a look at the internal dialogue between various entities, with the intention of leaving you with a clearer understanding of hip-hopification. We begin at Phase One, the enquiry stage, where teachers investigate how hip hop can be impactful and relevant to their students. Phase Two depicts a meeting of worlds where hip hop 'signs in' and enters education. Phase Three is storytelling, which features strongly in my Hip Hop Literacy program, which aims to make learning more fun and provide an understanding of hip hop, whilst simultaneously improving literacy skills. Phase Four embraces active engagement, which gives students part ownership of the performance and their thoughts and feelings, validating their expression irrespective of spelling and grammar. Phase Five is sharing outstanding students' verses that expose their vulnerability, writing skill and knowledge of self. My rebellious practice is to enter a world, set up my world within it, disrupt, understand, transform and empower in no particular order and then leave a whole new world behind. And that is Phase Six of my work and research – a new world!

Phase One: The Enquiry

Dear Breis,

Hi, my name is *&^$+'? @$%* and I am in charge of Year 5 & 6 in my school. Could I please have some more information re: these workshops? They sound fantastic for our students. What kinds of things do the workshops entail? Could there be a focus on the language within rap music as well as perception?

 | DOI:10.1163/9789004516069_032

Please feel free to contact me on this email address.
I look forward to hearing from you

Regards
*&^$+'? @$%

Dear *&^$+'? @$%,

Thank you for your email. The Hip Hop Literacy workshops look at what goes into creating a rap verse. The poetic devices used, a history of the art form, some written exercises and performances from the students and myself. We can work with up to four groups in a day.

Please let me know how many groups you'd like to take part during the day. Once you are happy to go ahead, I will send a booking form for you to fill in.

King regards
Breis

This continues until the school and I are both in agreement. I send a booking form, which is filled and returned along with a list of needed equipment and resources. This is mainly a microphone, PA system, USB port for a PowerPoint presentation, pens and paper. This then takes us to Phase Two.

Phase Two: A Meeting of Worlds

As an artist, I live in my own world. It's chaotic, rhythmical, exciting and mathematical. When I'm invited into another world, I take note of how that world operates and find a way of still operating the way I do but within the restrictions of said new world. As I approach the school I'll be working in, I remind myself of why I'm there.

Hip Hop and the MC

'It's the foundation of every nation, but what is the true meaning of education?' asked the MC.

Hip hop had been pacing up and down. On hearing the question, he paused and looked up and ahead as if looking into the future.

'Education is derived from the Latin word "educere" or "educare", which means to train or mould. It also means to draw out or to know', he replied.

'It sounds like education is there to guide us, or find what is already inside us', rapped the MC.

'In a way it is. Education draws out the internal hidden talent of a child or person. In the broader meaning it is what equips us to handle life.'

'I see how you flow and show what you know, but what has education got to do with me though?' interrogated the MC.

'In 1833, the British government made education compulsory for children working in factories (Factory Act 1833). They realised the more educated a nation gets, the more powerful it can become. When I was formed my purpose was to educate and to empower. When you were formed it was to educate others.' Hip Hop paused and looked the MC dead in the eye. 'You are more than what you think you are.'

'I was born to put knowledge of self over a beat, to educate disenfranchised youth on the street', the MC replied in agreement.

'And there's still more work for us to do', said Hip Hop, placing their hand on the MC's shoulder.

In my own life, education was always a priority of my strict Nigerian parents. It was drummed into my siblings and I that education was the most important thing and the one thing that would make our lives a lot easier in the future. I schooled in London until the age of eight and then lived in Nigeria for the next six years. I found the difference in teaching styles difficult and took a while to adjust. When I returned to London as a teenager, I had to readjust to the UK's style of teaching. It was a bit of a car wreck. How I got through my General Certificate of Secondary Education (GCSE), A Levels (Advanced Level qualifications) and a Bachelor of Science degree is still a mystery to me.

I'm greeted by the receptionist and asked to sign in to their world. As I sign in, I have officially entered this new world. I'm taken to a space where the workshop will occur, and I begin to set up equipment and rearrange the space to accommodate the activities I have set for them. I set up my world within theirs – hip hop within education. The mic is on and tested, the volume of the background beat is adjusted to match the volume of the mic. Then I wait for the students to arrive and to be introduced to them. The students arrive with looks of curiosity and intrigue. They settle down in their seats, looking at me, wondering what's in store. The teacher introduces me to the 200 seated students. I take centre stage and begin.

Phase Three: Storytelling

From as far back as a four-year-old I can remember always having a passion for writing and performing. This steadily grew throughout college and university and in the years after graduating when I decided to become a full-time artist.

One night after performing at a venue in Brixton, a poet friend of mine by the name of Malika Booker pointed out that the way I interacted with the audience would translate really well in the classroom. She proceeded to explain the work she did as a poet within education and encouraged me to think about running workshops. It seemed like a million miles away from what I believed to be doable and I abandoned the notion until a year later. This was when I decided to quit my regular job and make a living as an artist. I figured I could facilitate workshops whilst I was still getting my music career off the ground. I shadowed other spoken word artists who worked in schools, developed my style of delivery and in a few months I began delivering rap and poetry workshops in primary and secondary schools across the UK.

I combined my love of hip hop with my passion for education and devised a program called Hip Hop Literacy through my organisation Student of Life. The aim was to make learning more fun, and provide an understanding of hip hop whilst simultaneously improving literacy skills. Through the art of rap and movement, I was able to engage with hard-to-reach students. I got students creating raps around different topics and subjects. We published anthologies, shot music videos and had grand performances in front of an audience as outcomes for them. It proved to be a huge success with the children, teachers and parents alike. I would soon come to know this as hip hop education and I realised there were practitioners in America using this same approach. One professor in particular from Columbia University by the name of Chris Emdin was steeped deeply into the practice of using hip hop in the school curriculum. On Twitter, I came across a group of teachers and practitioners whose method of teaching was influenced by hip hop under the hashtag #HipHopEd. It was a community I was happy to be a part of and contribute towards. It reinforced the importance of the work I was doing and confirmed I was on the right path. I went on to further develop creative tools to engage students and transform learning experiences.

A few things I noticed along the way:

- Students got excited seeing an actual rapper/practitioner in their class. It made what they were learning even more real.
- It is important to dispel negative stereotypes around rap music.
- Rapping in other languages besides English, made EAL (English as an additional language) students feel included and empowered. I did this often, rapping in English, Yoruba and Pidgin English.
- There was a high level of engagement from students who normally didn't produce much.
- The growth in the students' confidence as a result of their participation was visible.

Hip is to know, it's a form of intelligence
To be hip is to be update and relevant
Hop is a form of movement; you can't just observe a hop
You gotta hop up and do it. Hip and hop is more than music
Hip is the Knowledge; Hop is the Movement
Hip and Hop is intelligent movement
(*KRS-One and Marley Marl, 2007*)

The MC & the Student

'What is hip hop?' the wide-eyed student asked the MC.

The Master of Ceremony was delighted with the question and eager to answer. 'Hip hop is a rebellious culture born out of the need to express and create', he began. 'It was birthed by African Americans and Latin Americans in the Bronx, New York in the 70s' (Chang, 2007).

'I thought it was a type of dance', interrupted the student.

'Well, it's more than just a type of dance. Hip hop is rap, it's art, it's an attitude. It gave the young people living in American ghettos a voice. It's a tool for social justice, for some it's a way out of the gang violence and poverty prevalent in their lives. For others it's pure entertainment. Its existence predates its birth, with certain elements existing before being named as they currently are.'

The student was in deep thought, taking in every word of the MC. 'The elements being rapping and dancing?'

'Yes, to be precise it's a combination of DJing, emceeing, graffiti art, and b-boying. There are other elements including beatboxing, street fashion, production, knowledge of self and entrepreneurialism. Each of these elements helped create a purpose for young people and helped them escape the harsh realities they were dealing with. For some participants who were dedicated, consistent and had a flair for their specialised practice, it would become a career.'

The student mentally replayed three words the MC had just mentioned: dedication, consistency and flair.

Phase Four: Active Engagement

Crossing borderlines with broader rhymes
I generate ideas that blow your mind

You see my awesome mind does more than rhyme
I'm thinking all the time with thoughts of mine
My thoughts are 3D and HD, *all combined*
Sharper than the spines on a porcupine
Signed, sealed and delivery is full of imagery
Vividly visualised through my eyes, spoken terrifically
I'm so unique my own shadow can't even mimic me
My visions make me think into infinity
Do things differently with authenticity
And aim high specifically
'cos inside of you and inside of me
There's a genius inside that no one can see
Do you know what you want and who you wanna be?
We're bigger than we think but it's hard to see
(BREIS, *'Think big'*)

After introducing myself and explaining the four main elements of hip hop, I demonstrate what I do by performing one of my songs, 'Think big'. The song is about encouraging people to believe in their capacity to achieve greatness. I teach them how to sing the chorus and encourage them to assist me at the appropriate place. This is important as I am now giving them part ownership of the performance. How good the overall performance turns out to be now depends on them performing well. Hip hop is all about performing, so it's important the students take part in the performance. They begin to loosen up and immerse themselves in the experience, simultaneously preparing themselves for other tasks ahead. After the performance I invite the students to take part in a quick writing exercise.

We look through the text of 'Think big' together and discuss the theme and how that applies to their lives. They discuss their imagination, their ability to dream, the potential they possess and mental health. We look at the imagery, various perspectives and what was interesting about them. We pick out the similes, metaphors, adjectives, the emotive language and observe how and when they are used. I give the class the option of creating their own 'Think big' verse or writing about someone who means a lot to them. After providing them with a few more triggers, the class begins to write. I urge them to focus on their thoughts and feelings as opposed to spelling and grammar. I validate their expression by emphasising that there is no wrong answer, only what they want to express.

Phase Five: Sharing

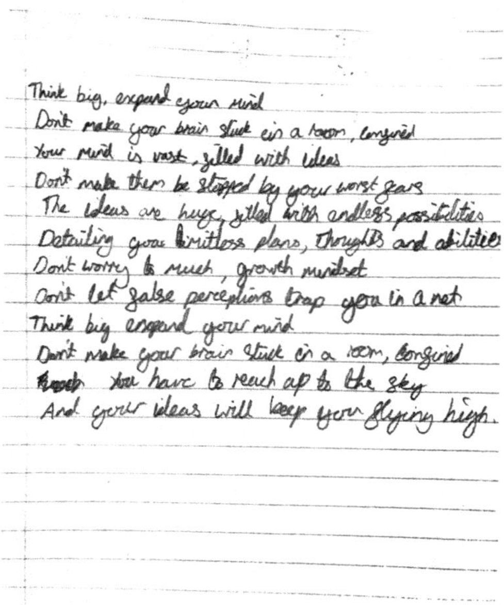

Think big, expand your mind
Don't make your brain stuck in a room, confined
Your mind is vast, filled with ideas
Don't make them be stopped by your worst fears
The ideas are huge, filled with endless possibilities
Detailing your limitless plans, thoughts and abilities
Don't worry to much, growth mindset
Don't let false perceptions trap you in a net
Think big expand your mind
Don't make your brain stuck in a room, confined
You have to reach up to the sky
And your ideas will keep you flying high.

FIGURE 24.1 Think Big verse written by a Year 6 student, Salcombe Primary School

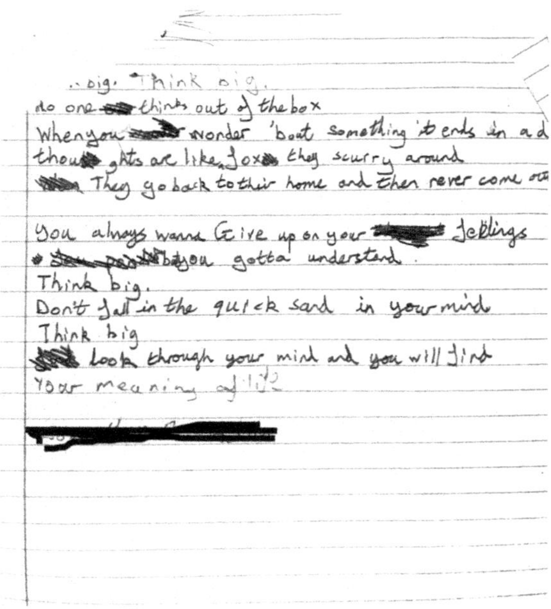

..big. Think big.
No one thinks out of the box
When you wonder 'bout something it ends in a d
thoughts are like fox they scurry around
They go back to their home and then never come out
You always wanna Give up on your feelings
you gotta understand
Think big.
Don't fall in the quick sand in your mind
Think big
look through your mind and you will find
Your meaning of life

FIGURE 24.2 Think Big verse written by Jonathon and Jacob, Year 6, Salcombe Primary School

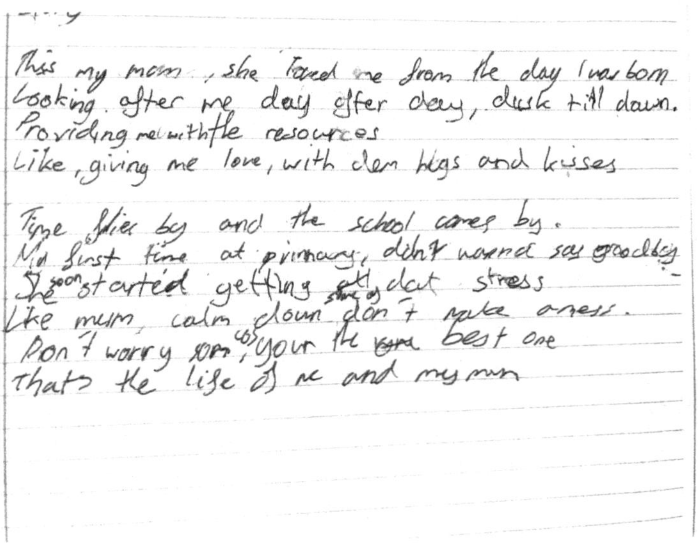
This my mom, she loved me from the day I was born
Looking after me day after day, dusk till dawn.
Providing me with the resources
Like, giving me love, with clem hugs and kisses

Time flies by and the school comes by.
My first time at primary, didn't wanna say goodbye
She soon started getting stressed out stress
Like mum, calm down don't make a mess.
Don't worry mum, cos your the best one
Thats the life of me and my mum

FIGURE 24.3 'Me and my Mum' verse written by Arda, Year 6, Salcombe Primary School

The outcome was an outstanding verse from each student that showed his or her vulnerability, writing skill and knowledge of self.

One by one I encourage each student to share their work in front of the class. Some read it like a poem; some perform it as a rap. They've gone from being the student to now being the MC. I take a back seat and allow the students to give their feedback after each verse they hear.

A young boy puts his hand up to read out his rap. He is easily the tallest boy in the class and looks older than he is. His rap is about his mum. He reads it out, as the class listens intently. He finishes the last sentence, 'that's the life of me and my mum', and the whole class erupts into a cacophony of claps, wows, smiles and even a teary eye from the teacher's assistant can be seen. The students express their delight at the story he has shared about someone who clearly means so much to him and continue to tell him what in particular they enjoyed about his rap. He is seen, his voice is heard, and he is acknowledged and validated.

It's the end of the session and I ask the students what their favourite part of the session was. For some it was hearing a professional artist perform. For some it was what they were able to come up with themselves. For the teachers it was seeing how engaged the students were and how much more they now knew about some of their students.

The MC & the Teacher

The classroom was filled with most of the teachers in the school. There were over 20 teachers in attendance, all eager to share experiences and learn new skills that they could implement in their respective classes. The MC was speaking to them about the importance of creativity in the class. One of the English teachers, a few rows from the front, raised her hand to ask a question: 'Could you tell us a bit more about hip hop education?'

The MC smiled, took a quick look at his notes and proceeded to answer. 'Hip hop education is looking at the creative, vibrant energy of hip hop and applying it in the classroom.'

The MC went on his laptop and pressed play. A hip hop instrumental played through the speakers. He observed the body language of some of the teachers. 'Immediately you heard this music, some of you started bobbing your head. I saw a couple of smiles creep out and some of you tensed up. This is the energy of hip hop. This energy can be used and utilised in many ways', said the MC.

'My approach to conducting workshops in schools is to look at the task at hand through a hip hop lens, specifically that of an MC (rap artist). To some degree, being a good MC is similar to being a good teacher.'

The group laughed. The MC paused and smiled again.

'An MC stands in front of an audience; a teacher stands in front of their class or audience. An MC must command the attention of the crowd; teachers must command the attention of their students. An MC must dazzle with their skills, engage the audience and get them to participate; a teacher must do the same. Interaction and inclusion are integral parts of my stage shows. As much as possible I get my audience to take part in the experience. Hip hop is about participation, so a session should never be one sided. There will be times when things will go wrong on stage and you have to improvise (freestyle); similarly a teacher's lesson plan may not be effective enough in the moment and they will therefore need to think on their feet to keep the lesson alive.'

'It's my job as an MC to gauge an audience and see what's working, what's not and what's missing. To know when to switch gears, when to ask the crowd to repeat after me or rap along with me. To gauge whether they've had enough, whether they need a break, when to get them energised or when to bring the energy levels down to a place of introspection. The legendary GOAT (Greatest Of All Time) MC, Rakim said, "To me, MC means move the crowd" (Eric B. & Rakim, 1986). The way you do that is by connecting with your audience. Being in tune with them, articulating and expressing their views in a way they wish they could. It's about understanding where they're coming from, their surroundings, their culture, their world. With that insight you're able to connect with them and steer them to a place where they can learn in a safe space. My experience as an MC is what I bring to the classroom. It's what I call the hip-hopification of education. It's exciting, transformative and nerve racking all at the same time.'

The MC gauged the energy levels of the room.

'Who's up for a challenge?' he shouted. A few teachers responded. He repeated the question, this time more emphatically.

'Who's up for a challenge?!'

'Me!' They all shouted in response.

'Good ... Every MC has to have a cool stage name. So right now I want you to create yours. Take the letters of your name and turn them into words, until you have a phrase, slogan or mantra that fits you as a person.'

The teachers mumbled their ideas to one another as they grabbed their pens and started scribbling words down.

'You have three minutes to complete the task.'

The beat bellowed in the back as the scribes scribbled their syllables.

With creative intervention, there is a possibility that hard-to-reach students will get excited by lessons, feel like they are intelligent and capable of achieving more than they ever thought. I have so much respect for the amazing work teachers do, and what I do is in no way a critique of their work. It's more of an add-on. I produced the Hip Hop Literacy program to bring something different to a child's learning experience. Some schools have pushed back against what we do. To a few, the mere mention of hip hop throws up negative tropes of misogyny, homophobia, violence, etc. and therefore puts some head teachers off. They see hip hop music only through what the mainstream media machine promotes to the public. 'How can such an unruly element be used in my school?' they ask. I've had other teachers invite us in and realise that not only is the content positive, inspirational and aspirational, but it manages to engage pupils who teachers struggle to reach. What the culture of hip hop does is make your voice count. It makes your words and lived experience matter. It makes you visible in a world that treats you like you're invisible.

Like I said, one of the key approaches to my delivery is connecting with the participants. Meeting them where they're at and understanding their viewpoints and experiences is just as important as what I have to deliver. Their input and perspective are what makes the work work. I had a session in a challenging Pupil Referral Unit and had a workshop with five young men who weren't exactly elated to find themselves in the session. One young man in particular was devoted to letting me know that he wasn't interested and wasn't about to make the session an easy one. I set a writing task and all he kept talking about were his smoking and narcotic activities. Now normally these experiences would be denied, excluded and forbidden, but I saw an opening to connect with him despite my distaste for his obsession. This was a chance to be rebellious in my approach.

Explaining to him the power of metaphors, I encouraged him to write about his 'passion' but to substitute it for something less incriminating like flowers. He began writing; the teacher and teacher's assistant were confused. He finished writing his piece and at the end he couldn't wait to share it with everyone. He relished the fact that everybody praised him for his work, but nobody knew what he was really talking about. This filled him with glee. It wasn't so much the task, it was more about the fact that in this instance, in this environment, his voice was not silenced or dismissed like it normally would be. He was just redirected. When an MC is flowing, they have to flow according to what the beat is doing. Not fight it but flow with it. Similarly, I try to teach according to the energy of the group I have and not resist what they're bringing to the party. Hip hop has always been a voice for the silenced. Alongside punk music, rap is the soundtrack to protests. In the 70s it may have been the Sex Pistol's 'God save the Queen', but in the student protests of December 2010 at Parliament Square it was rapper Lethal Bizzle's song 'Pow! (Forward)' that was the anthem (Hancox, 2011). In America it was Kendrick Lamar's 'Alright' that became the protest song for the Black Lives Matter movement. Rap can be a rallying cry to galvanise people and a middle finger to the establishment and all forms of injustice. In America, it is an essential tool even politicians no longer ignore. It speaks to the masses, cuts through the noise and speaks directly to the people.

> This art form, RAP should be revered and studied in schools the same way the poetry of Shakespeare et al. is still studied. Rap captures the zeitgeist of modern-day trials, tribulations and triumphs of everyday people. (BREIS, 2020, p. 151)

Phase Six: A New World

My rebellious practice is to enter a world, set up my world within it, disrupt, understand, transform and empower in no particular order and then leave a whole new world behind.

Imagine if education could solve most of our world problems today? If we could solve the problems of the world through education, wouldn't that be an amazing and exciting prospect? Yet education isn't being utilised in this way. Ultimately, hip hop education is thinking outside the box to fix a problem, mixing different ideas together, taking something old and making it new.

As practitioners, researchers and educators, it's important to update our systems like we tend to do with our smart phone operating systems. Our models must exhort educationalists to be open-minded in approach, to take into account the diversity of our environments and be inclusive. Over the past twenty years or so, many textbooks in school have been called out for containing racially stereotypical information/propaganda. Textbooks and teaching materials need to be updated and remixed to reflect the times and to promote equity. Some approaches to teaching and learning are antiquated and no longer prepare or enrich their participants as they may once have done.

Education is meant to prepare us for the 'real world', yet many leave educational institutions not knowing much about most things they need to. Things such as how to be in a loving relationship, how to be a parent, keeping personal finances healthy, knowing and understanding who you are, and a myriad of soft skills needed to navigate life and work. If education is there to help us in the 'real world' then surely we need to understand more about ourselves. For me, this is where hip hop can play an important role. One of the pillars of hip hop is *knowledge of self*. Understanding who we are and how to operate in this world has always been part of the program. Making this a fundamental part of learning will be crucial to our future well-being.

Heavenly sent to me so it was meant to be
I'm already mentally who I'm meant to be eventually
They couldn't see this entity's intensity immensity
Didn't invest in me, but that wasn't my destiny
Don't mess with me, God-given energy
To crush my enemy like a centipede, but I'm friendly
the mic is my girl. At 10 to 3, secret assignments to MC
I'll do it for free but first pay my rent for me
I'm ebony and everybody's telling me
How to be, I won't let it be a dent in me
Let me be me, the best in me is yet to be
Don't need an ID card to show you my identity
In a class of my own I tend to be essentially
A student of life, it's elementary
Not me, but a conduit I get to be
The Word in me is next to me; spell my name

This world is full of lies, everybody's in a guise
Despise and diss guys in disguise that spit lies
A bit wise behind my eyes and behind my disguise
I'm a fat guy mistaking MCs for mince pies

Throw your hands in the air, reach for the skies
I rise till I realise: I am the prize
But don't be surprised when I enter-prise
I'm blessed, I'm a blessing, I'm blessing in disguise
Disguised in a body – soul, spirit
My whole lyric no limit, so go get it
Why did he did it? 'cos flows is good for his health
Bona fide Rhymes Exist In Self
(BREIS, *'Identity'*)

References

BREIS. (2020). *Diary of a creative mind.* Student of Life Publishing.

Chang, J. (2007). *Can't stop, won't stop: A history of the hip hop generation.* Ebury Press.

Eric, B., & Rakim. (1986). Eric B. is president [Song]. On *Paid in full.* Zakia Records.

Hancox, D. (2011, February 4). Pow! Anthem for kettled youth. *The Guardian.* https://www.theguardian.com/music/2011/feb/03/pow-forward-lethal-bizzle-protests

KRS-One and Marley Marl. (2007). *Hip hop lives* [Album]. Koch Records.

Part 4: Reflective Questions

Tatjana Dragovic

Linking to Futures of Teaching and Learning

1. What is the level of rebelliousness that is acceptable in our established educational institutions? How would rebelliousness look in your professional practice?

2. Are you aware of your and/or your colleagues' implicit leadership theories? How do they influence educational practices?

3. When was the last time you have contradicted yourself? What would happen if we were to allow ourselves to do that more frequently in educational contexts?

4. How do you recognize and experience radical trust and playfulness in your everyday life? How would teaching and learning practices look and feel if they were to embody radical trust and playfulness? What learning lays in experiences of radical trust and playfulness?

5. What would Hip-Hopification add to your professional practice?

6. What is your relationship like with not-knowing? Imagine education and not-knowing being in a long-lasting and loving relationship. How would we recognize that they are if we were to observe teaching and learning practices?

7. What would magic and illusion add to your professional practice?

8. What can we transfer from the past education to the present education in order to co-create future-making education?

 | DOI:10.1163/9789004516069_033

EPILOGUE

What happened here: Writing with a Rebellious Community

Pamela Burnard, Elizabeth Mackinlay and Trisha McCrae

Abstract

The capacity to write rebelliously, in varying registers and voices, tempos and volumes, as we have seen featured across this book, is boundaryless. As writers, whether within or beyond academia, we simultaneously perform and materialize We-ness and I-ness. We come to you the reader, risk-taking and vulnerable, in the process of writing. For us, all academic writing is/should be a conscious strategy to push boundaries, to disrupt, to rupture conventions. This is so essential, that its very repetition signals the reader to attend both to its message and meaning. So, in this brief and final rebellious act, we move between departing radically from academic writing to arriving at a new academic endeavor; a transaction between reader and text produced by poem-as-event.

DOI:10.1163/9789004516069_034

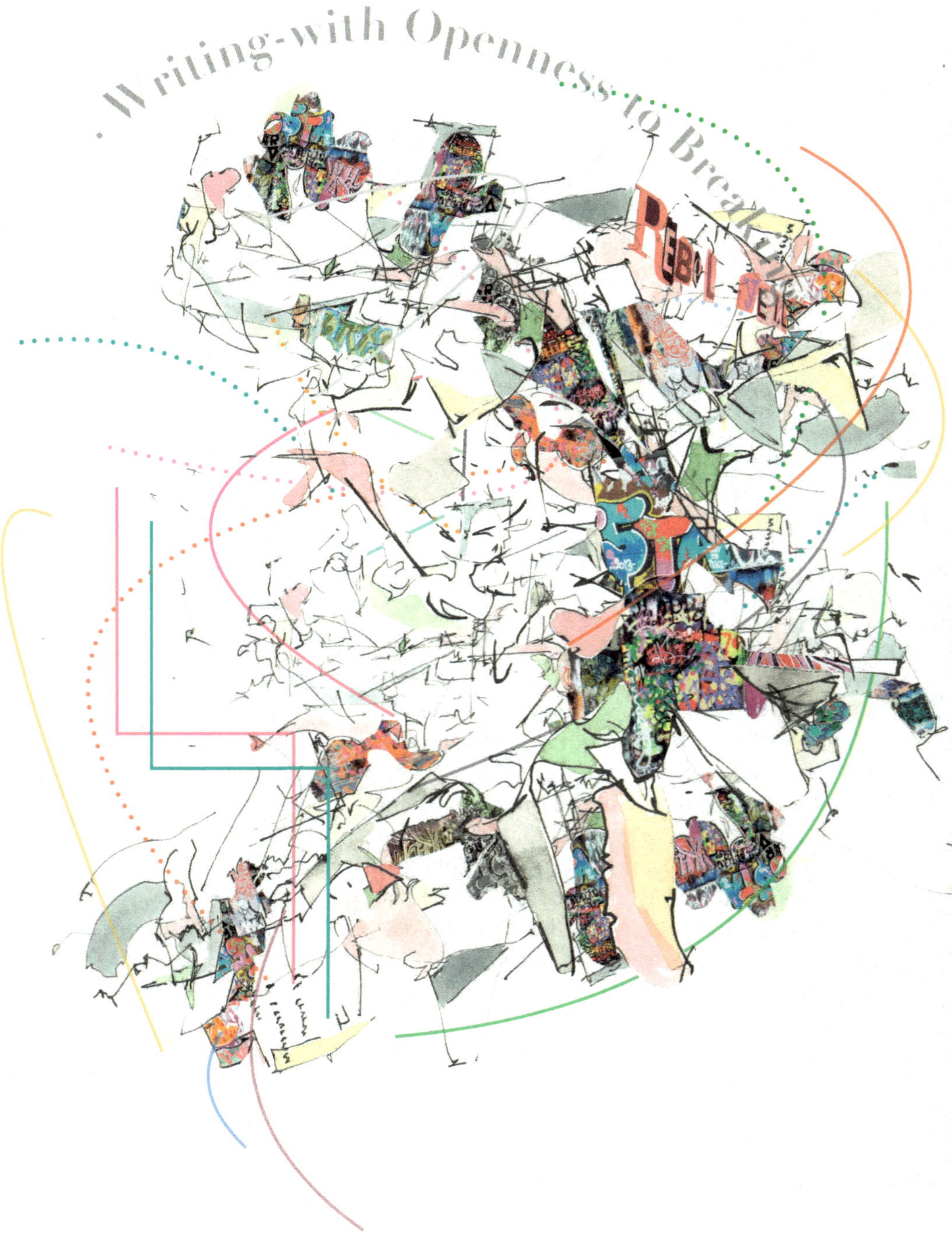
Writing-with Openness to Break

Introduction: What happened here?

There were. What happened here? There were radical departures
there were first drafts that went through a metamorphosis
there were new lines of flight reconfigured—there were.

With/in these. What happened here? With/in these
embodied sites with/in disruption. With/in these ecologies
eruptive encounter. Between y-our being knowing doing—with/in.

Encounters. What happened here? Encounters of rebellious coupling
with research. Encounters of rupture and re-vision critical encounters of
critique in crisis. Encounters and innovative creation—and encounters.

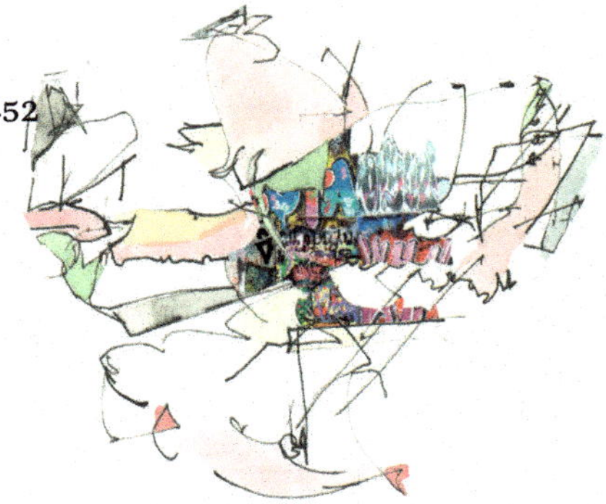

Departures in writings. What happened here? Departures in writings of resistance enacted departures in writing process and flux cutting performingmattering in relationality—departures in writings.

Emergence. What happened here? Emergence of a new way of doing being a writing community in communion, emergence of multiplic-plural-divers-ities of unimagined possibilities —emergence.

Dear reader,

And, we end this book as we began in an epistolatry fashion; it seems an elegant way to close the invitation to open rebellion we have offered you in academic research and writing. Yet, unlike many insurgencies which falter and fizzle out quickly, we see this rebellion as an uprising which is "forever on the way"—in this "comings together of ceaseless composition" in research and writing, we have dared to defamiliarize the ordinary in a search for and in order to give credence to alternative realities.

We hope that you have sensed the *kind* of academic research and writing community we are building; unified, whole, multiple and in complete resistance of the binaries that threaten to separate us. We are a community in so far as we have rebellion in common, and yet, we see ourselves as so much more; we are, in fact, in tight knit, gracious and relational communion *as* "we". Ken Gale (2018) suggests such relationality is one which "can no longer live in domains of practice based upon those sharpened hierarchies that frame the 'researcher' and the 'researched' as somehow separate categories of difference and that are in relationships that are somehow already formed by their discursively constructed, interactive dimensionality". Rooted and routed towards this relational response-and-sense-ability, we have embraced our re-actions, en-actions and pro-actions as researchers and researched and have come full circle—we have arrived, wide awake to the rebellion.

And, if you are in any doubt—and we certainly welcome the principle of uncertainty as rebellious because it too, in the folds of its dark unknowns, is also a location of possibility—return to the cover image of this book and let yourself fall into the waves it creates in your mind. Let yourself permission to be reminded of who and what we are in rebellious academic research and writing communion.

Let yourself be reminded that in the wording and worldings contained within this book, we have gathered our shared potential as a collective force "becoming-with" and taking new" 'lines of flight". Let yourself be inspired, as we are, to new ways of seeing yourself, new ways of encountering new research and writing that perform radical departures from the academy. Let yourself willfully reach your arm, armed and in arms, to stand against those forces—call them what you will, neoliberal and capitalist, colonial and imperial, white and patriarchal—that seek to constrain, contain and cancel us out. Let yourself come with us—come together with us in writing community as communion and weave multiple lines of flight.

And, you see, writing is itself a "line of flight" originating from one voice to another; the writer to reader—from us to you. As authors, in this book we are writing openly, vulnerably and critically about our own conditions and contexts; the ones that matter, that ones that have come to matter most, and those that must matter if what we write about the world is to matter at all. In daring to fly, we have watched each other spread our writing wings—posied on the precipice about to leap into the abyss, beautiful and terrifying in composition, composure and compassion—and have found ourselves learning, living, loving and becoming enlightened by new ways to word the world. And yet we know—for we have felt it deeply in our bodies, hearts and minds—that each time we take to the air there is always the risk of falling and our flight line becoming a faultline. Shaking with fear as pointing and punitive fingers condemn us as failures, our wings wrap around one another and our collective perspectives and practices enables to fly right over the barriers that are placed before us.

And for us, one of the critical issues in the future of teaching and learning is encouraging rebellious researchers to willfully find new ways to do the work that re/turns and frames a line of flight that is wise, loving, relational and non-violent all at once in its orientation to the world. In order to explore these lines of flight, we need to pay attention; we *need* to disrupt, we need to enact new and creative ruptures, we need to actively engage in practices that depart radically from taken-for-granted and common sense significations. This our radical *need* for roots and routes; we unearth them here in lines of flight across, with/in, between and through new disrusive-material-affective terrains, in this case the discursive-material-affective terrains of research and writing in and beyond the academy.

And now, to paraphrase feminist-speculative-science fiction writer Ursula K. Le Guin, "You cannot take what you have not given, and you must give yourself. You cannot buy the rebellion. You cannot make the rebellion. You can only *be* the rebellion. It is in your spirit, or it is nowhere". And let us not forget that we are not alone in this rebellion, we are in *kind* with our more than human kin too. We think and wonder, are you now positioned with us, paused, on the edge of this expanse prepared to research and write in rebellion? How, where, with whom and why might the next communion of rebellious researchers-as-writers-as-readers-as-imaginers exchange and etch ourselves as each other in relationality with scholarly and globally sustainable collaborations of future writing communities? This is our provocation to you: fly, imagine, give, become.

Yours in rebellion,
Pamela, Elizabeth and Trisha.

References

Deleuze, G., & Guattari, F. (1980). *A thousand plateaus: Capitalism and schizophrenia*. Minneapolis, MN: University of Minnesota Press.

Gale, K. (2018). *Madness as methodology: Bringing concepts to life in contemporary theorising and inquiry*. London: Routledge.

Greene, M. (1995). *Releasing the imagination: Essays on education, the arts, and social change*. San Francisco, CA: Jossey-Bass.

Le Guin, U. K. (1974). *The dispossessed*. London: Gollancz.

Rosenblatt, L. (1964). The poem as event. *College English, 26*, 23–25.

Simmons, N., & Singh, A. (2019). (Eds.) *Critical collaborative communities: Academic writing partnerships, groups and retreats*. (Critical Issues in the Future of Learning and Teaching Series, Vol. 17). Leiden, The Netherlands: Brill | Sense.

GOB SPIT
REBEL YELL
Doing Rebellious Research in and Beyond the Academy
INTOXICATING

Glossary

affect there are many ways to conceptualise 'affect' and we offer the following definitions: 1) Emotions and qualitatively experienced feelings seen as vital to shaping social values, gender ideals, and collective groups; 2) a pre-personal intensity that shifts the capacity for a body (of any kind) to think, feel, and act in relation with other bodies. Whether considered as subjective emotion or impersonal intensity, affects circulate amongst bodies in ways that are collectively modulated and yet largely unconscious.

anarchism a political orientation typified by noncompliance with authority of any kind.

agential cuts a concept coined by theoretical physicist Karen Barad to describe 'momentary stabilizations', doings, rather than beings. Agential cuts enact that which is inside and outside of phenomena in a single movement. They are two-folded movements that produce the very boundaries through which something is made 'inside' and 'outside', 'this' and 'that', of the phenomena.

animism an ontological orientation and cultural belief in the inherent 'personhood' or 'soul' of nonhuman entities, such as animals, plants, mountains, rivers, and ritual objects. There are myriad varieties of animism practiced by Indigenous cultures on every continent, with various cultural and spiritual animisms also forming an important facet of many contemporary Asian societies.

appetition a concept coined by process philosopher A. N. Whitehead to describe the creaturely desire for vibrant contrasts and differentials of experience.

art of dosages a phrase used by the philosophers Gilles Deleuze and Felix Guattari to describe the art of calibrating the coefficient of chaos (or 'deterritorialisation') that a body can withstand without destroying itself.

art of life a phrase used by Whitehead to describe the art of orientating oneself toward vivid contrasts of experience.

assemblage developed by Felix Guattari and Gilles Deleuze, assemblage theory frames socio-ecological complexity through an emphasis on the fluidity, exchangeability, and multiplicity of becomings through which entities enter into connectivity and generate new collaborative realities.

attention a concept drawn from the philosophy of French Feminist Simone Weil which means 'waiting, pausing, suspending thought' and thereby 'paying attention'.

being-in-the-world an existential concept which was first introduced by Martin Heidegger and refers to a state of living with a highly meaningful orientation, an existence that aims to achieve personal growth.

becoming Deleuze and Guattari argue that the concept of 'becoming' is not one of imitation or analogy, it is generative of a new mode of existence that is a function of difference rather than resemblances. The process is one of removing the element from its original functions and bringing about new ones.

carnival a traditional celebration carried out every year since the early 19th century on the islands of Trinidad and Tobago, with wide-ranging variations in many cities worldwide. The Trinidadian tradition of Carnival is typified by highly elaborate costumes (‘*mas*’), steelpan orchestras, and ritual stick-fighting, and has historically developed as a vibrant expression of Black resistance to white supremacy and the dominance of European social and political constructs. See also *J'Ouvert.*

composting a philosophical, political and practical process put forward by Donna Haraway for undoing the relations of domination that subordinate nonhuman lives to human interests.

contrast Whitehead's term for the felt-sense of disjunctive togetherness (or ‘clashing intensities’) carried by events.

de/re/territorialization in Deleuze and Guattari's critical theory of goephilosophy, ‘deterritorialization’ is the process by which a social relation of components, a territory, has its current organization and context altered, mutated or destroyed. The components then constitute another new relation and become reterritorialized.

diffraction a concept used by physicists to describe interference patterns generated by a confluence of material forces. The term has achieved a new currency through the work of feminist theorist and physicist Karen Barad, who has drawn theoretical links between diffraction phenomena observed at the quantum level and feminist studies of science, culture, sexuality, and gender.

divination a concept used by education scholar Maggie MacLure to describe speculative inquiry as an apprenticeship with occult signs and events, akin in some ways to witchcraft and other esoteric practices that demand a ‘leap’ into the unknowable.

drabbles short works of fiction of exactly 100 words which explicitly aim to tell a story in a confined space in a way that is short, sharp and snappy.

DRAW a rebellious academic writing movement DRAW (Departing Radically in Academic Writing) movement which began in early November 2019 at the University of Queensland and was led by rebellious daughters of the academy Associate Professor Elizabeth Mackinlay and her doctoral student Karen Madden.

ethico-onto-epistemological the notion of ‘ethico-onto-epistem-ology’ was first coined by physicist-philosopher Karen Barad to point at the inseparability of ethics, ontology and epistemology when engaging in (scientific) knowledge production, with scientific practices, and with the world itself and its inhabitants – human and non-human beings.

extinction the end of a lifeworld, a way of living, a society, an ecosystem, a mode of existence.

FOLleadOWing/folLEADowing developed and explored by the leaders of an international business organisation and Tatjana Dragovic during a three-year long Leadership Development Programme, it is defined as the processes of following and leading being merged into one simultaneous process. Following and Leading co-exist and co-habituate only to be slightly distinguished through alternating the 'boldness' of parts of the word thus enabling 'following' to lead and 'leading' to follow.

gamelan a traditional musical instrument used throughout South East Asia, consisting of approximately 50 orchestral percussion elements that are tuned and played as a single unit. The composition and tuning of each gamelan is highly individualised according to local contexts and rituals. Gamelan often play a central role in their communities, and continue to be accorded a sense of animist agency or 'personhood' on South-East Asian islands such as Java and Bali.

going all city a phrase commonly used by illegal graffiti writers to describe all night 'bombings' of an entire city with graffiti tags. Usage of the term arose from the illegal graffiti scene in the Bronx, NY in the 1970s.

hip-hopification of education defined and practiced by BREIS (Brother Reaching Each Inner Soul), Hip-Hopification of Education is looking at the creative, vibrant energy of Hip Hop and applying it in the classroom. It is about captivating audience with lyrical wizardry and a command of a chosen topic. It is about participation, interaction, inclusion, improvisation, connecting with and steering audience towards a safe space where they can learn.

image-inary a sphere of immersive, collaborative experimentation through which an ecology of images are sensed, fabulated, assembled, fragmented, recomposed, projected, and exchanged.

implicit leadership theories a cognitive network of everyday concepts containing the traits and behaviours of leaders used by individual followers to interpret and explain their leader's behaviour. As each individual can have their own implicit leadership theory, the same behaviour can be interpreted differently by different individuals.

intra-action a Baradian term used to replace 'interaction,' which necessitates pre-established bodies that then participate in action with each other. Intra-action understands agency as not an inherent property of an individual or human to be exercised, but as a dynamism of forces.

J'Ouvert a French term meaning 'break of day' marking the beginning of Carnival celebrations, usually at 4am, on the Caribbean islands of Trinidad and Tobago.

Kuikoru an Indigenous people from the Mato Grosso region of Brazil who have inhabited the Amazonian rainforest along the Upper Xingu River for over a thousand years.

line of flight a term developed by Gilles Deleuze and Félix Guattari to refer to the indiscernible possibility of escape, the elusive moment when change happens when a threshold between two is crossed.

manifesto a statement in which someone makes their beliefs, motives, intentions or views easy for people to ascertain.

margem a Portuguese word with a variety of English meanings, including 'edge', 'band', 'shore', 'margin', and 'chance'.

micropolitics a concept developed by Felix Guattari to describe a sphere of political activity that operates through the affective, unconscious, and vital drives. The concept was developed further through Guattari's collaborations with Gilles Deleuze. It is contrasted with the sphere of macropolitics, which reduces political agency and thought to the experience of the bounded human subject.

minor a concept initially developed by Gilles Deleuze and Felix Guattari to describe 'minor literatures' and 'minor languages' that operate in the cracks between majoritarian regimes of signification and subjectification.

pluriverse a concept that has developed out of onto-political struggles for Indigenous land rights in Latin America, with strong links to the Zapatista movement's call for a 'world where many worlds fit'. The pluriverse acknowledges that different worlds are brought into existence through the ontological practices that constitute them. It challenges western humanist ideals of universal values by showing how radically incommensurable worlds can co-exist (often uneasily) without reducing their onto-political differences.

politics of hap a concept developed by feminist Sara Ahmed to refer to a way of discovering an unexpected sense of joy that can displace regulative happiness.

posthuman/post-human a concept originating in the fields of science fiction, futurology, contemporary art, and philosophy to describe a state or condition in which human life is inseparable from nature, thus disrupting claims of human exceptionalism or 'man as the measure of all things'.

post-qualitative inquiry a concept proposed predominantly by education scholar Elizabeth St Pierre to describe new approaches to social inquiry that break completely with traditional qualitative methodologies. St Pierre argues that such a break with qualitative methodology is necessary if social researchers are to adequately respond to post-structuralist, new materialist, and posthumanist deconstructions of the liberal humanist subject.

radical from the fourteenth-century Latin word *radicalis* meaning 'of or having roots', the source from which the vitality of life is drawn and to be rooted in something real.

readicide the systematic killing of the joy of reading.

refrain according to Deleuze and Guattari, the refrain is a rhythmic operation that connects with a moment of emergence out of chaos. The refrain helps the person to navigate that moment, creating certain stability, close to the source of chaos or helps to launch the person away from it.

ritual a collection of practices through which particular sets of worldly relations are brought into being and sustained for varying durations.

speculative fabulation Donna Haraway's concept which refers to a mode of attention, a theory of history and a practice of worlding that blurs the sharpness of existing meanings and interpretations. It frees the mind to reach/invent new dimensions within the same physical appearance.

surface a non-hierarchical plane of experience that is thoroughly immanent, with no transcendent positions.

worlding a particular blending of the material and the semiotic that removes the boundaries between subject and environment; the way we experience the world as an event.

writing to it from the work of Jonathan Wyatt and Ken Gale, this concept is not just about the creation of new concepts in writing, it is about the act itself of bringing concepts to life in writing by doing something with them and making them work.

Index